THE SEVEN DEADLY SINS 17

nakaba suzuki presents

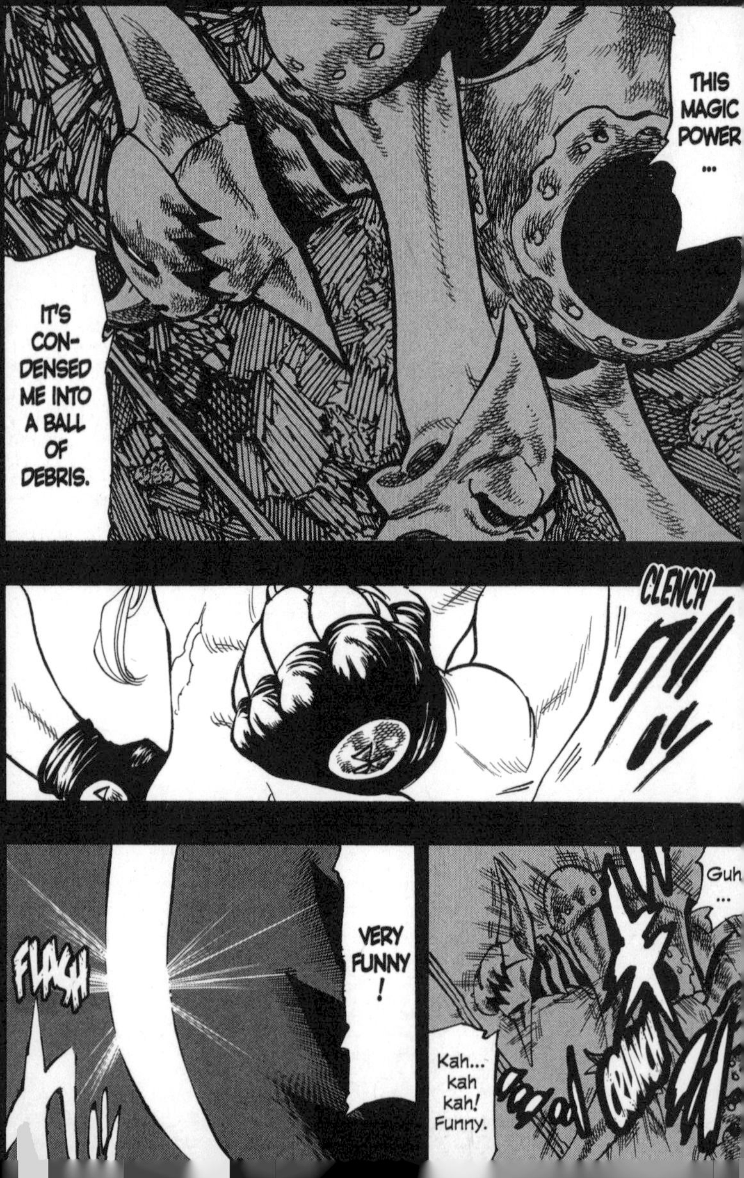
THIS MAGIC POWER ...
IT'S CON-DENSED ME INTO A BALL OF DEBRIS.
CLENCH
Guh ...
CRUNCH
Kah... kah kah! Funny.
VERY FUNNY !
FLASH

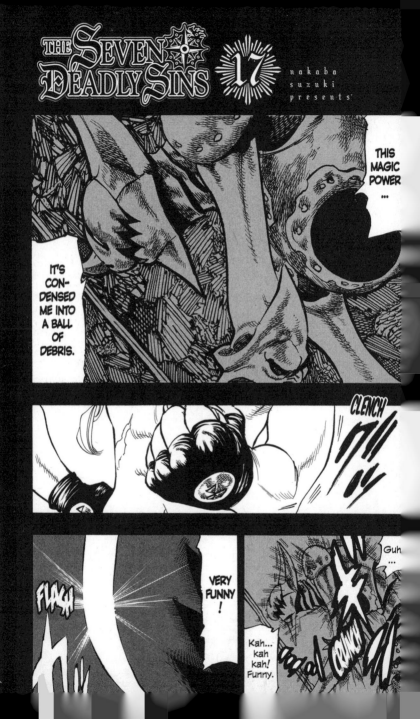

CONTENTS

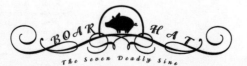

BOAR HAT
The Seven Deadly Sins

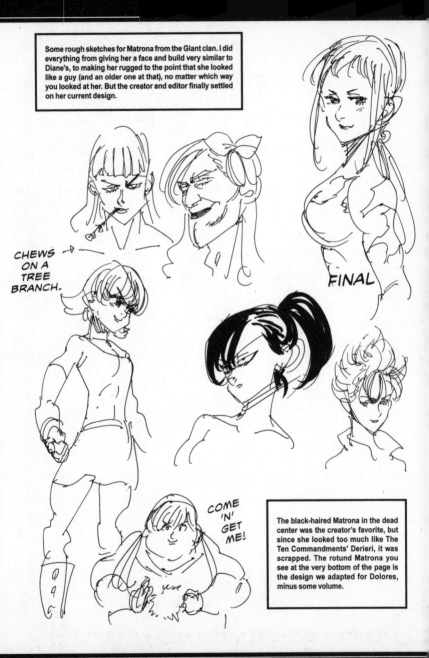

Some rough sketches for Matrona from the Giant clan. I did everything from giving her a face and build very similar to Diane's, to making her rugged to the point that she looked like a guy (and an older one at that), no matter which way you looked at her. But the creator and editor finally settled on her current design.

CHEWS ON A TREE BRANCH.

FINAL

COME 'N' GET ME!

The black-haired Matrona in the dead center was the creator's favorite, but since she looked too much like The Ten Commandments' Derieri, it was scrapped. The rotund Matrona you see at the very bottom of the page is the design we adapted for Dolores, minus some volume.

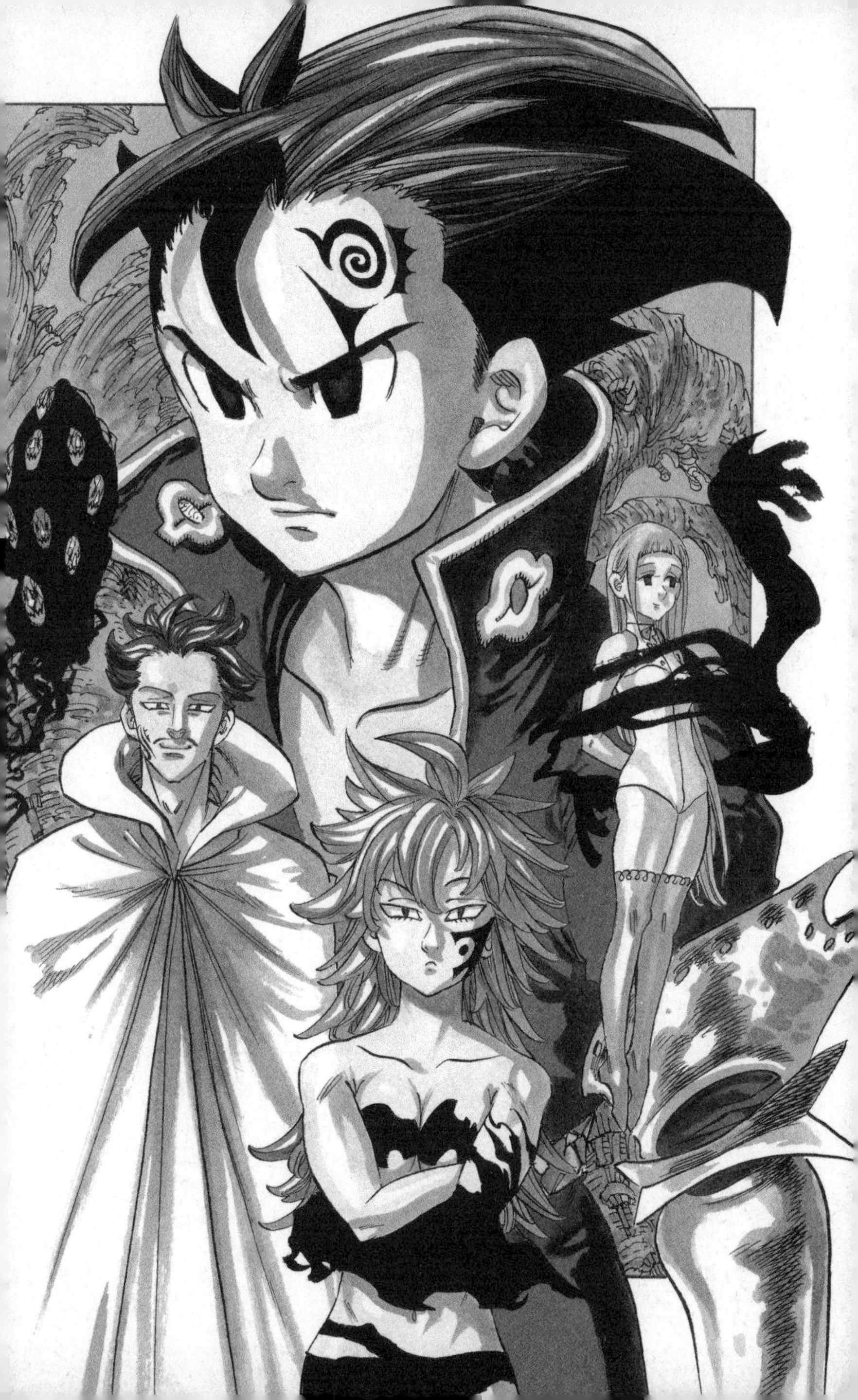

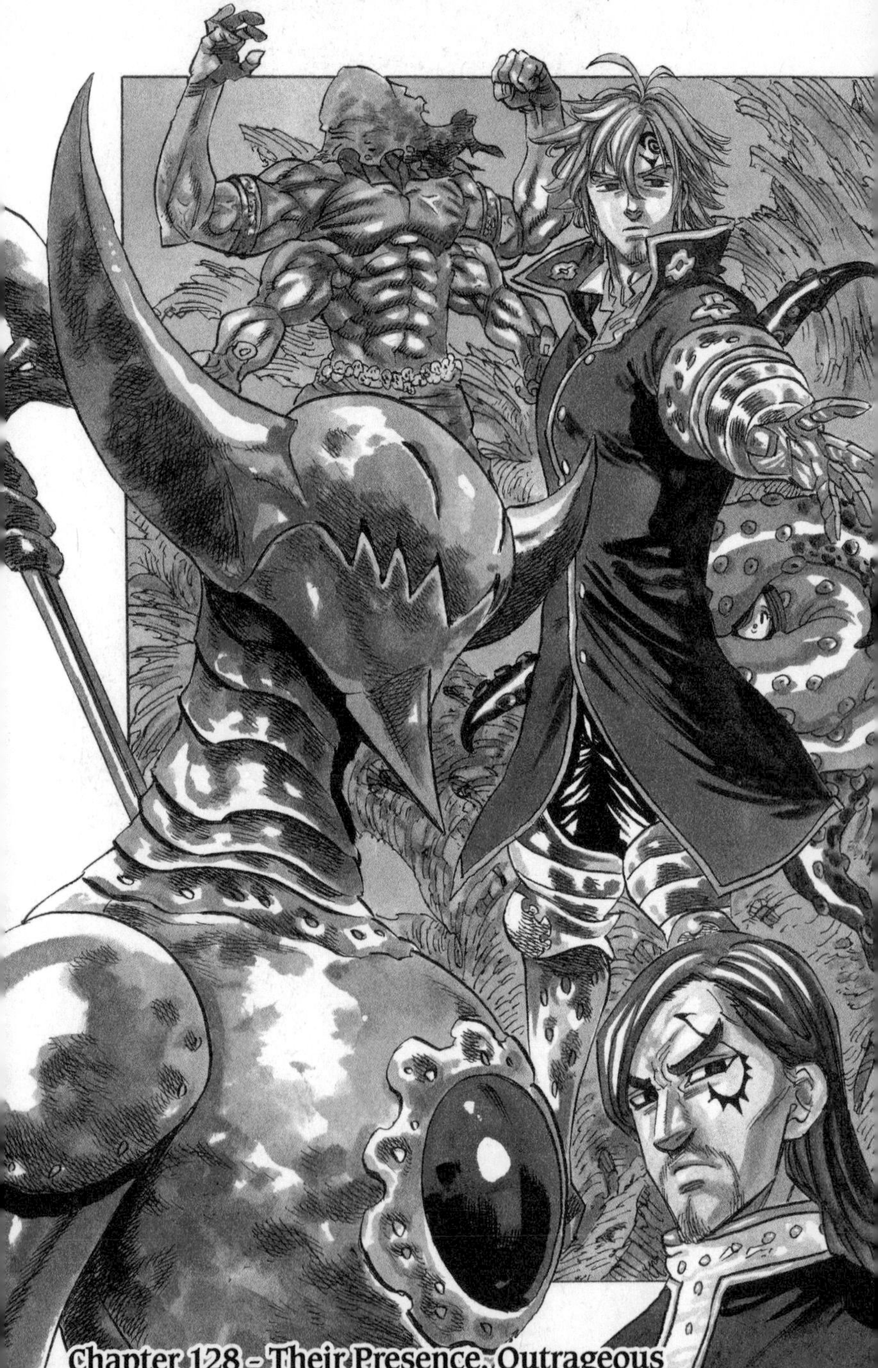

Chapter 128 - Their Presence, Outrageous

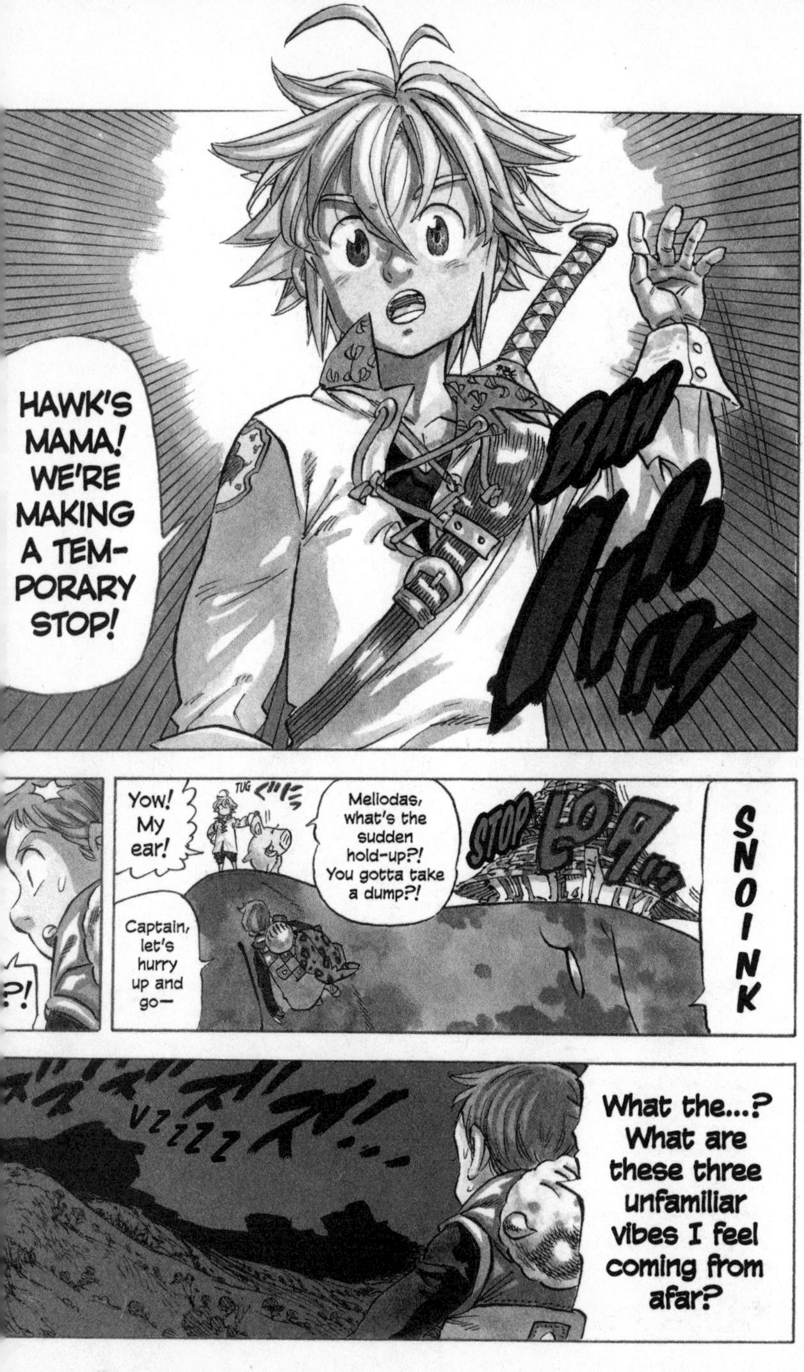
HAWK'S MAMA! WE'RE MAKING A TEM-PORARY STOP!
SNOINK
STOP
Meliodas, what's the sudden hold-up?! You gotta take a dump?!
TUG
Yow! My ear!
Captain, let's hurry up and go—
?!
What the...? What are these three unfamiliar vibes I feel coming from afar?
VZZZZZ

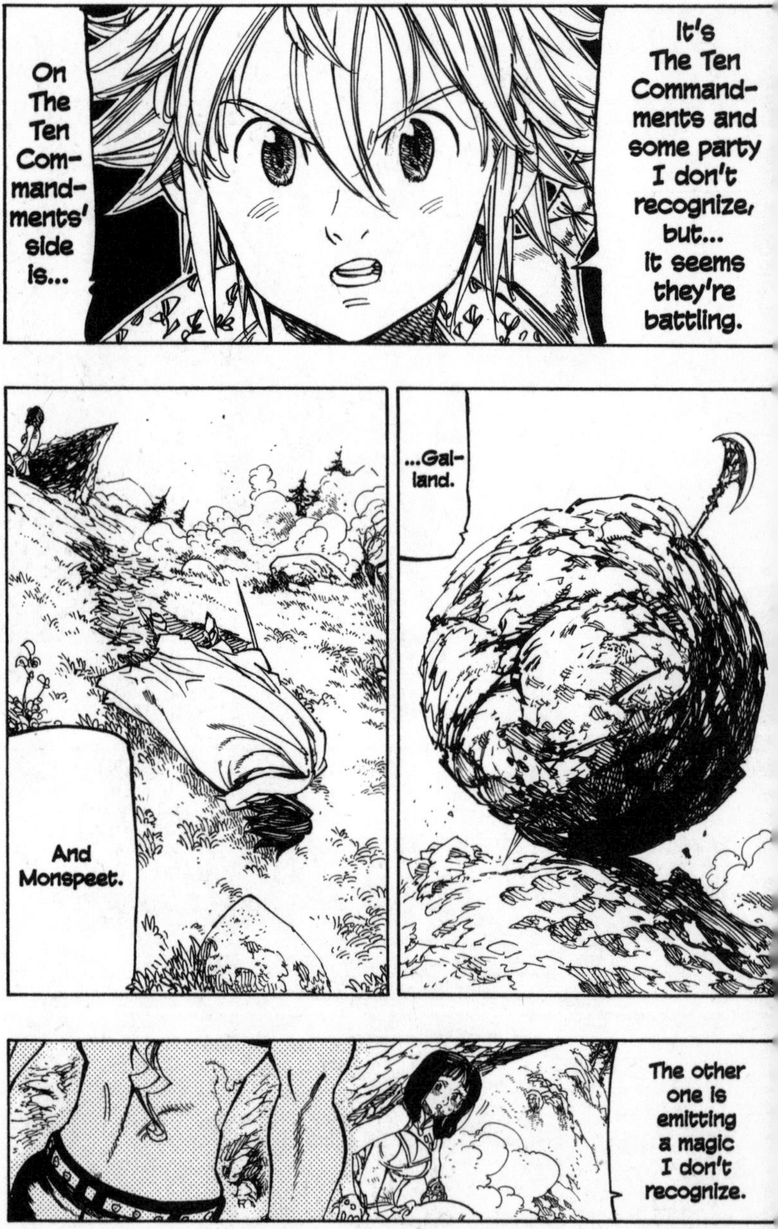
It's The Ten Commandments and some party I don't recognize, but... it seems they're battling.
On The Ten Commandments' side is...
...Galland.
And Monspeet.
The other one is emitting a magic I don't recognize.

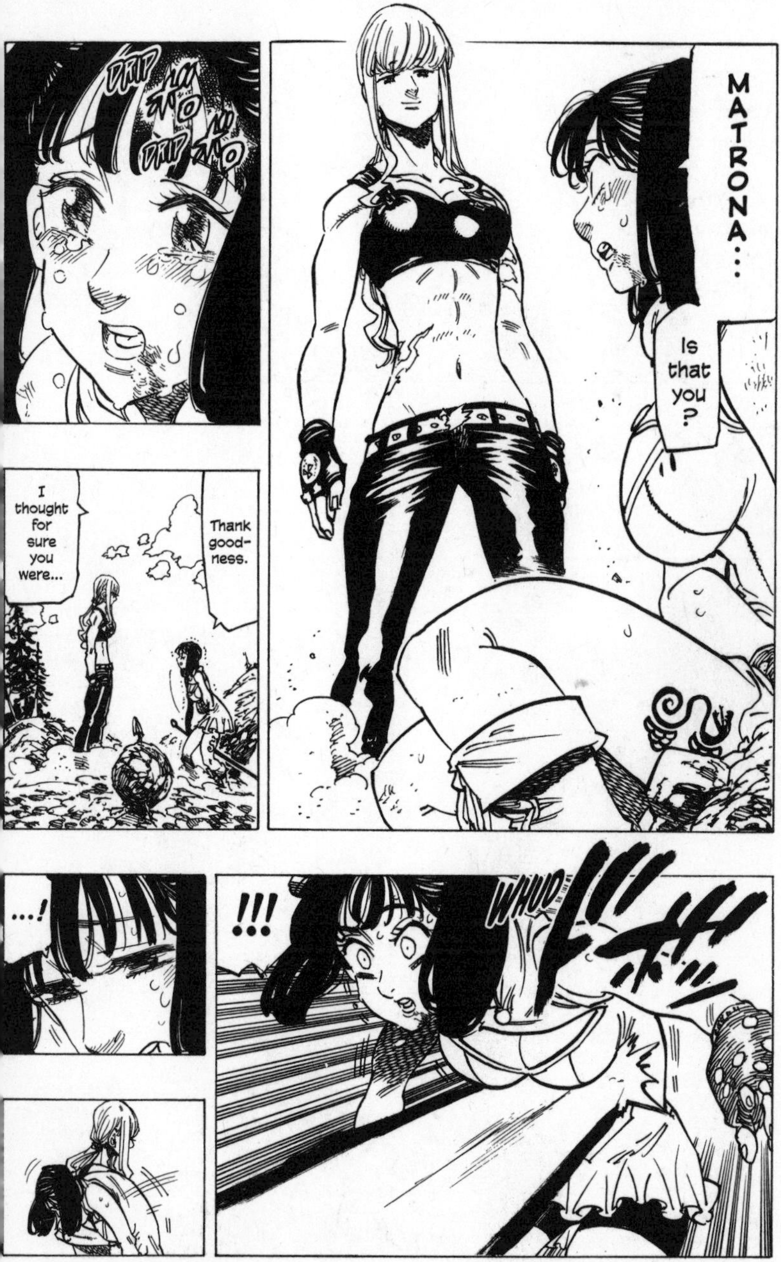
MATRONA...
Is that you?
DRIP
DRIP
Thank goodness.
I thought for sure you were...
!!!
WHUD
...!

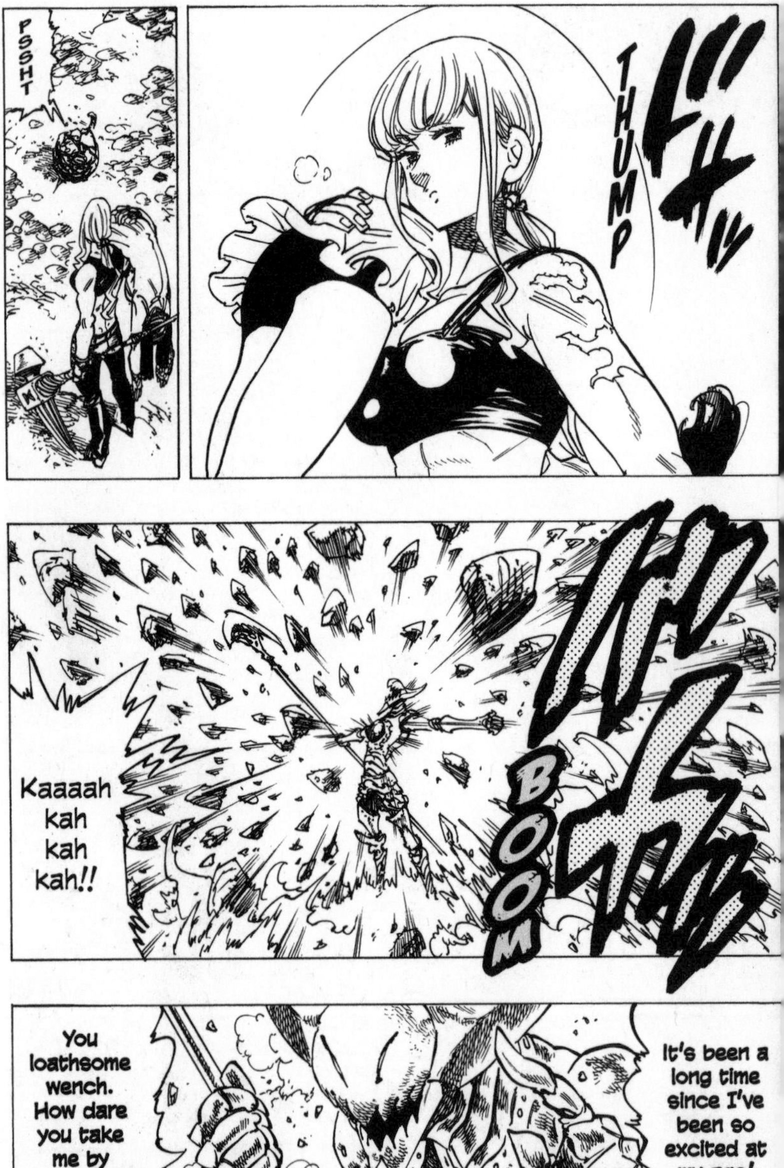

THUMP
PSSHT
BOOM
Kaaaah kah kah kah!!
It's been a long time since I've been so excited at my age!
You loathsome wench. How dare you take me by surprise?!

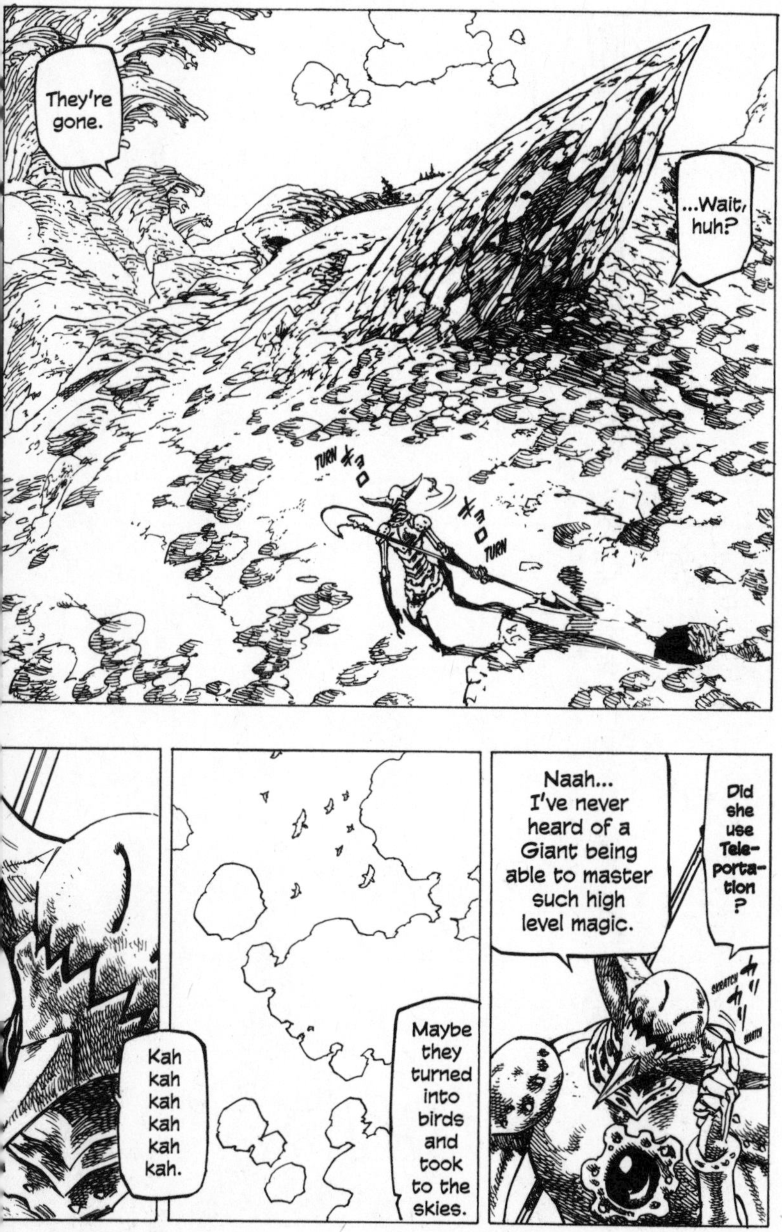
They're gone.
...Wait, huh?
TURN
TURN
Did she use Teleportation?
Naah... I've never heard of a Giant being able to master such high level magic.
SKRATCH
SKRATCH
Maybe they turned into birds and took to the skies.
Kah kah kah kah kah kah.

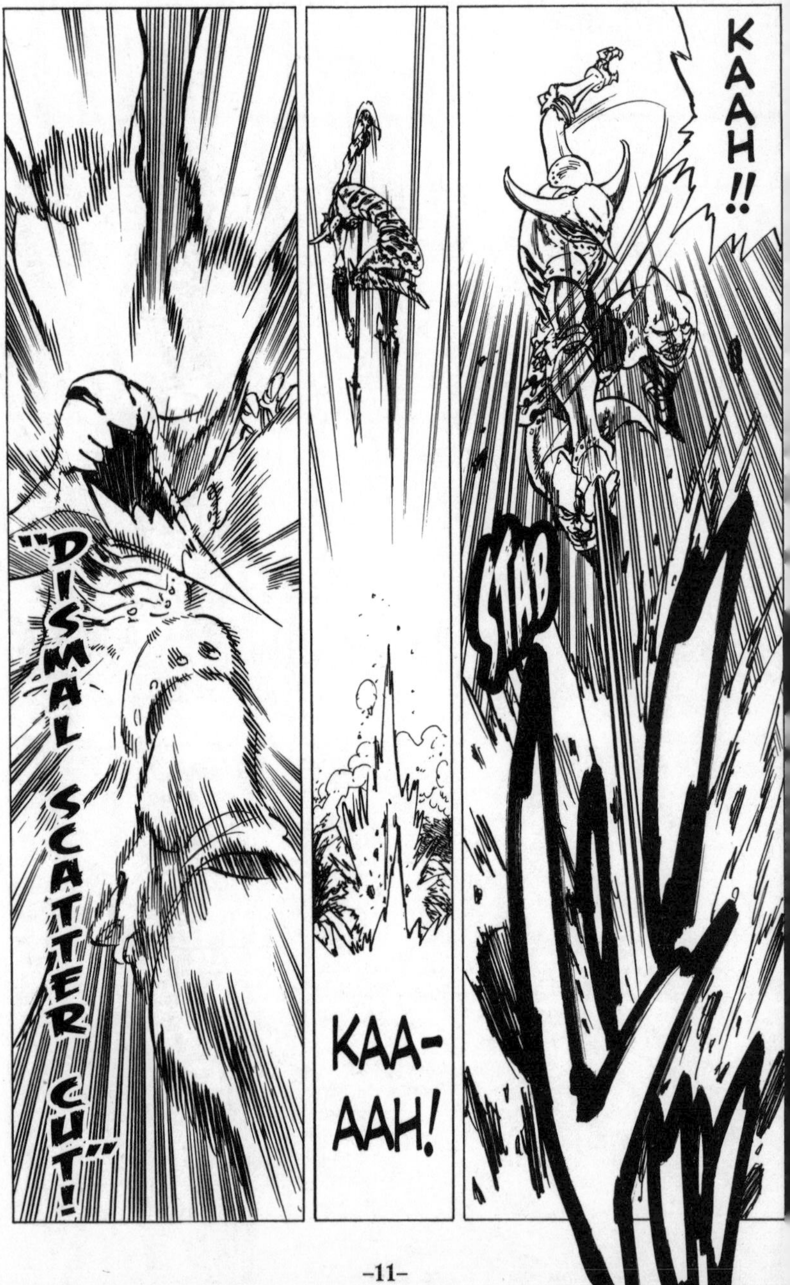
KAAH!!
STAB
KAA-AAH!
"DISMAL SCATTER CUT"!

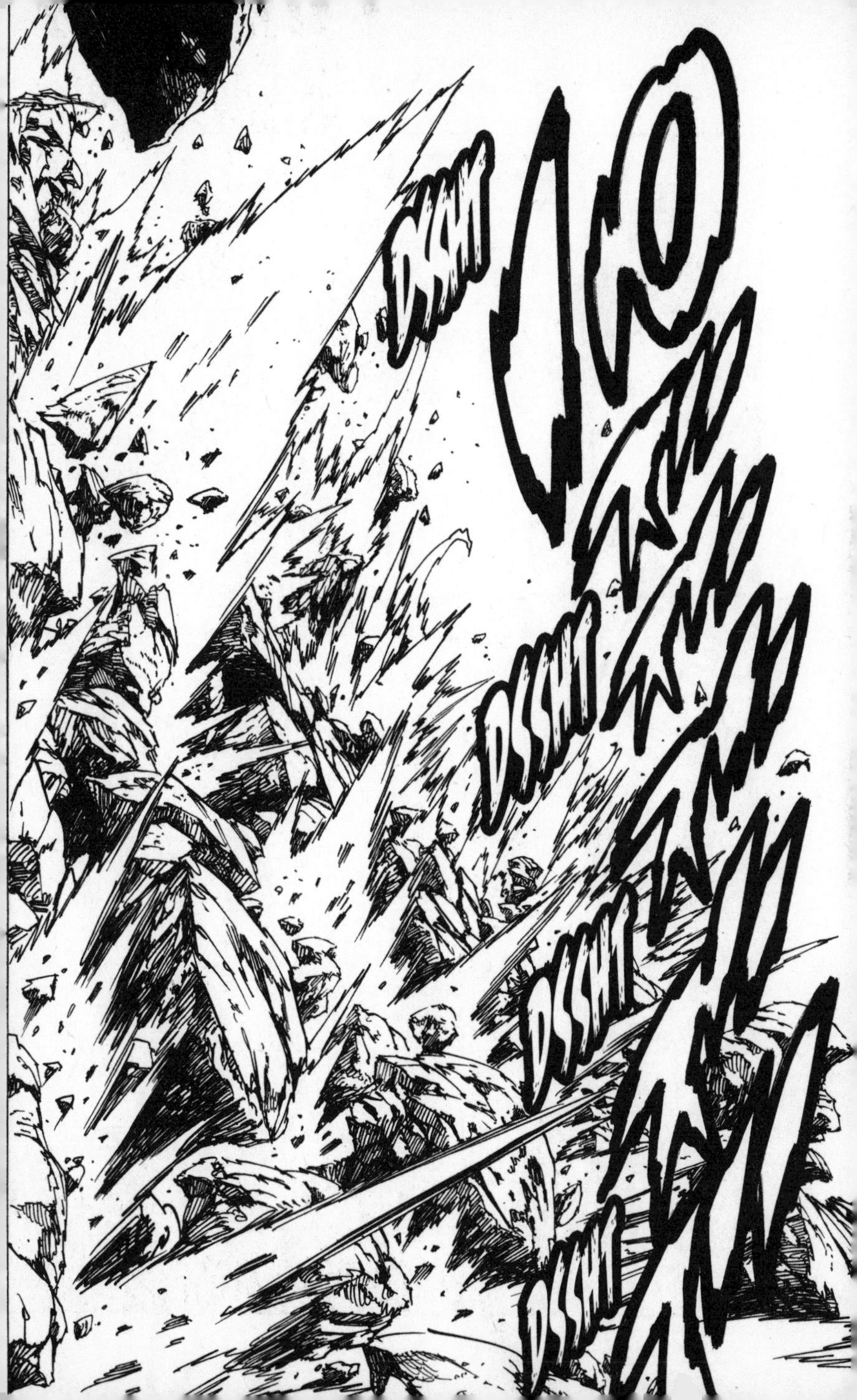
DSHT
DSHT
DSHT
DSHT

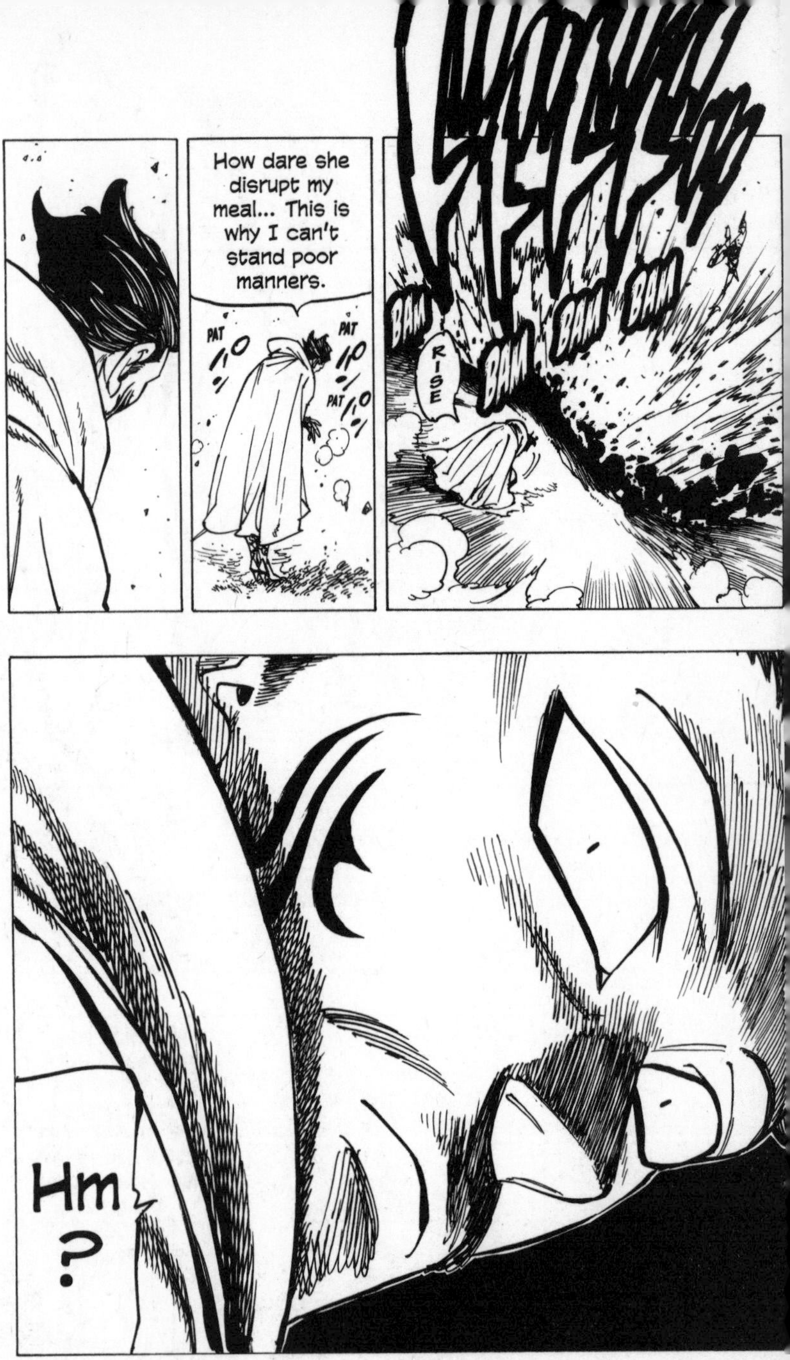
BAM
BAM
BAM
BAM
BAM
RISE
How dare she disrupt my meal... This is why I can't stand poor manners.
PAT
PAT
PAT
Hm?

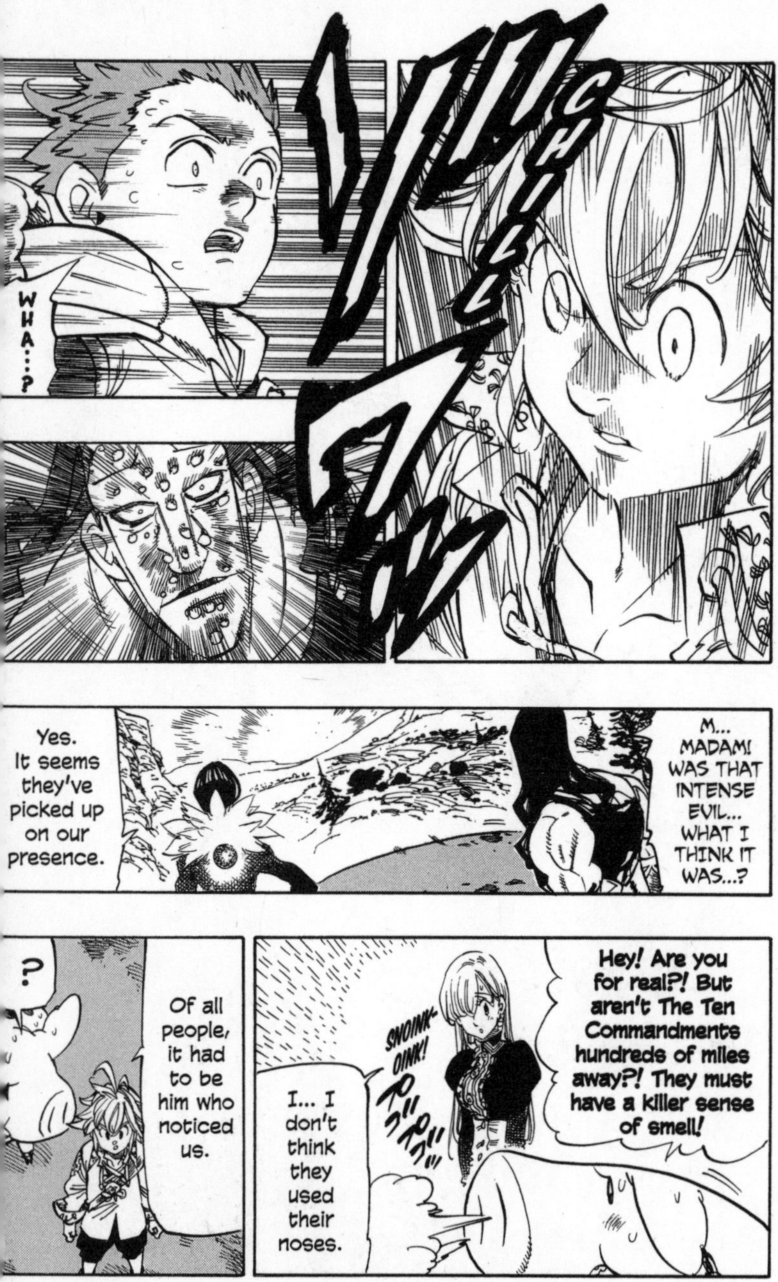
CHILL
WHA...?
M... MADAM! WAS THAT INTENSE EVIL... WHAT I THINK IT WAS...?
Yes. It seems they've picked up on our presence.
Hey! Are you for real?! But aren't The Ten Commandments hundreds of miles away?! They must have a killer sense of smell!
SNOINK-OINK!
I... I don't think they used their noses.
?
Of all people, it had to be him who noticed us.

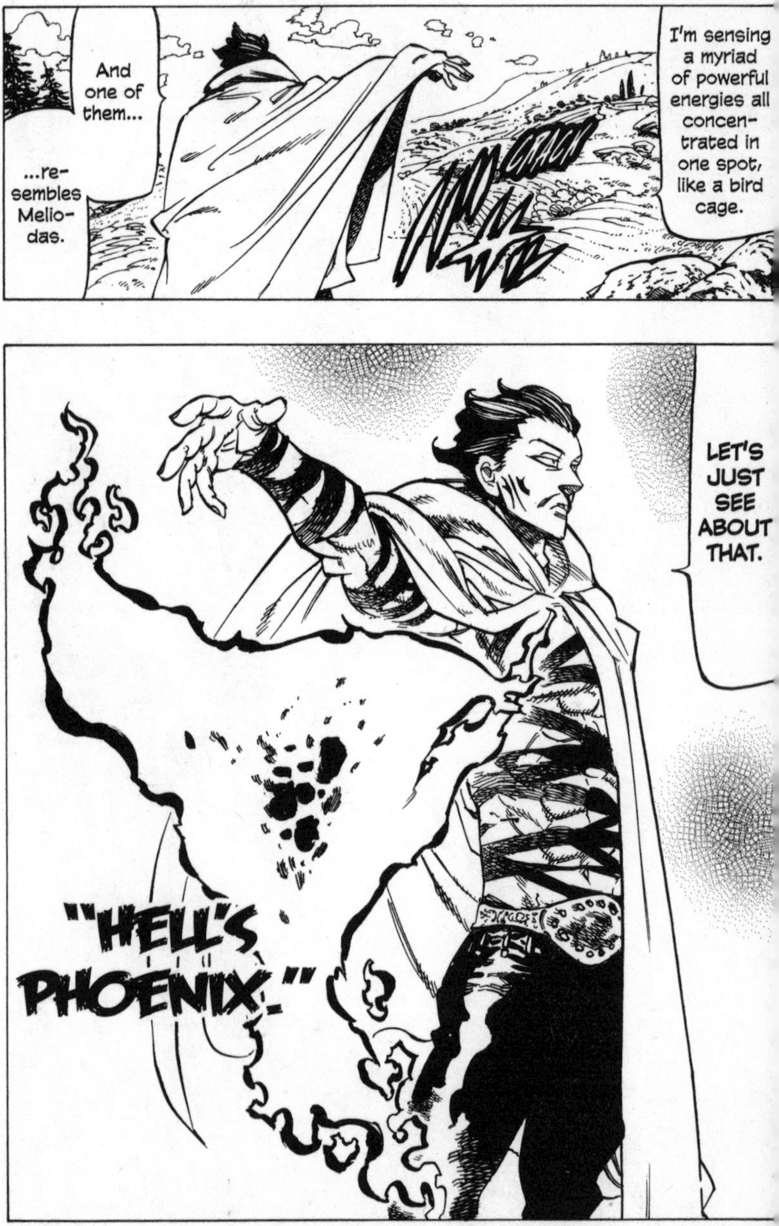
I'm sensing a myriad of powerful energies all concentrated in one spot, like a bird cage.
And one of them...
...resembles Meliodas.
LET'S JUST SEE ABOUT THAT.
"HELL'S PHOENIX."

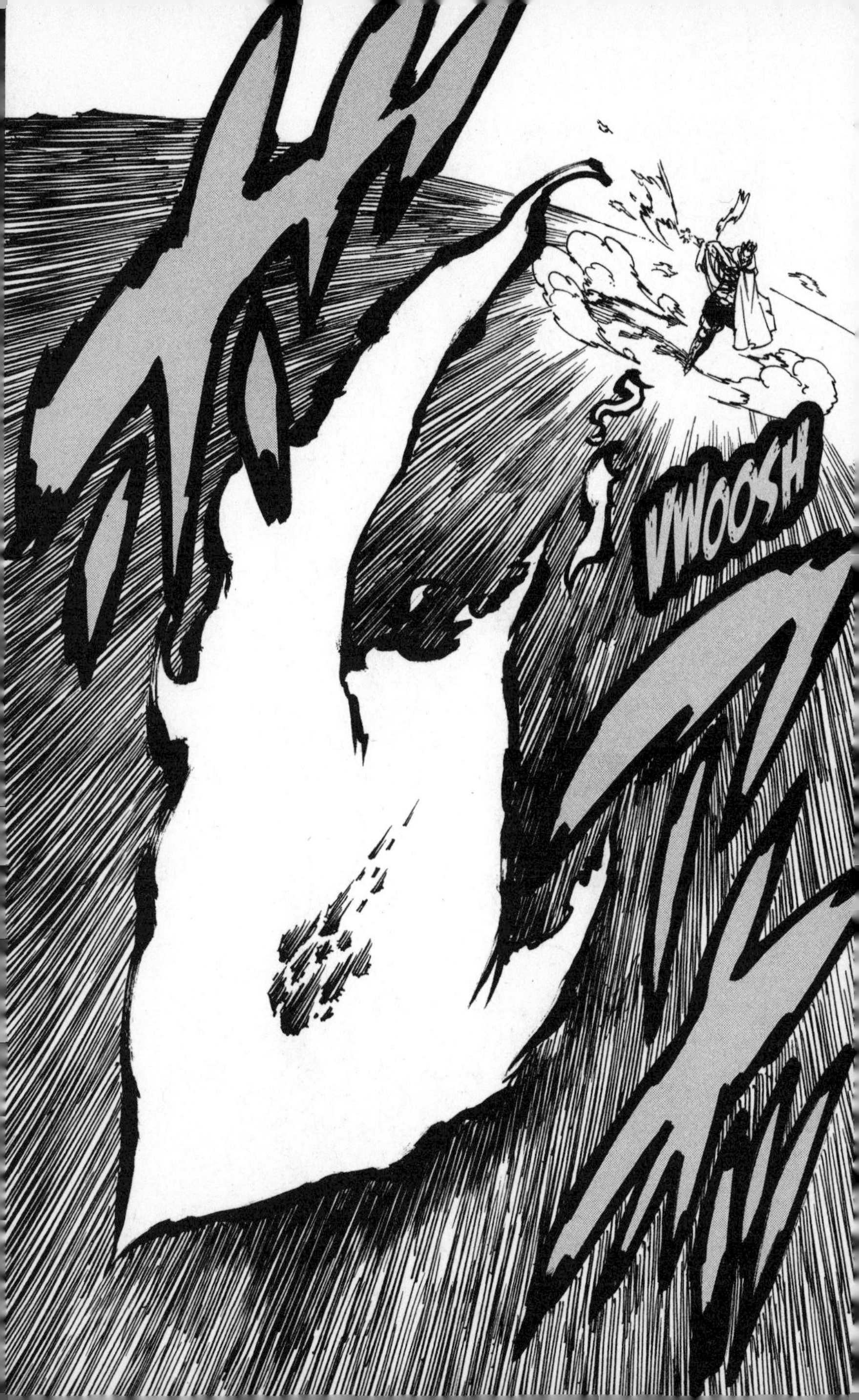
VWOOSH

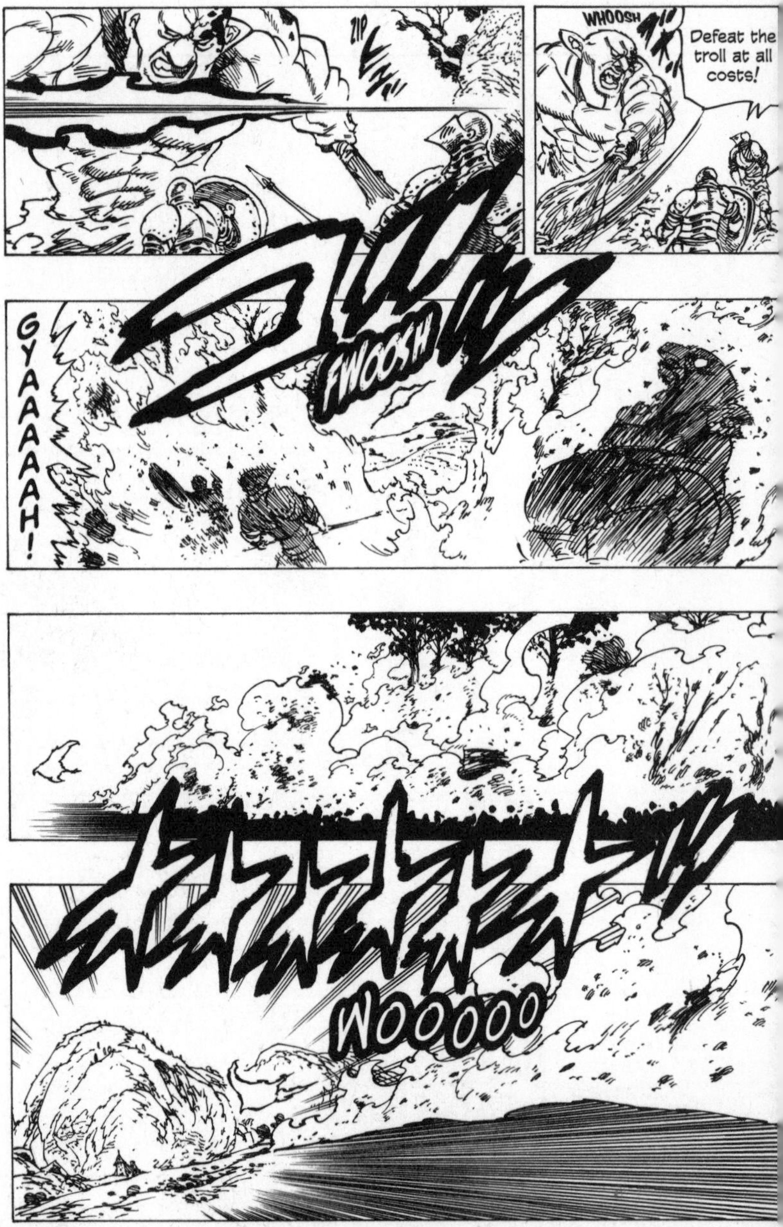
WHOOSH
Defeat the troll at all costs!
ZIP
GYAAAAAAH!
FWOOSH
WOOOOO

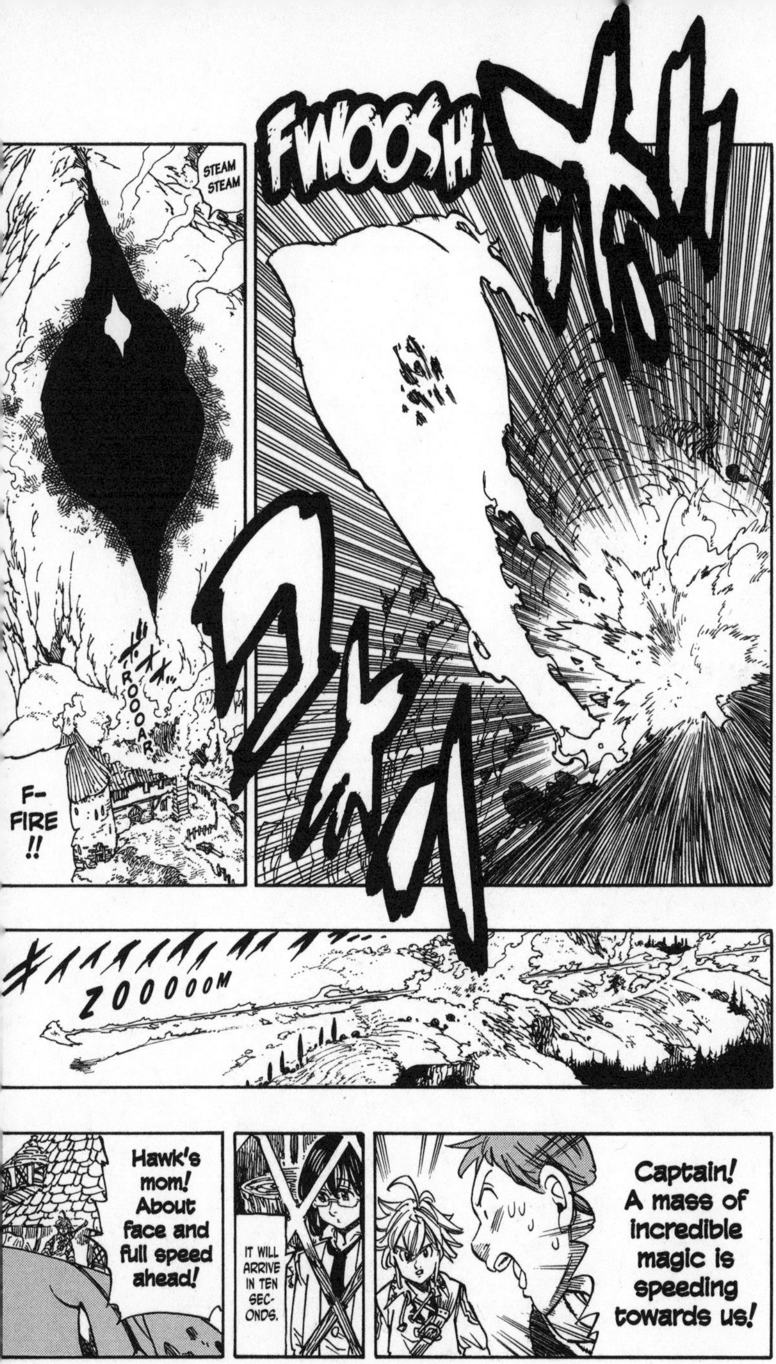
FWOOSH
STEAM
STEAM
ROOOOAR
F-FIRE!!
ZOOOOOM
Captain! A mass of incredible magic is speeding towards us!
IT WILL ARRIVE IN TEN SECONDS.
Hawk's mom! About face and full speed ahead!

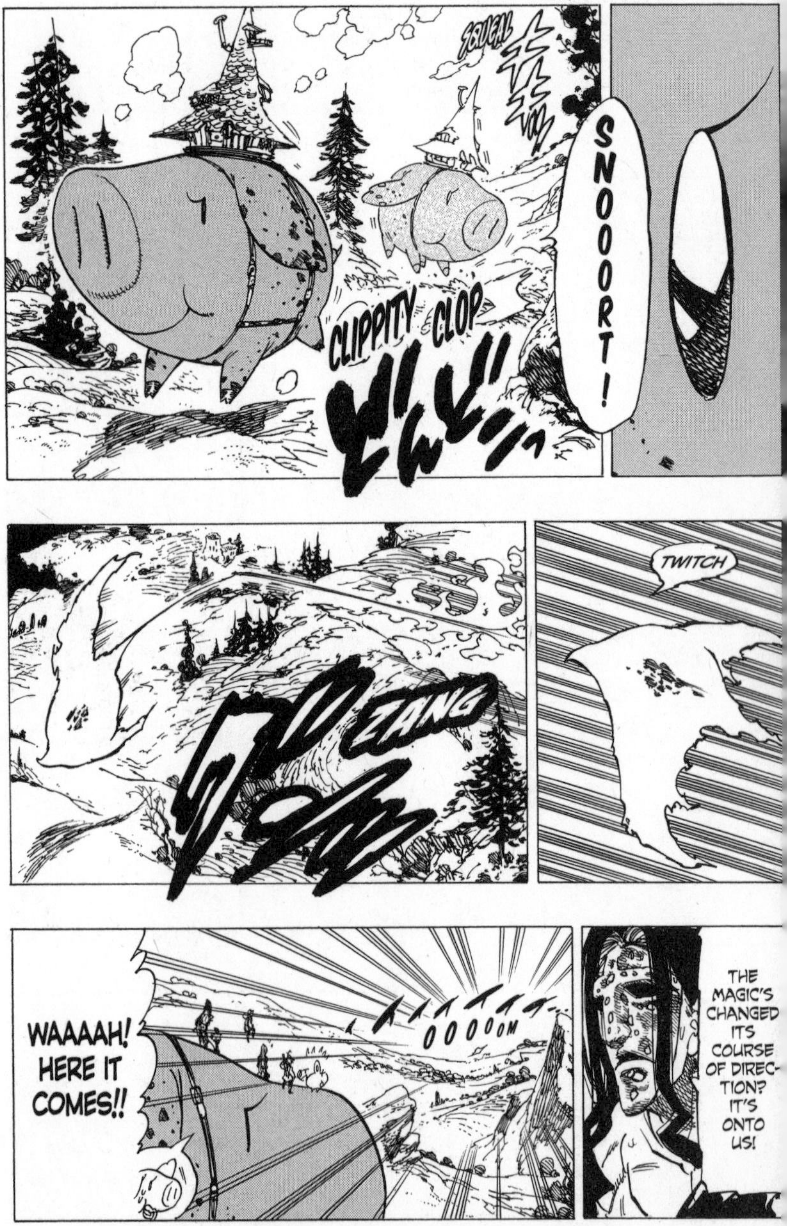
SNOOOORT!
SQUEAL
CLIPPITY CLOP
TWITCH
ZANG
THE MAGIC'S CHANGED ITS COURSE OF DIRECTION? IT'S ONTO US!
WAAAAH! HERE IT COMES!!
OOOOOM

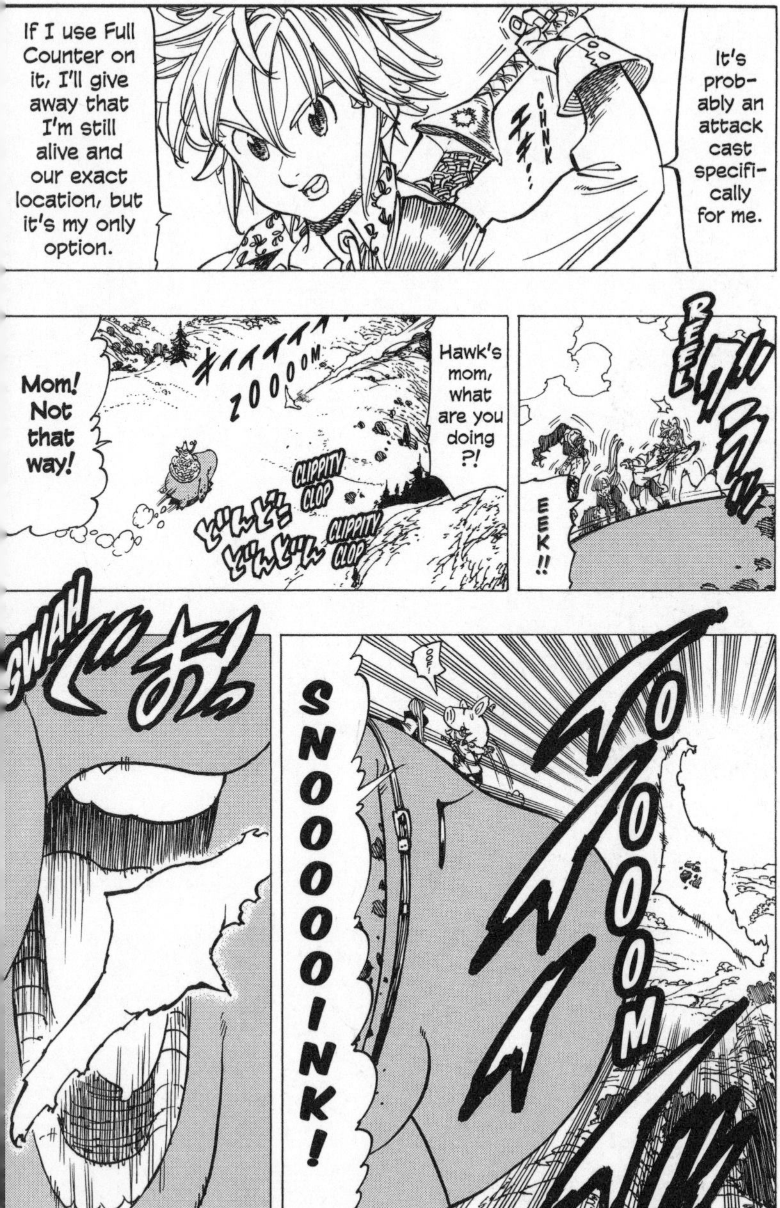
It's probably an attack cast specifically for me.
CHNK
If I use Full Counter on it, I'll give away that I'm still alive and our exact location, but it's my only option.
REEL
EEK!!
Hawk's mom, what are you doing?!
ZOOOOM
CLIPPITY CLOP
CLIPPITY CLOP
Mom! Not that way!
OOF!
OOOOM
SNOOOOOINK!
GWAH

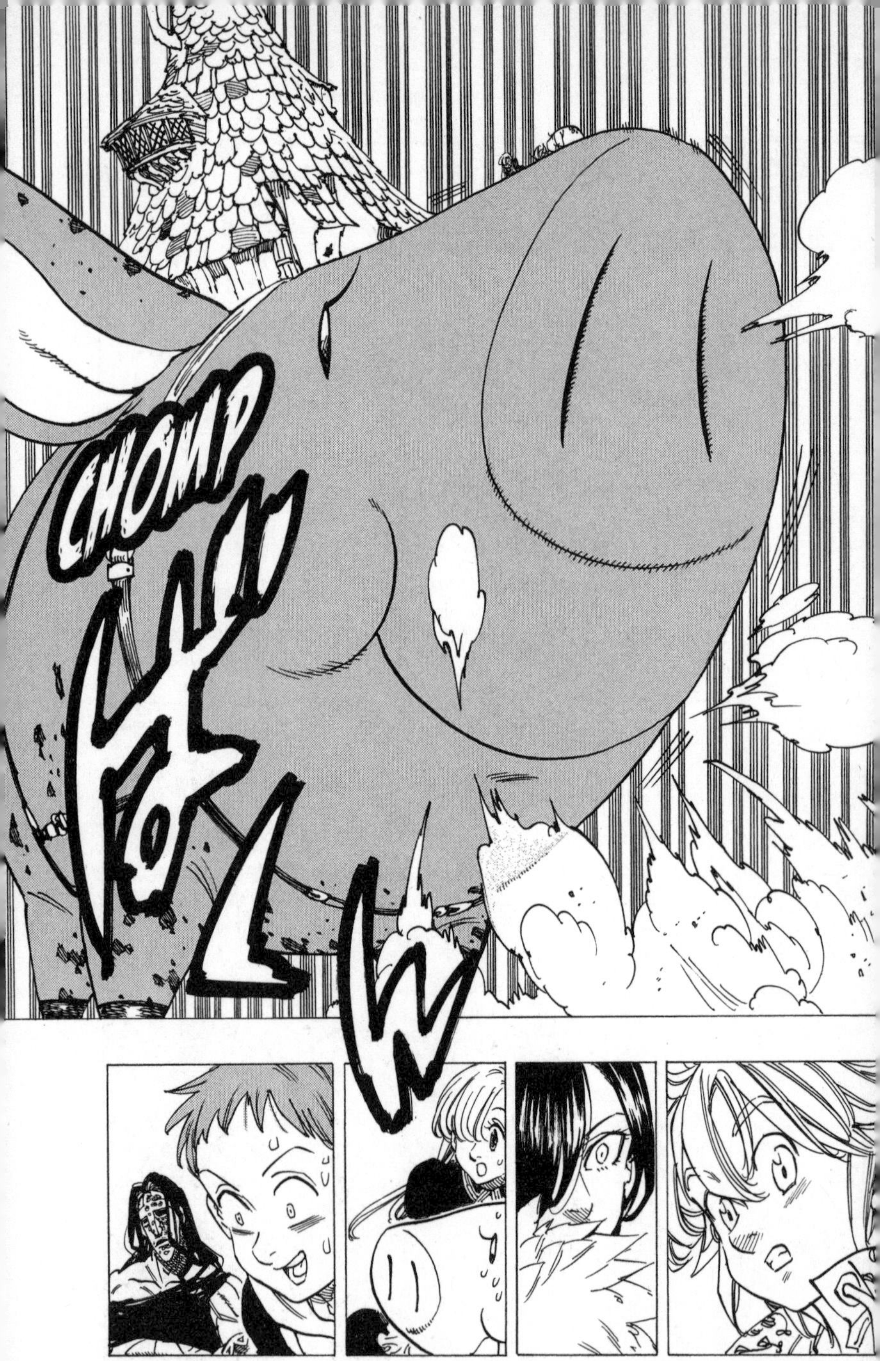

CHOMP

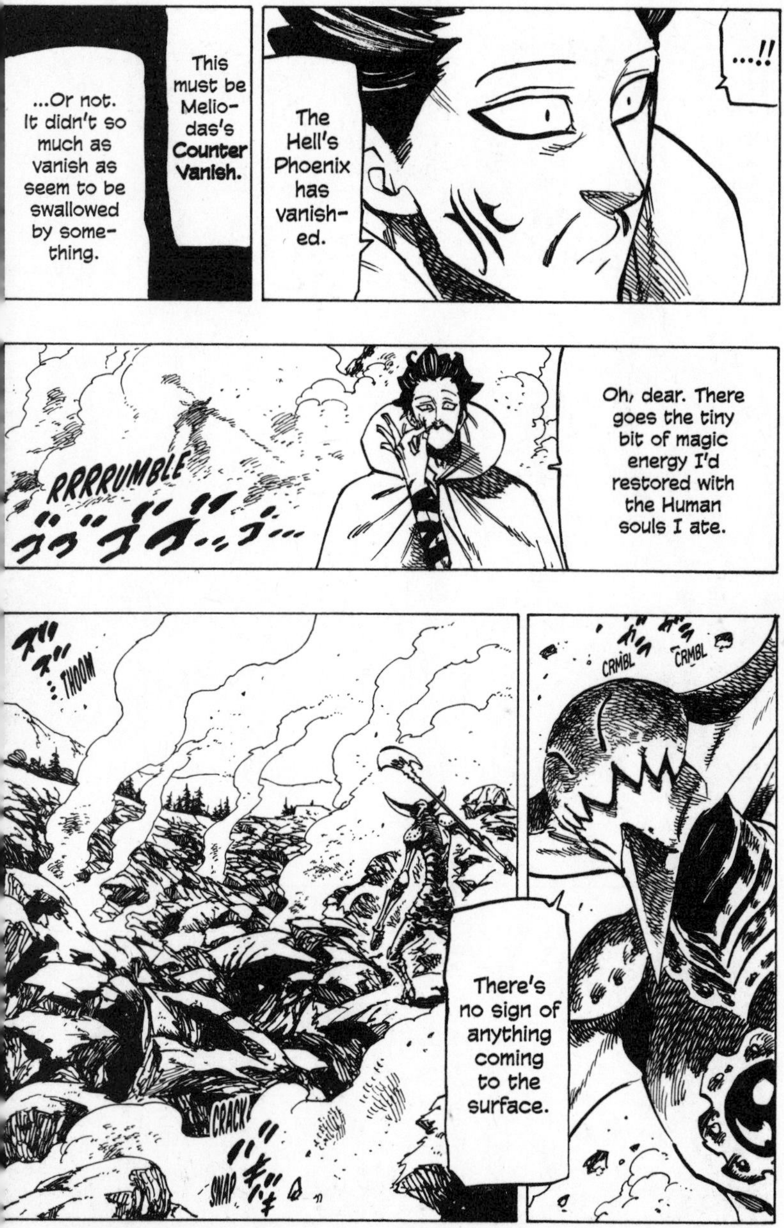
...!!
The Hell's Phoenix has vanish-ed.
This must be Melio-das's **Counter Vanish.**
...Or not. It didn't so much as vanish as seem to be swallowed by some-thing.
Oh, dear. There goes the tiny bit of magic energy I'd restored with the Human souls I ate.
RRRRUMBLE
CRMBL
CRMBL
There's no sign of anything coming to the surface.
THOOM
CRACK
SNAP

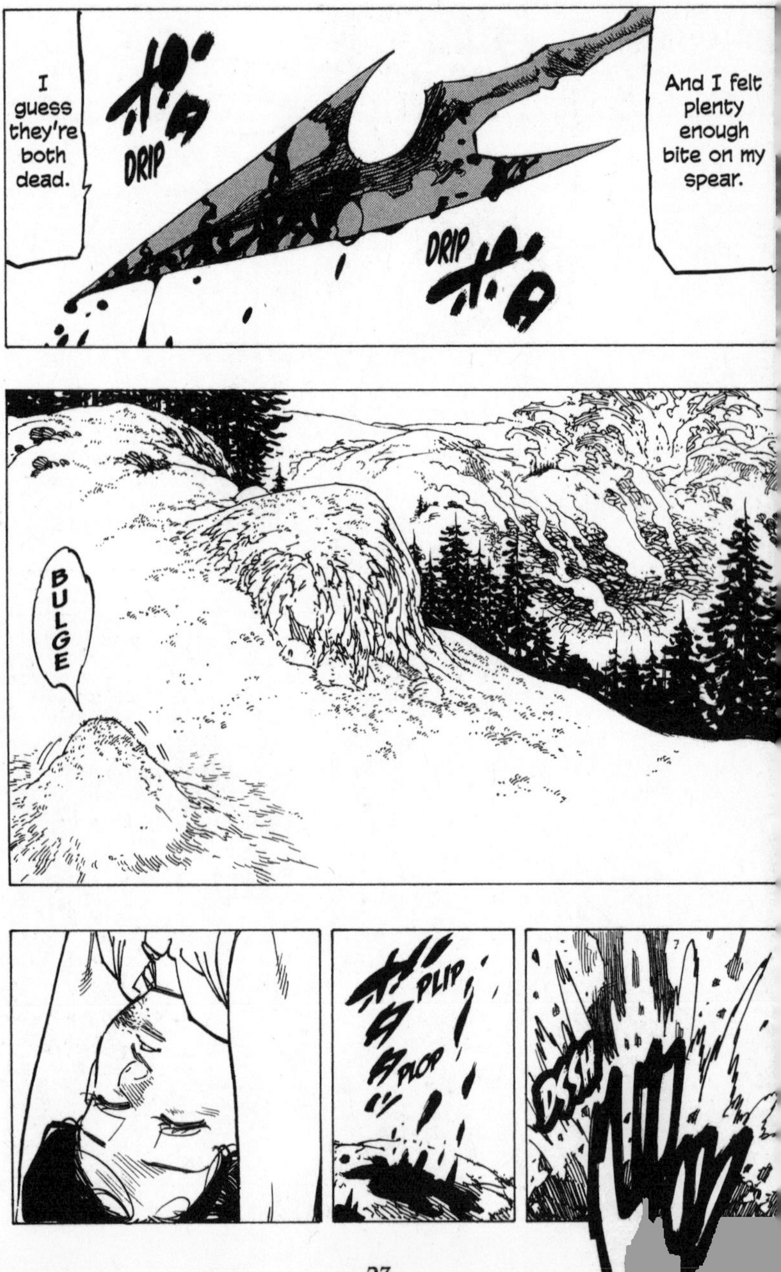
And I felt plenty enough bite on my spear.
DRIP
I guess they're both dead.
DRIP
BULGE
DSSH
PLIP
PLOP

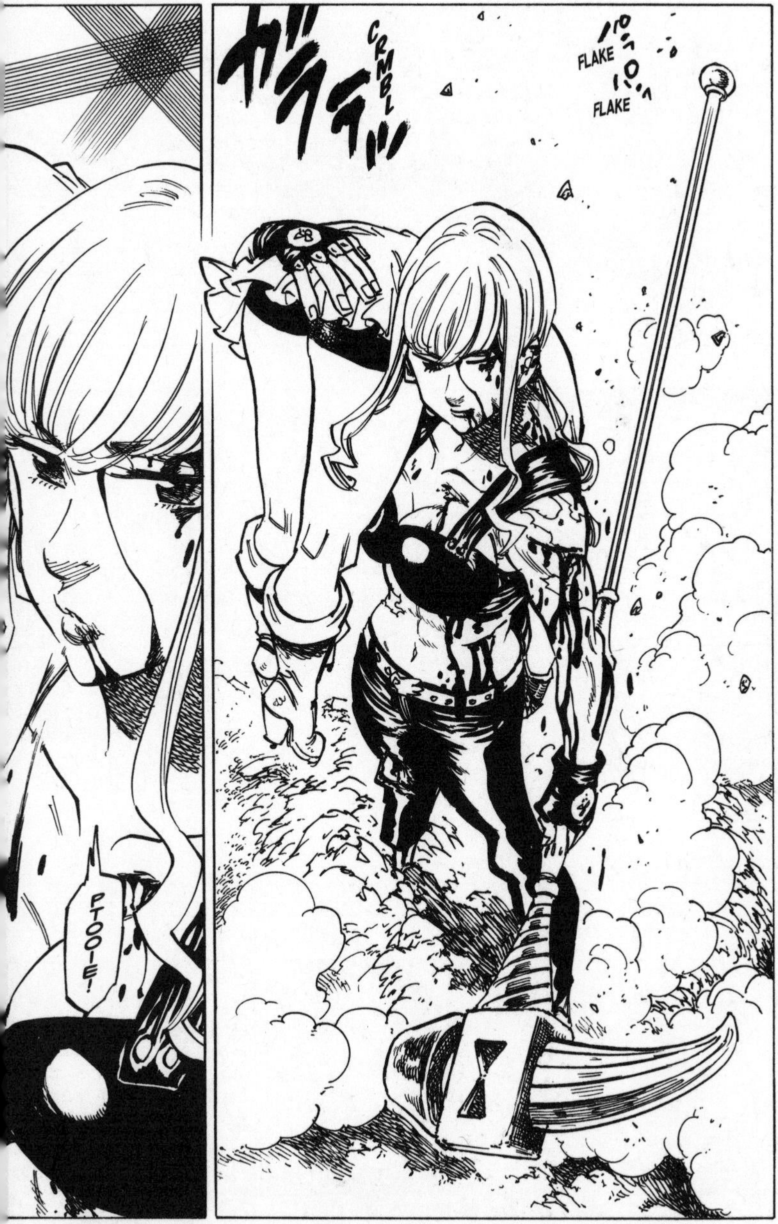
CRMBL
FLAKE
FLAKE
PTOOIE!

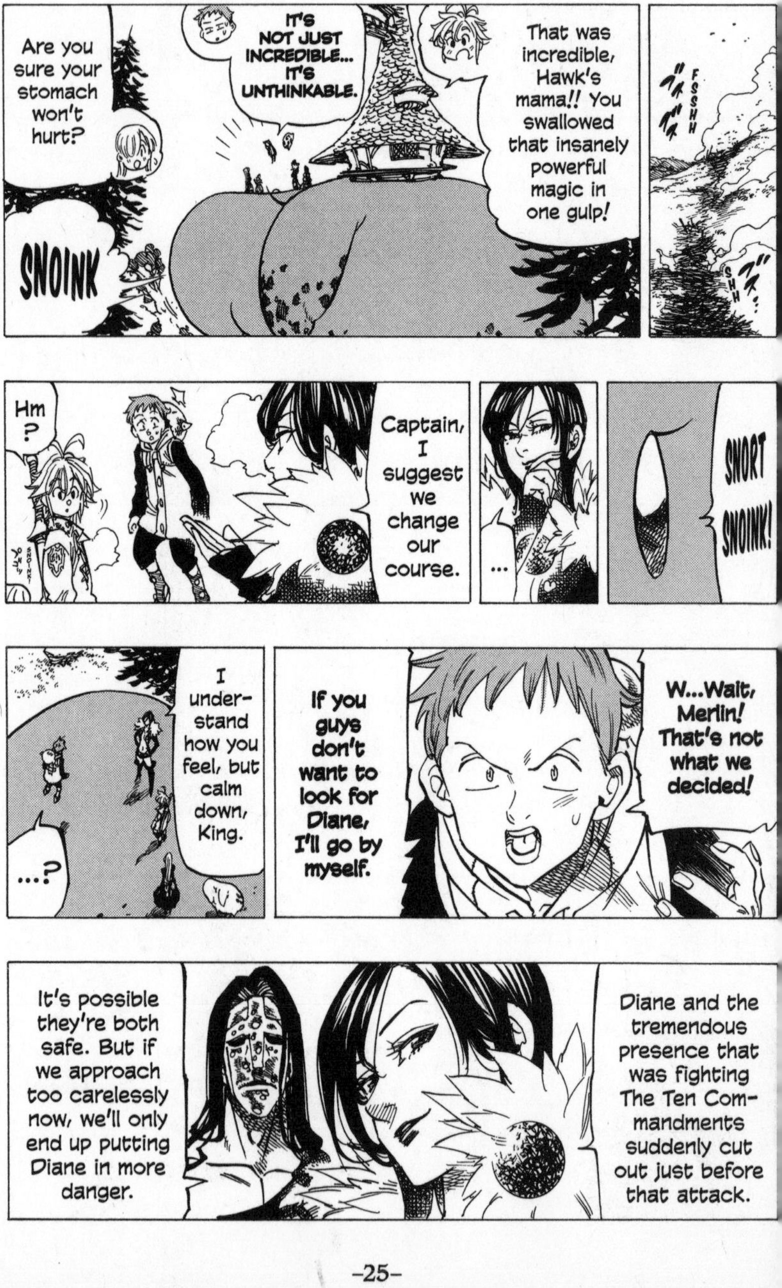
FSSHH
SHH
That was incredible, Hawk's mama!! You swallowed that insanely powerful magic in one gulp!
IT'S NOT JUST INCREDIBLE... IT'S UNTHINKABLE.
Are you sure your stomach won't hurt?
SNOINK
SNORT SNOINK!
...
Captain, I suggest we change our course.
Hm ?
W...Wait, Merlin! That's not what we decided!
If you guys don't want to look for Diane, I'll go by myself.
I understand how you feel, but calm down, King.
...?
Diane and the tremendous presence that was fighting The Ten Commandments suddenly cut out just before that attack.
It's possible they're both safe. But if we approach too carelessly now, we'll only end up putting Diane in more danger.

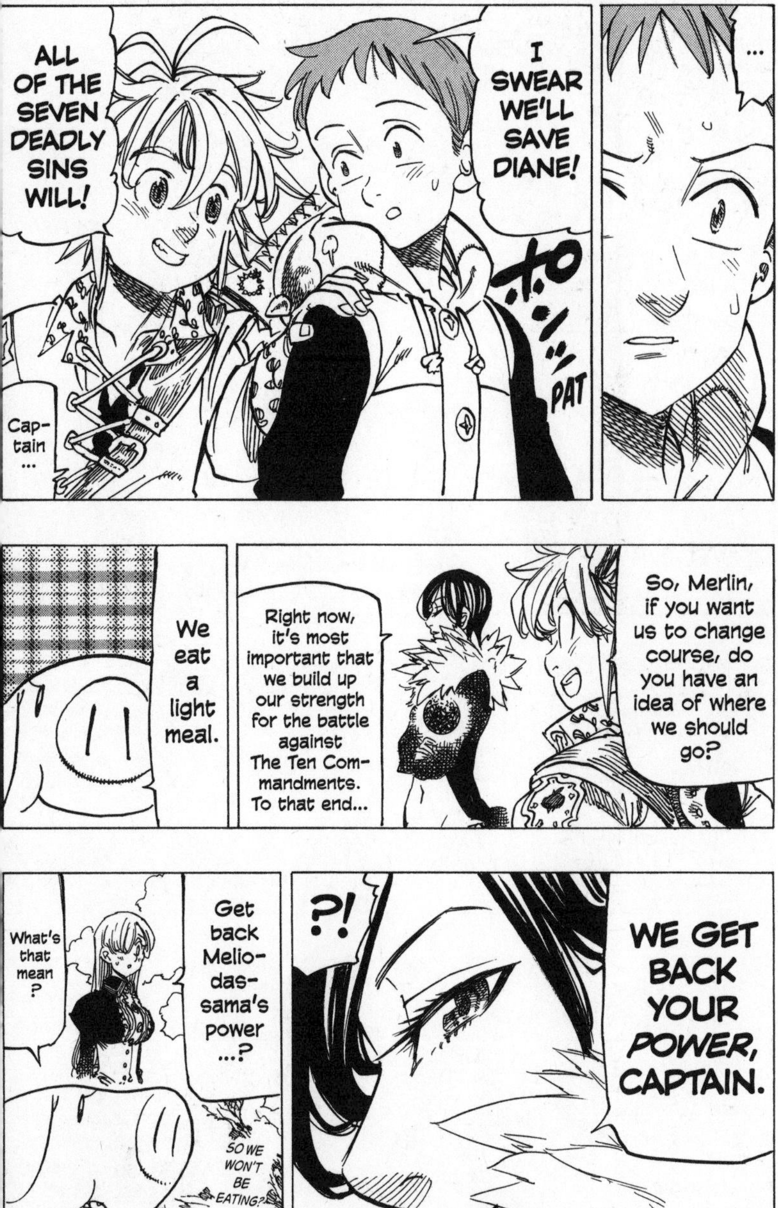
...
I SWEAR WE'LL SAVE DIANE!
ALL OF THE SEVEN DEADLY SINS WILL!
PAT
Captain...
So, Merlin, if you want us to change course, do you have an idea of where we should go?
Right now, it's most important that we build up our strength for the battle against The Ten Commandments. To that end...
We eat a light meal.
WE GET BACK YOUR POWER, CAPTAIN.
?!
Get back Meliodas-sama's power...?
What's that mean?
SO WE WON'T BE EATING?

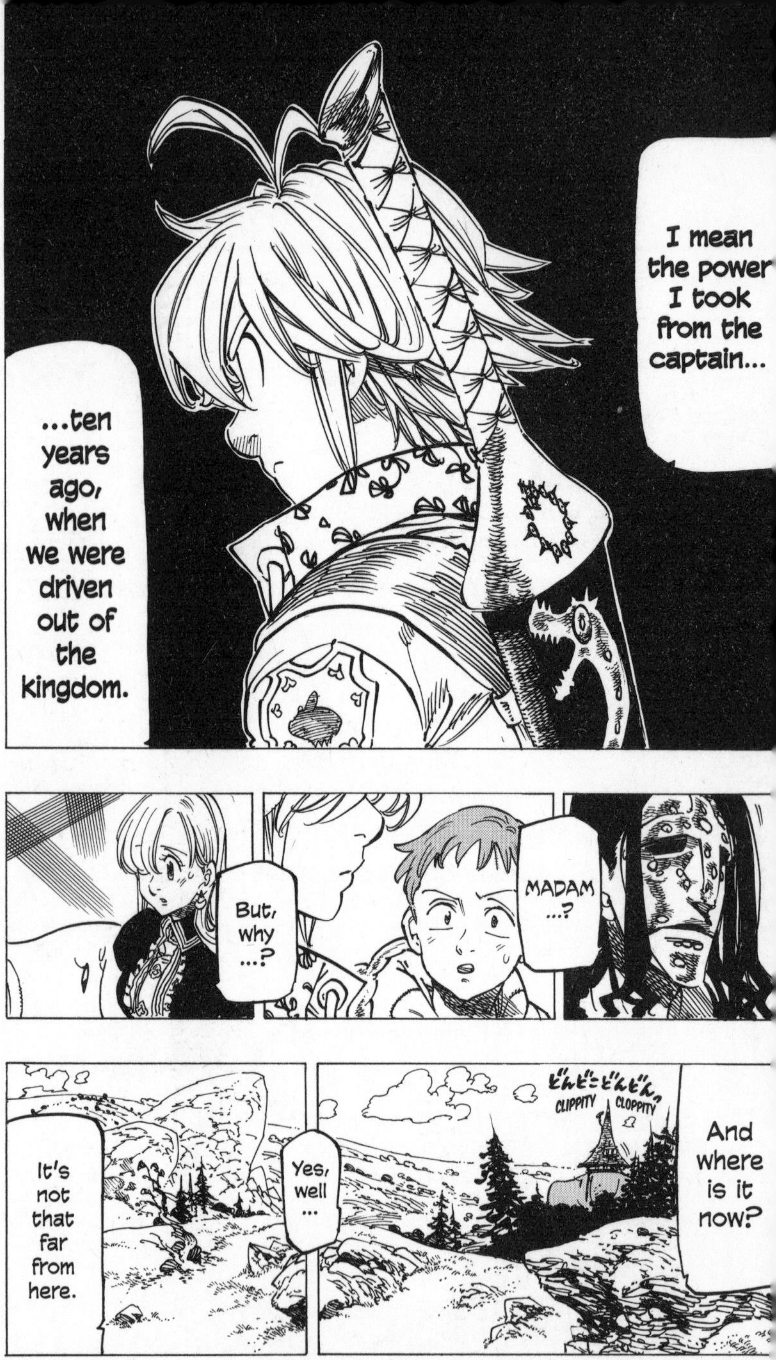
I mean the power I took from the captain...
...ten years ago, when we were driven out of the kingdom.
MADAM ...?
But, why ...?
どんどこどんどん
CLIPPITY CLOPPITY
And where is it now?
Yes, well ...
It's not that far from here.

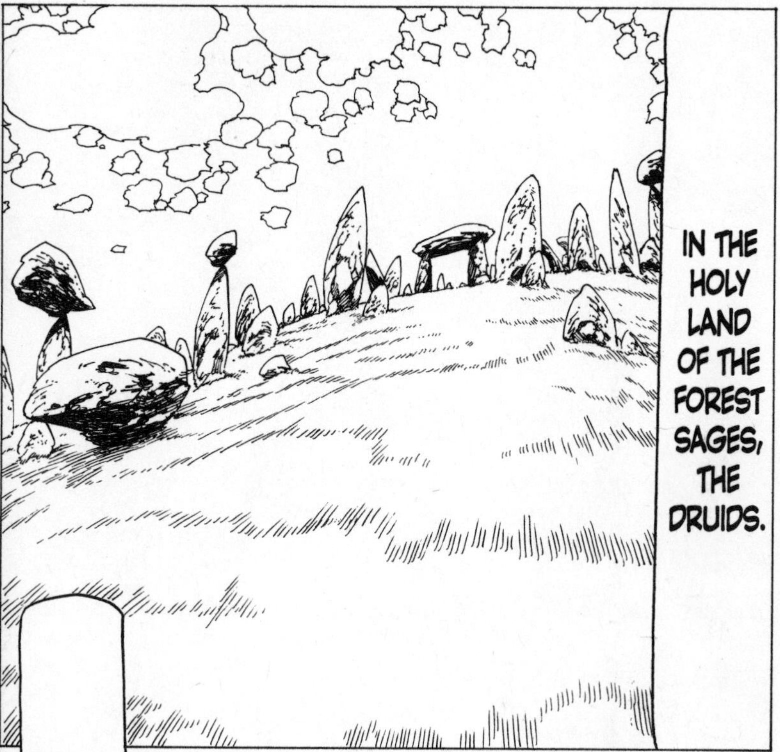
IN THE HOLY LAND OF THE FOREST SAGES, THE DRUIDS.
ISTAL.
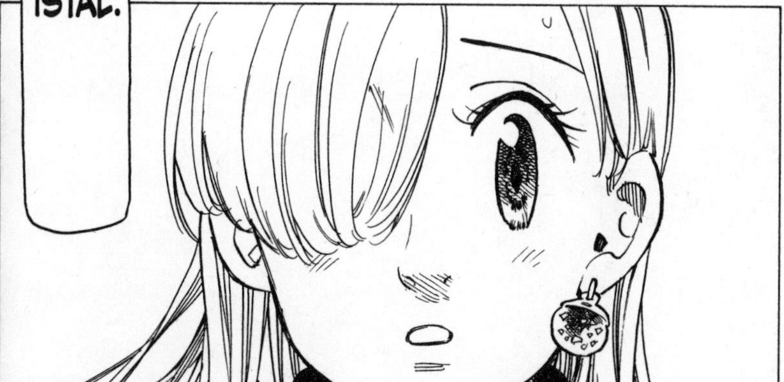

Chapter 129 - The Druids' Holy Land

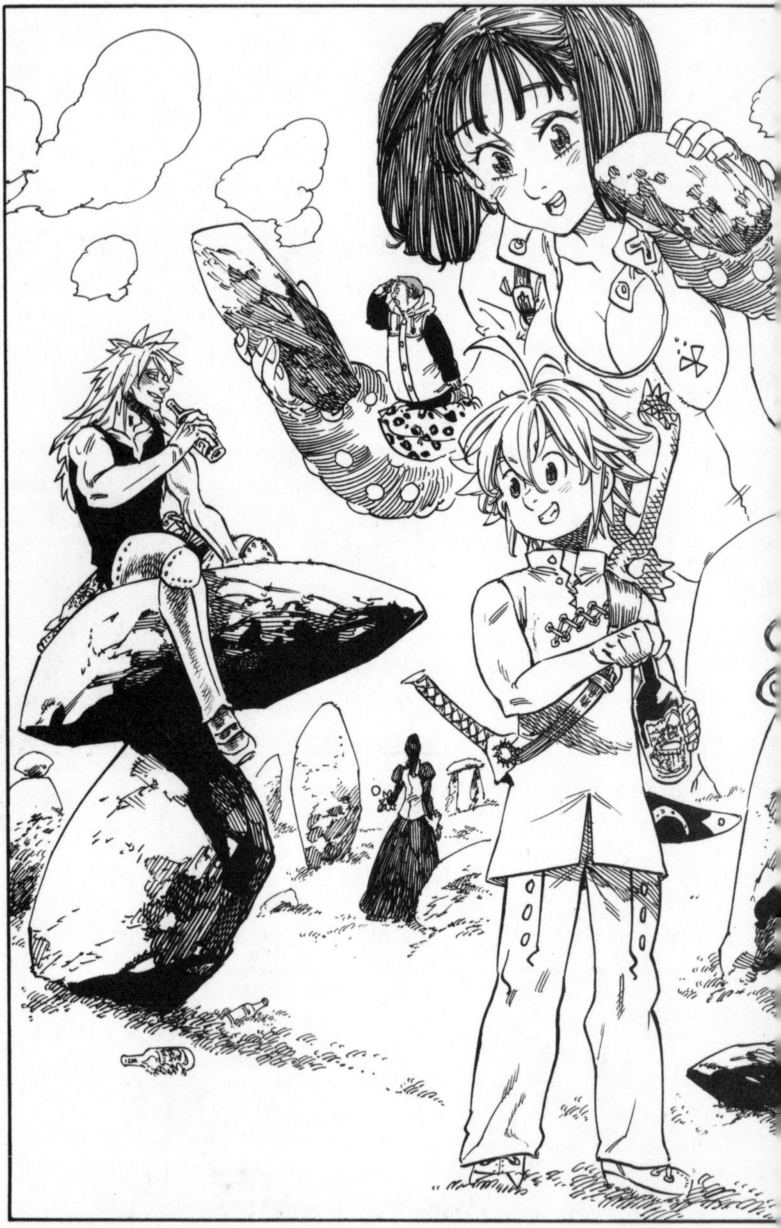

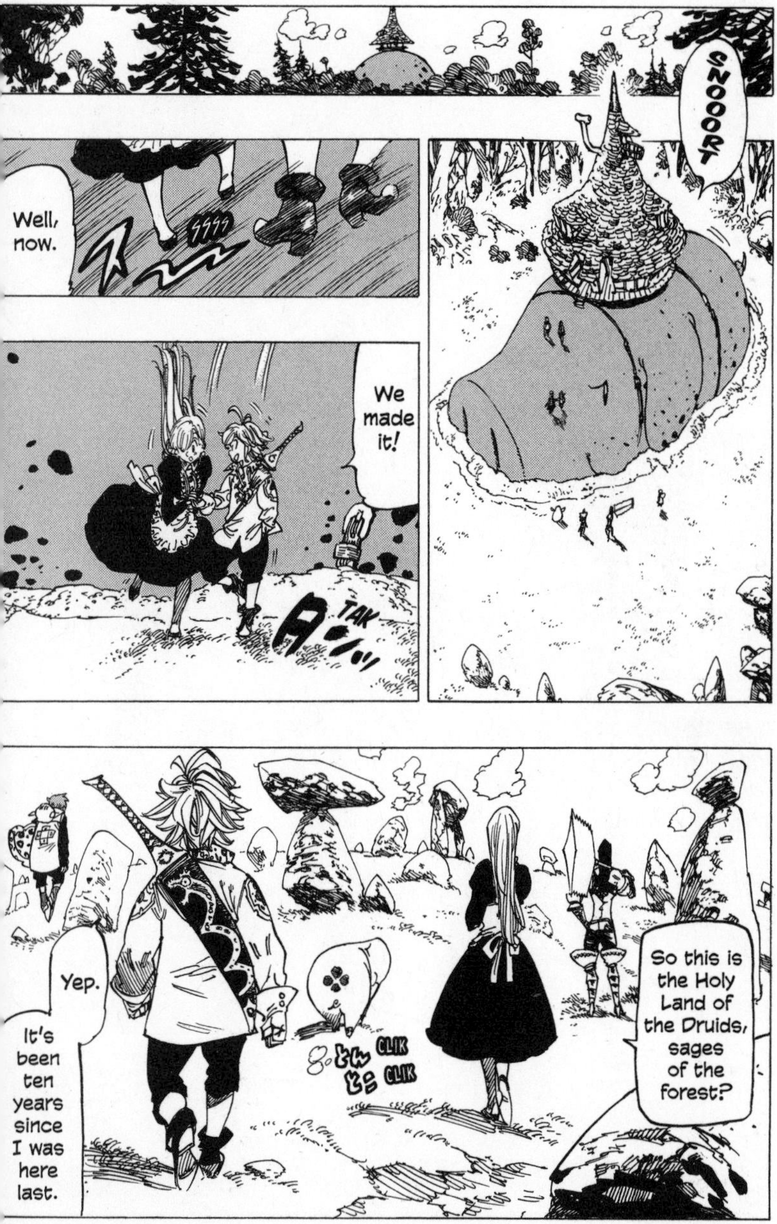
SNOOORT
Well, now.
We made it!
TAK
So this is the Holy Land of the Druids, sages of the forest?
CLIK
CLIK
Yep.
It's been ten years since I was here last.

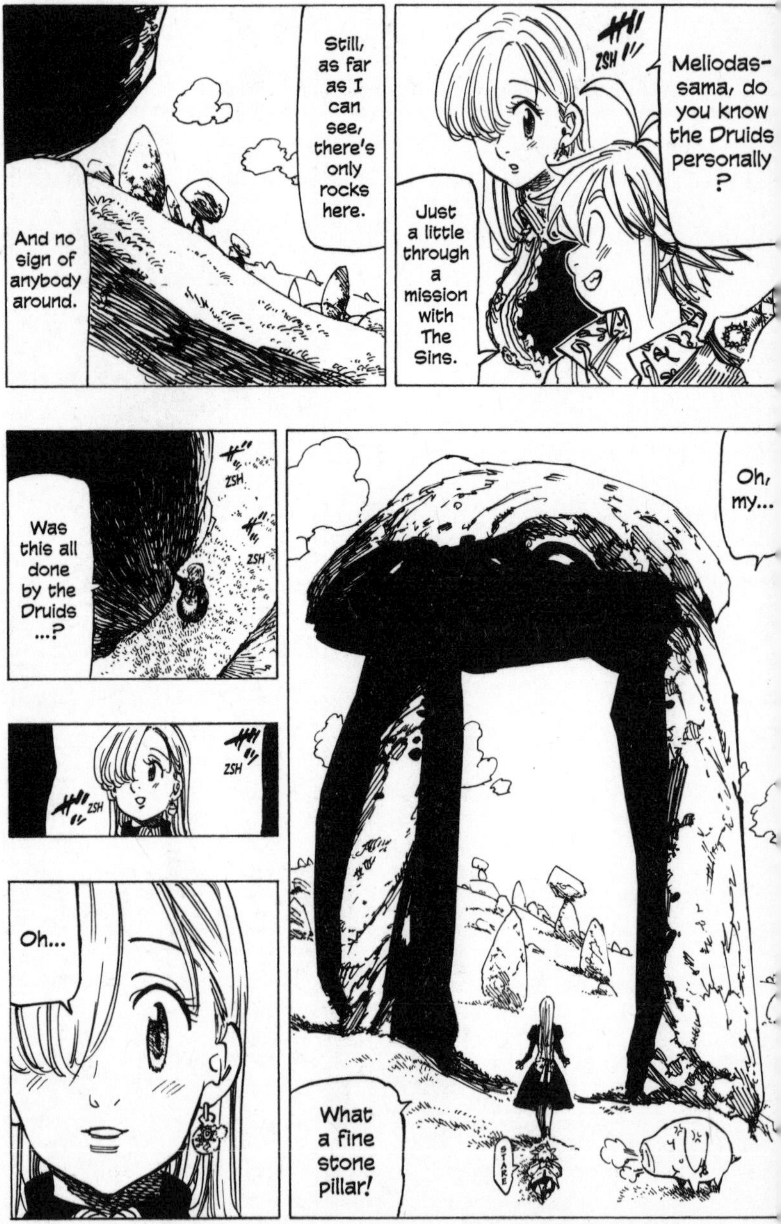
ZSH
Meliodas-sama, do you know the Druids personally?
Just a little through a mission with The Sins.
Still, as far as I can see, there's only rocks here.
And no sign of anybody around.
Oh, my...
What a fine stone pillar!
STARE
ZSH
ZSH
Was this all done by the Druids ...?
ZSH
ZSH
Oh...

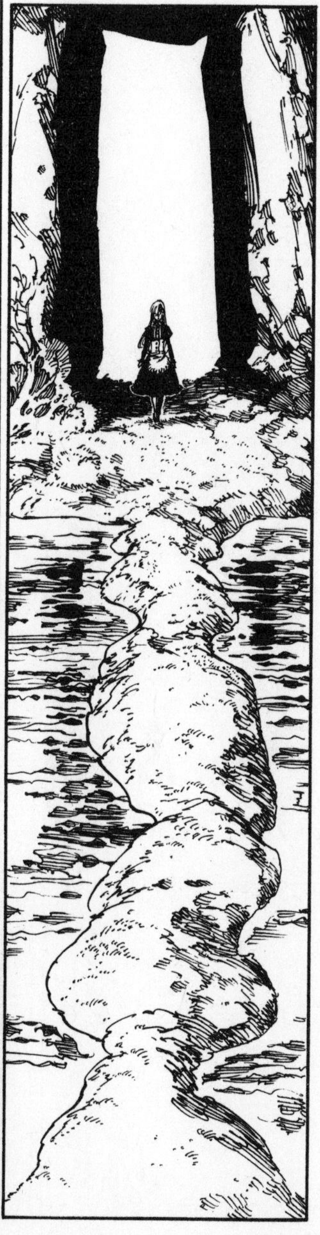
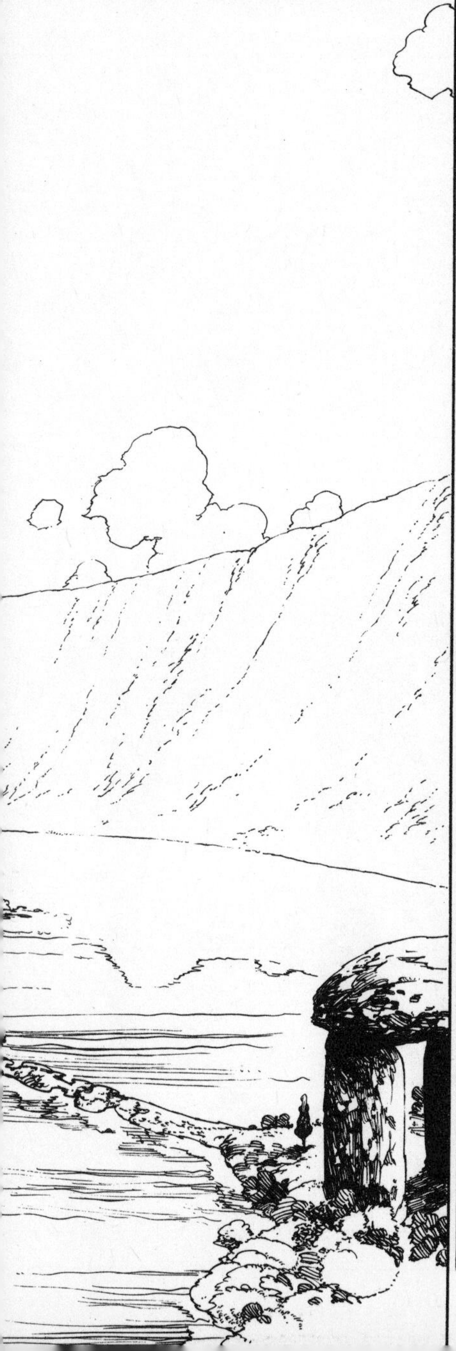

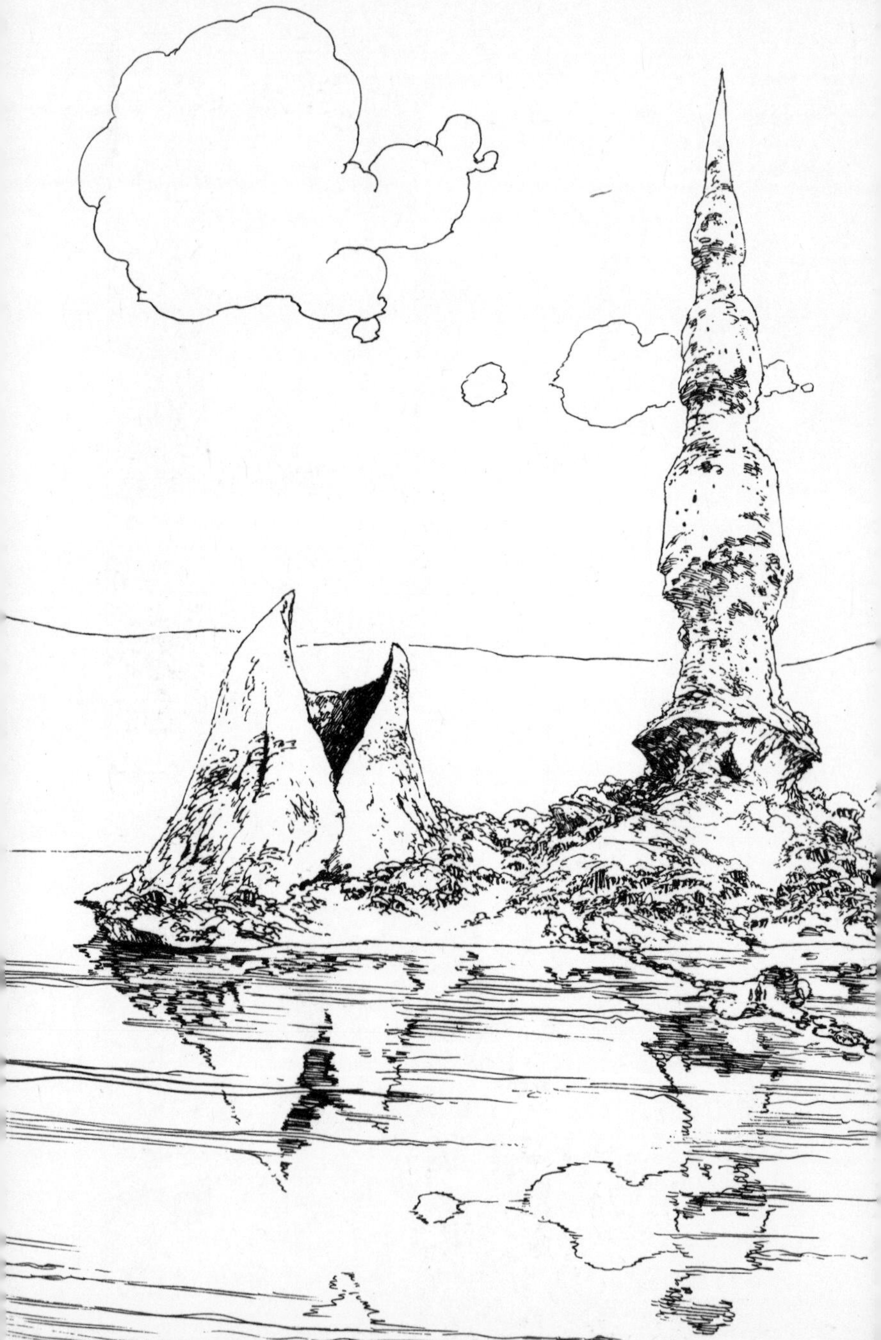

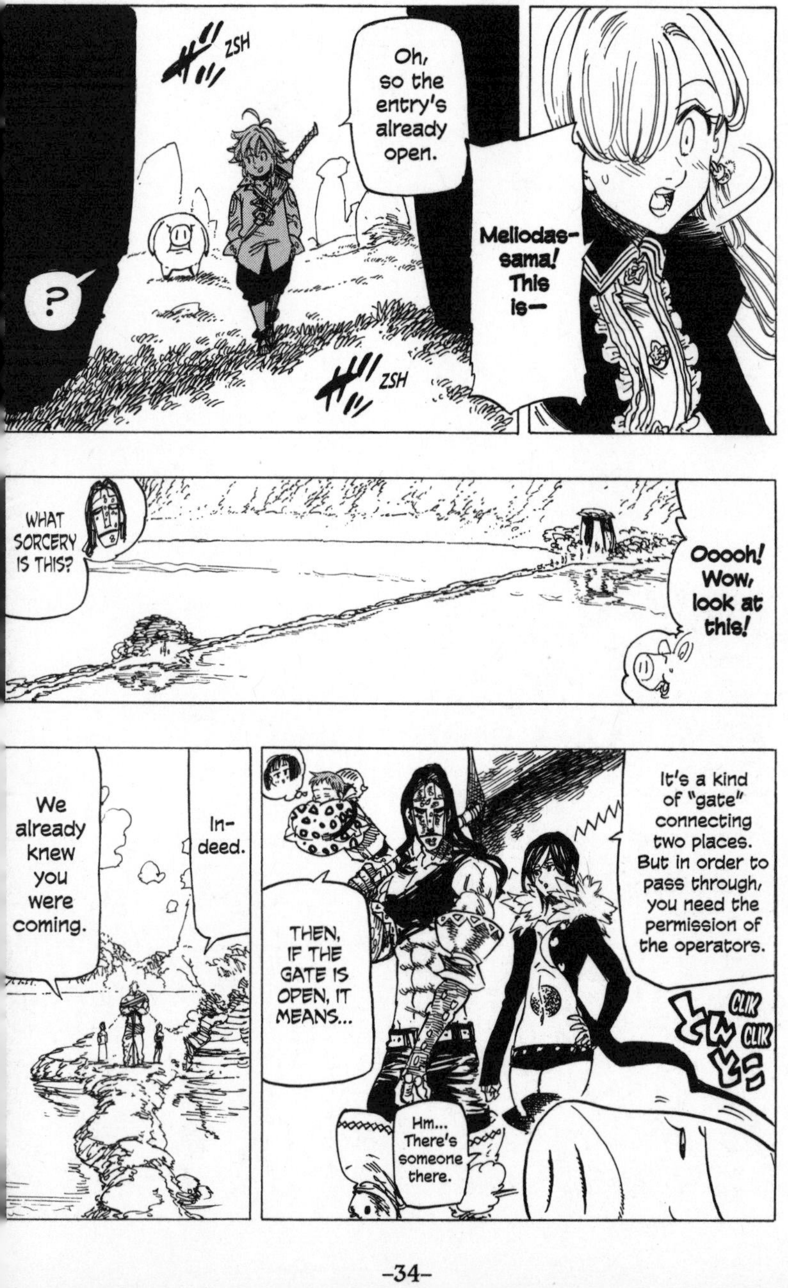

Meliodas-sama! This is—
ZSH
Oh, so the entry's already open.
?
ZSH
Ooooh! Wow, look at this!
WHAT SORCERY IS THIS?
It's a kind of "gate" connecting two places. But in order to pass through, you need the permission of the operators.
CLIK CLIK
THEN, IF THE GATE IS OPEN, IT MEANS...
Hm... There's someone there.
In-deed.
We already knew you were coming.

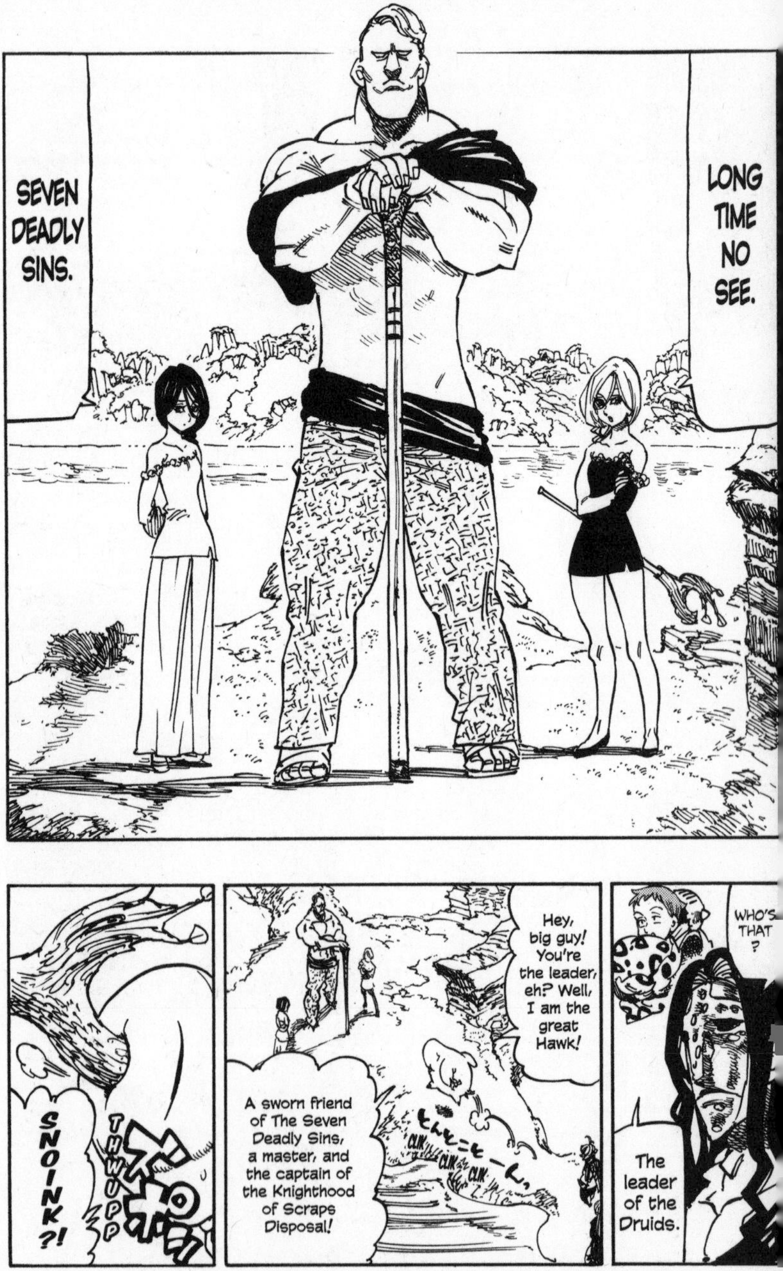
LONG TIME NO SEE.
SEVEN DEADLY SINS.
WHO'S THAT?
The leader of the Druids.
Hey, big guy! You're the leader, eh? Well, I am the great Hawk!
A sworn friend of The Seven Deadly Sins, a master, and the captain of the Knighthood of Scraps Disposal!
とんとことーん
CLIK CLIK CLIK
THWUPP
SNOINK?!

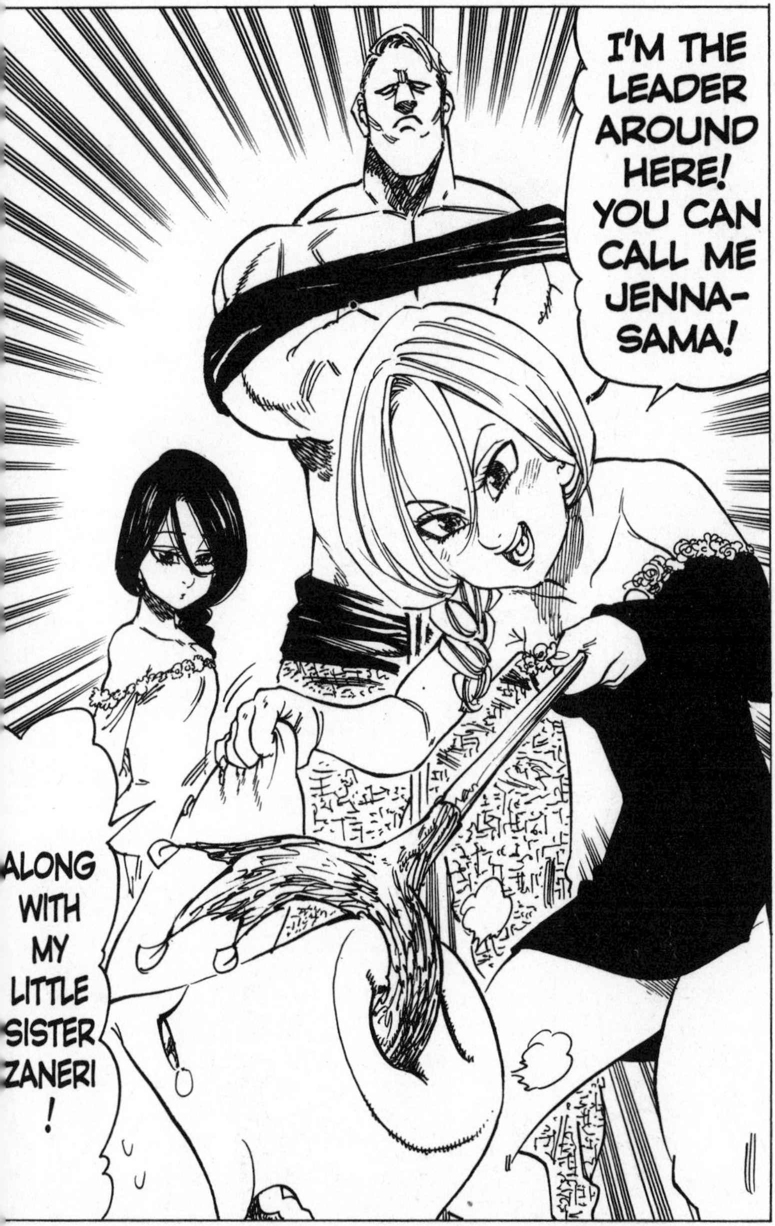
I'M THE LEADER AROUND HERE! YOU CAN CALL ME JENNA-SAMA!
ALONG WITH MY LITTLE SISTER ZANERI!

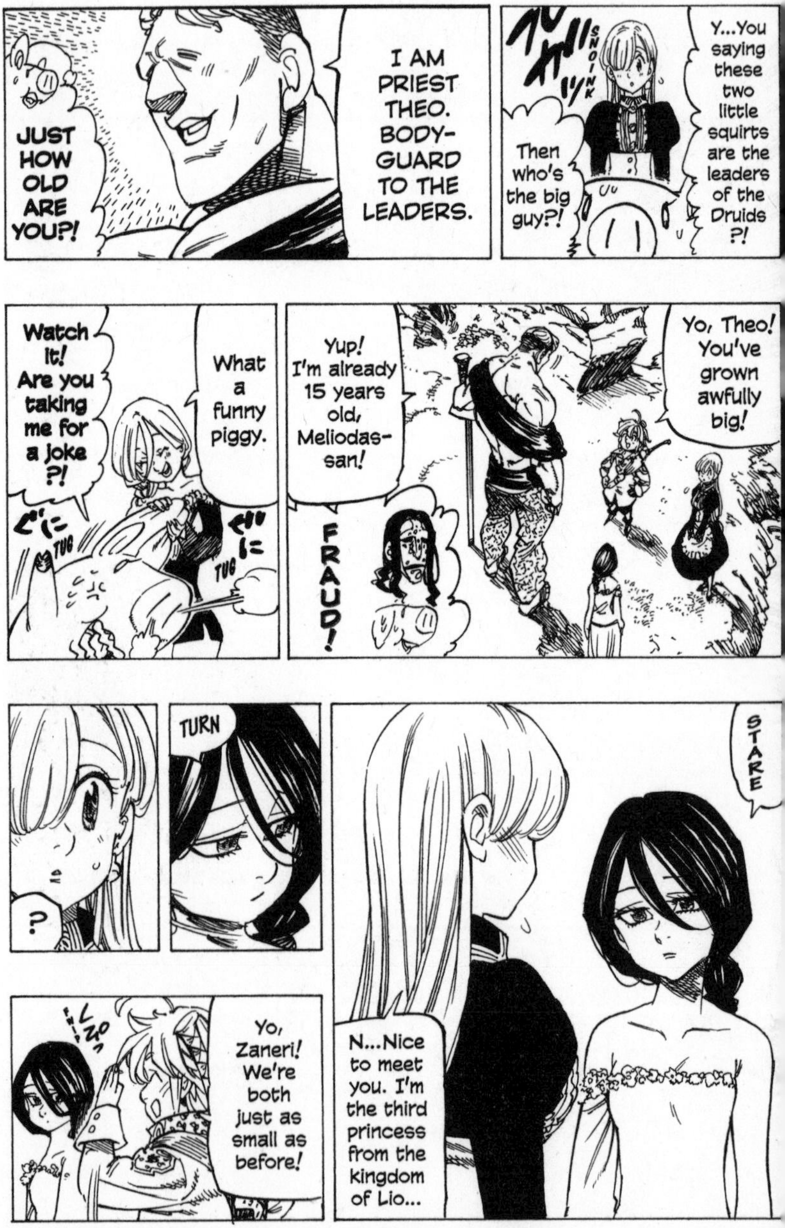
SNOINK
Y...You saying these two little squirts are the leaders of the Druids?!
Then who's the big guy?!
I AM PRIEST THEO. BODY-GUARD TO THE LEADERS.
JUST HOW OLD ARE YOU?!
Yo, Theo! You've grown awfully big!
Yup! I'm already 15 years old, Meliodas-san!
FRAUD!
What a funny piggy.
Watch it! Are you taking me for a joke?!
TUG
TUG
STARE
N...Nice to meet you. I'm the third princess from the kingdom of Lio...
TURN
?
Yo, Zaneri! We're both just as small as before!

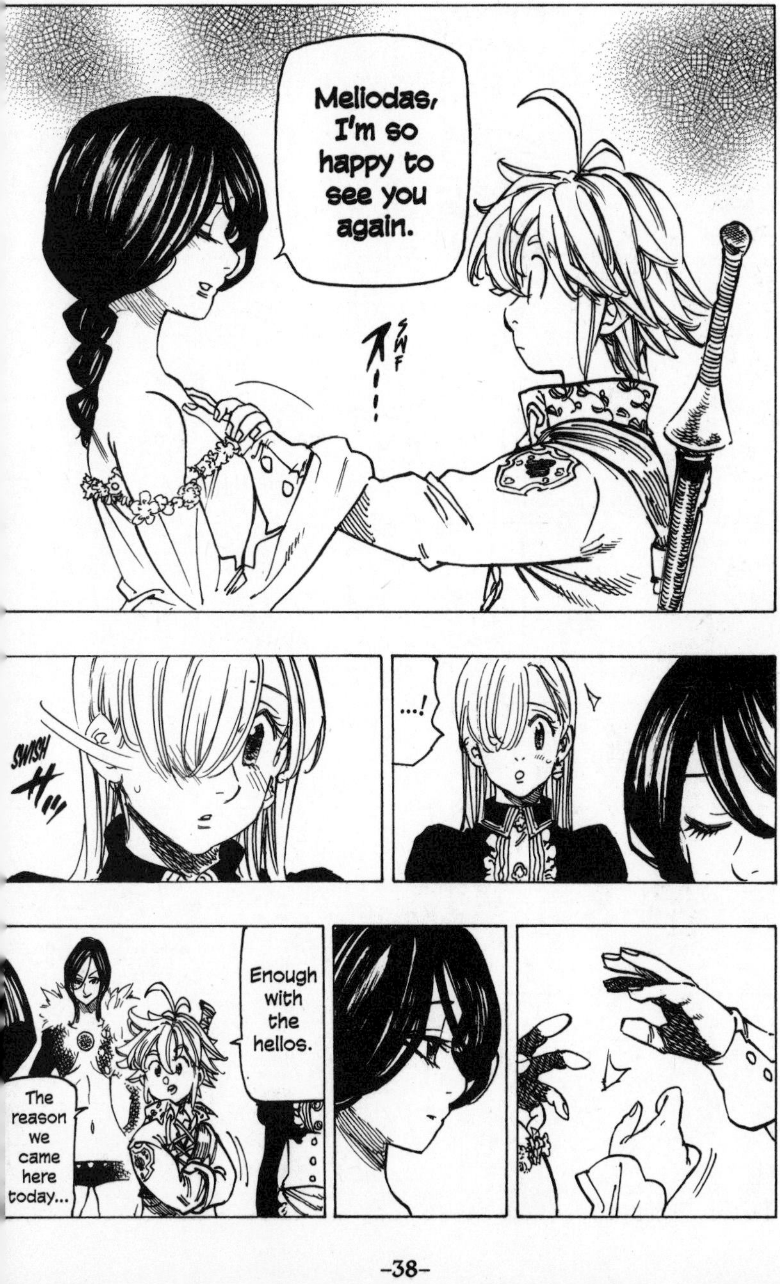
Meliodas, I'm so happy to see you again.
SWF
...!
SWISH
Enough with the hellos.
The reason we came here today...

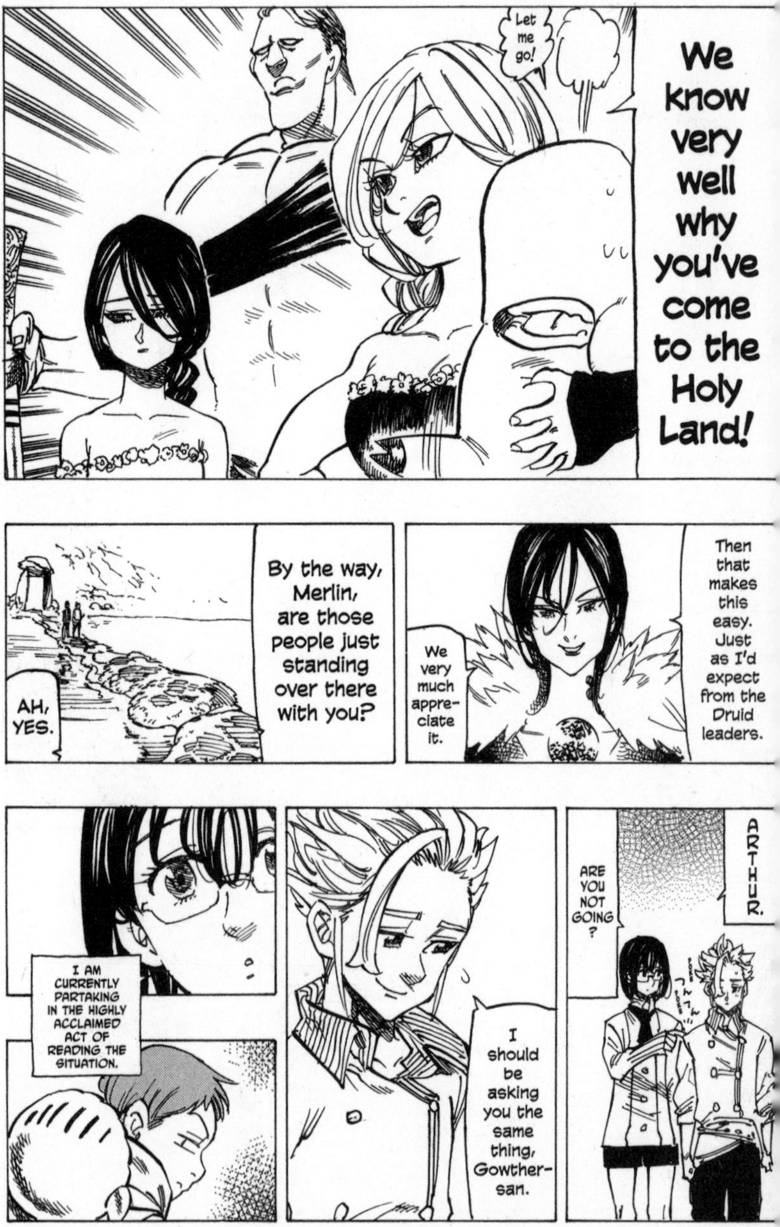
We know very well why you've come to the Holy Land!
Let me go!
Then that makes this easy. Just as I'd expect from the Druid leaders.
We very much appreciate it.
By the way, Merlin, are those people just standing over there with you?
AH, YES.
ARTHUR.
ARE YOU NOT GOING?
I should be asking you the same thing, Gowther-san.
I AM CURRENTLY PARTAKING IN THE HIGHLY ACCLAIMED ACT OF READING THE SITUATION.

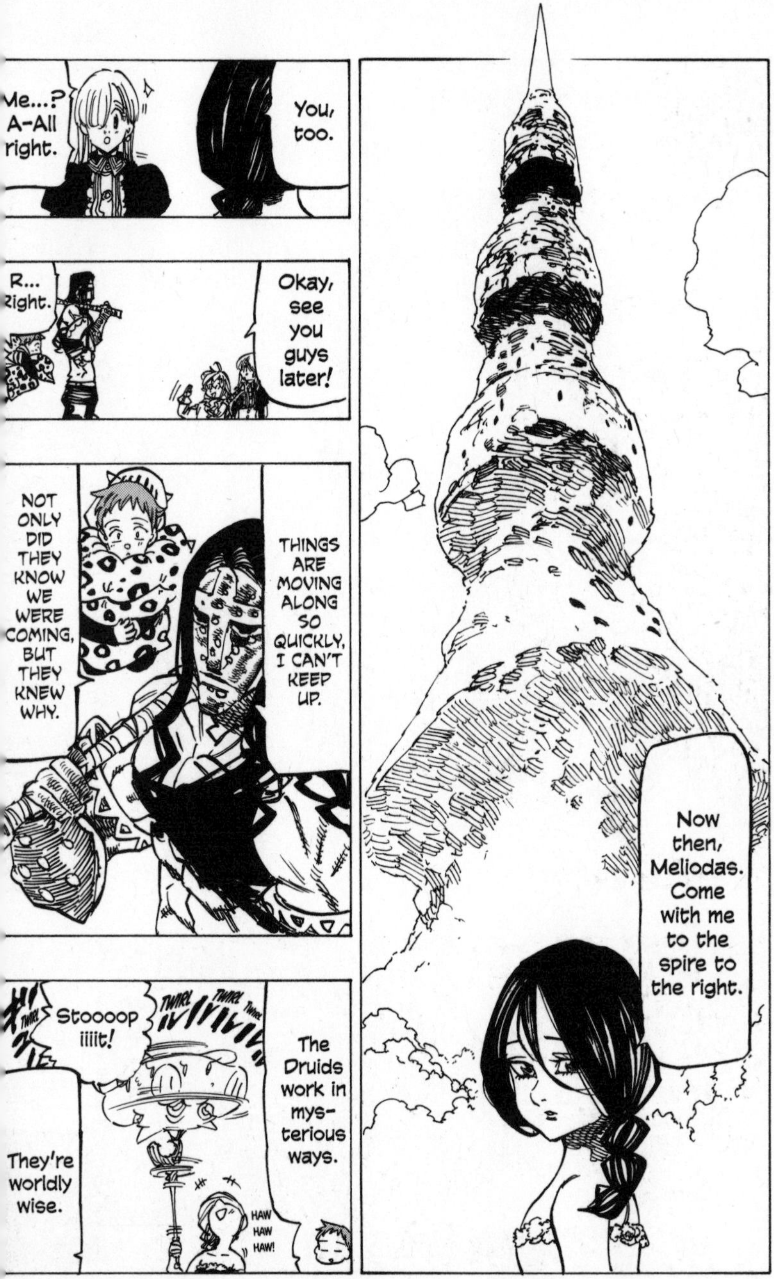

Now then, Meliodas. Come with me to the spire to the right.
You, too.
Me...? A-All right.
Okay, see you guys later!
R... Right.
THINGS ARE MOVING ALONG SO QUICKLY, I CAN'T KEEP UP.
NOT ONLY DID THEY KNOW WE WERE COMING, BUT THEY KNEW WHY.
TWIRL TWIRL Twirl
Stoooop iiiit!
The Druids work in mys-terious ways.
They're worldly wise.
HAW HAW HAW!

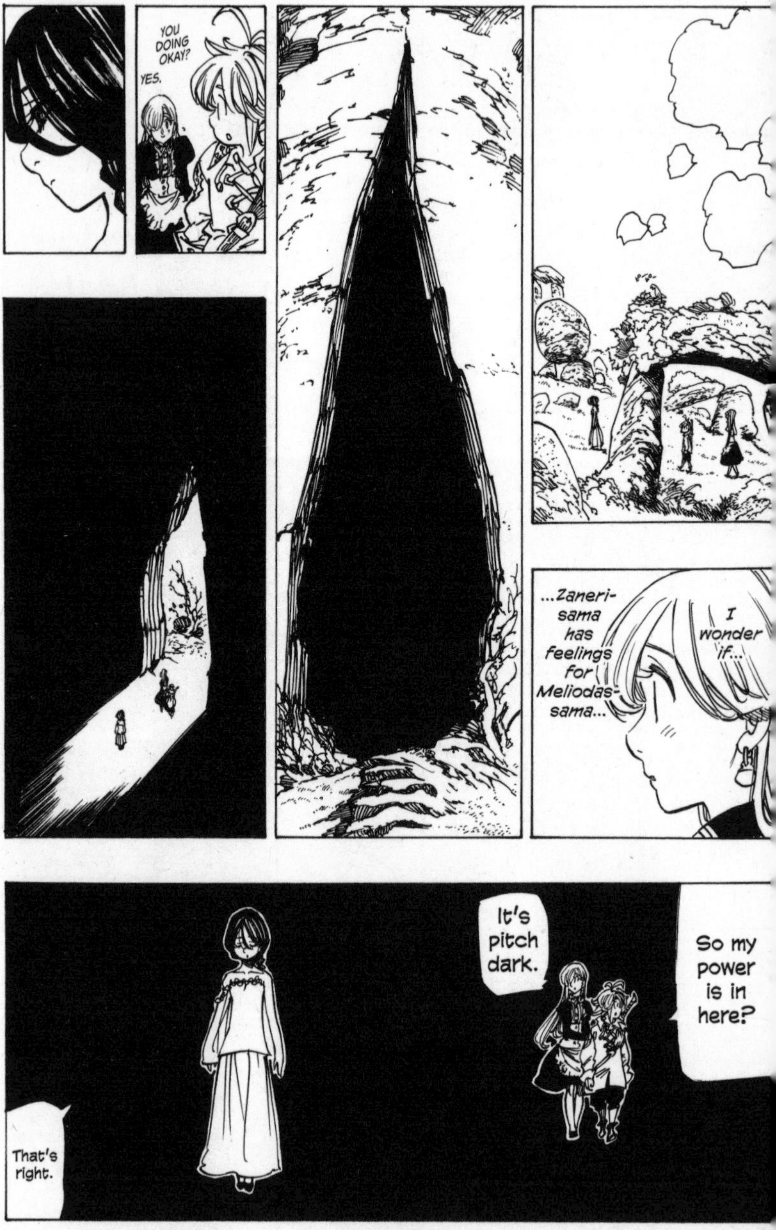
I wonder if...
...Zaneri-sama has feelings for Meliodas-sama...
YOU DOING OKAY?
YES.
So my power is in here?
It's pitch dark.
That's right.

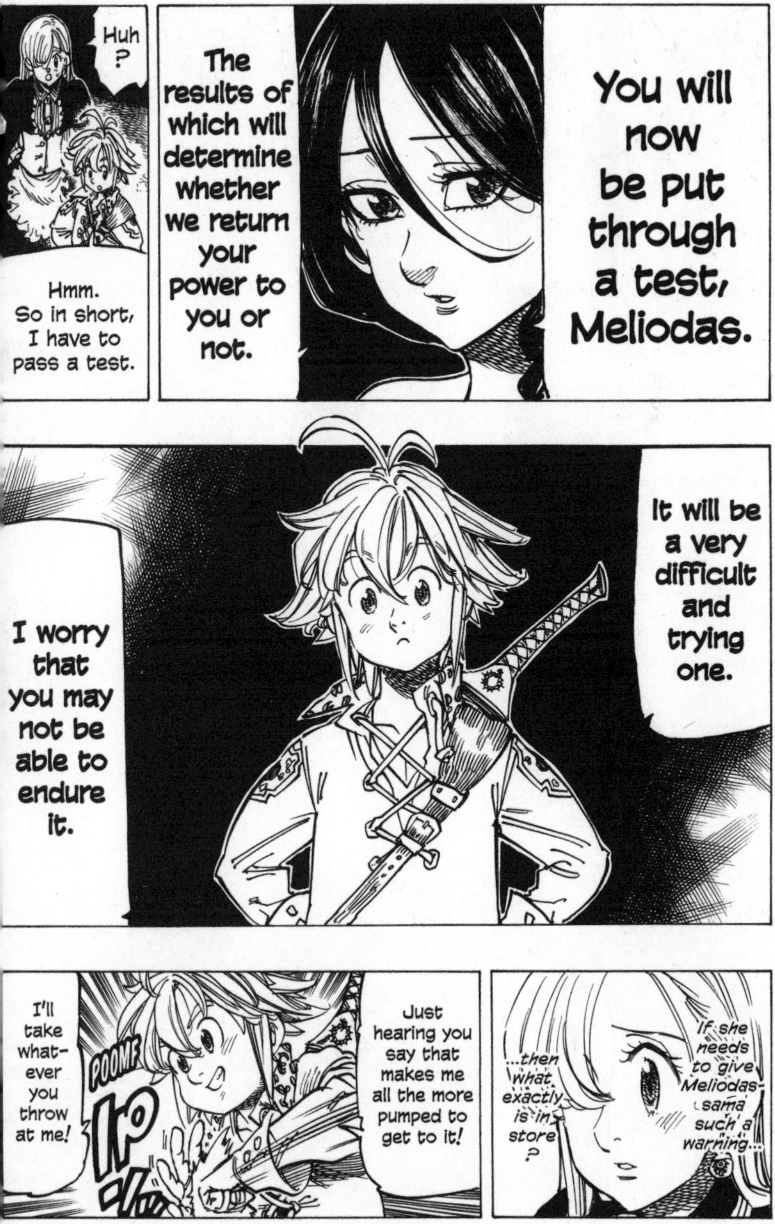
You will now be put through a test, Meliodas.
The results of which will determine whether we return your power to you or not.
Huh?
Hmm. So in short, I have to pass a test.
It will be a very difficult and trying one.
I worry that you may not be able to endure it.
If she needs to give Meliodas-sama such a warning...
...then what exactly is in store?
Just hearing you say that makes me all the more pumped to get to it!
I'll take whatever you throw at me!
POOMF

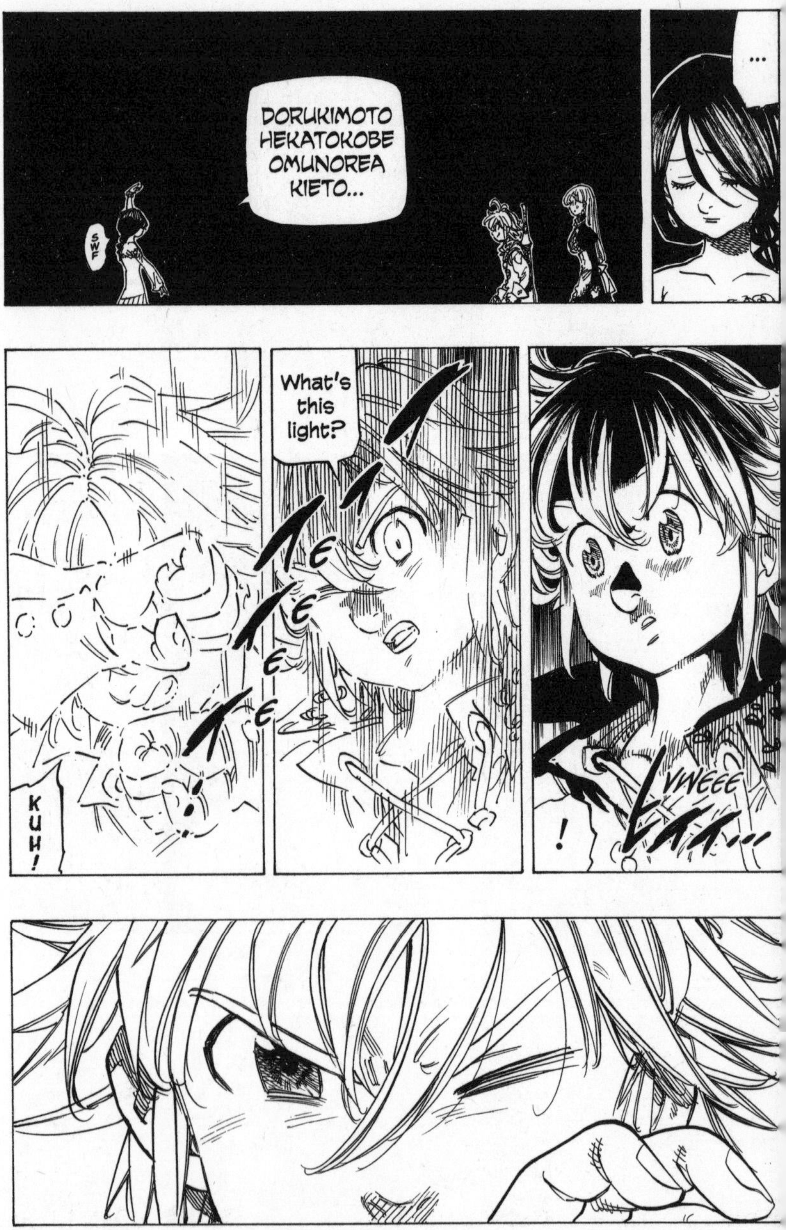
...
DORUKIMOTO HEKATOKOBE OMUNOREA KIETO...
SWF
!
VWEEE
What's this light?
KUH!

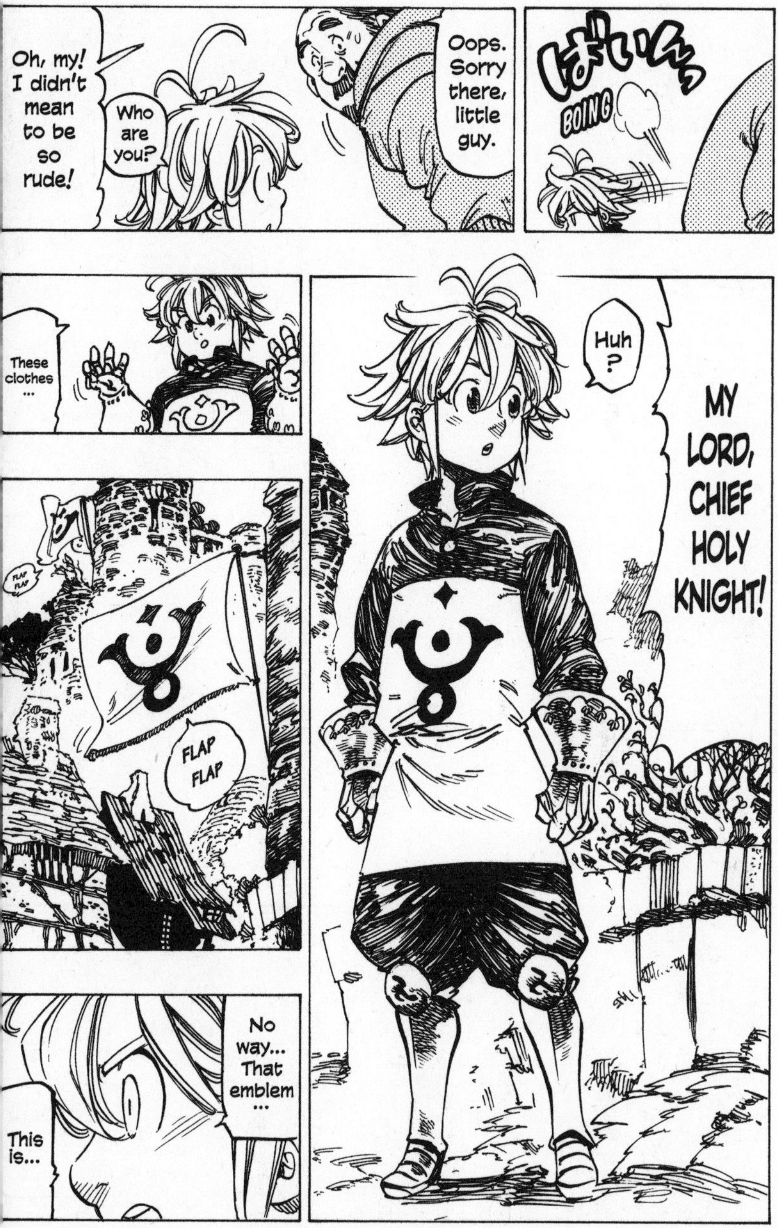
BOING
Oops. Sorry there, little guy.
Oh, my! I didn't mean to be so rude!
Who are you?
MY LORD, CHIEF HOLY KNIGHT!
Huh?
These clothes...
FLAP FLAP
FLAP FLAP
No way... That emblem...
This is...

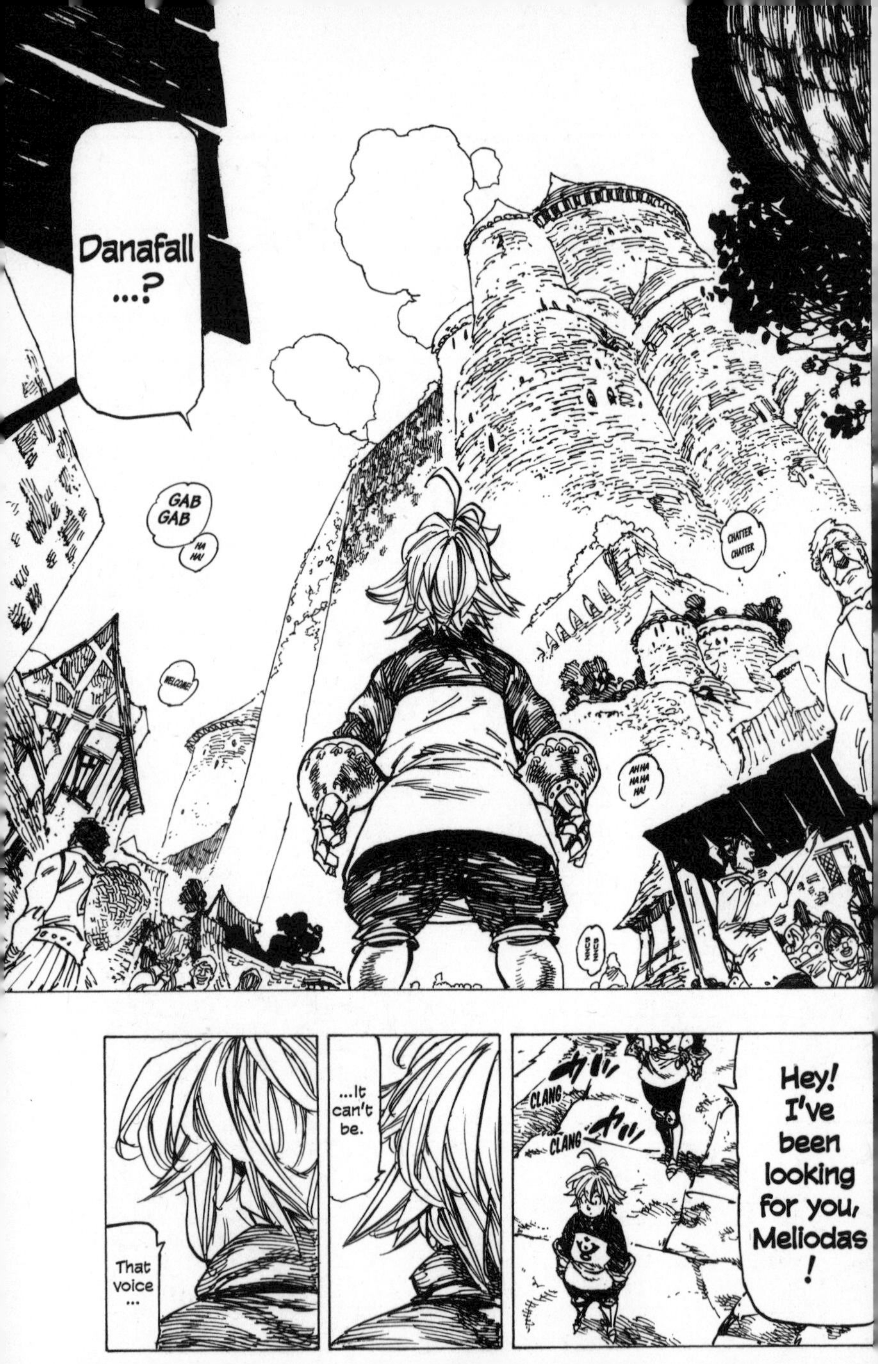
Danafall ...?
CHATTER CHATTER
AH HA HA HA HA!
GAB GAB
HA HA!
WELCOME!
Hey! I've been looking for you, Meliodas!
CLANG
CLANG
...It can't be.
That voice ...

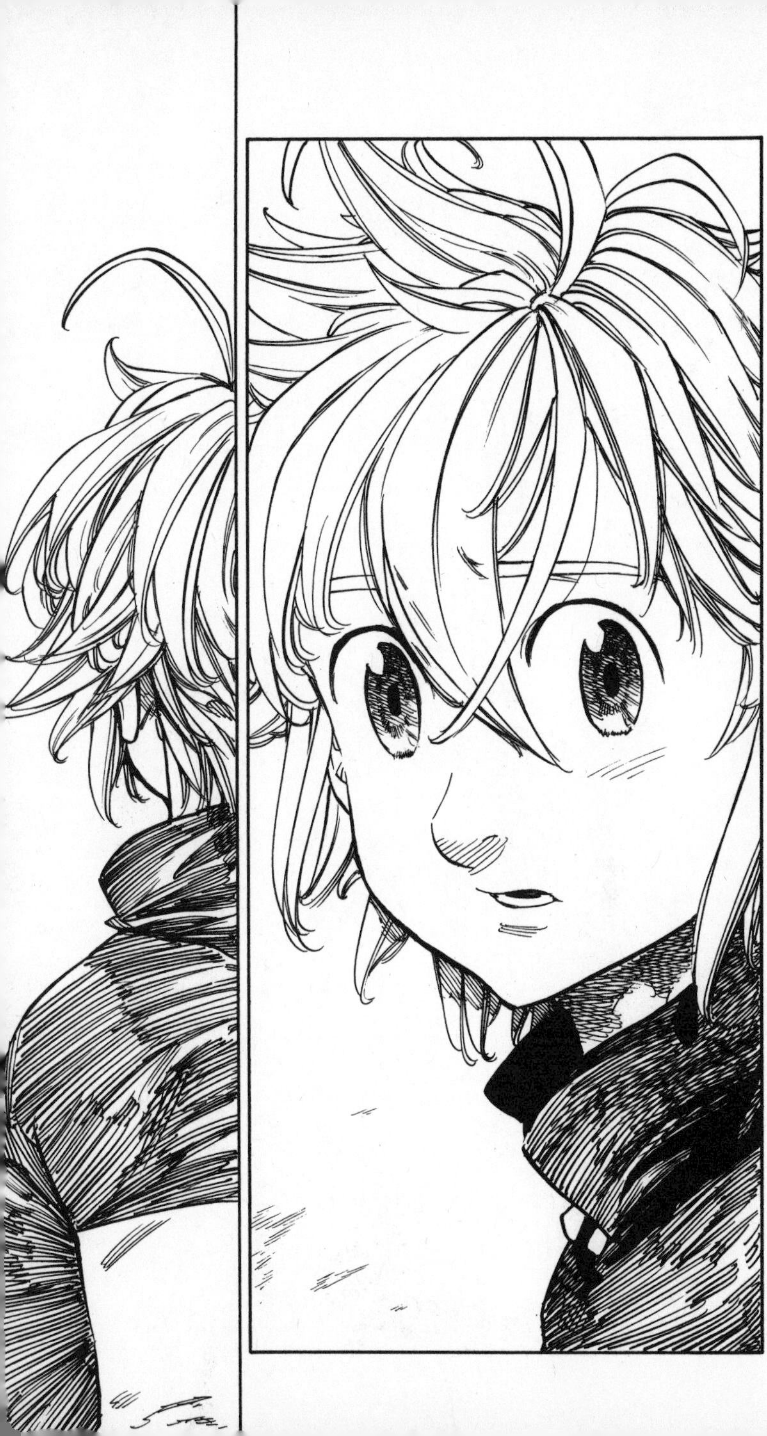

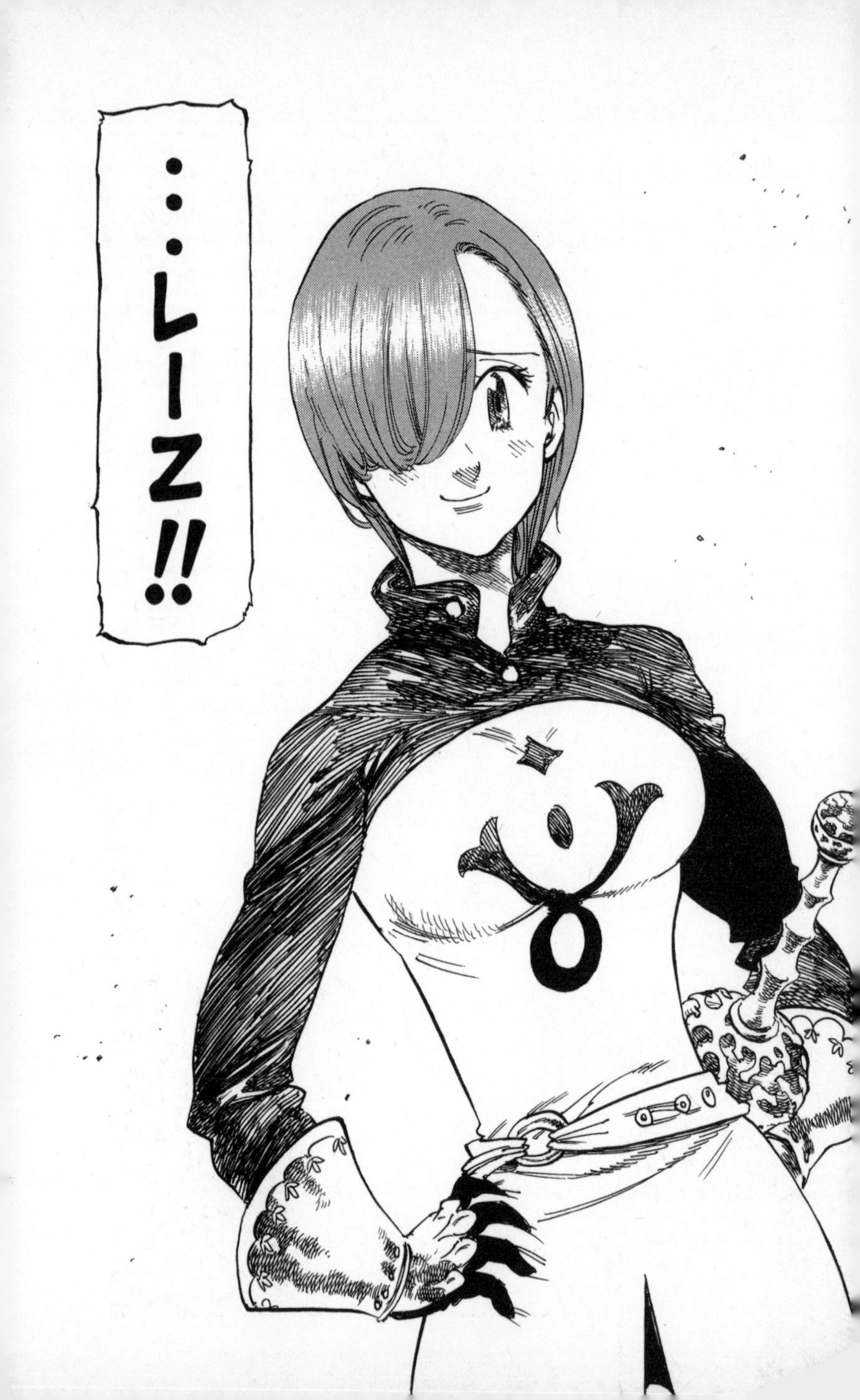
...LIZ!!

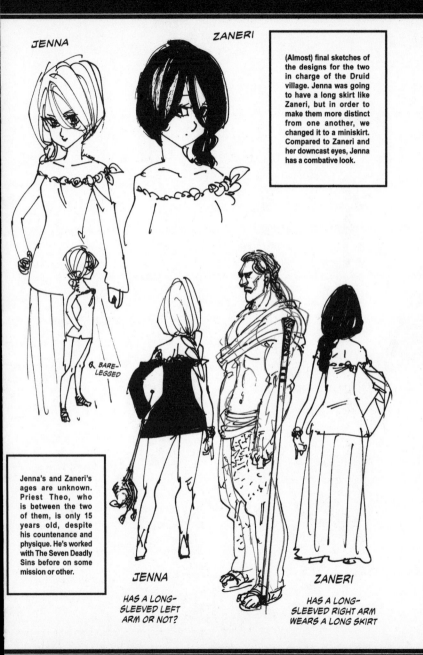

JENNA

ZANERI

(Almost) final sketches of the designs for the two in charge of the Druid village. Jenna was going to have a long skirt like Zaneri, but in order to make them more distinct from one another, we changed it to a miniskirt. Compared to Zaneri and her downcast eyes, Jenna has a combative look.

BARE-LEGGED

Jenna's and Zaneri's ages are unknown. Priest Theo, who is between the two of them, is only 15 years old, despite his countenance and physique. He's worked with The Seven Deadly Sins before on some mission or other.

JENNA

HAS A LONG-SLEEVED LEFT ARM OR NOT?

ZANERI

HAS A LONG-SLEEVED RIGHT ARM WEARS A LONG SKIRT

Chapter 130 - The Pain of Being Softly Pierce

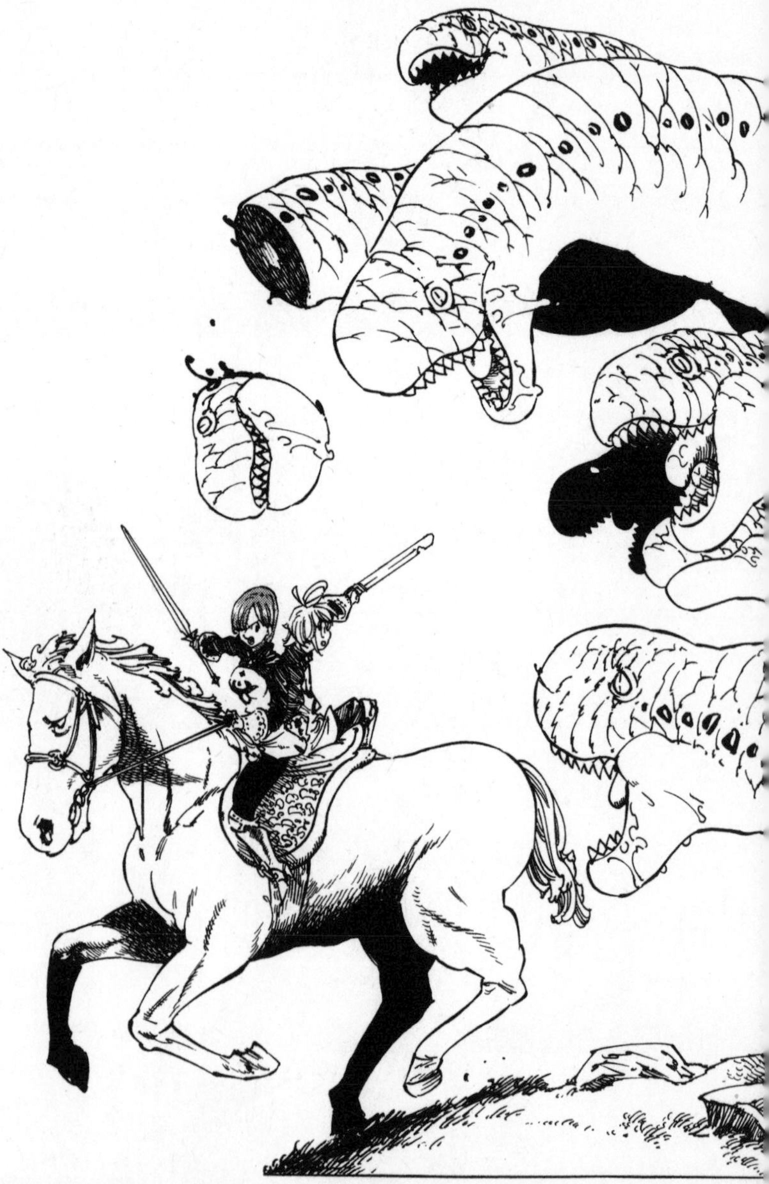

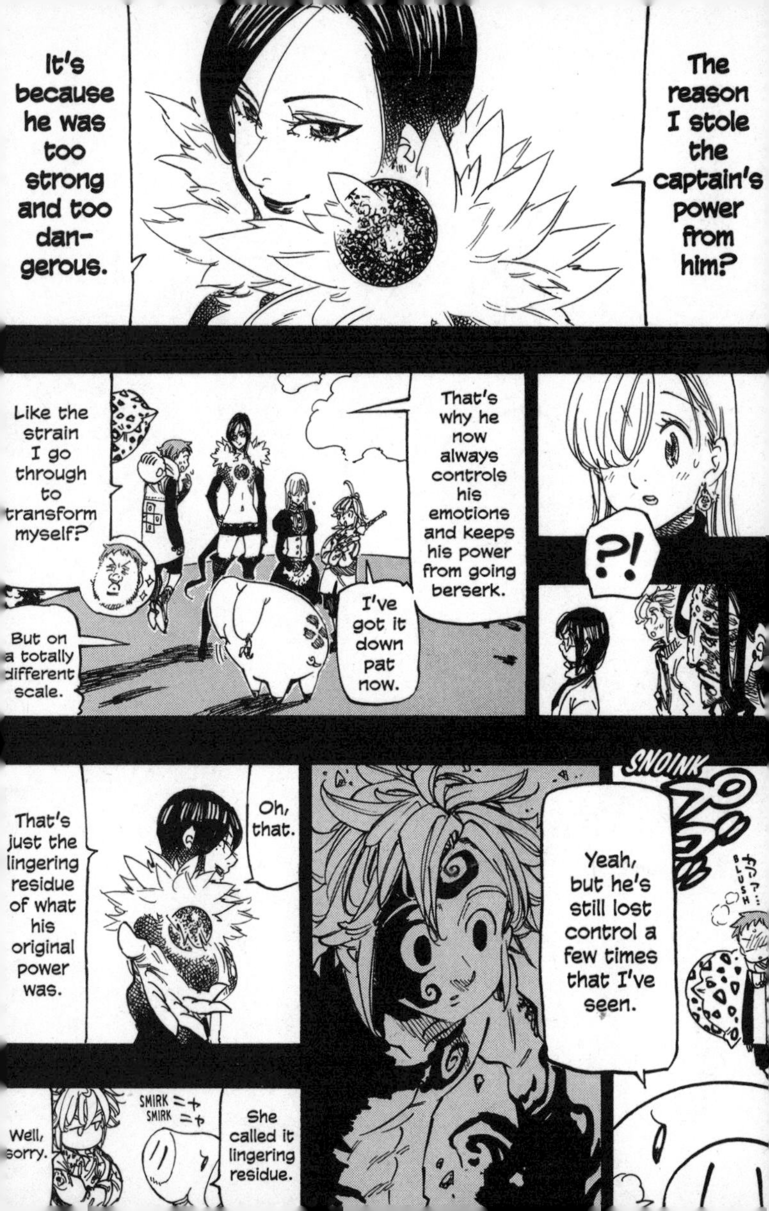
The reason I stole the captain's power from him?
It's because he was too strong and too dangerous.
?!
That's why he now always controls his emotions and keeps his power from going berserk.
I've got it down pat now.
Like the strain I go through to transform myself?
But on a totally different scale.
SNOINK
BLUSH
Yeah, but he's still lost control a few times that I've seen.
Oh, that.
That's just the lingering residue of what his original power was.
She called it lingering residue.
SMIRK SMIRK
Well, sorry.

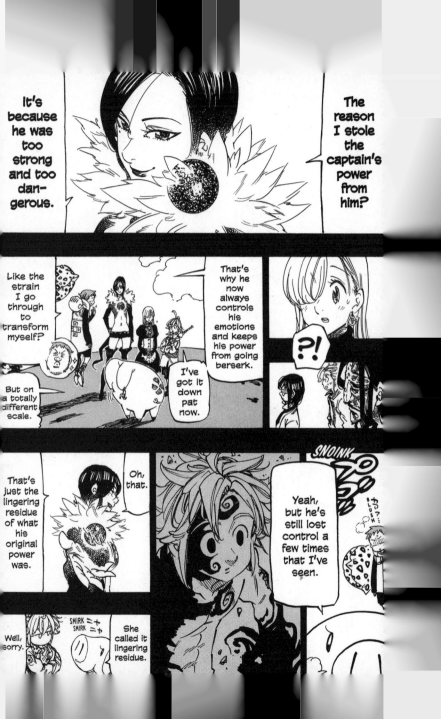

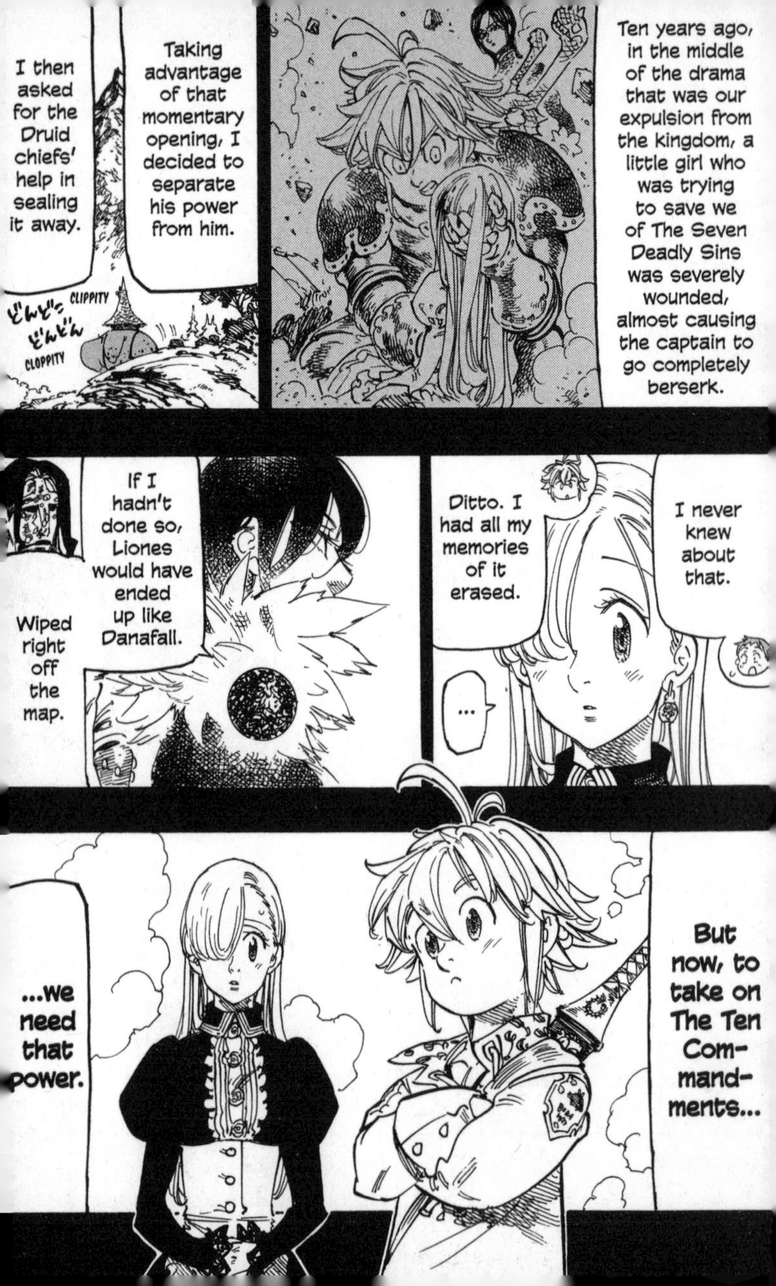

Ten years ago, in the middle of the drama that was our expulsion from the kingdom, a little girl who was trying to save we of The Seven Deadly Sins was severely wounded, almost causing the captain to go completely berserk.
Taking advantage of that momentary opening, I decided to separate his power from him.
I then asked for the Druid chiefs' help in sealing it away.
どんどこ CLIPPITY
どんどん CLIPPITY
I never knew about that.
Ditto. I had all my memories of it erased.
...
If I hadn't done so, Liones would have ended up like Danafall.
Wiped right off the map.
But now, to take on The Ten Commandments...
...we need that power.

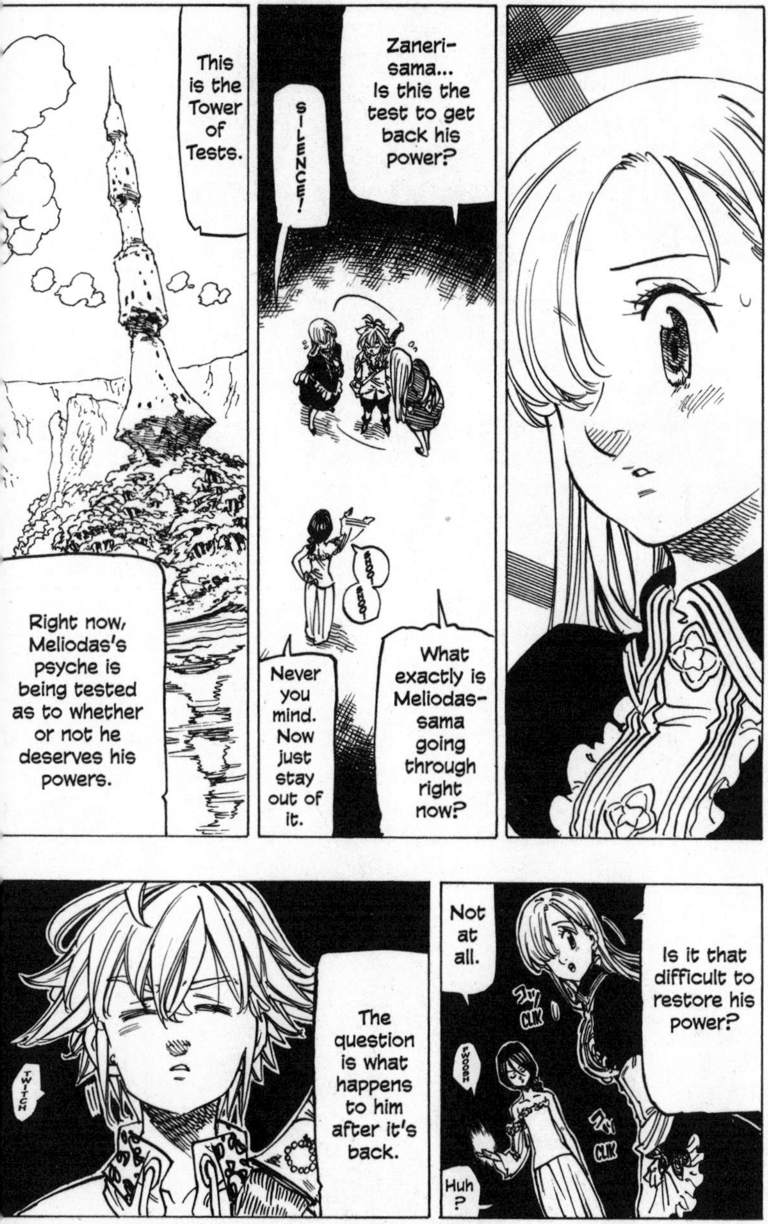
Zaneri-sama... Is this the test to get back his power?
SILENCE!
What exactly is Meliodas-sama going through right now?
Never you mind. Now just stay out of it.
This is the Tower of Tests.
Right now, Meliodas's psyche is being tested as to whether or not he deserves his powers.
Is it that difficult to restore his power?
Not at all.
CLIK
FWOOSH
CLIK
Huh?
The question is what happens to him after it's back.
TWITCH

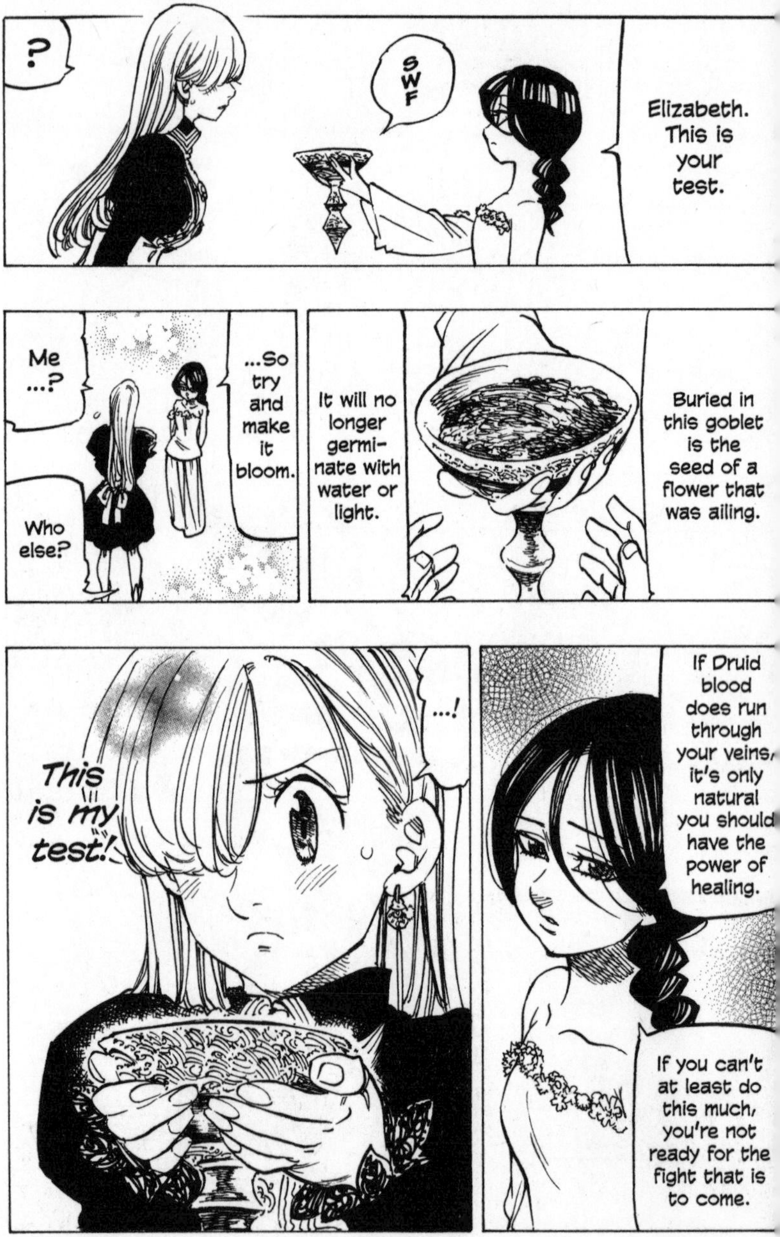
Elizabeth. This is your test.
SWF
?
Buried in this goblet is the seed of a flower that was ailing.
It will no longer germinate with water or light.
...So try and make it bloom.
Me ...?
Who else?
If Druid blood does run through your veins, it's only natural you should have the power of healing.
If you can't at least do this much, you're not ready for the fight that is to come.
...!
This is my test!

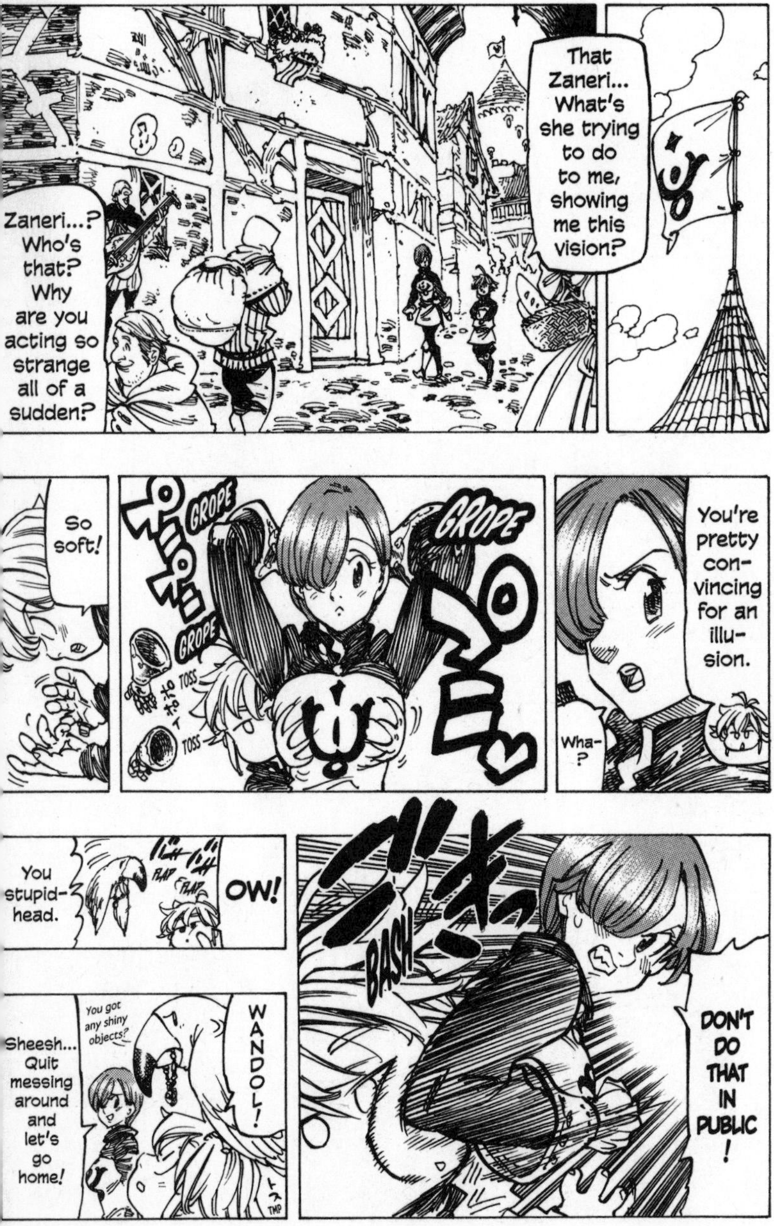
That Zaneri... What's she trying to do to me, showing me this vision?
Zaneri...? Who's that? Why are you acting so strange all of a sudden?
You're pretty convincing for an illusion.
Wha-?
GROPE
GROPE
GROPE
TOSS
TOSS
So soft!
BASH
DON'T DO THAT IN PUBLIC!
OW!
FLAP
FLAP
You stupid-head.
WANDOL!
You got any shiny objects?
Sheesh... Quit messing around and let's go home!
TMP

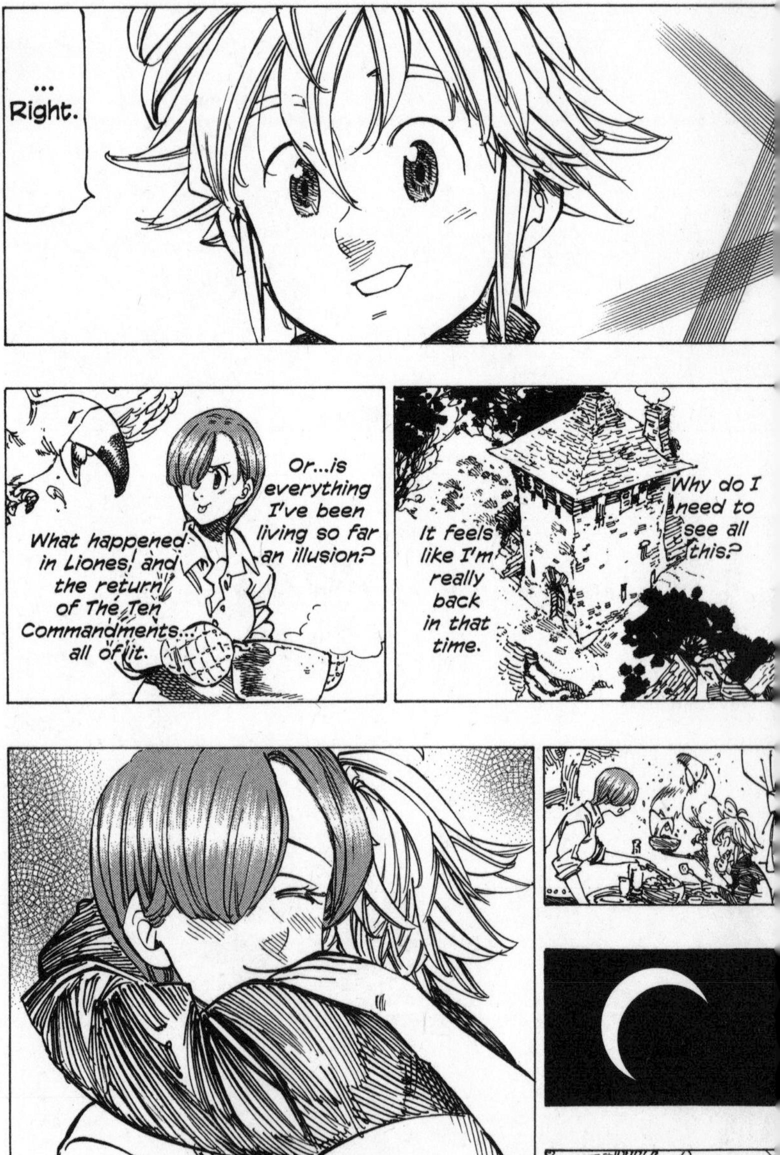

... Right.
Why do I need to see all this?
It feels like I'm really back in that time.
Or...is everything I've been living so far an illusion?
What happened in Liones, and the return of The Ten Commandments... all of it.

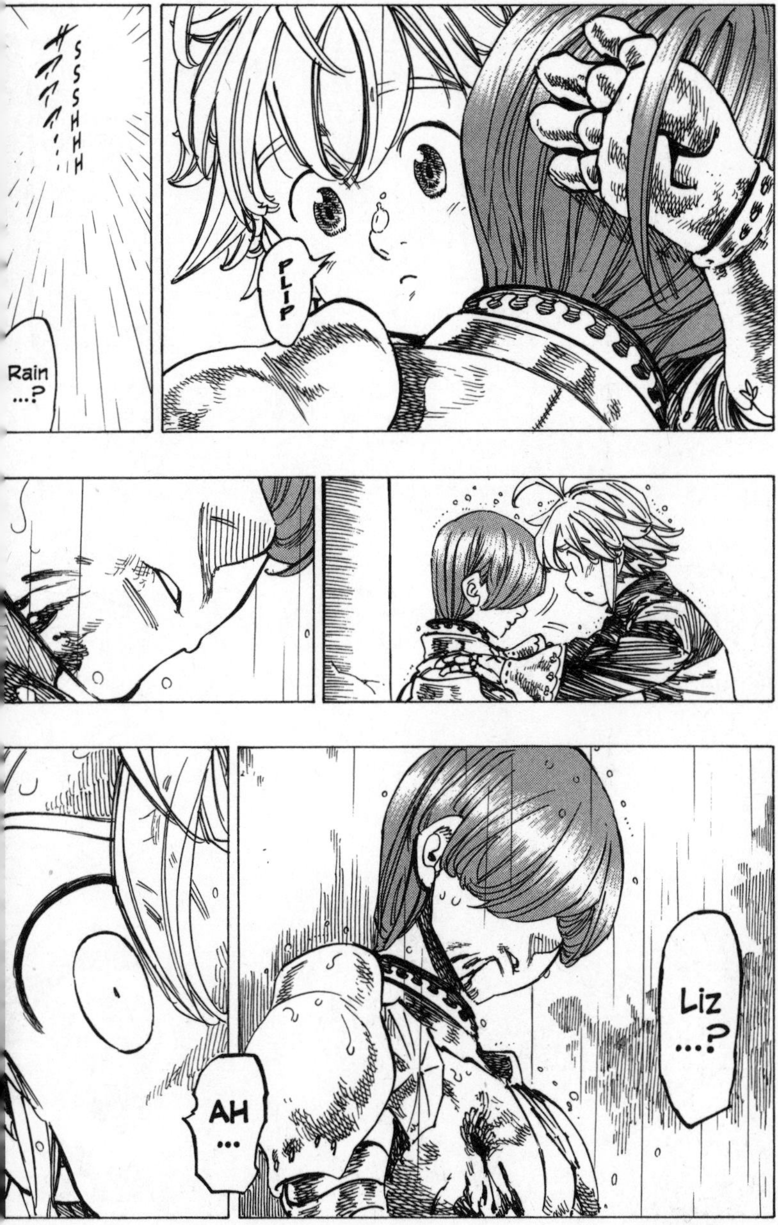
PLIP
SSSHHH
Rain ...?
Liz ...?
AH ...

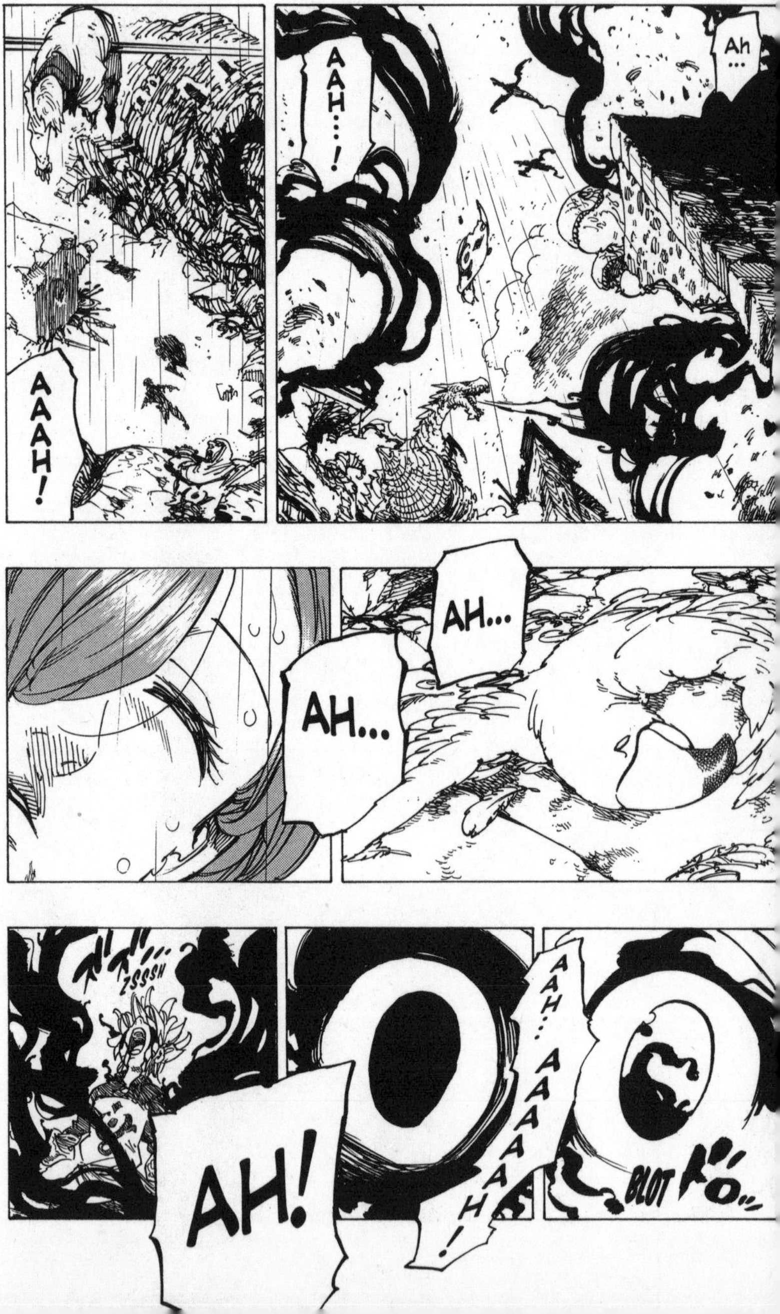
Ah...
AAH...!
AAAAH!
AH...
AH...
BLOT
AAH... AAAAAH!
ZSSSH
AH!

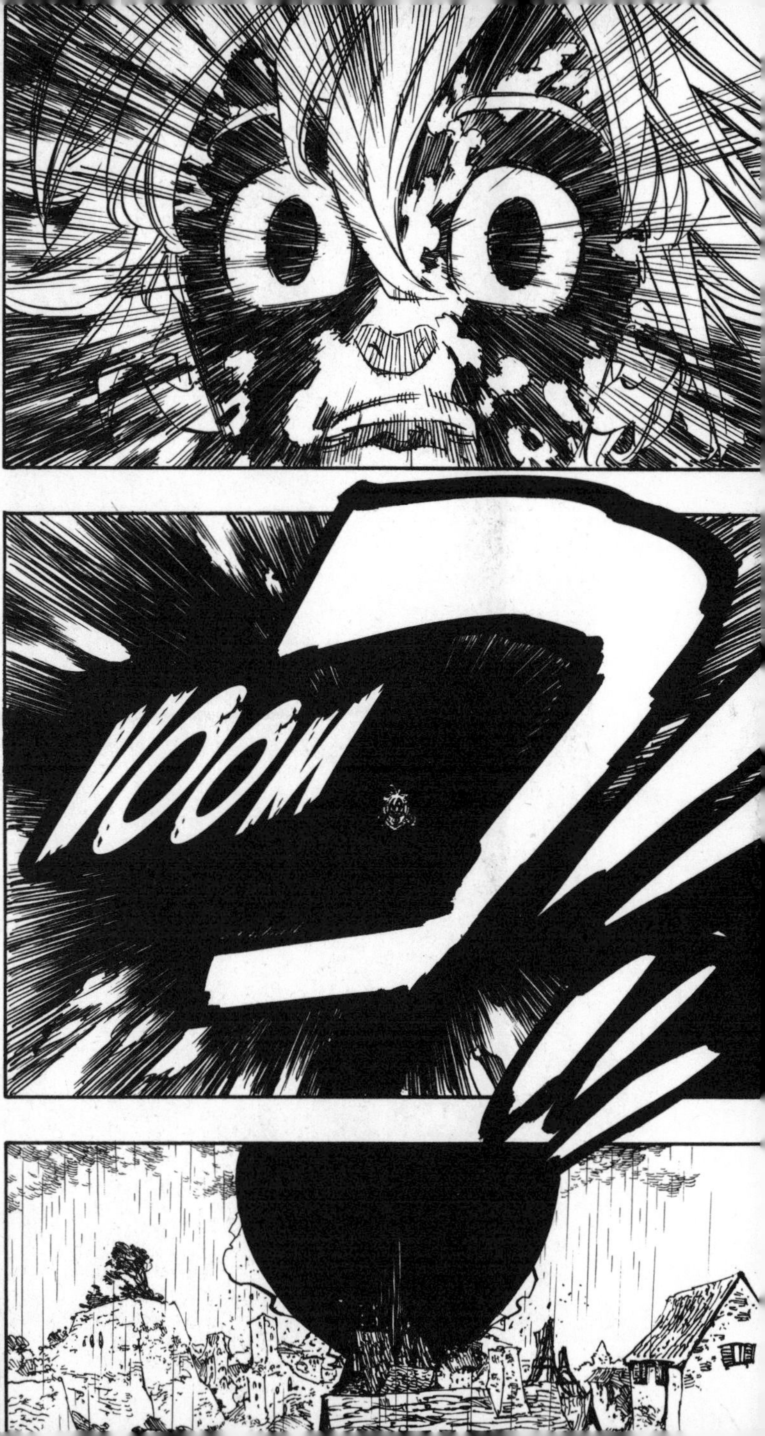
VOOM

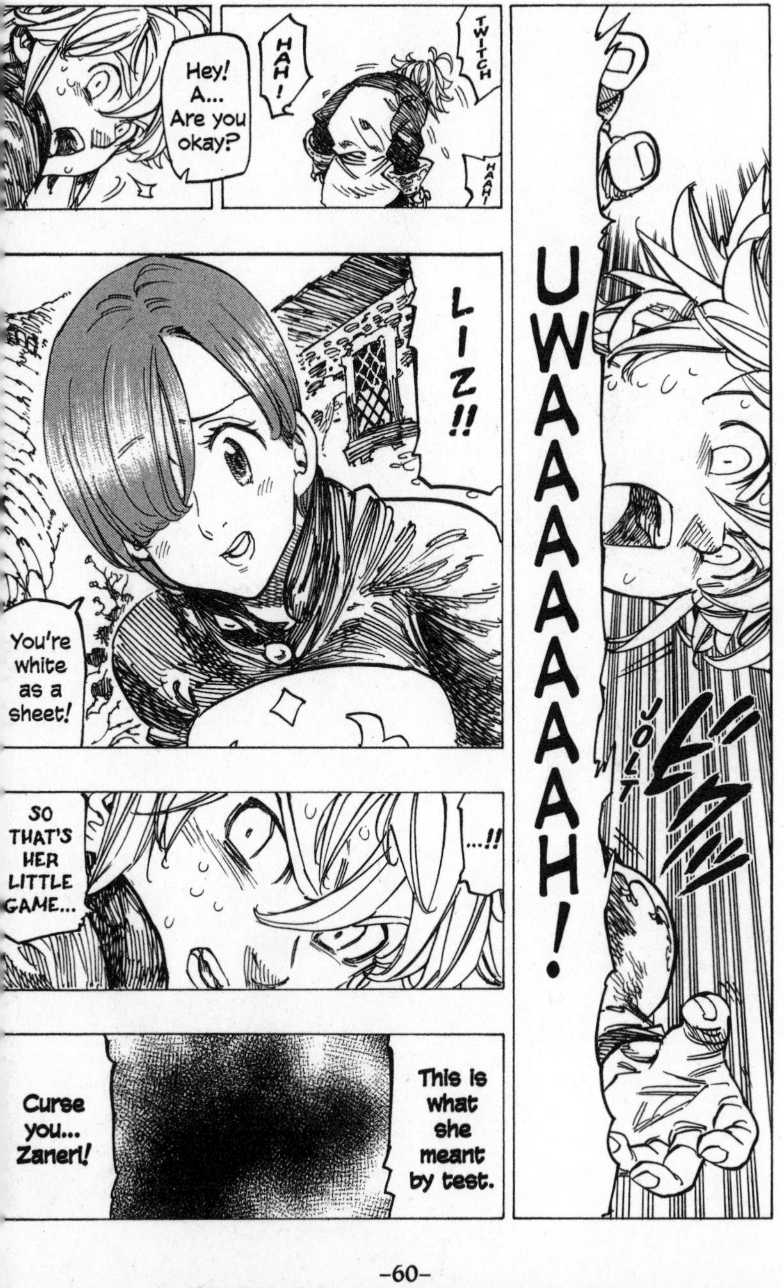
UWAAAAAAAH!
JOLT
TWITCH
HAH!
HAAH!
Hey! A... Are you okay?
LIZ!!
You're white as a sheet!
...!!
SO THAT'S HER LITTLE GAME...
This is what she meant by test.
Curse you... Zaneri!

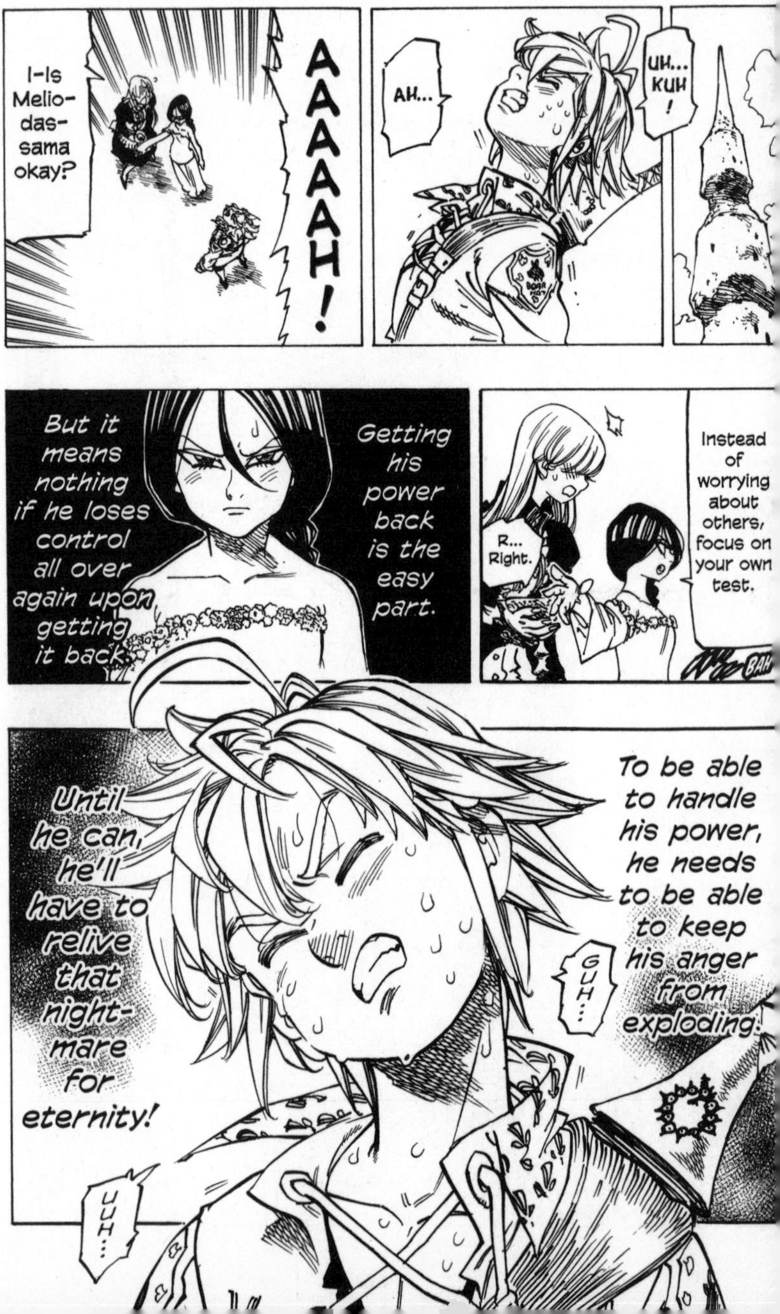
UH... KUH!
AH...
AAAAAH!
I-Is Melio-das-sama okay?
Instead of worrying about others, focus on your own test.
R... Right.
BAH
Getting his power back is the easy part.
But it means nothing if he loses control all over again upon getting it back.
To be able to handle his power, he needs to be able to keep his anger from exploding.
GUH...
Until he can, he'll have to relive that night-mare for eternity!
UUH...

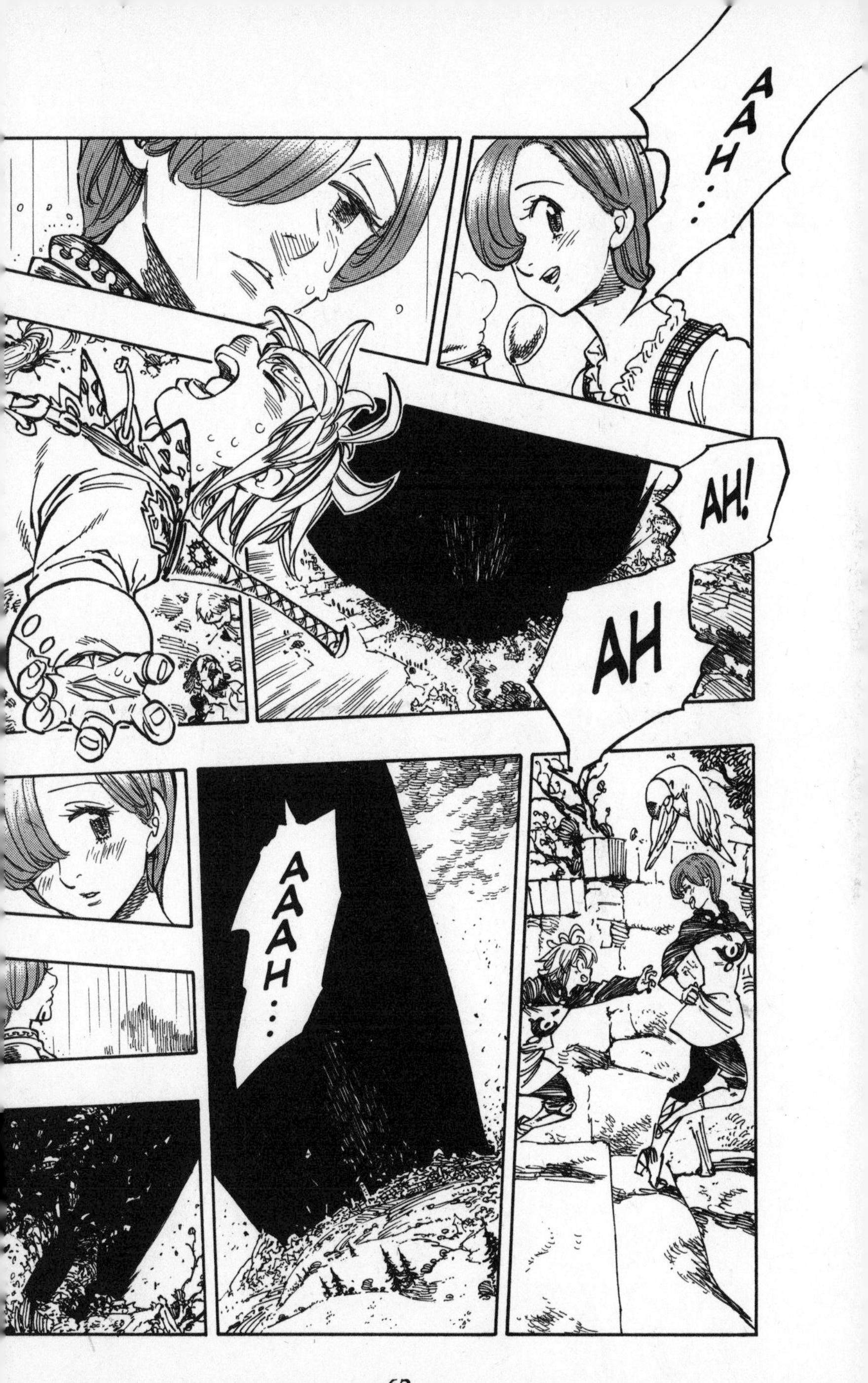
AAAH...
AH!
AH
AAAAH...

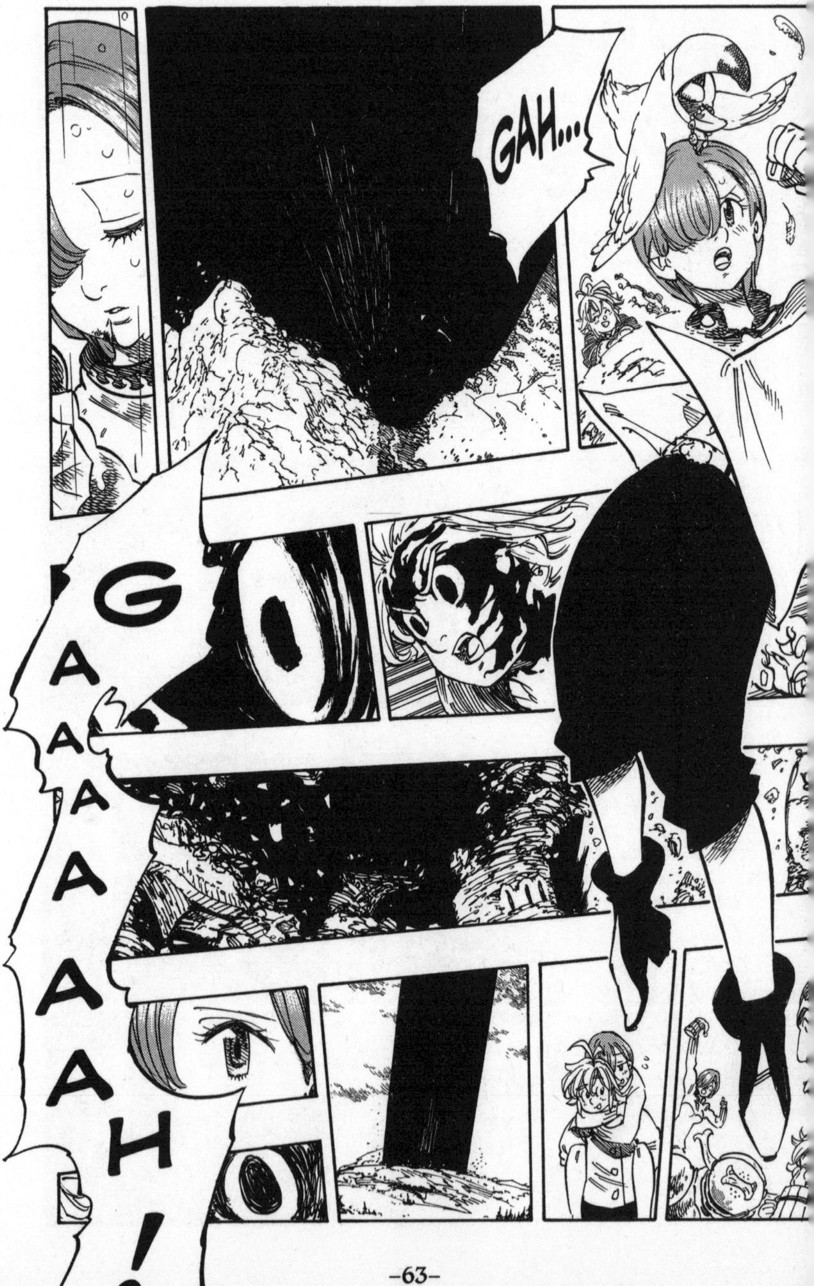
GAH...
GAAAAAAAH!

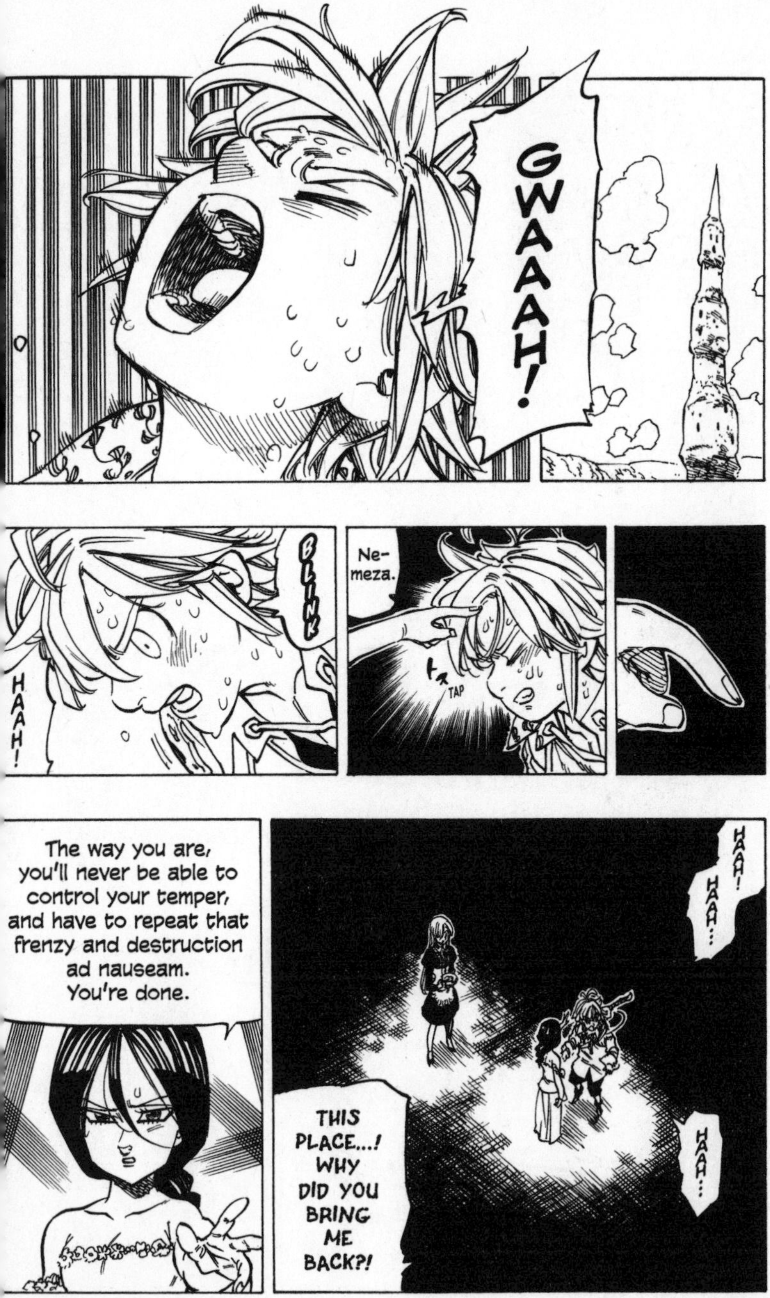
GWAAAH!
Ne-meza.
TAP
BLINK
HAAAH!
HAAH! HAAH...
HAAH...
THIS PLACE...! WHY DID YOU BRING ME BACK?!
The way you are, you'll never be able to control your temper, and have to repeat that frenzy and destruction ad nauseam. You're done.

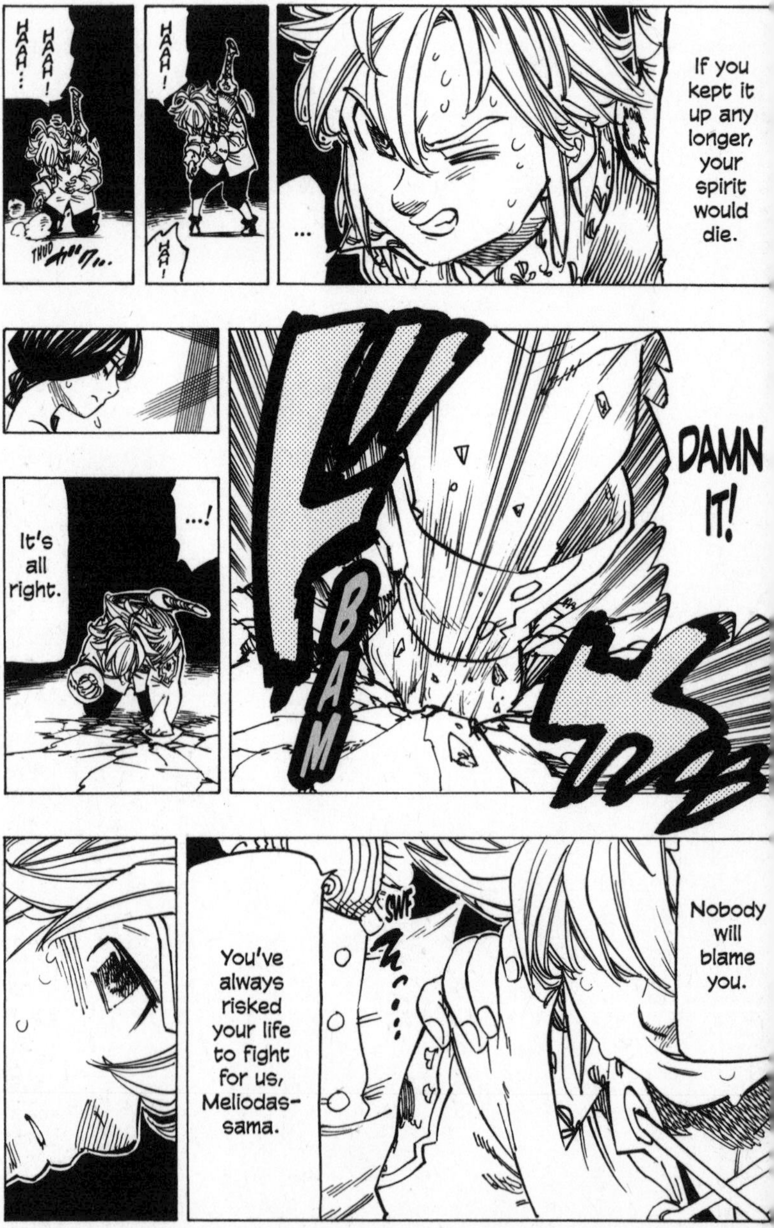
If you kept it up any longer, your spirit would die.
...
HAAH!
HAAH!
HAAH!
HAAH...
THUD
DAMN IT!
BAM
...!
It's all right.
Nobody will blame you.
SWF
...
You've always risked your life to fight for us, Meliodas-sama.

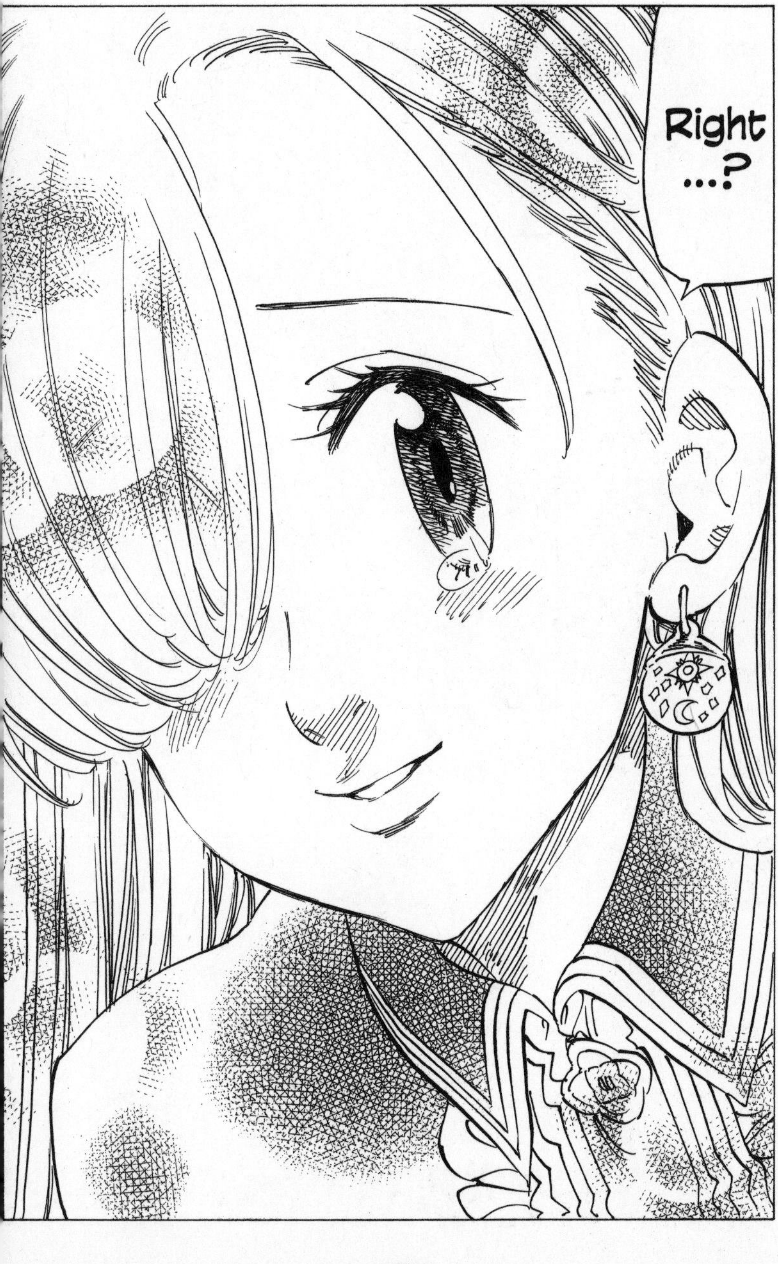
Right
...?

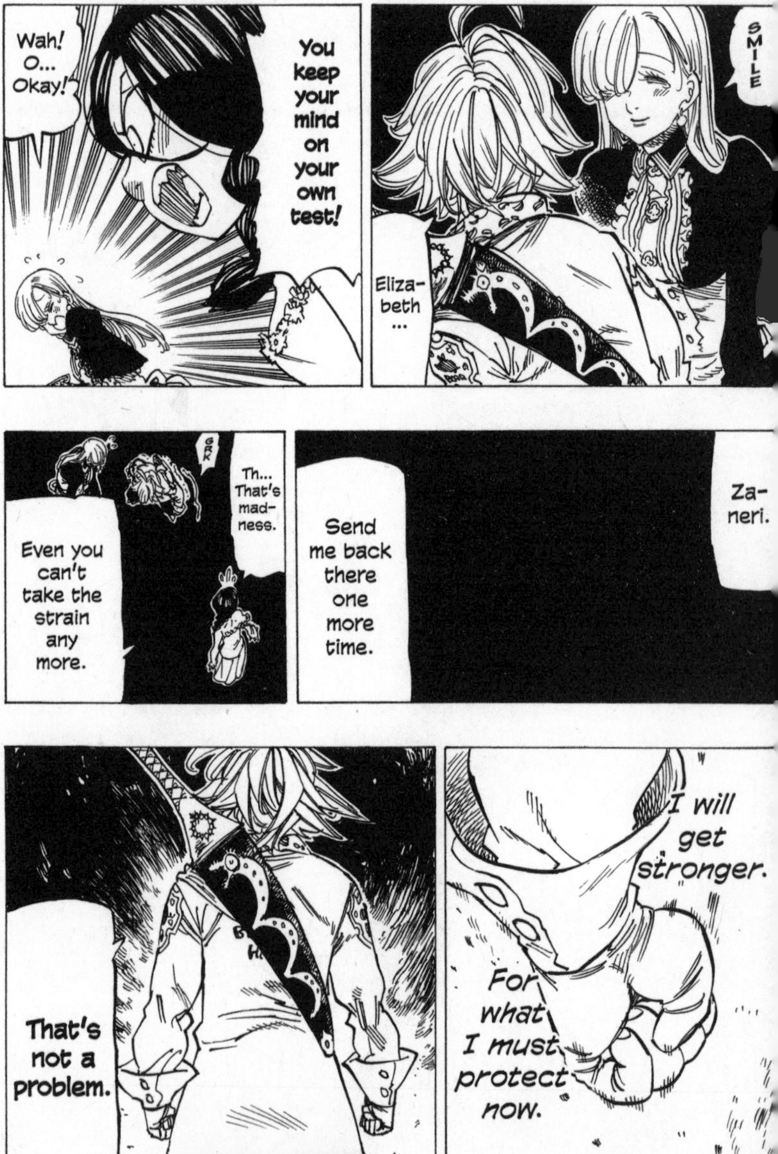
SMILE
Elizabeth...
You keep your mind on your own test!
Wah! O... Okay!
Za-neri.
Send me back there one more time.
Th... That's madness.
GRK
Even you can't take the strain any more.
I will get stronger.
For what I must protect now.
That's not a problem.

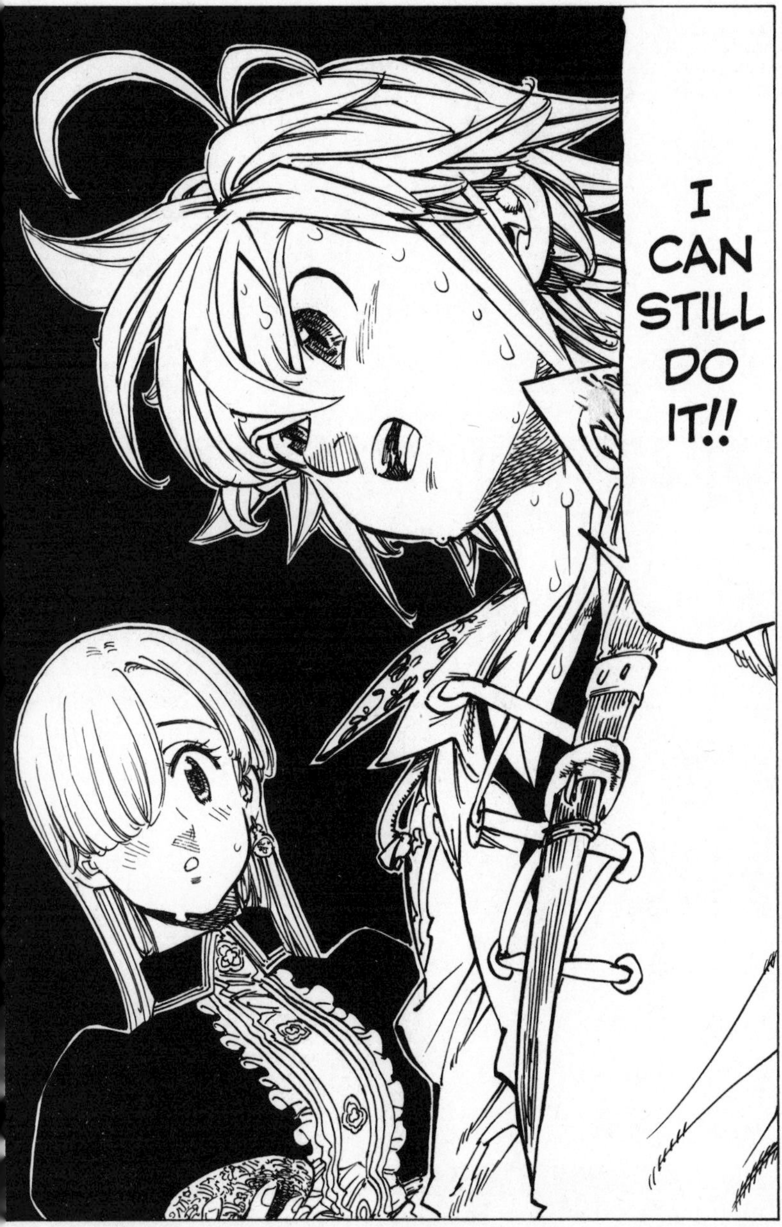
I CAN STILL DO IT!!

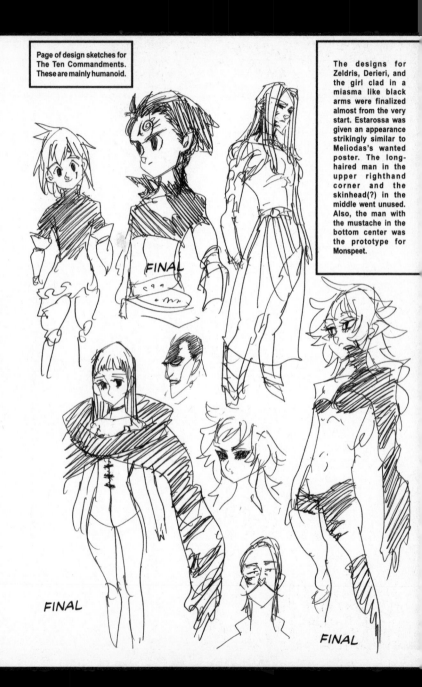

Page of design sketches for The Ten Commandments. These are mainly humanoid.

The designs for Zeldris, Derieri, and the girl clad in a miasma like black arms were finalized almost from the very start. Estarossa was given an appearance strikingly similar to Meliodas's wanted poster. The long-haired man in the upper righthand corner and the skinhead(?) in the middle went unused. Also, the man with the mustache in the bottom center was the prototype for Monspeet.

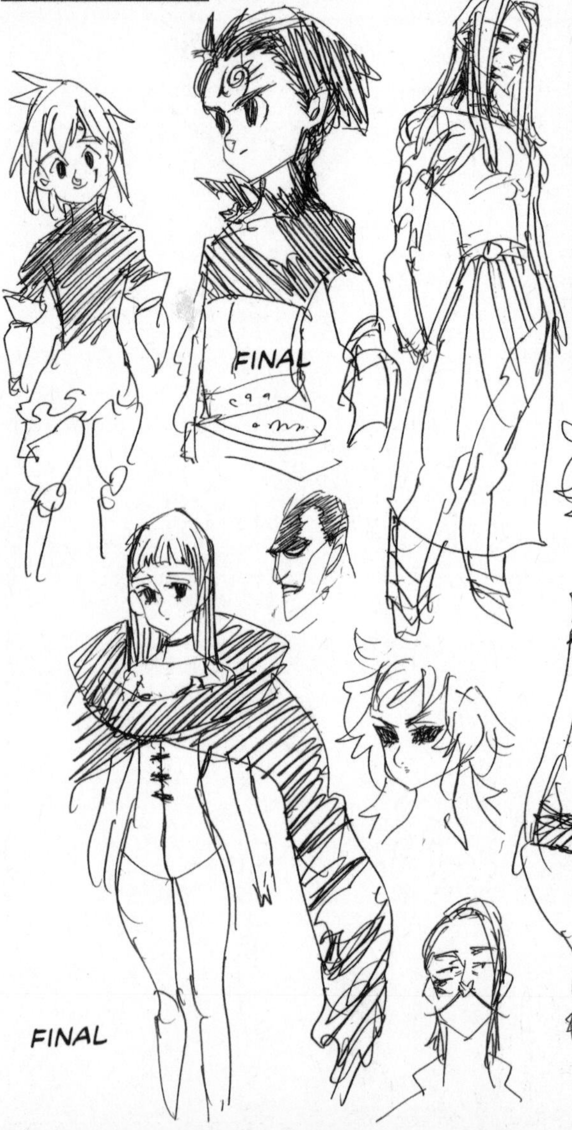
FINAL
FINAL

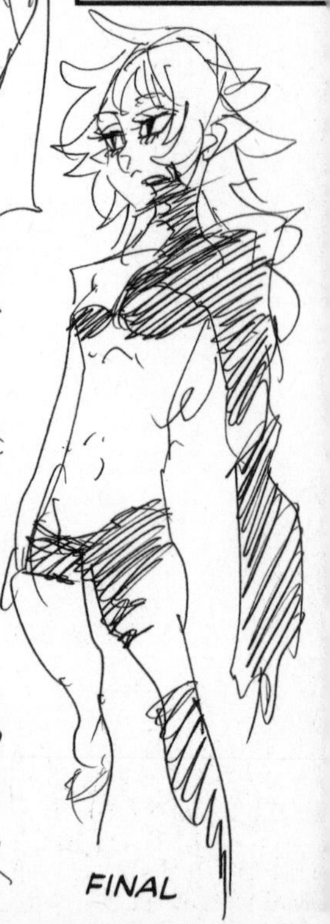
FINAL

Chapter 131 - A Promise To A Loved One

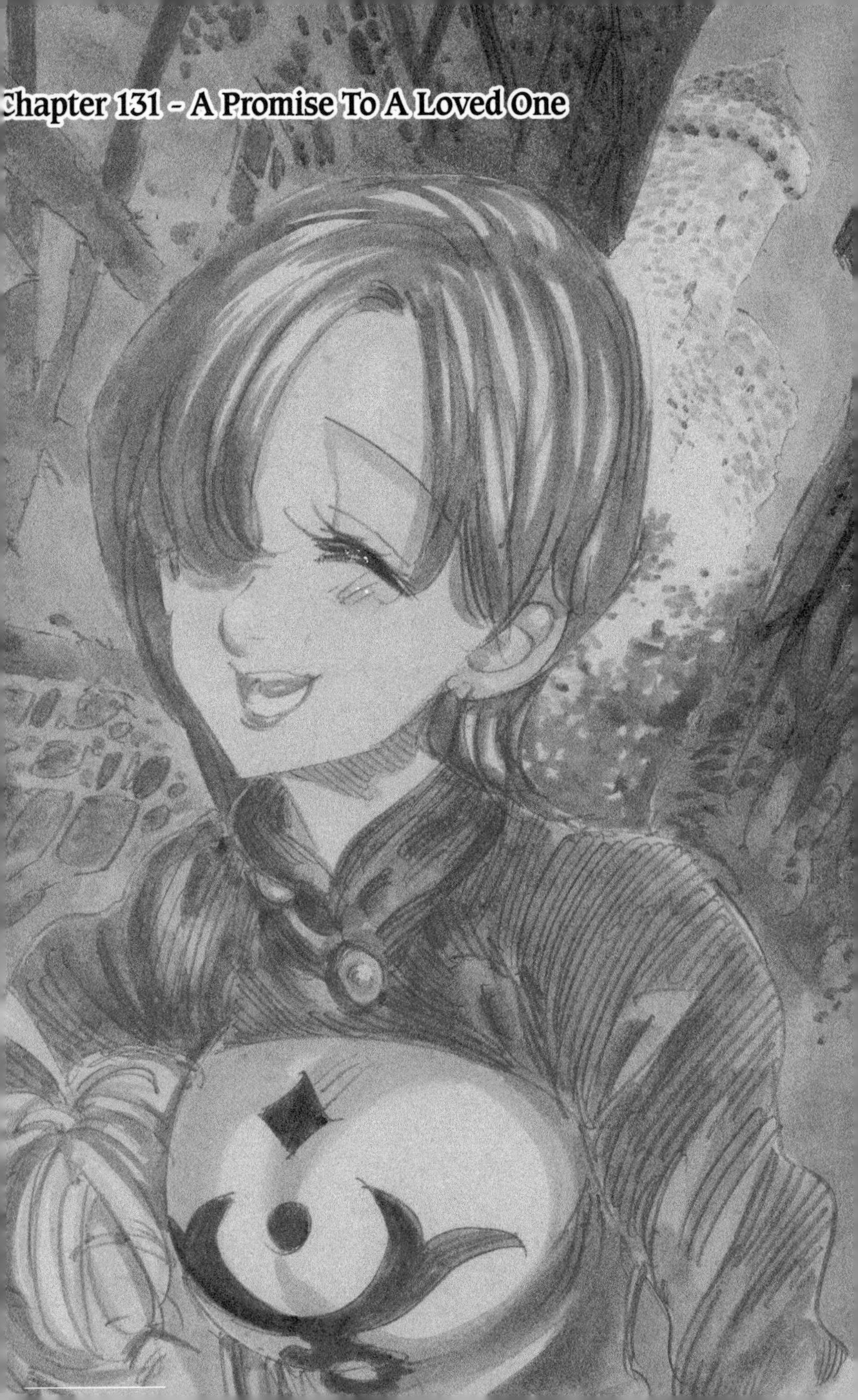

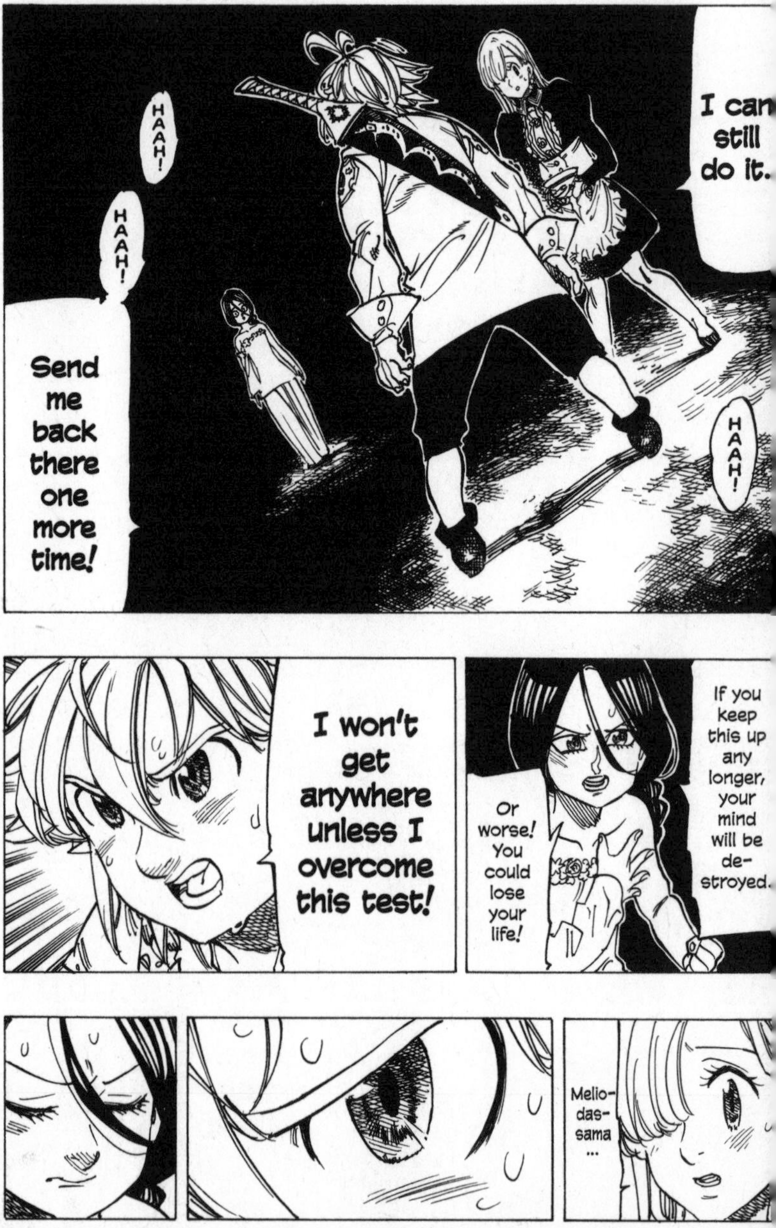
I can still do it.
HAAH!
HAAH!
HAAH!
Send me back there one more time!
If you keep this up any longer, your mind will be de-stroyed.
Or worse! You could lose your life!
I won't get anywhere unless I overcome this test!
Melio-das-sama...

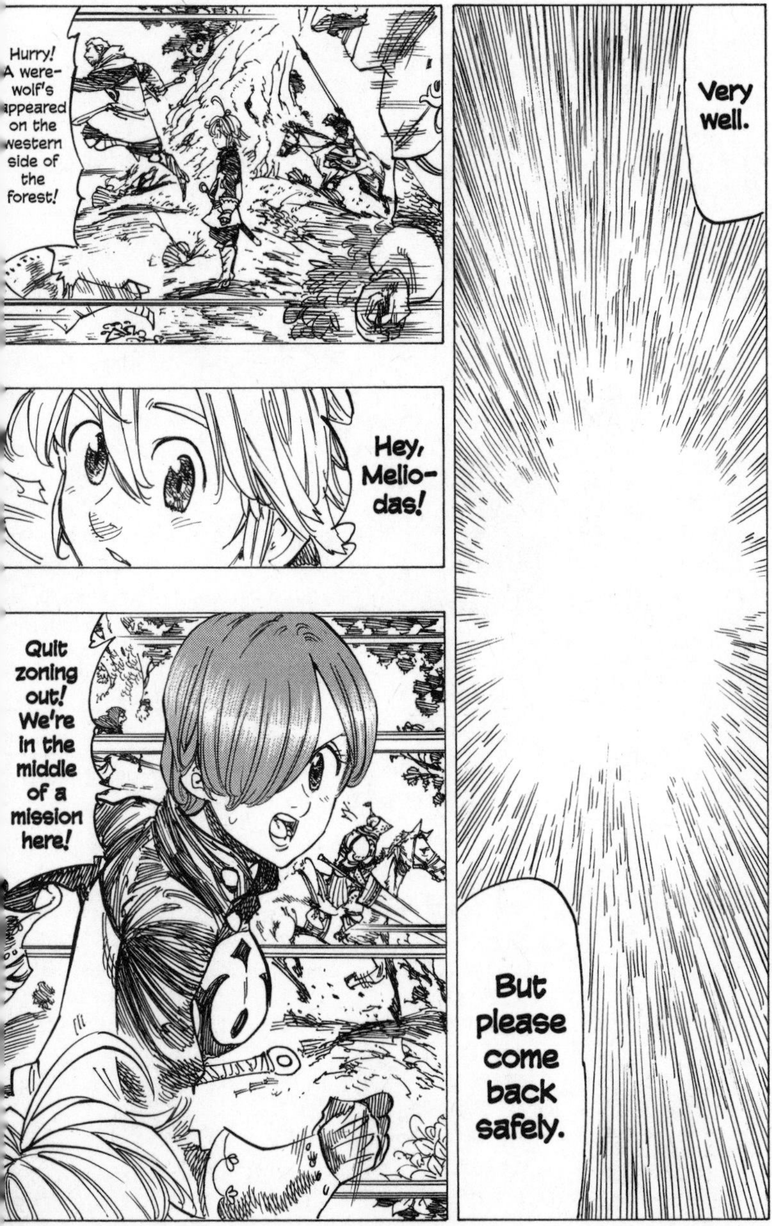
Very well.
But please come back safely.
Hurry! A were-wolf's appeared on the western side of the forest!
Hey, Melio-das!
Quit zoning out! We're in the middle of a mission here!

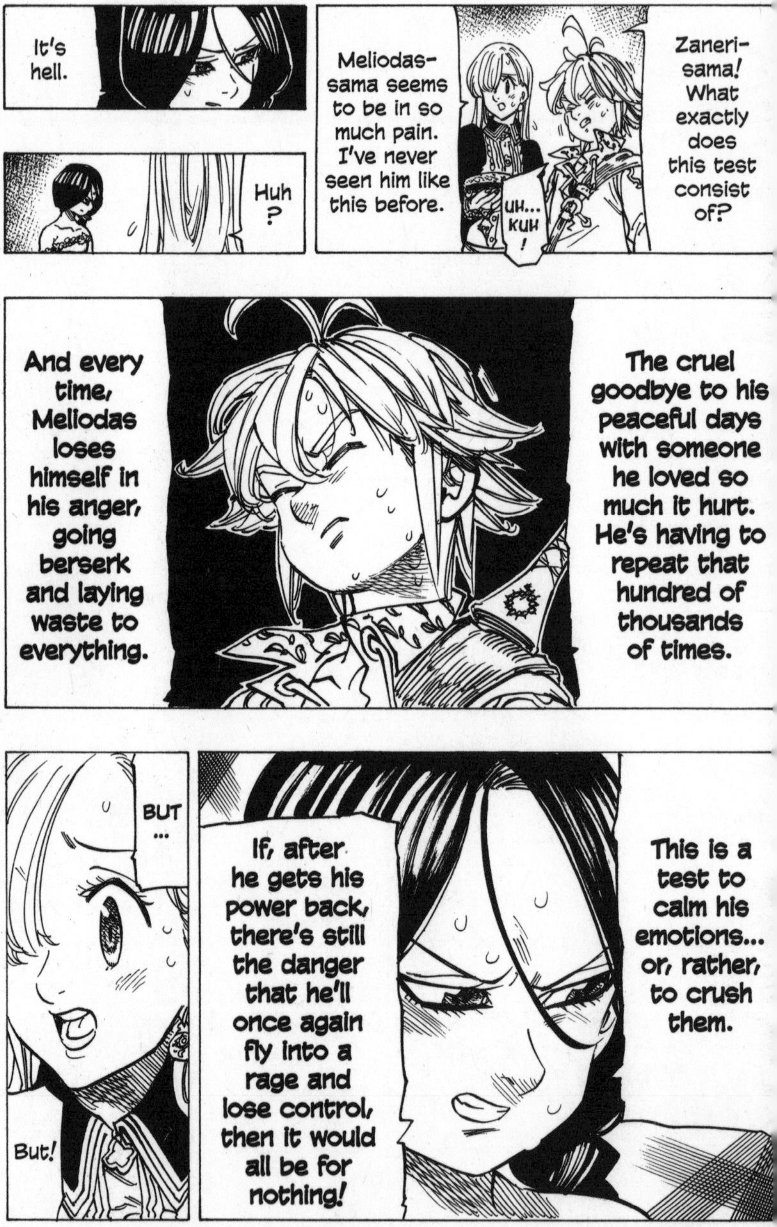
Zaneri-sama! What exactly does this test consist of?
Meliodas-sama seems to be in so much pain. I've never seen him like this before.
UH... KUH!
It's hell.
Huh?
The cruel goodbye to his peaceful days with someone he loved so much it hurt. He's having to repeat that hundred of thousands of times.
And every time, Meliodas loses himself in his anger, going berserk and laying waste to everything.
This is a test to calm his emotions... or, rather, to crush them.
If, after he gets his power back, there's still the danger that he'll once again fly into a rage and lose control, then it would all be for nothing!
BUT...
But!

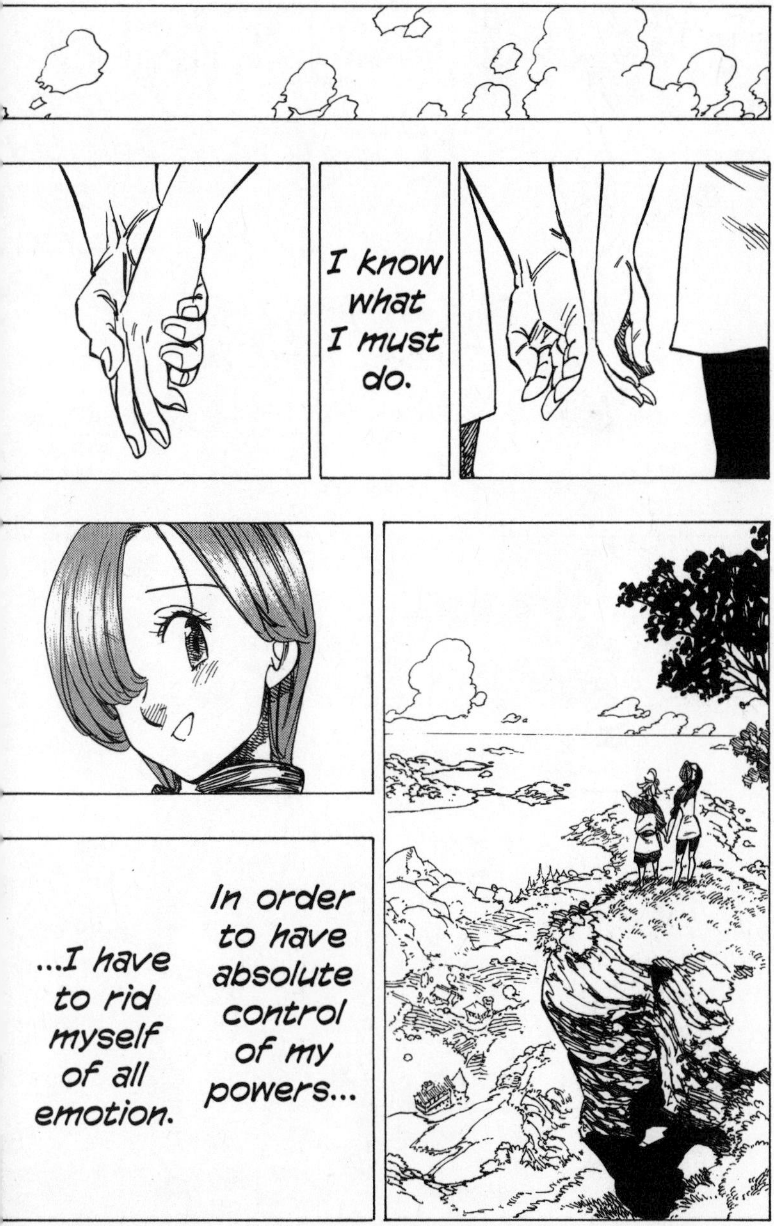
I know what I must do.
In order to have absolute control of my powers...
...I have to rid myself of all emotion.

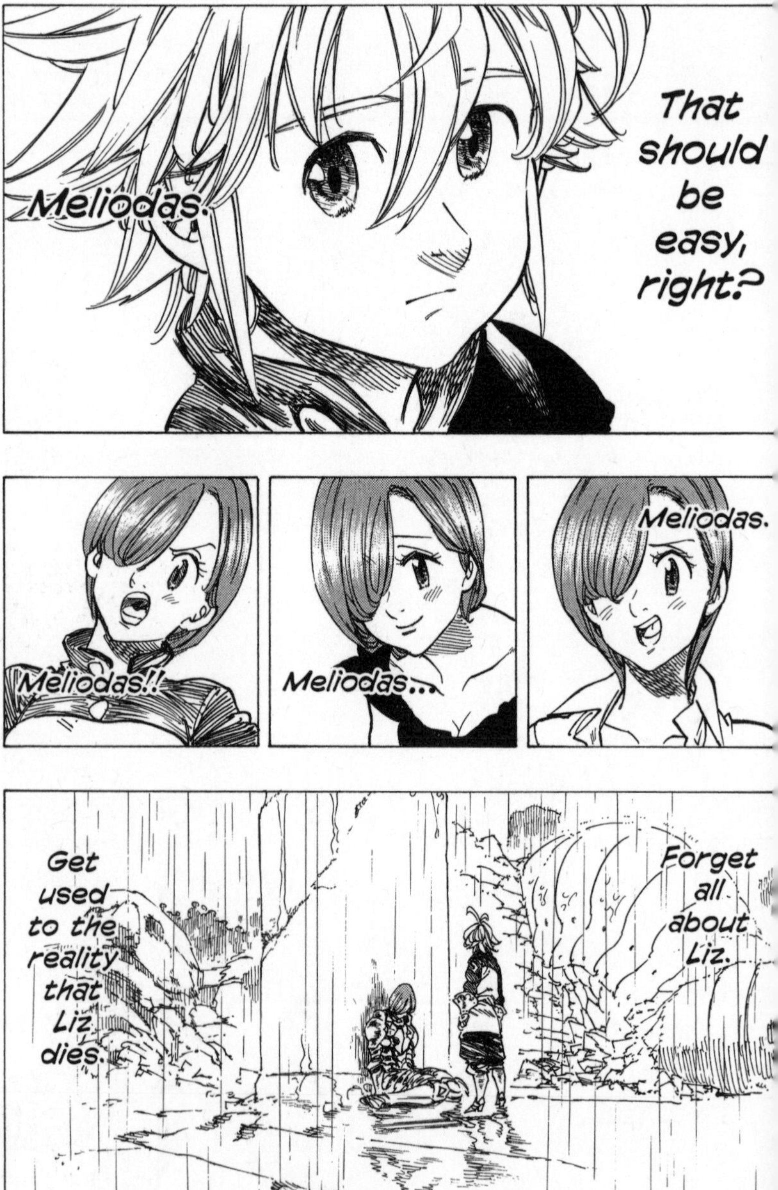
That should be easy, right?
Meliodas.
Meliodas.
Meliodas...
Meliodas!!
Forget all about Liz.
Get used to the reality that Liz dies.

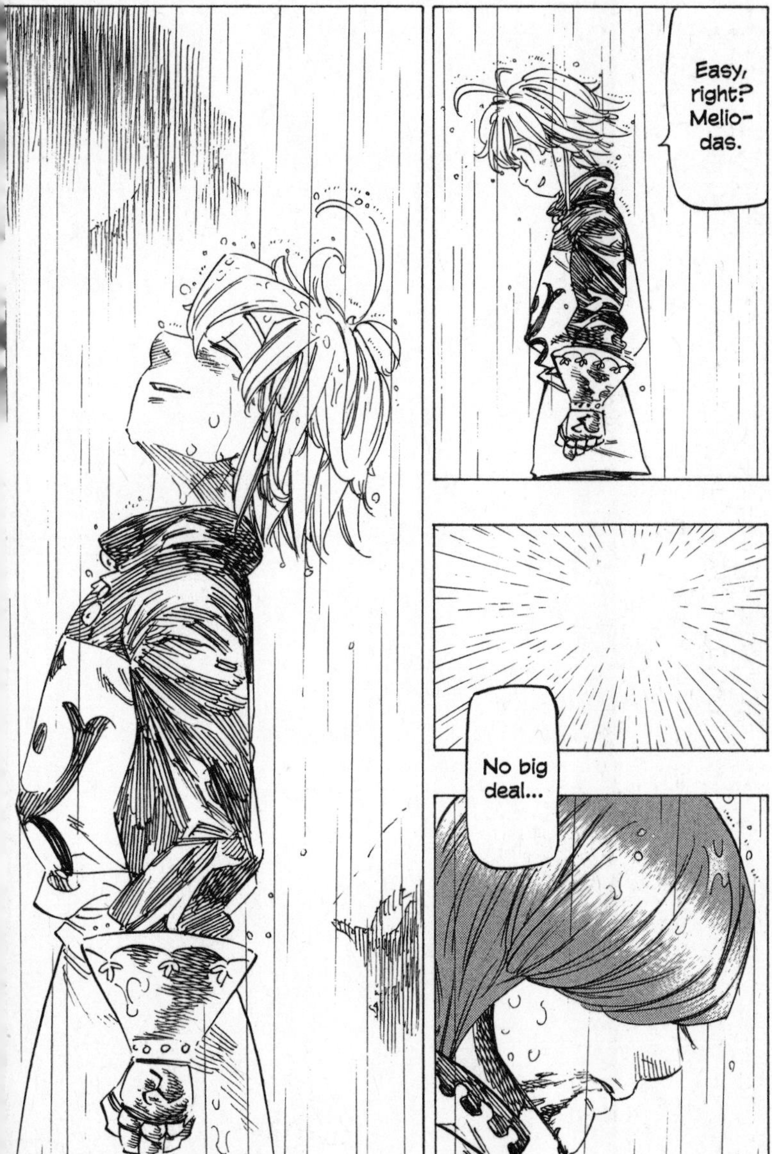
Easy, right? Melio-das.
No big deal...

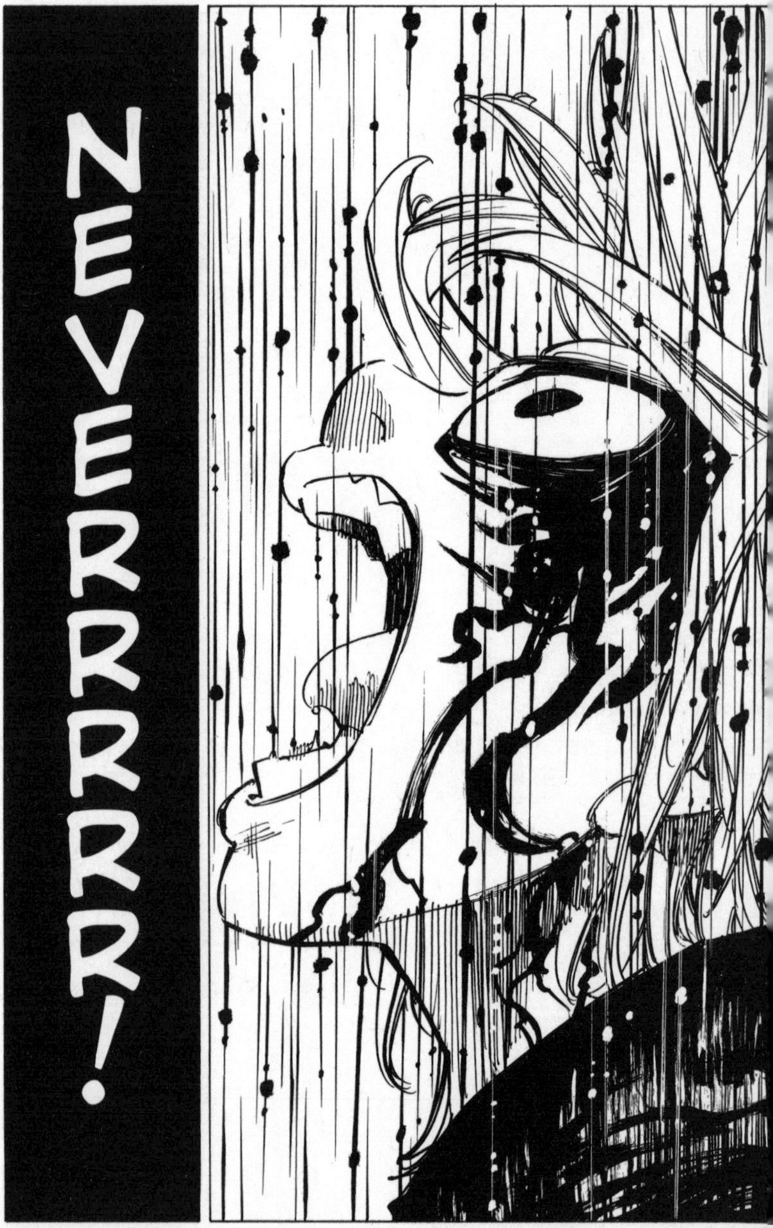
NEVERRR!

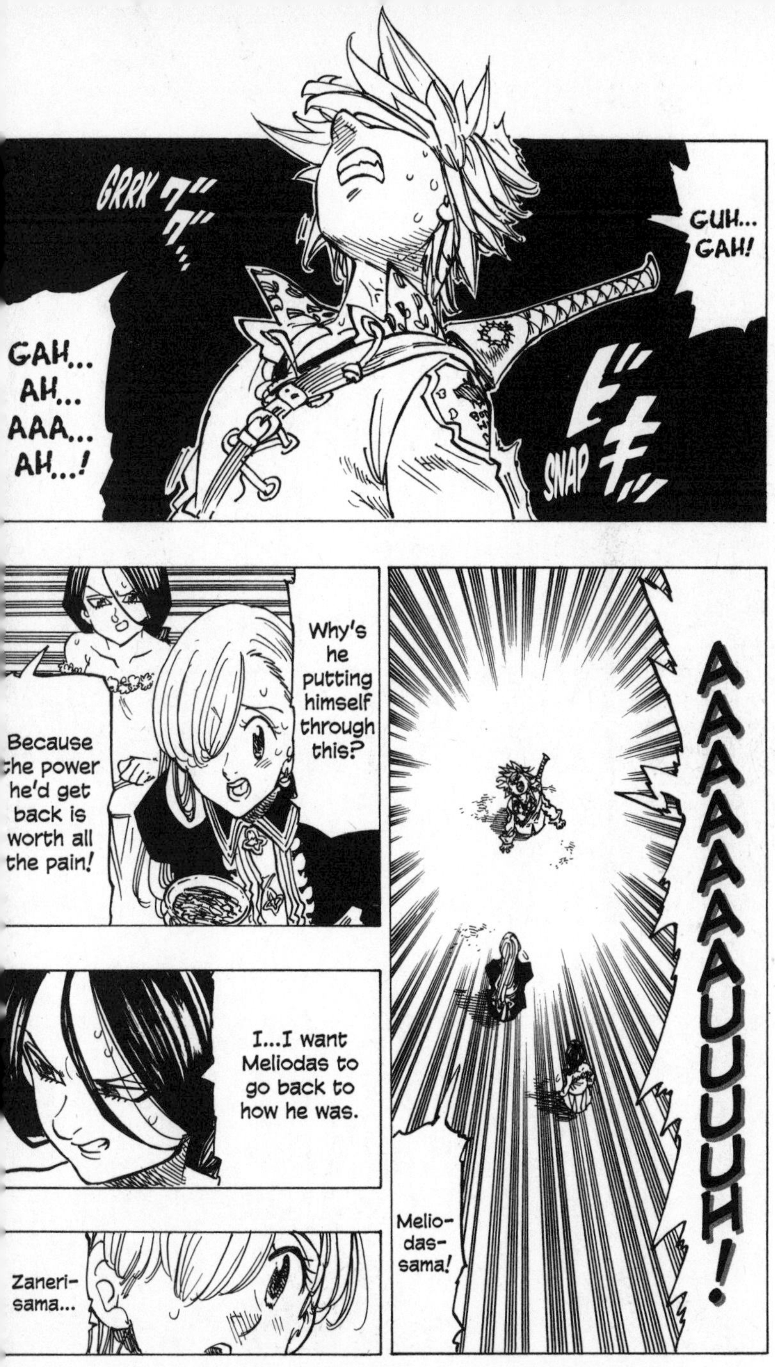

GUH... GAH!
GRRK
GAH... AH... AAA... AH...!
SNAP
AAAAAAAUUUH!
Melio-das-sama!
Why's he putting himself through this?
Because the power he'd get back is worth all the pain!
I...I want Meliodas to go back to how he was.
Zaneri-sama...

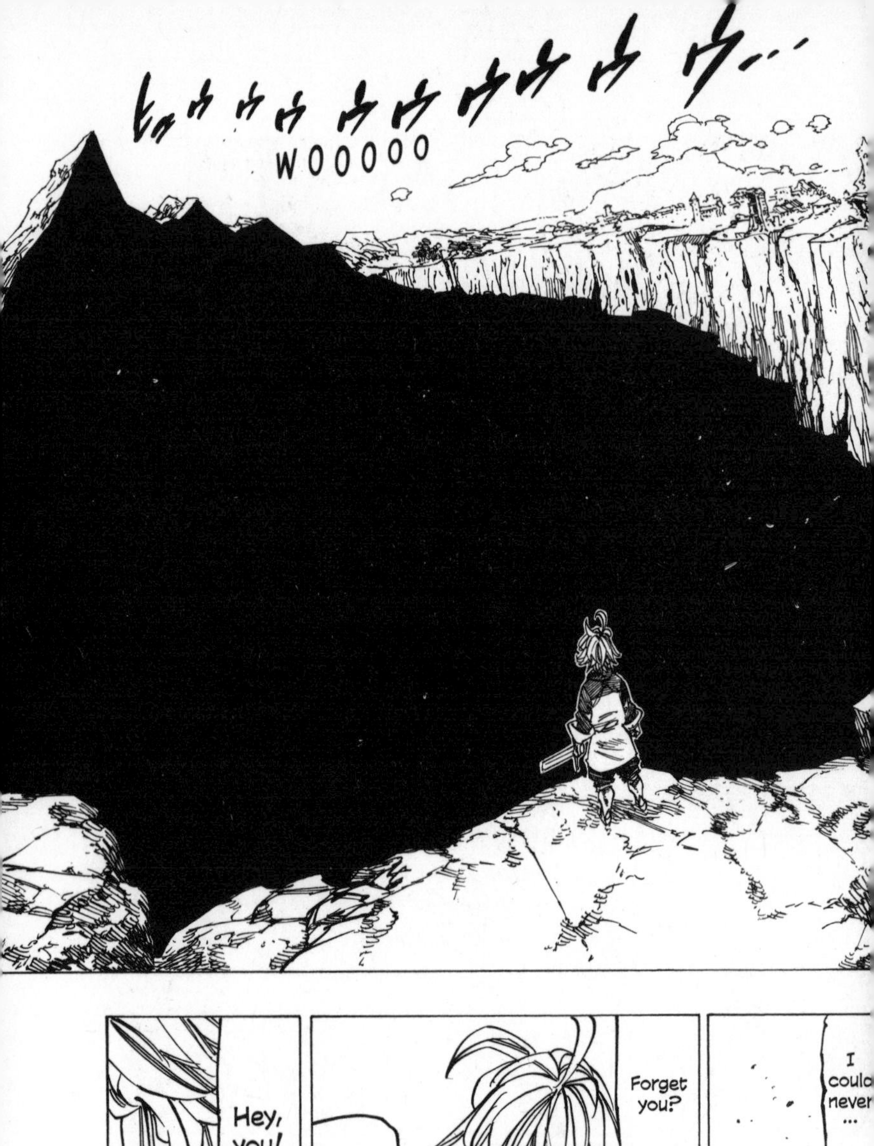
ヒュウウウウウウウウウ…
WOOOOO
I could never...
...do it...
Forget you?
Get used to losing you?
Hey, you!

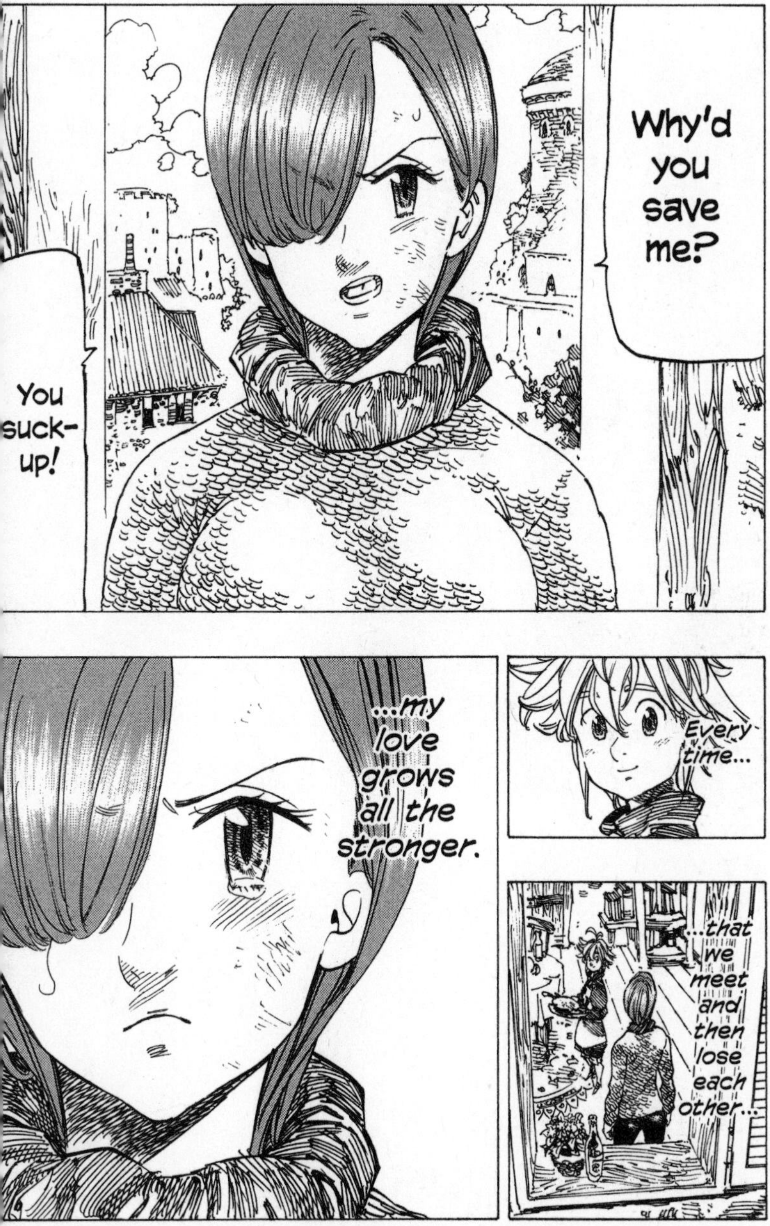
Why'd you save me?
You suck-up!
Every time...
...that we meet and then lose each other...
...my love grows all the stronger.

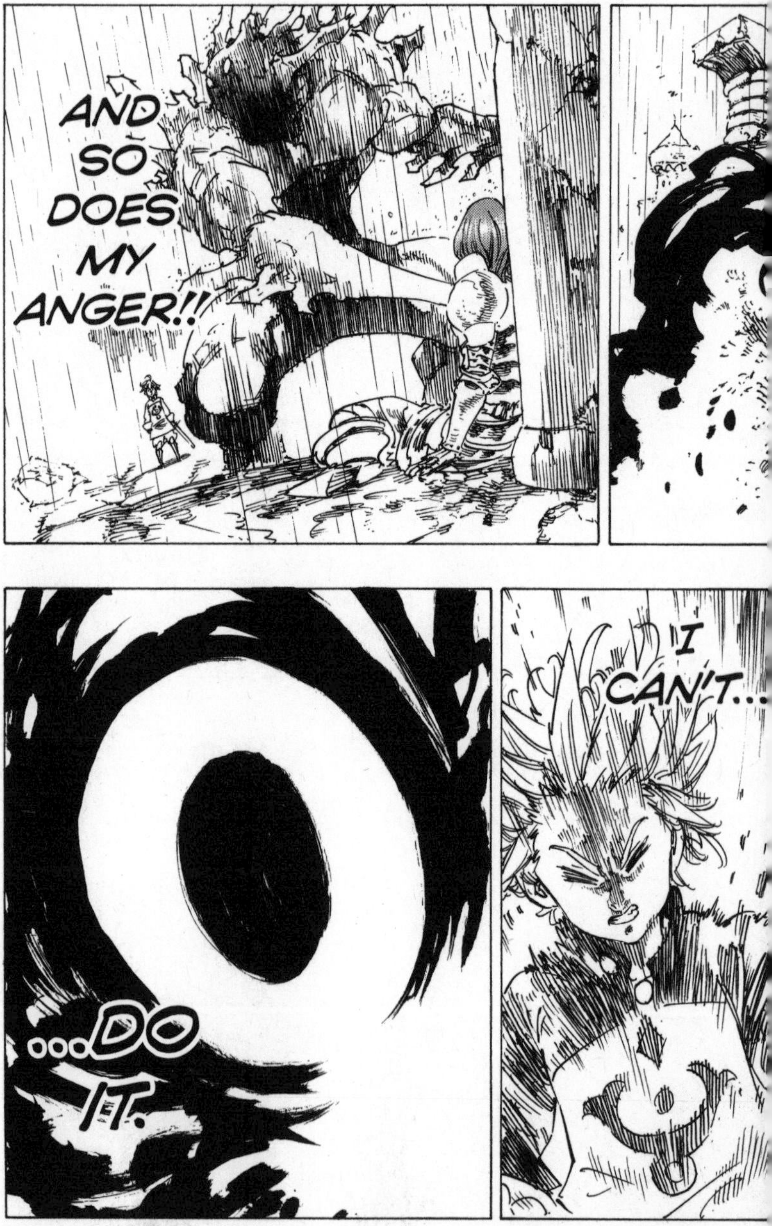
AND SO DOES MY ANGER!!
I CAN'T...
...DO IT.

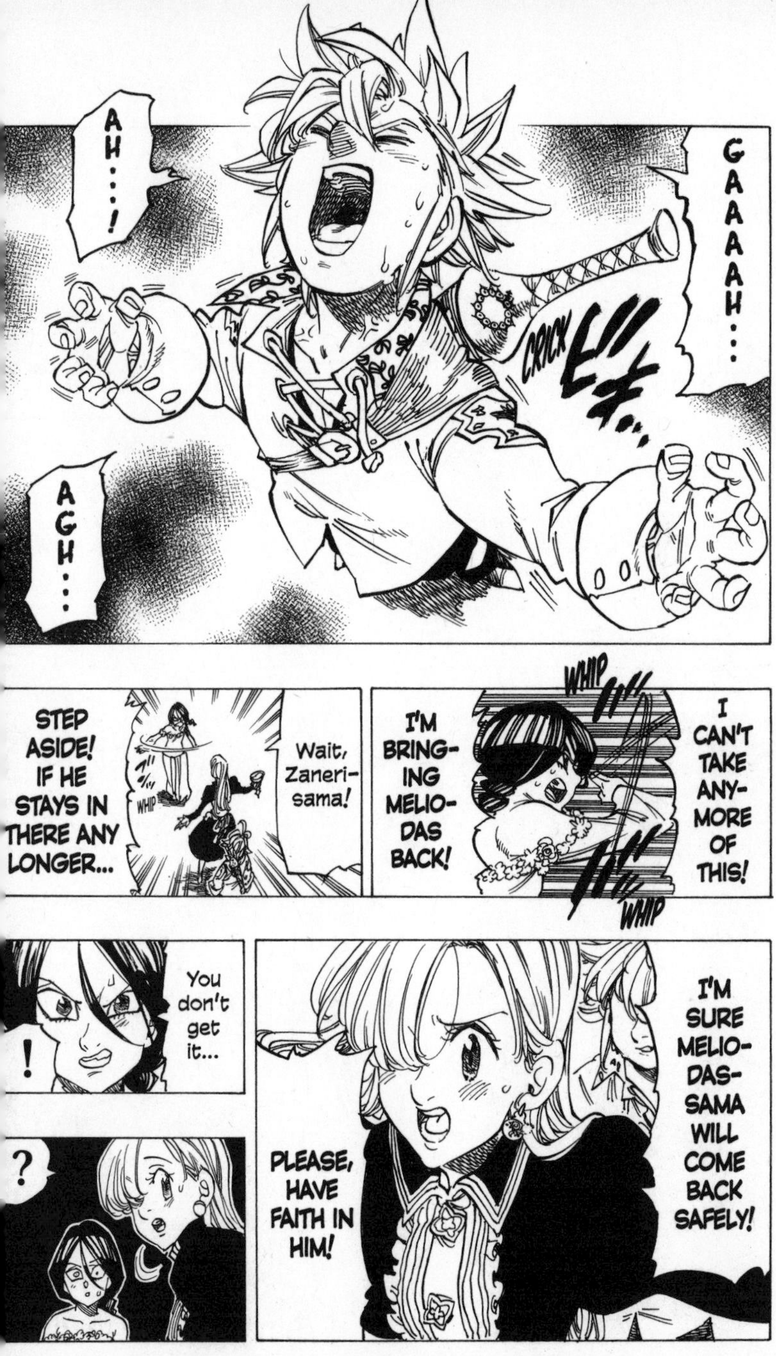

GAAAAH...
AH...!
CRICK
AGH...
I CAN'T TAKE ANYMORE OF THIS!
WHIP
I'M BRINGING MELIODAS BACK!
WHIP
Wait, Zaneri-sama!
WHIP
STEP ASIDE! IF HE STAYS IN THERE ANY LONGER...
I'M SURE MELIODAS-SAMA WILL COME BACK SAFELY!
PLEASE, HAVE FAITH IN HIM!
You don't get it...
!
?

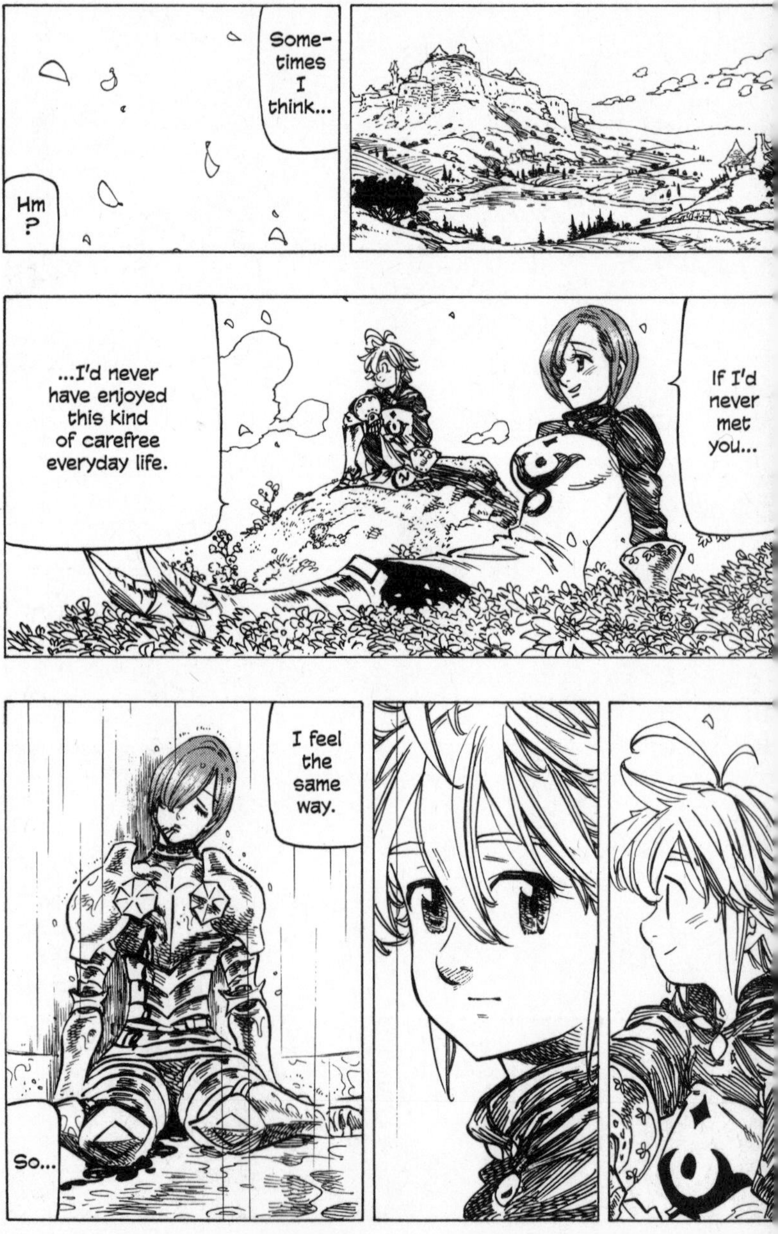

Some-times I think...
Hm?
If I'd never met you...
...I'd never have enjoyed this kind of carefree everyday life.
I feel the same way.
So...

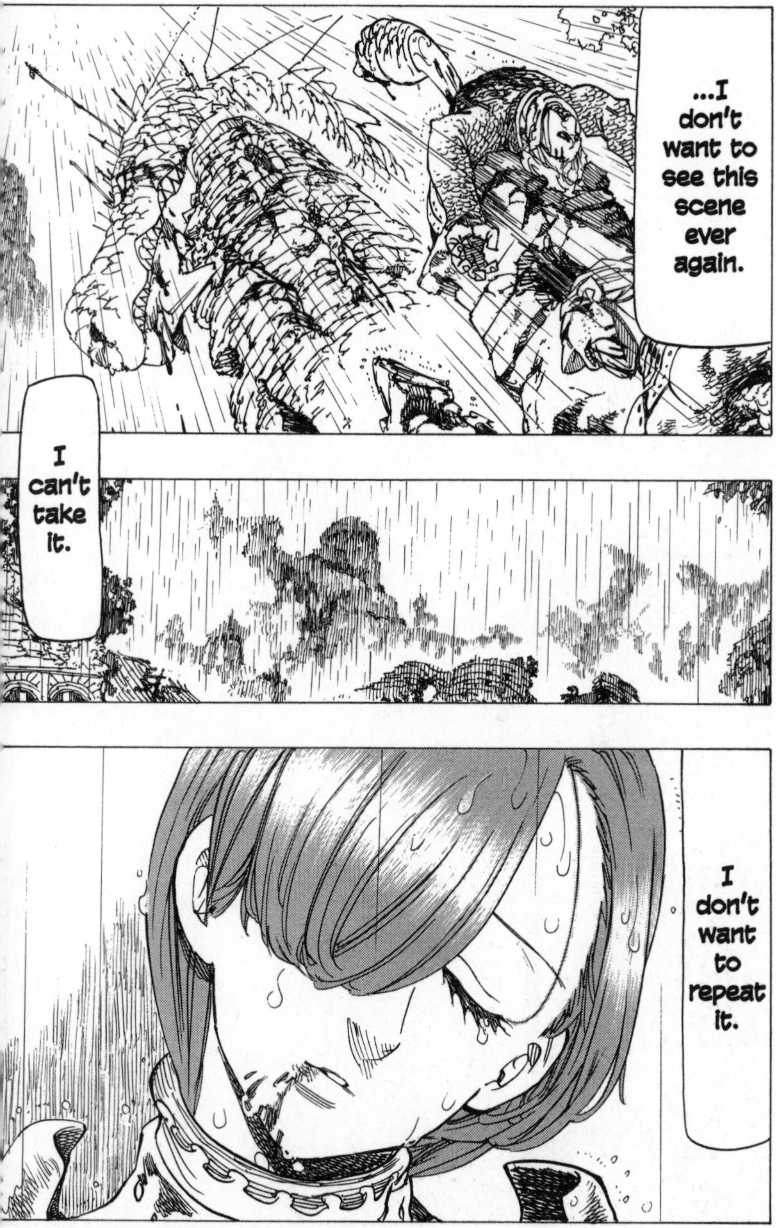
...I don't want to see this scene ever again.
I can't take it.
I don't want to repeat it.

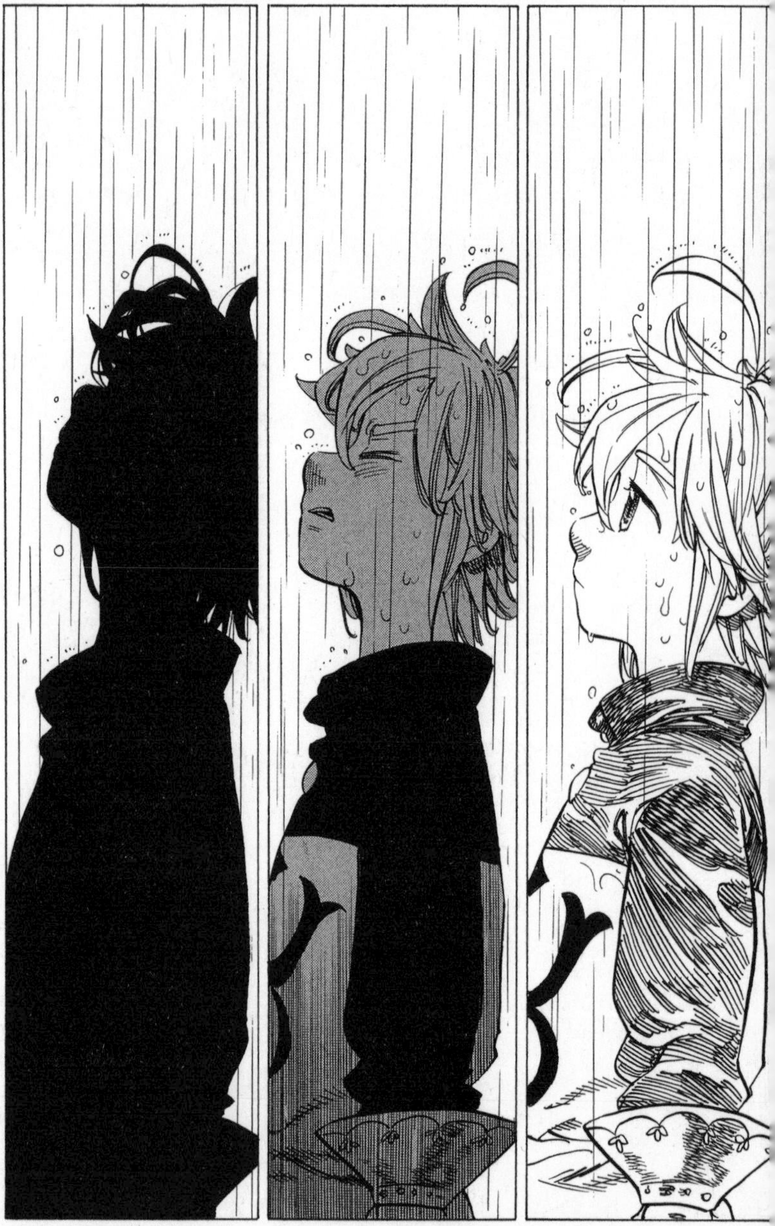

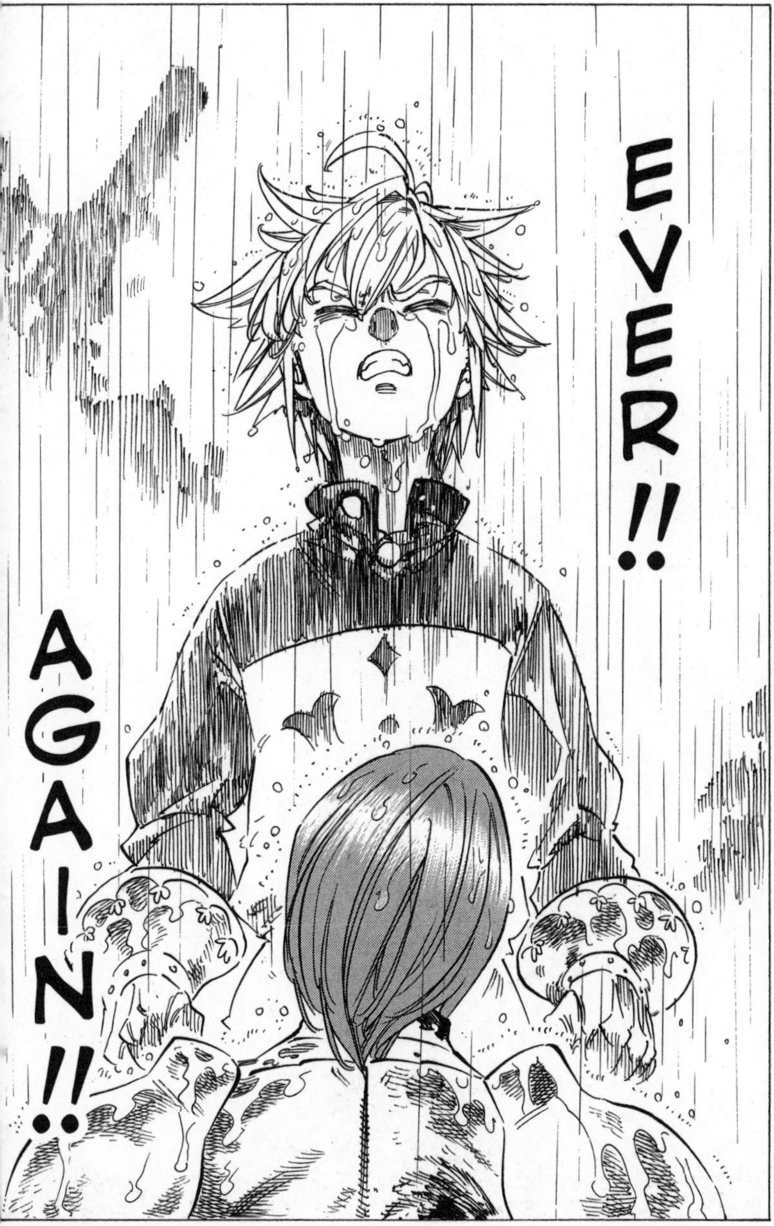
EVER!!
AGAIN!!

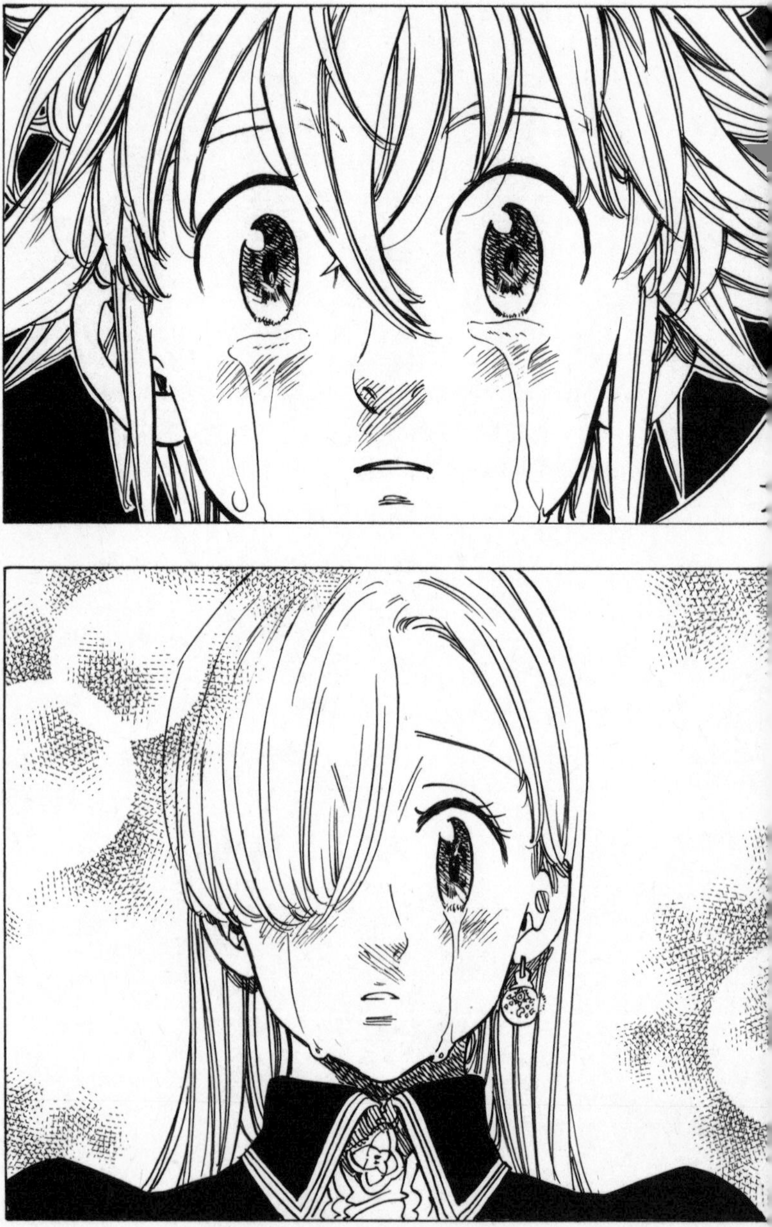

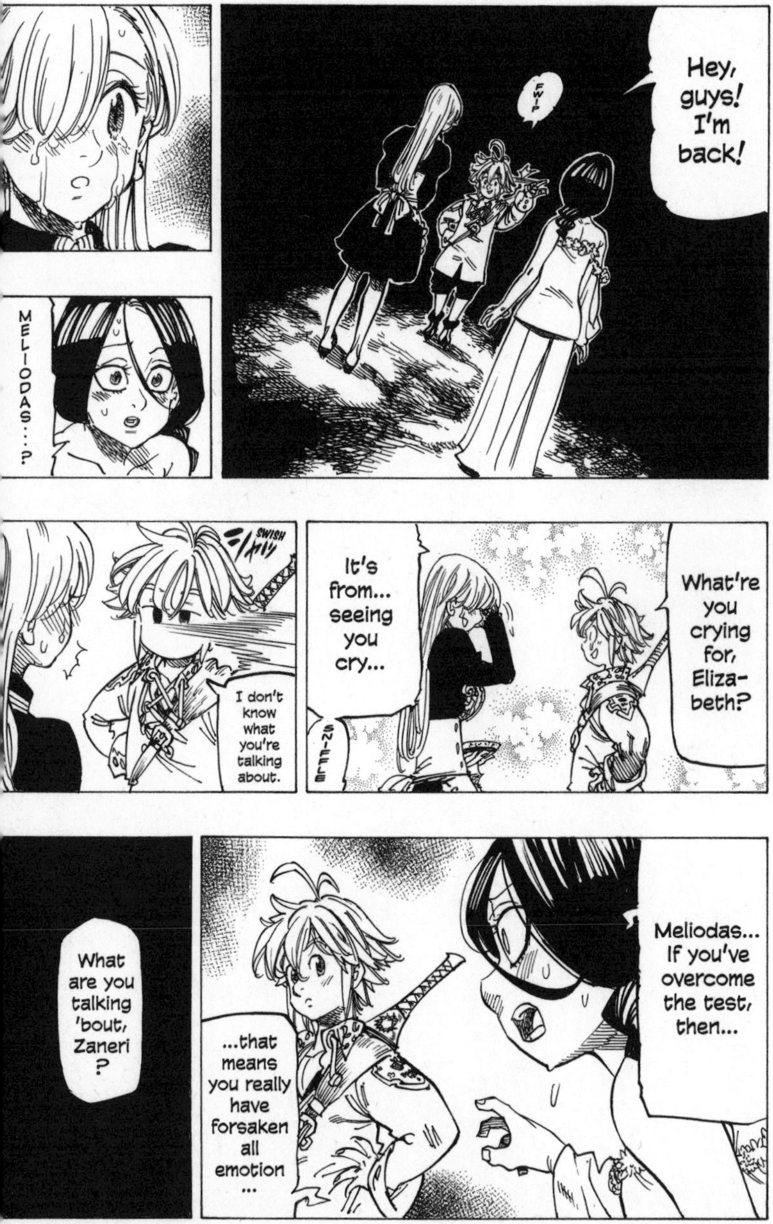
Hey, guys! I'm back!
FWIP
MELIODAS...?
What're you crying for, Elizabeth?
It's from... seeing you cry...
SNIFFLE
SWISH
I don't know what you're talking about.
Meliodas... If you've overcome the test, then...
...that means you really have forsaken all emotion...
What are you talking 'bout, Zaneri?

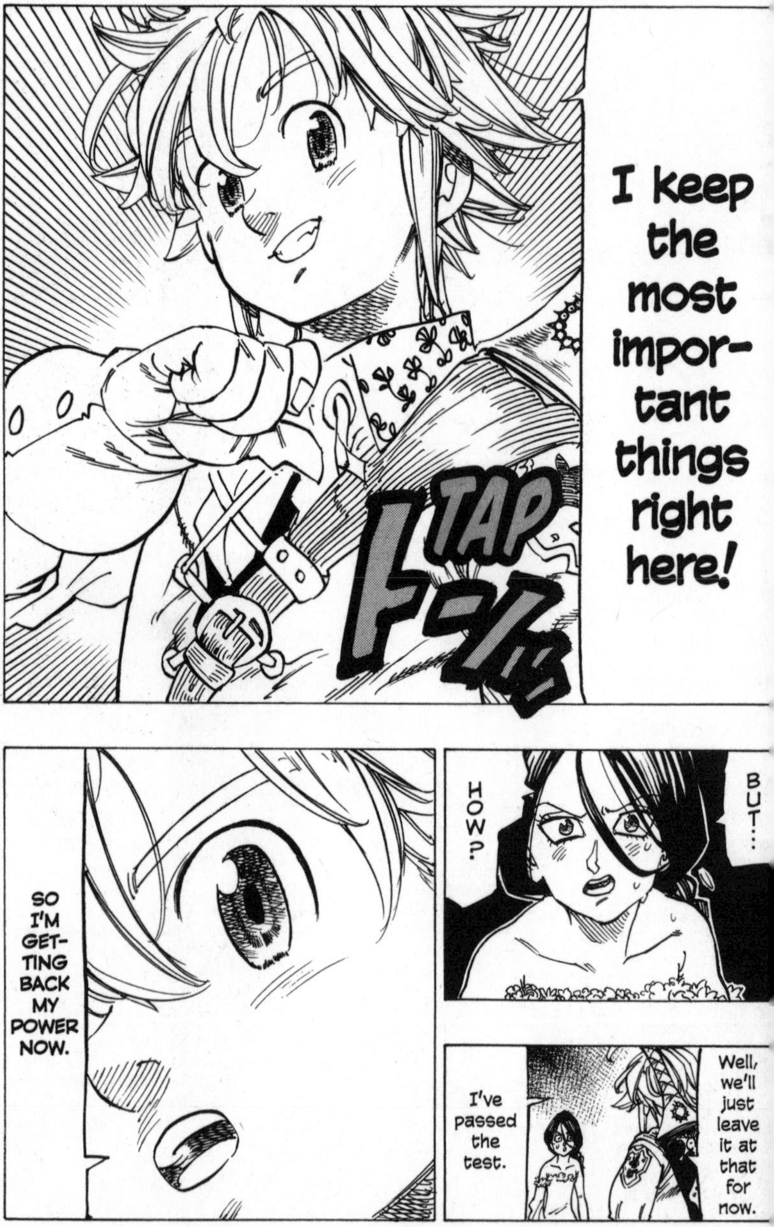
I keep the most important things right here!
TAP
BUT...
HOW?
Well, we'll just leave it at that for now.
I've passed the test.
SO I'M GETTING BACK MY POWER NOW.

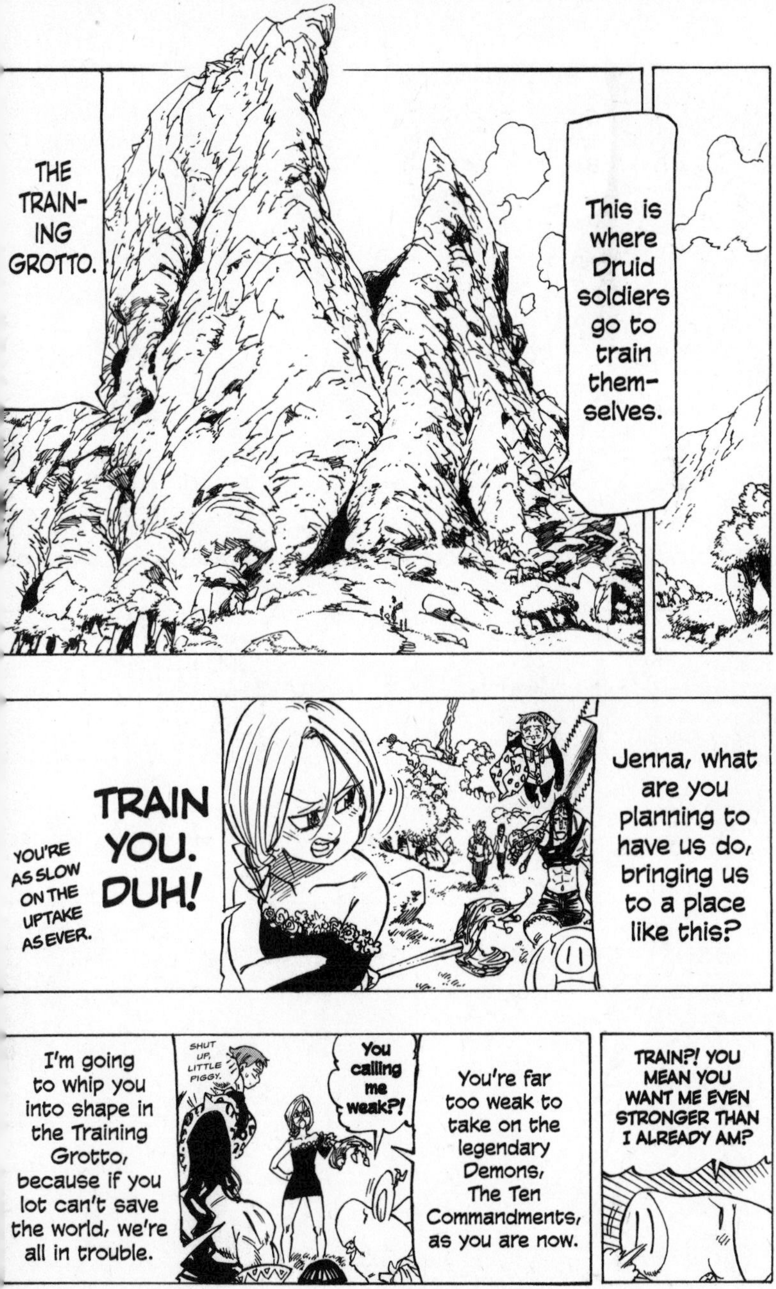
This is where Druid soldiers go to train themselves.
THE TRAINING GROTTO.
Jenna, what are you planning to have us do, bringing us to a place like this?
TRAIN YOU. DUH!
YOU'RE AS SLOW ON THE UPTAKE AS EVER.
TRAIN?! YOU MEAN YOU WANT ME EVEN STRONGER THAN I ALREADY AM?
You're far too weak to take on the legendary Demons, The Ten Commandments, as you are now.
You calling me weak?!
SHUT UP, LITTLE PIGGY.
I'm going to whip you into shape in the Training Grotto, because if you lot can't save the world, we're all in trouble.

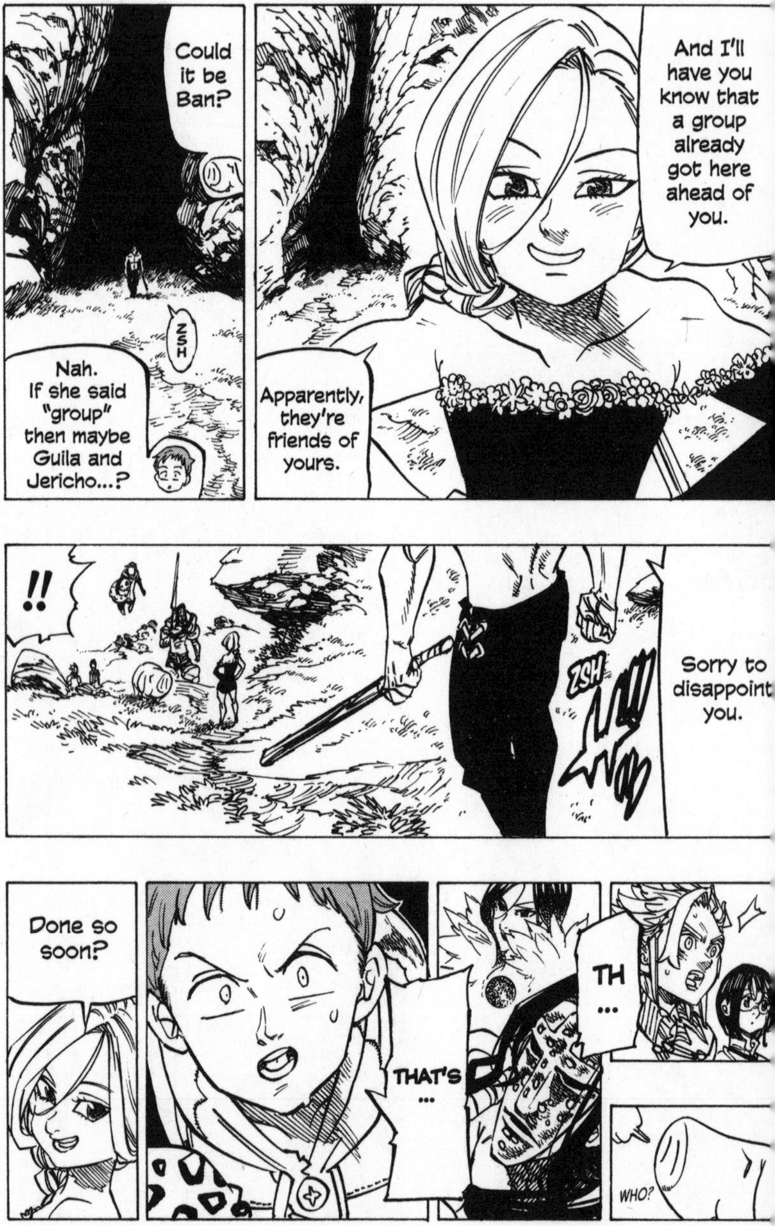
And I'll have you know that a group already got here ahead of you.
Apparently, they're friends of yours.
Could it be Ban?
ZSH
Nah. If she said "group" then maybe Guila and Jericho...?
Sorry to disappoint you.
ZSH
!!
TH ...
WHO?
THAT'S ...
Done so soon?

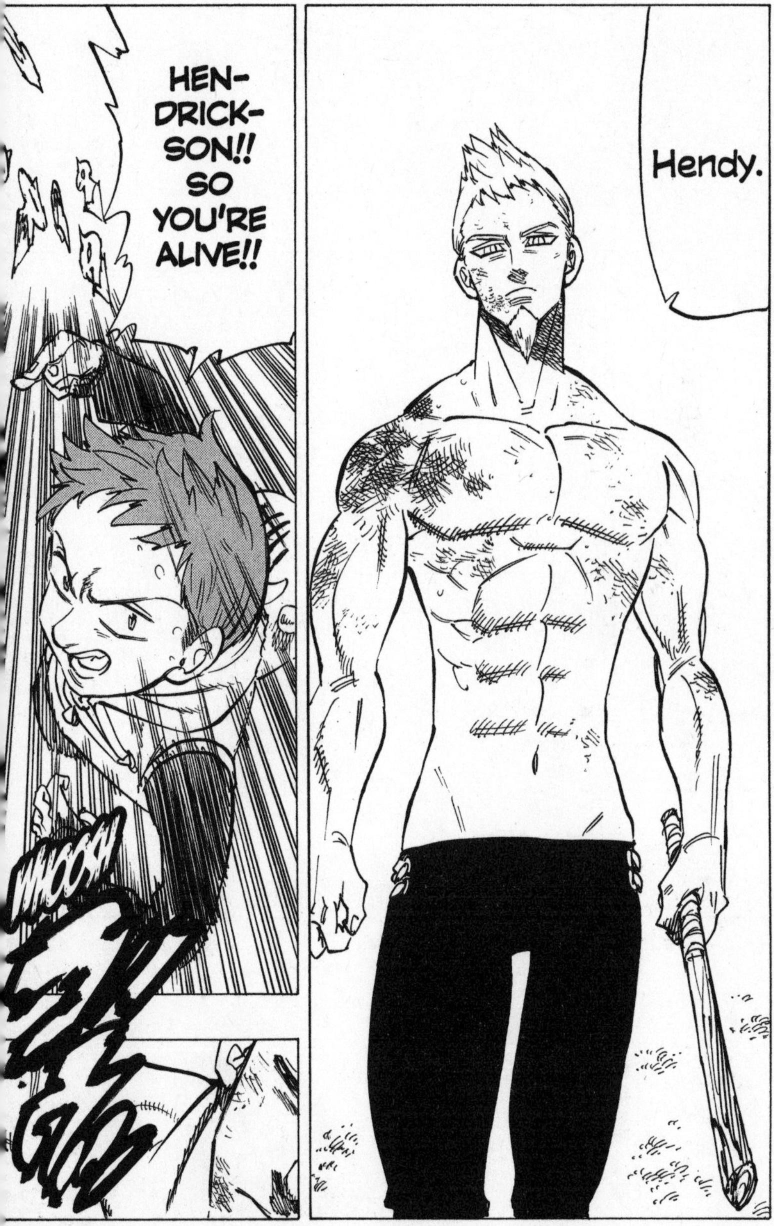
Hendy.
HEN-DRICK-SON!! SO YOU'RE ALIVE!!

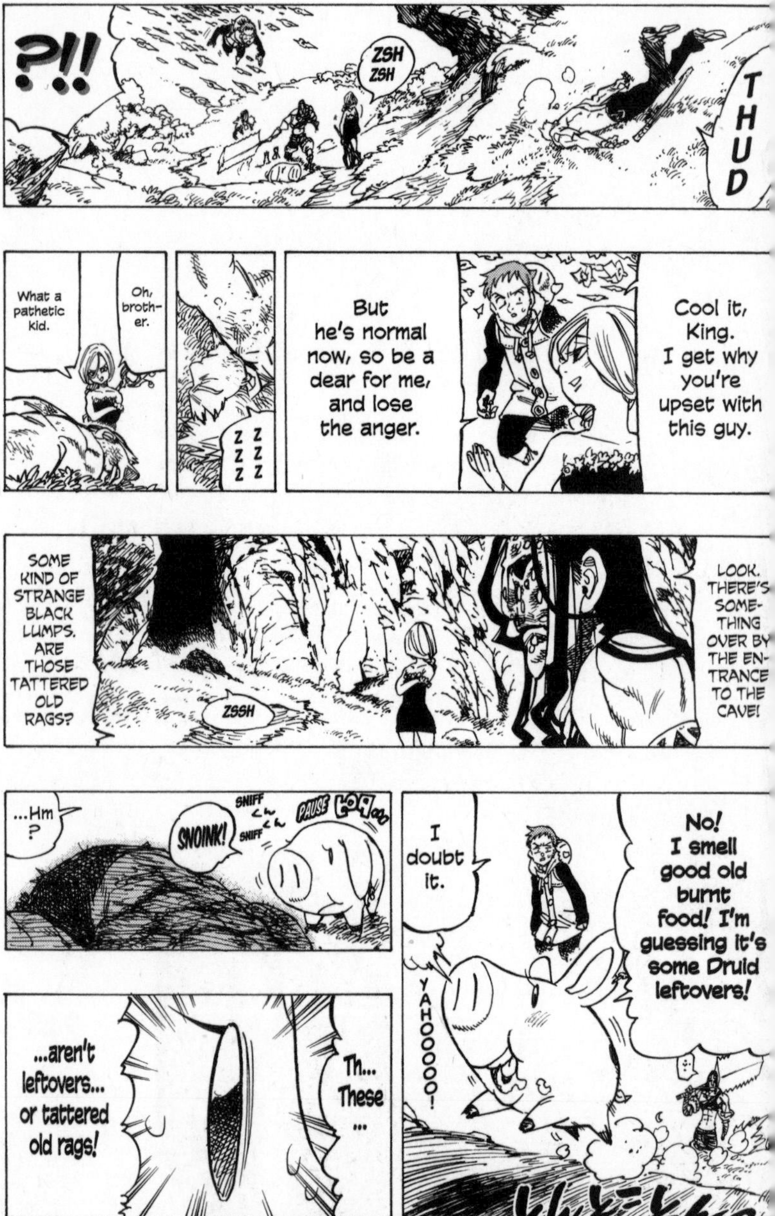
THUD
ZSH ZSH
?!!
Cool it, King. I get why you're upset with this guy.
But he's normal now, so be a dear for me, and lose the anger.
Z Z Z Z Z Z
Oh, brother.
What a pathetic kid.
LOOK. THERE'S SOMETHING OVER BY THE ENTRANCE TO THE CAVE!
ZSSH
SOME KIND OF STRANGE BLACK LUMPS. ARE THOSE TATTERED OLD RAGS?
No! I smell good old burnt food! I'm guessing it's some Druid leftovers!
I doubt it.
YAHOOOOOO!
CLIK CLIK CLIK
PAUSE
SNIFF SNIFF
SNOINK!
...Hm?
Th... These...
...aren't leftovers... or tattered old rags!

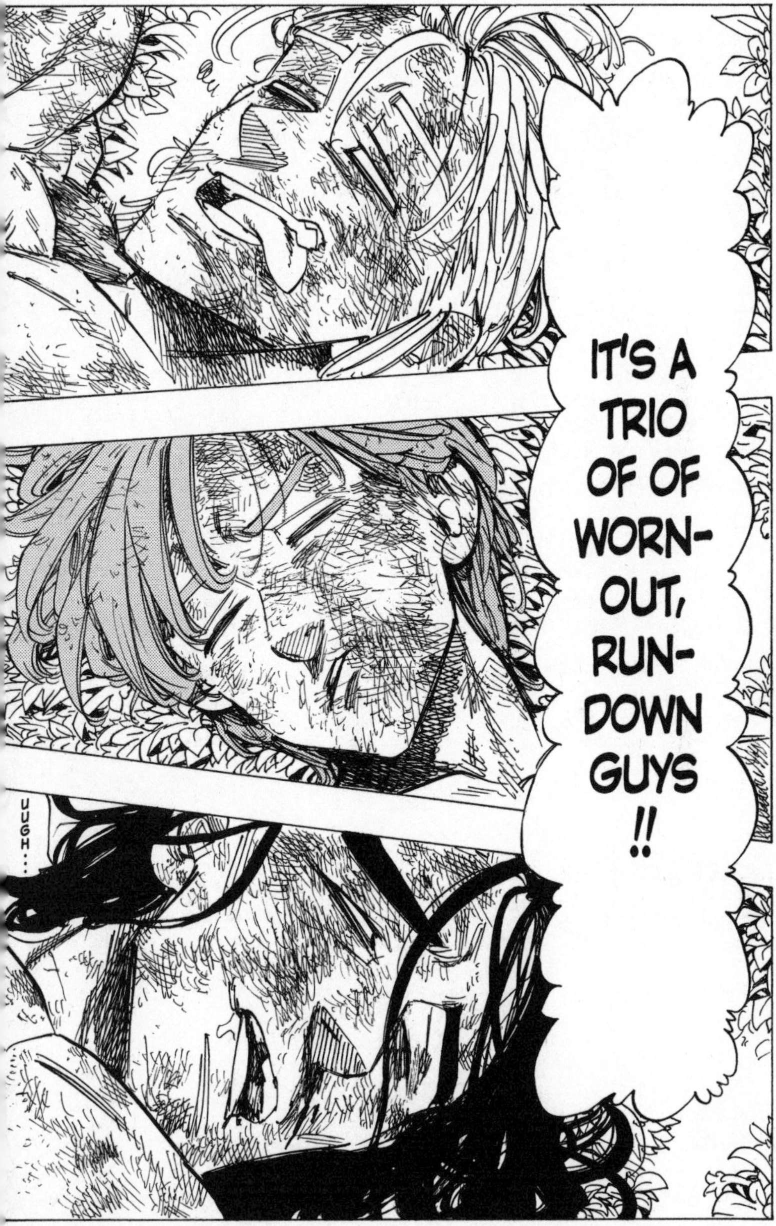
IT'S A TRIO OF OF WORN-OUT, RUN-DOWN GUYS !!
UUGH...

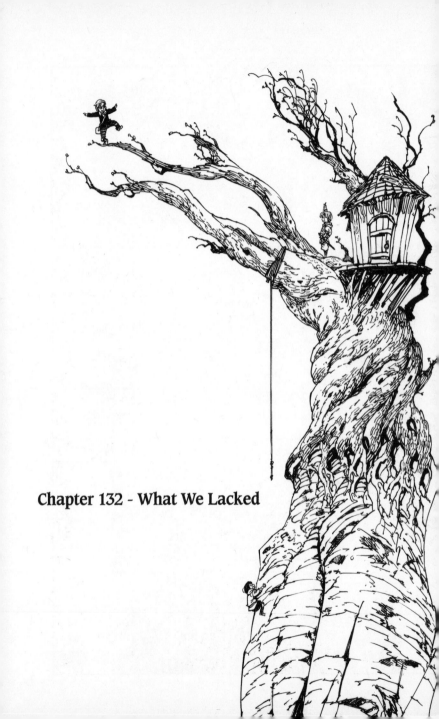

Chapter 132 - What We Lacked

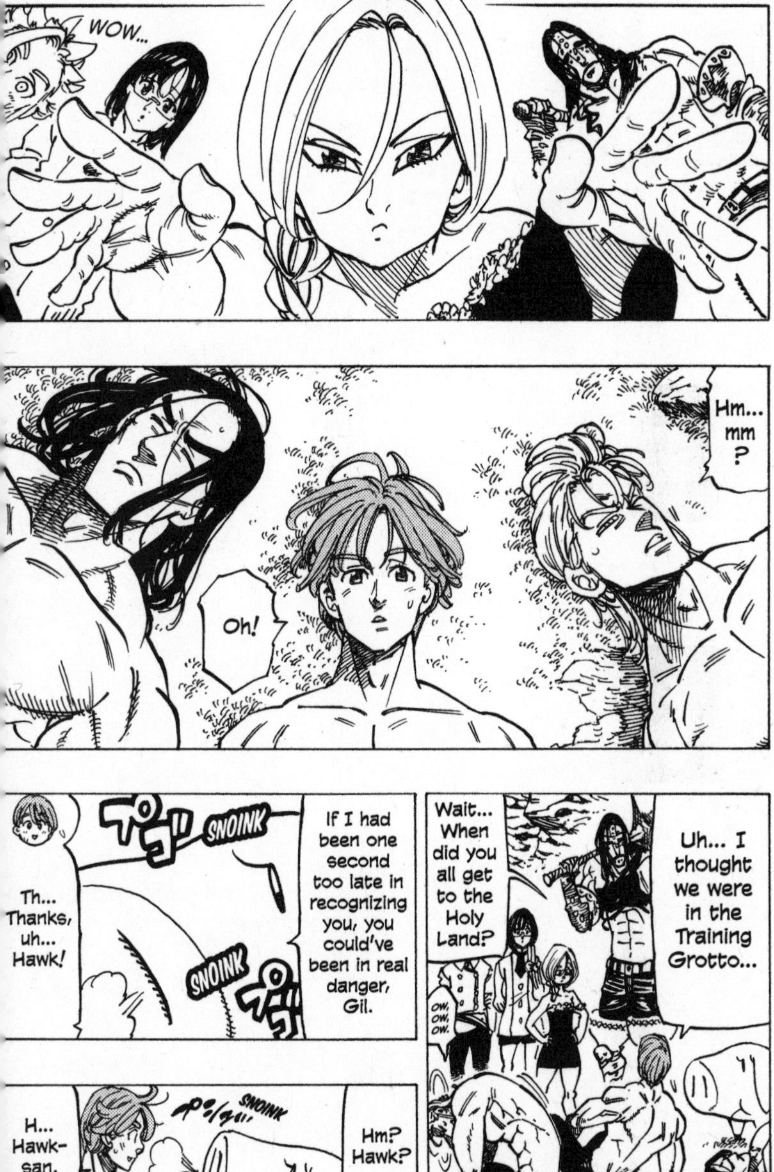
WOW...
Hm... mm ?
Oh!
Uh... I thought we were in the Training Grotto...
Wait... When did you all get to the Holy Land?
OW, OW, OW.
If I had been one second too late in recognizing you, you could've been in real danger, Gil.
SNOINK
SNOINK
Th... Thanks, uh... Hawk!
Hm? Hawk?
SNOINK
H... Hawk-san.

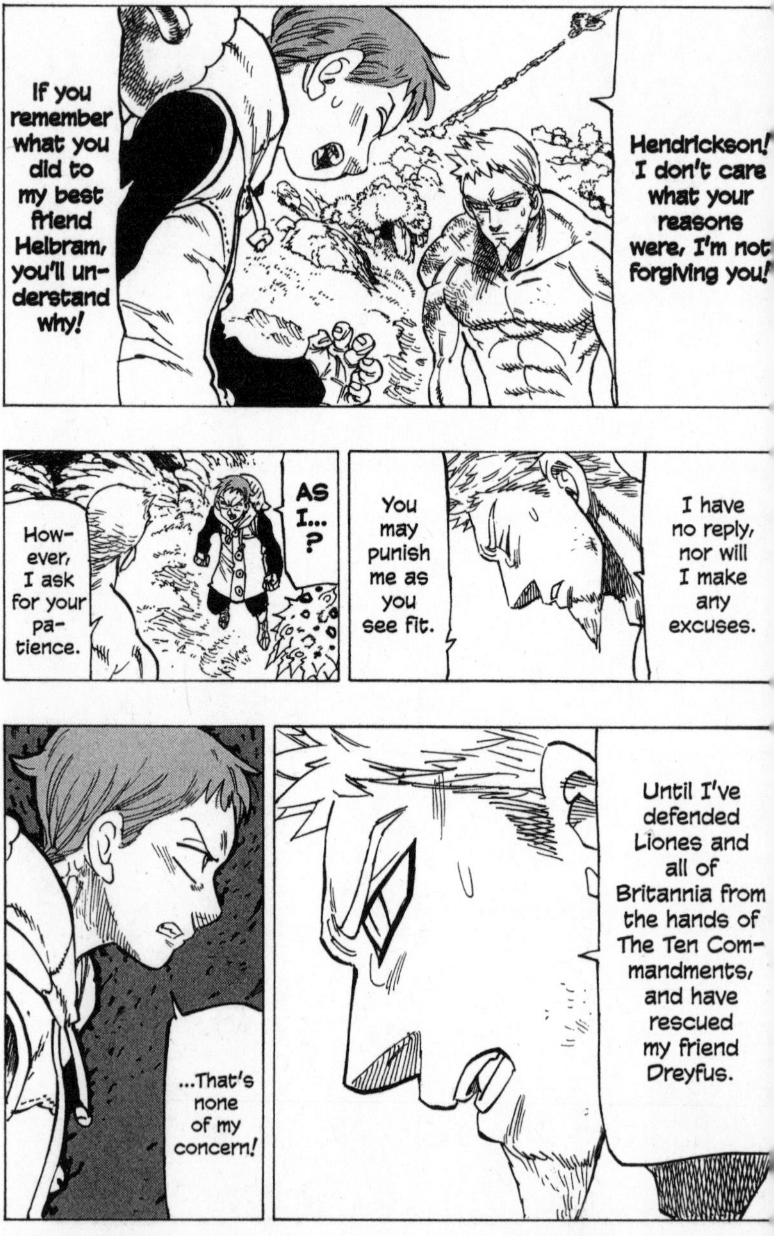

Hendrickson! I don't care what your reasons were, I'm not forgiving you!
If you remember what you did to my best friend Helbram, you'll understand why!
I have no reply, nor will I make any excuses.
You may punish me as you see fit.
AS I...?
However, I ask for your patience.
Until I've defended Liones and all of Britannia from the hands of The Ten Commandments, and have rescued my friend Dreyfus.
...That's none of my concern!

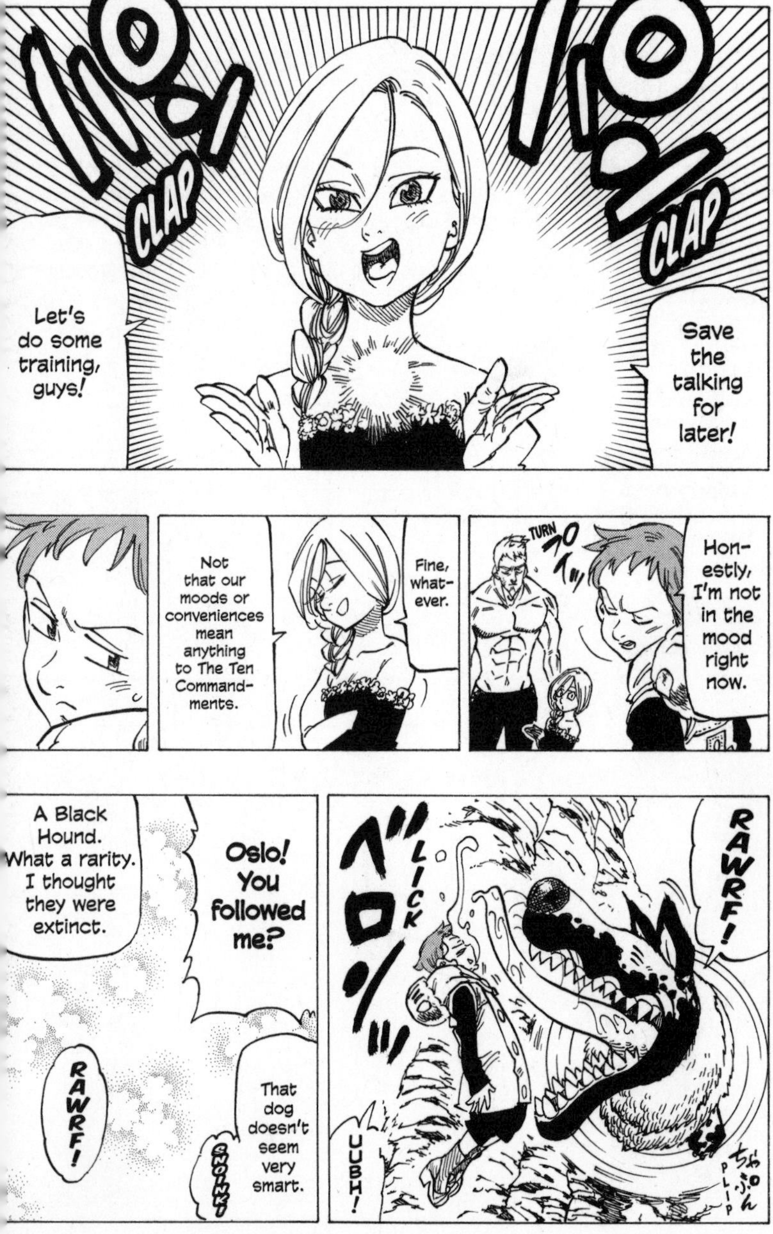

CLAP
CLAP
Save the talking for later!
Let's do some training, guys!
TURN
Honestly, I'm not in the mood right now.
Fine, whatever.
Not that our moods or conveniences mean anything to The Ten Commandments.
RAWRF!
LICK
UUBH!
PLIP
Oslo! You followed me?
A Black Hound. What a rarity. I thought they were extinct.
RAWRF!
That dog doesn't seem very smart.
SNOINK!

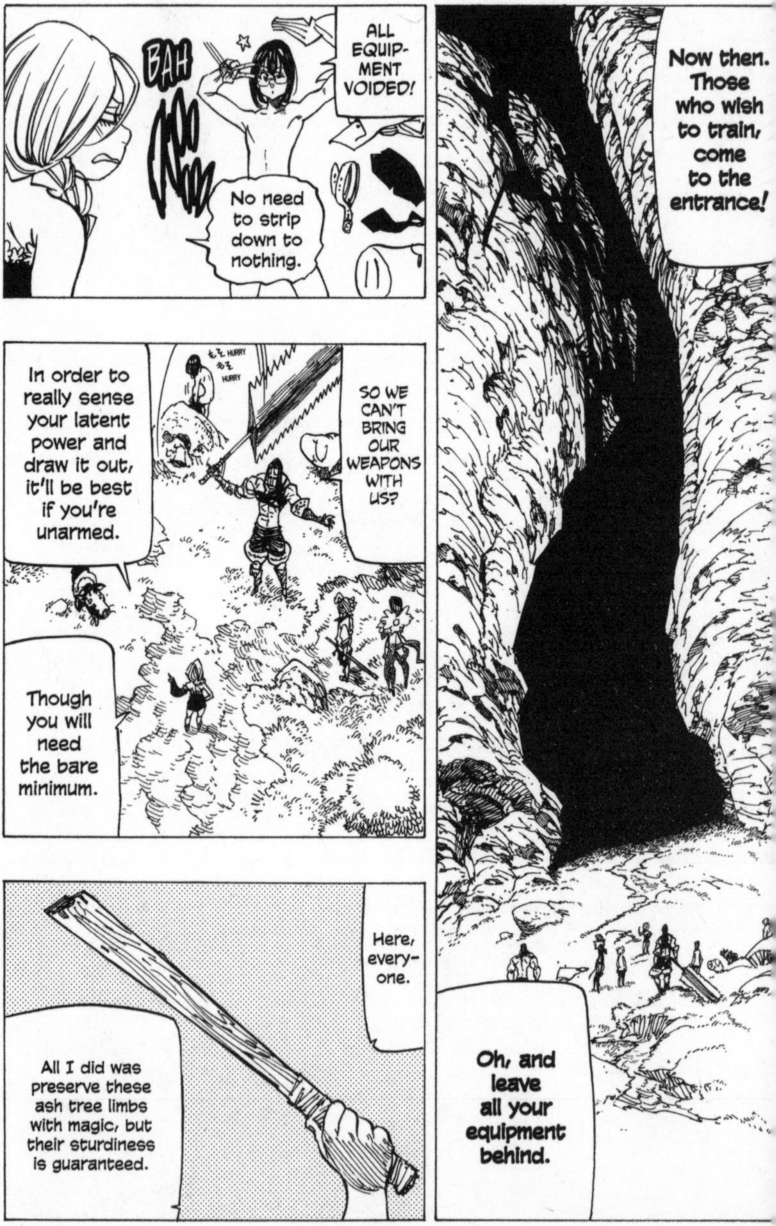
Now then. Those who wish to train, come to the entrance!
Oh, and leave all your equipment behind.
ALL EQUIPMENT VOIDED!
BAH
No need to strip down to nothing.
SO WE CAN'T BRING OUR WEAPONS WITH US?
HURRY HURRY
In order to really sense your latent power and draw it out, it'll be best if you're unarmed.
Though you will need the bare minimum.
Here, everyone.
All I did was preserve these ash tree limbs with magic, but their sturdiness is guaranteed.

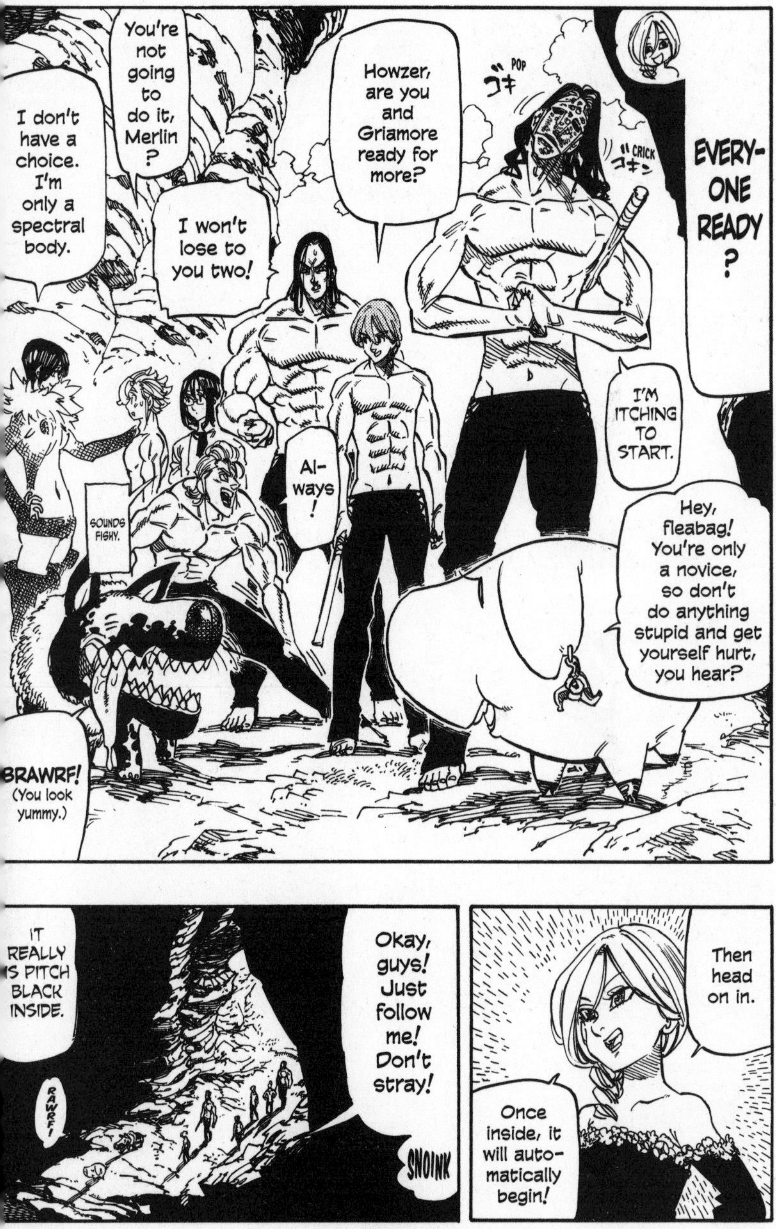
EVERY-ONE READY?
ゴキ POP
ゴキン CRICK
Howzer, are you and Griamore ready for more?
You're not going to do it, Merlin?
I don't have a choice. I'm only a spectral body.
I won't lose to you two!
I'M ITCHING TO START.
Al-ways!
Hey, fleabag! You're only a novice, so don't do anything stupid and get yourself hurt, you hear?
SOUNDS FISHY.
BRAWRF! (You look yummy.)
Then head on in.
Once inside, it will auto-matically begin!
Okay, guys! Just follow me! Don't stray!
SNOINK
IT REALLY IS PITCH BLACK INSIDE.
RAWRF!

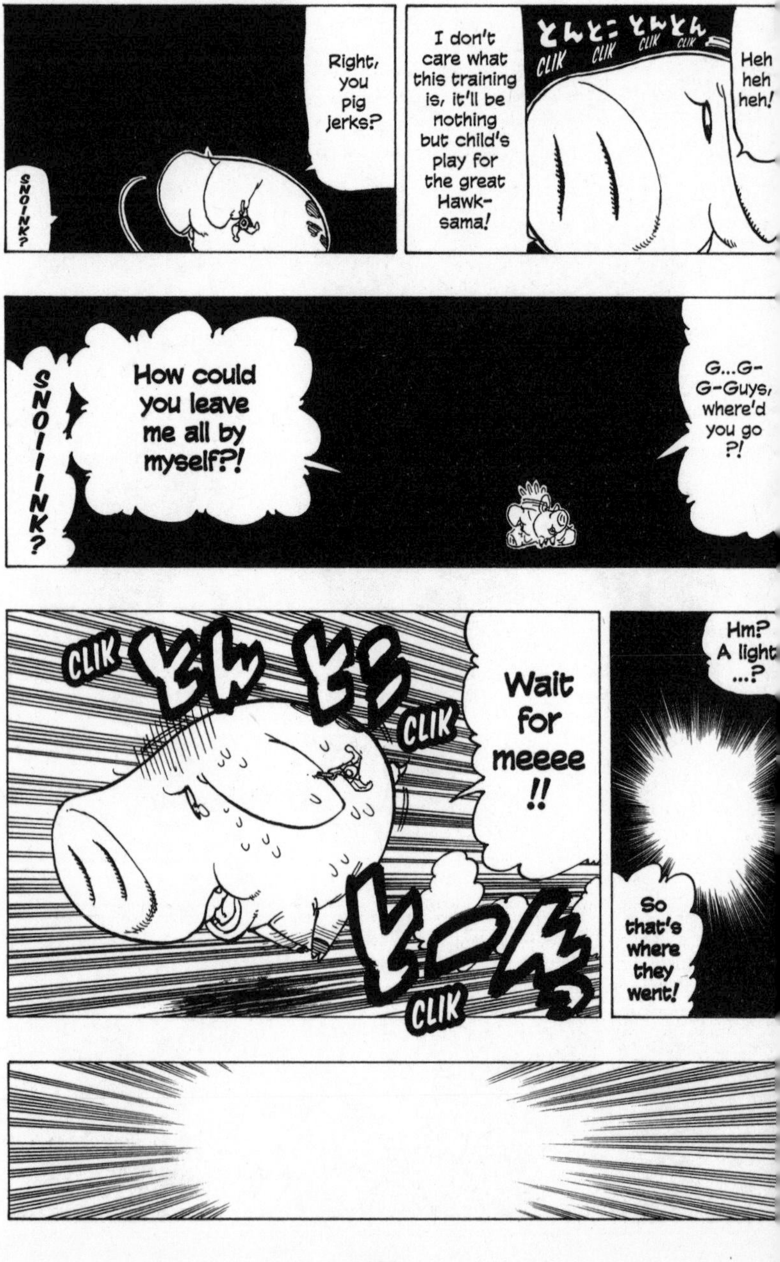
Heh heh heh!
CLIK CLIK CLIK CLIK
I don't care what this training is, it'll be nothing but child's play for the great Hawk-sama!
Right, you pig jerks?
SNOINK?
G...G-G-Guys, where'd you go?!
How could you leave me all by myself?!
SNOIIIINK?
Hm? A light...?
So that's where they went!
Wait for meeee!!
CLIK
CLIK
CLIK

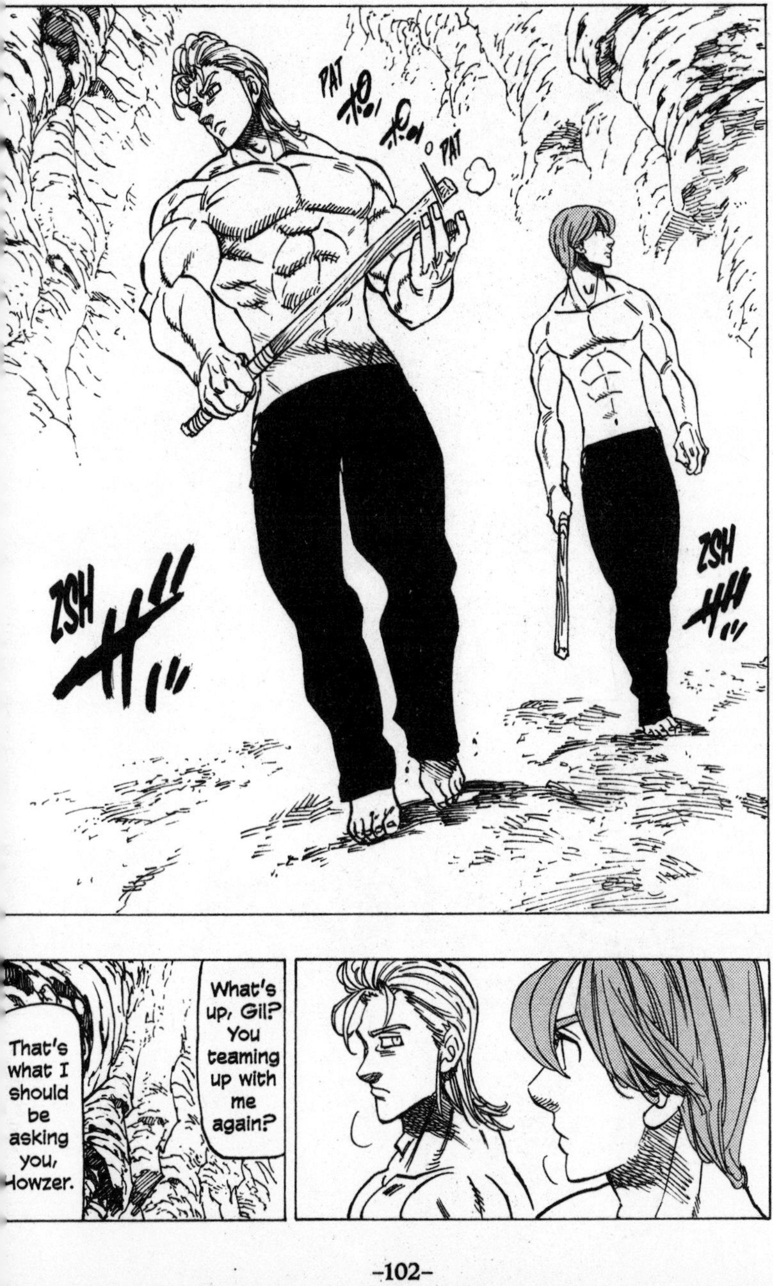
PAT
PAT
ZSH
ZSH
What's up, Gil? You teaming up with me again?
That's what I should be asking you, Howzer.

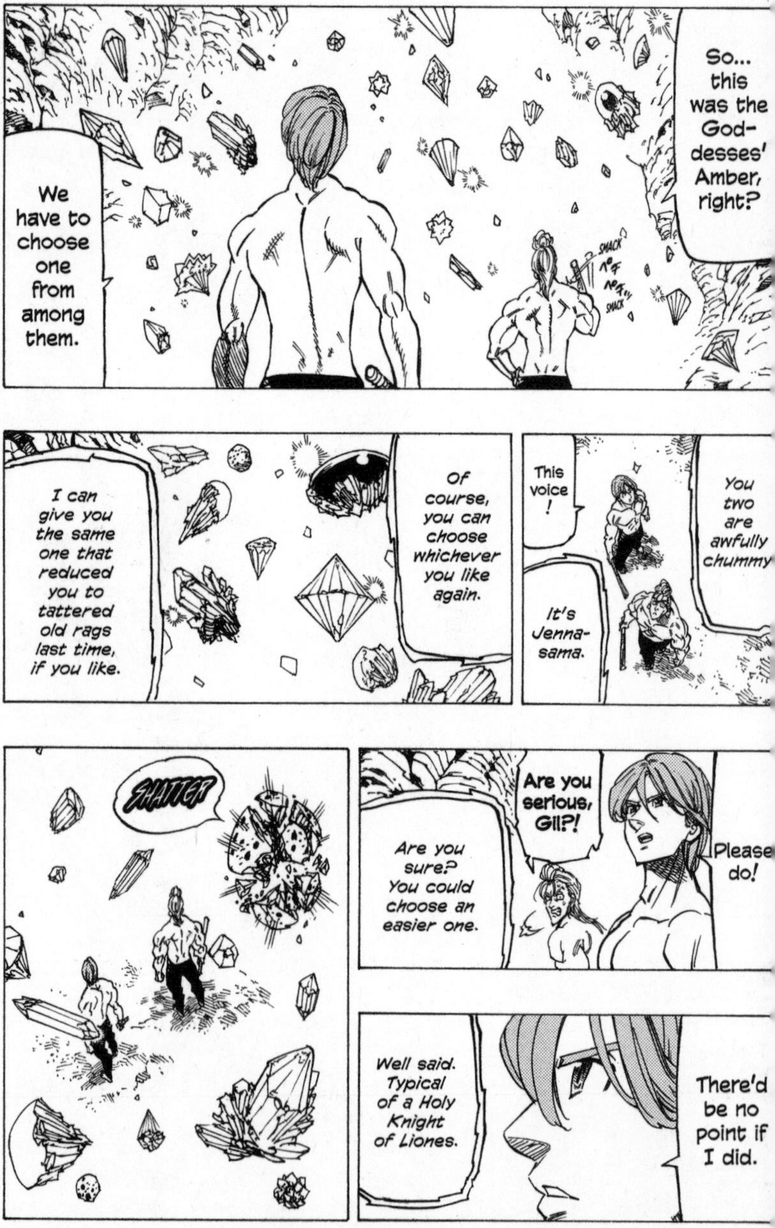

So... this was the God-desses' Amber, right?
SMACK ペチ ペチ SMACK
We have to choose one from among them.
You two are awfully chummy
This voice!
It's Jenna-sama.
Of course, you can choose whichever you like again.
I can give you the same one that reduced you to tattered old rags last time, if you like.
Please do!
Are you serious, Gil?!
Are you sure? You could choose an easier one.
There'd be no point if I did.
Well said. Typical of a Holy Knight of Liones.
SHATTER

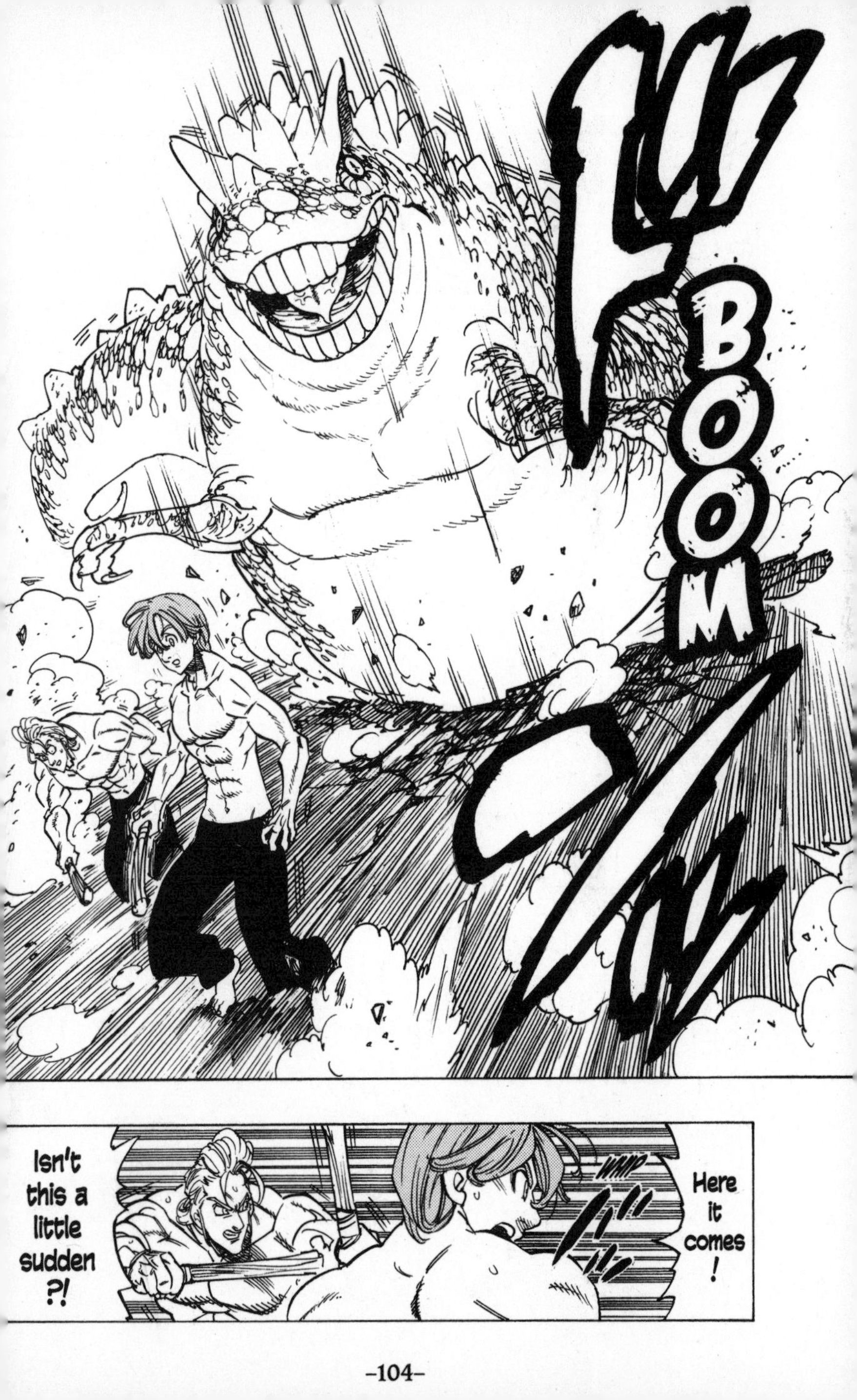
BOOM
Here it comes!
WHIP
Isn't this a little sudden?!

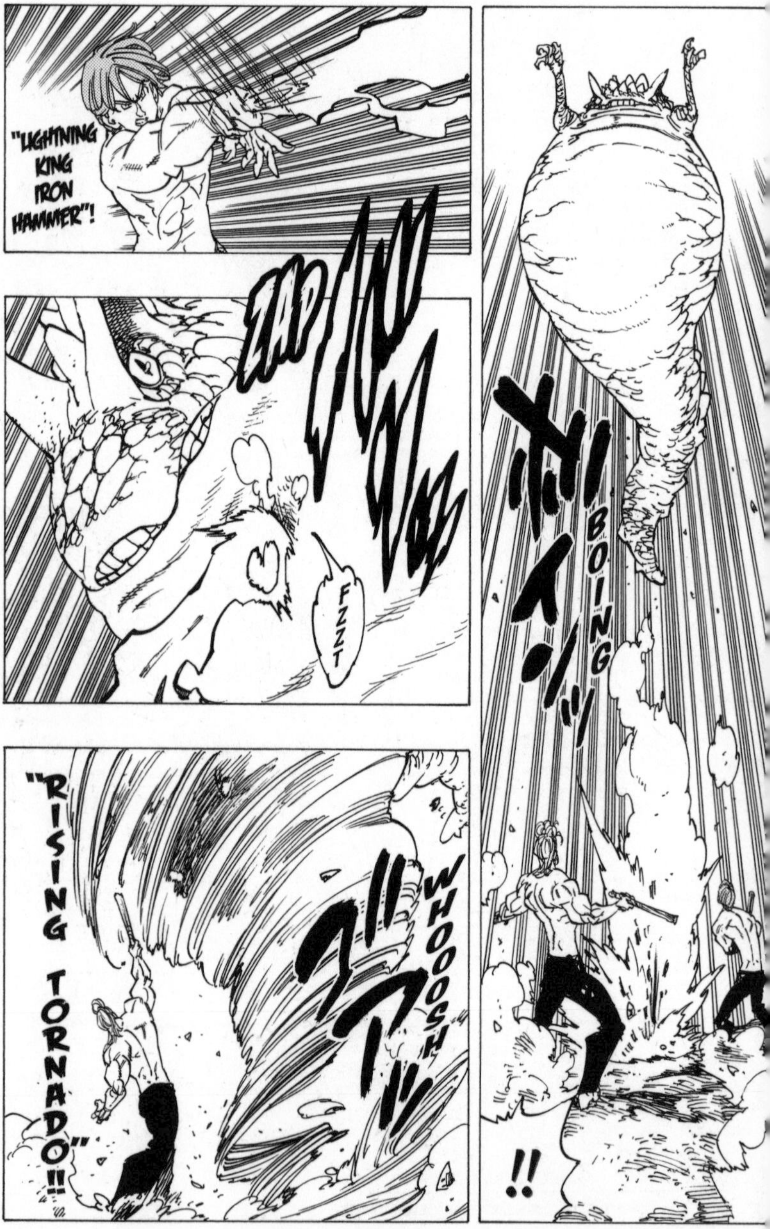
ボイン
BOING
!!
"LIGHTNING KING IRON HAMMER"!
ZAP
FZZT
"RISING TORNADO"!!
WHOOOOSH

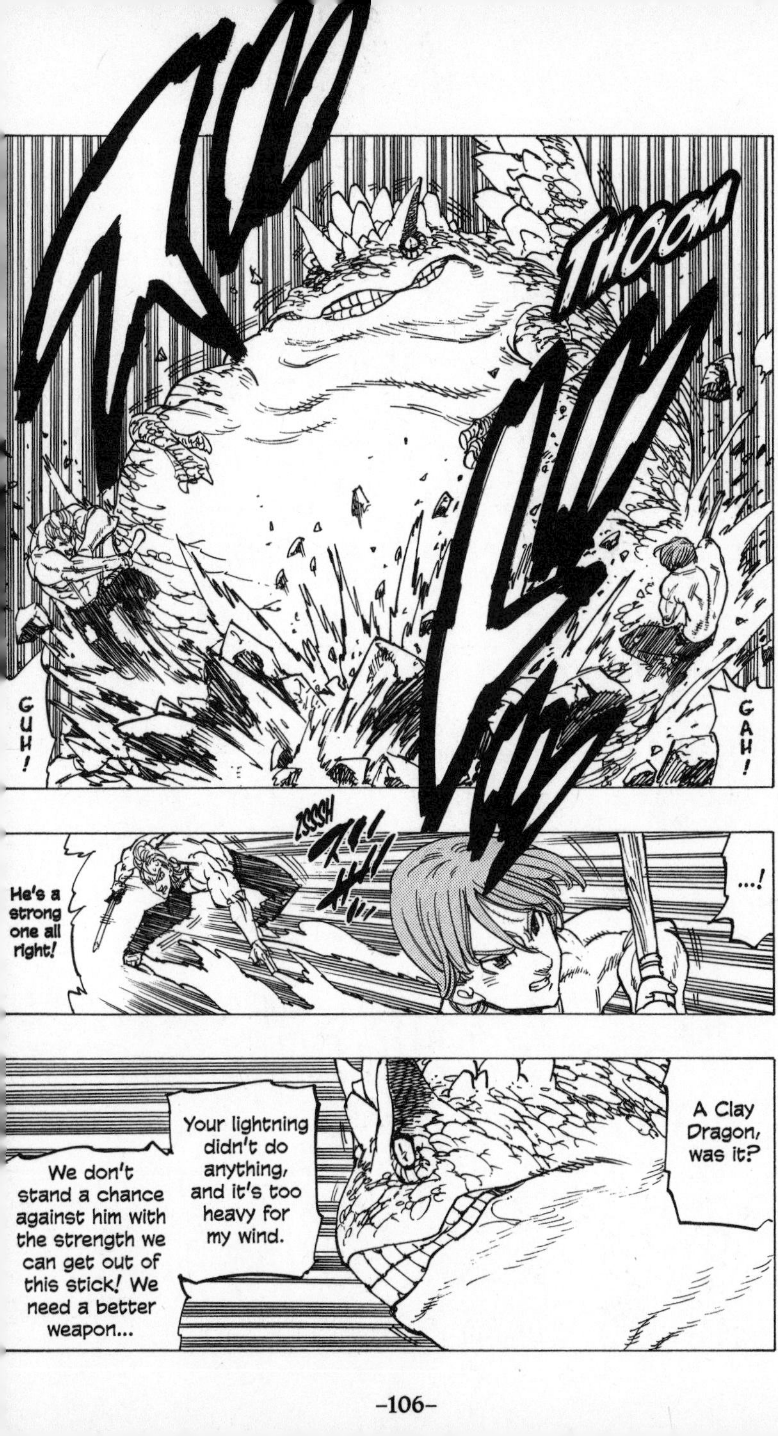
THOOM
GAH!
GUH!
...!
ZSSSH
He's a strong one all right!
A Clay Dragon, was it?
Your lightning didn't do anything, and it's too heavy for my wind.
We don't stand a chance against him with the strength we can get out of this stick! We need a better weapon...

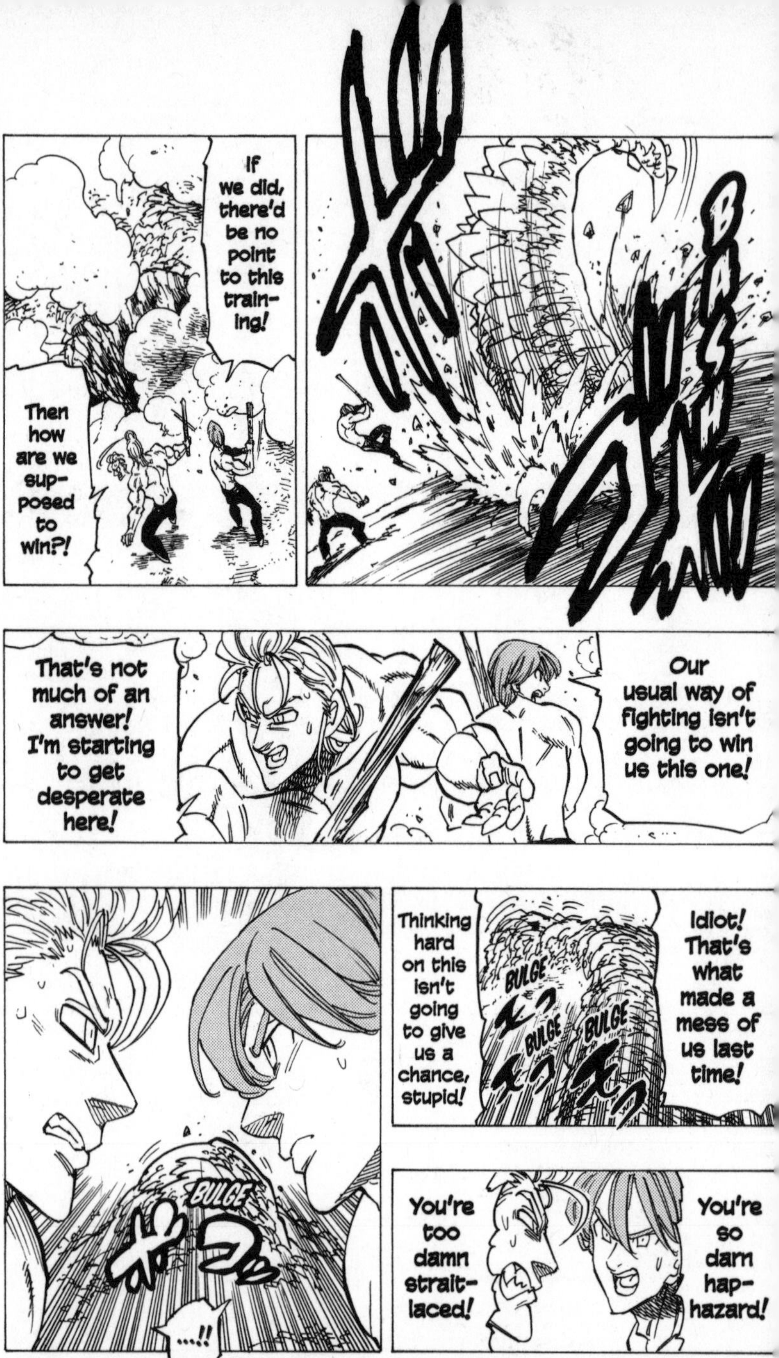
BASH
If we did, there'd be no point to this training!
Then how are we supposed to win?!
Our usual way of fighting isn't going to win us this one!
That's not much of an answer! I'm starting to get desperate here!
Idiot! That's what made a mess of us last time!
Thinking hard on this isn't going to give us a chance, stupid!
BULGE
BULGE
BULGE
You're so darn haphazard!
You're too damn strait-laced!
BULGE
....!!

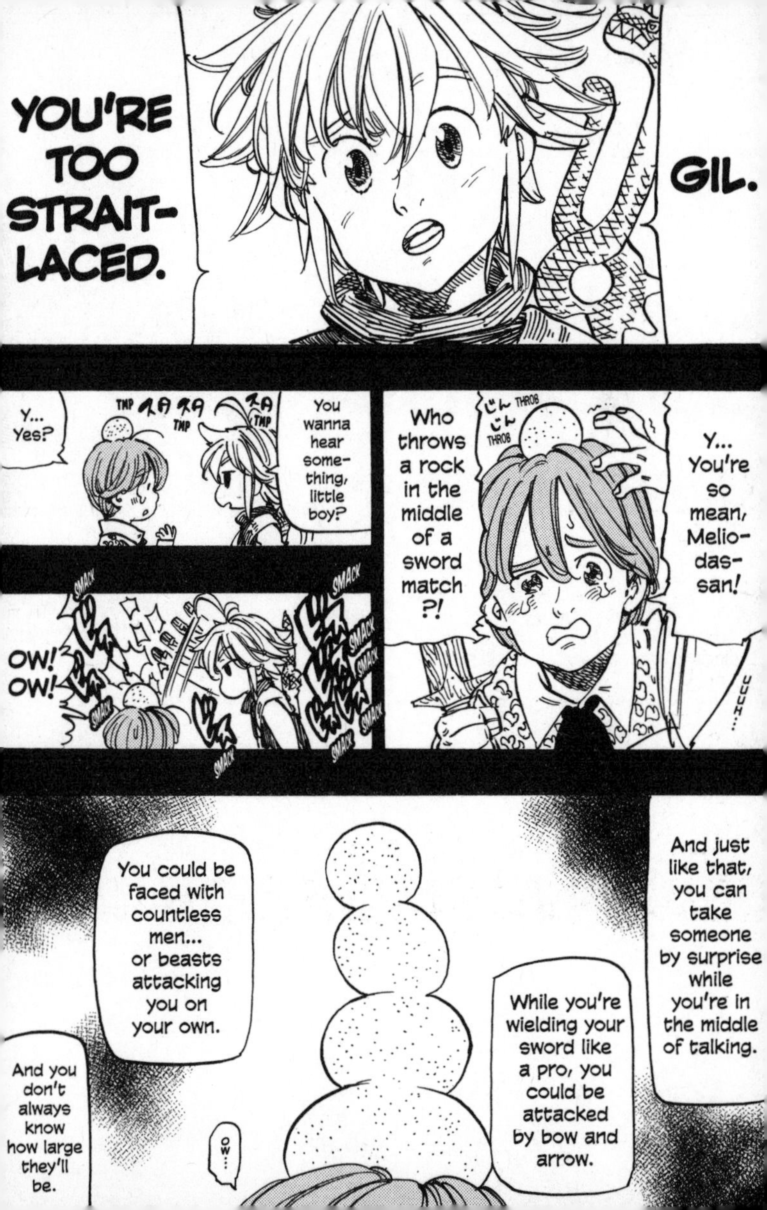
GIL.
YOU'RE TOO STRAIT-LACED.
Y... You're so mean, Meliodas-san!
じんじん THROB THROB
Who throws a rock in the middle of a sword match?!
UUUH...
You wanna hear something, little boy?
スタ TMP スタ TMP スタ TMP
Y... Yes?
SMACK SMACK SMACK SMACK SMACK SMACK SMACK
OW! OW!
And just like that, you can take someone by surprise while you're in the middle of talking.
While you're wielding your sword like a pro, you could be attacked by bow and arrow.
You could be faced with countless men... or beasts attacking you on your own.
OW...
And you don't always know how large they'll be.

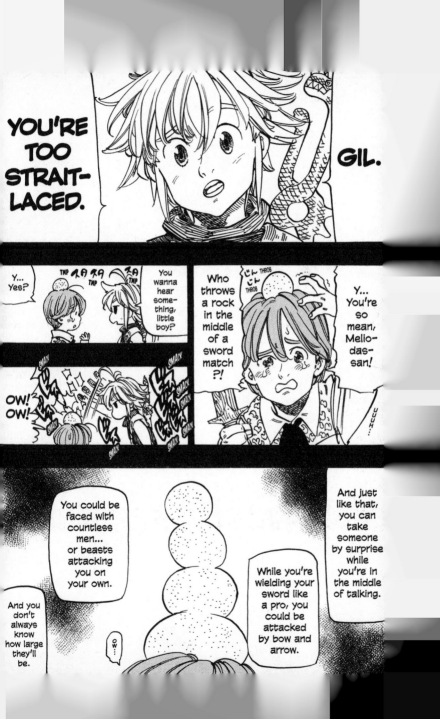

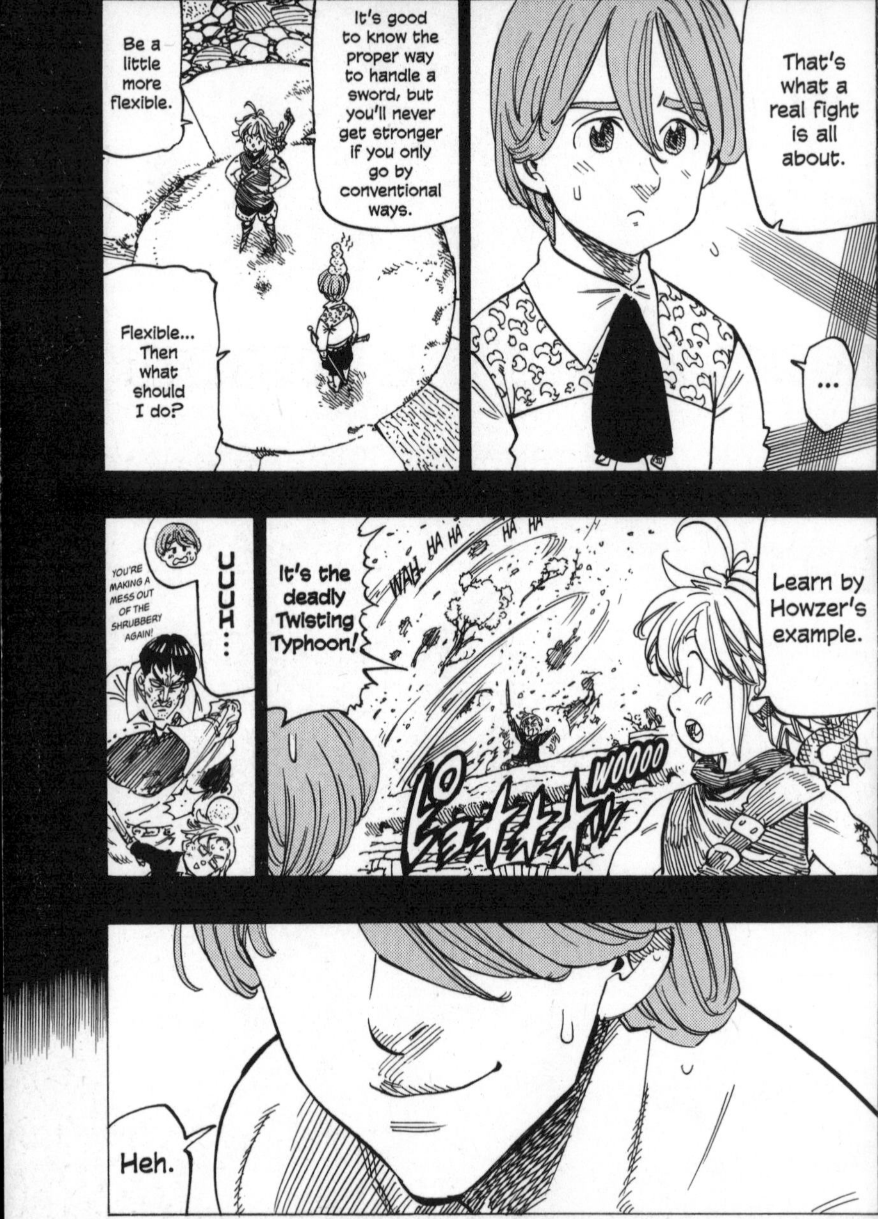
That's what a real fight is all about.
...
It's good to know the proper way to handle a sword, but you'll never get stronger if you only go by conventional ways.
Be a little more flexible.
Flexible... Then what should I do?
Learn by Howzer's example.
WAH HA HA HA HA
It's the deadly Twisting Typhoon!
WOOOO
UUUH...
YOU'RE MAKING A MESS OUT OF THE SHRUBBERY AGAIN!
Heh.

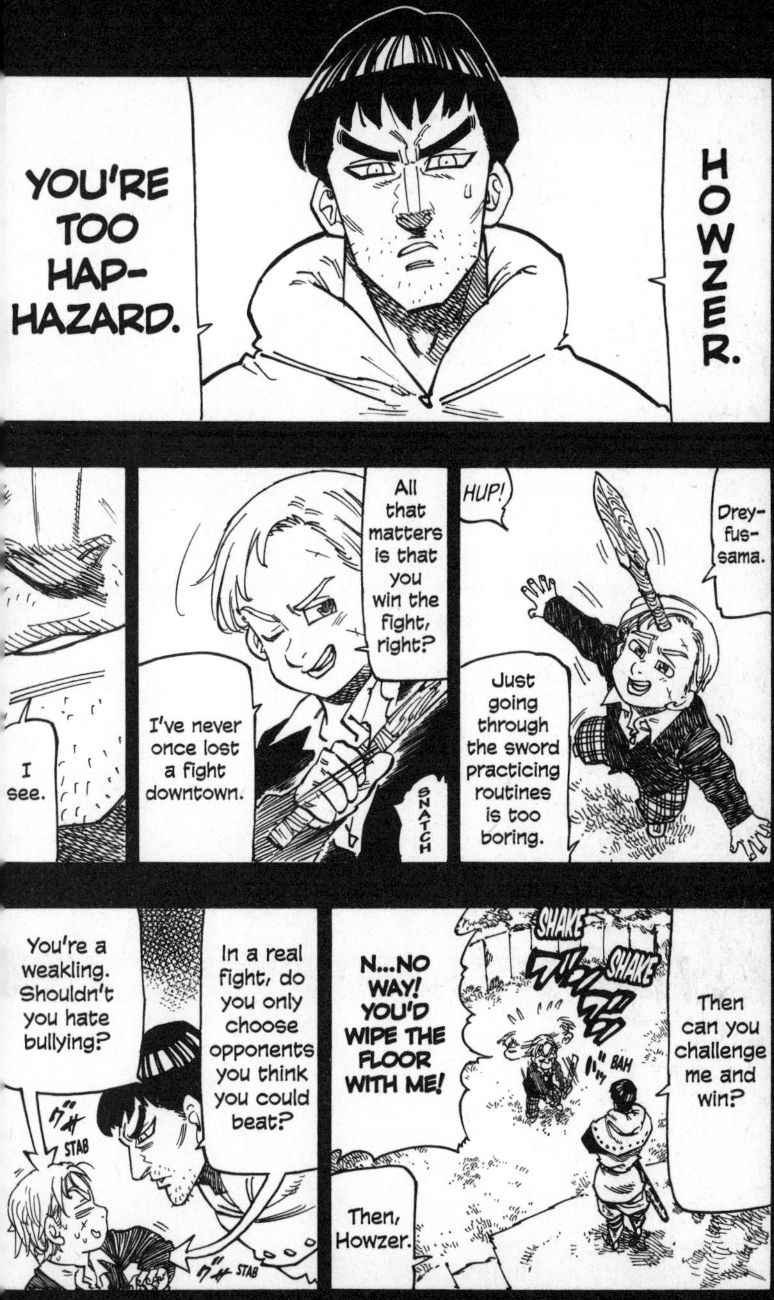
HOWZER.
YOU'RE TOO HAP-HAZARD.
Drey-fus-sama.
HUP!
Just going through the sword practicing routines is too boring.
All that matters is that you win the fight, right?
SNATCH
I've never once lost a fight downtown.
I see.
Then can you challenge me and win?
SHAKE
SHAKE
BAH
N...NO WAY! YOU'D WIPE THE FLOOR WITH ME!
Then, Howzer.
In a real fight, do you only choose opponents you think you could beat?
You're a weakling. Shouldn't you hate bullying?
STAB
STAB

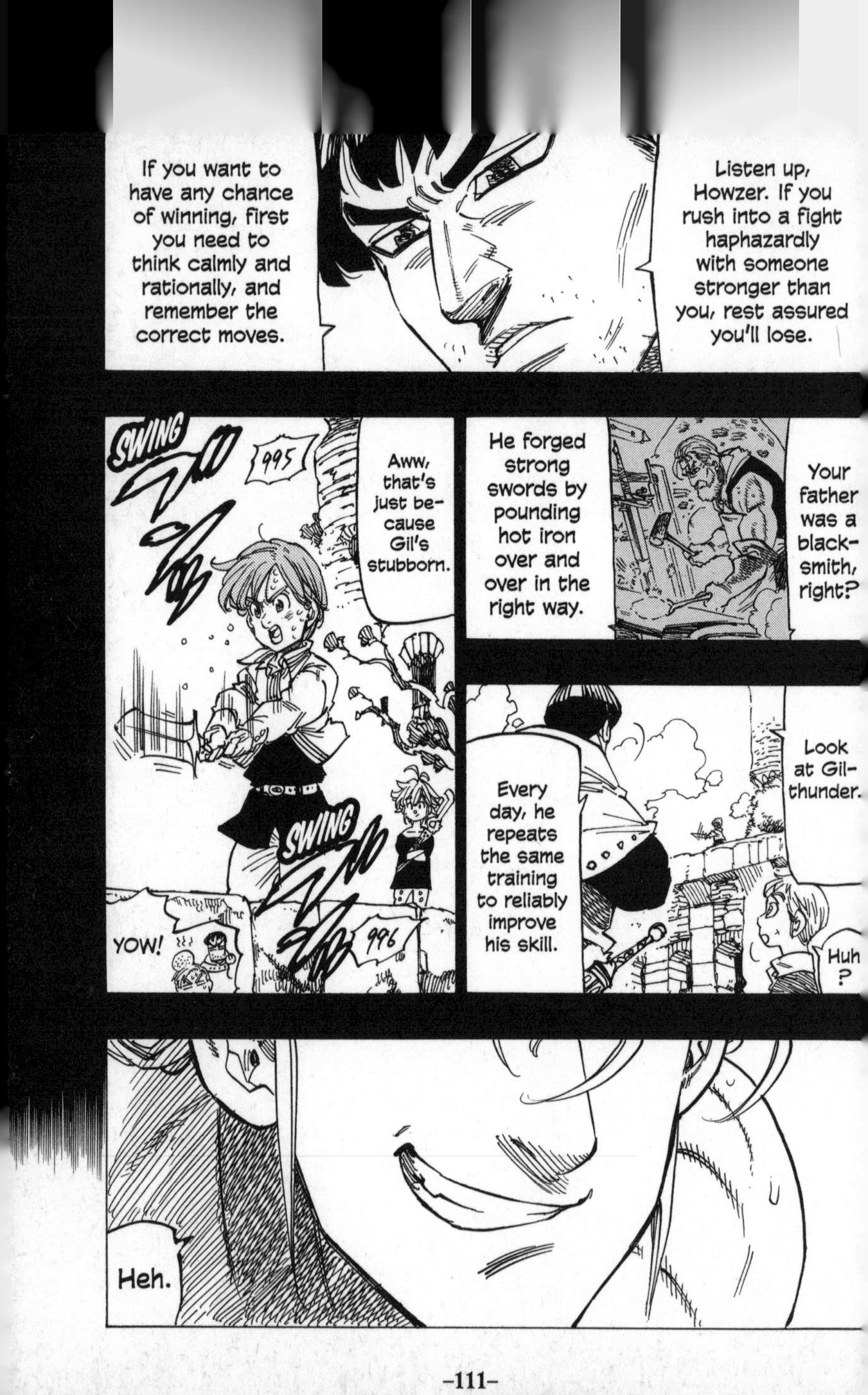

Listen up, Howzer. If you rush into a fight haphazardly with someone stronger than you, rest assured you'll lose.
If you want to have any chance of winning, first you need to think calmly and rationally, and remember the correct moves.
Your father was a blacksmith, right?
He forged strong swords by pounding hot iron over and over in the right way.
Look at Gilthunder.
Huh?
Every day, he repeats the same training to reliably improve his skill.
Aww, that's just because Gil's stubborn.
SWING
995
SWING
996
YOW!
Heh.

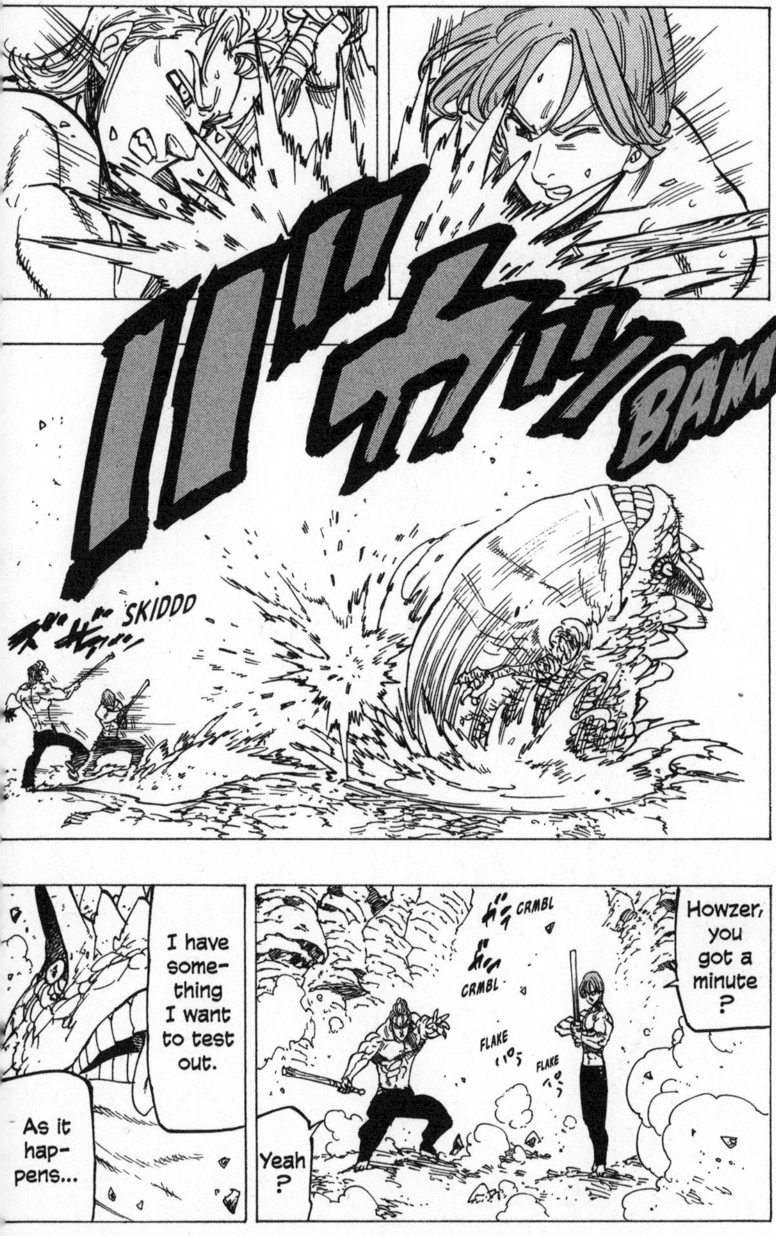
BAM
SKIDDD
Howzer, you got a minute?
CRMBL
CRMBL
FLAKE
FLAKE
Yeah?
I have something I want to test out.
As it happens...

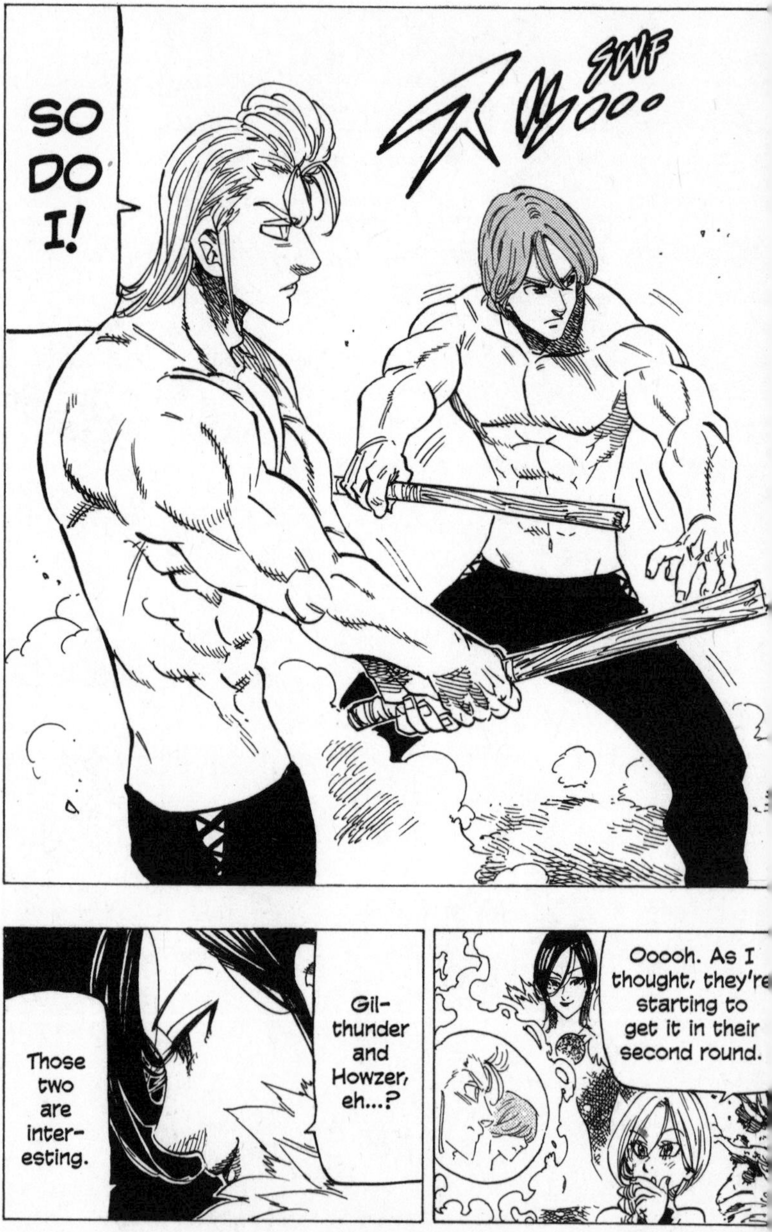
SWF
SO DO I!
Ooooh. As I thought, they're starting to get it in their second round.
Gil-thunder and Howzer, eh...?
Those two are inter-esting.

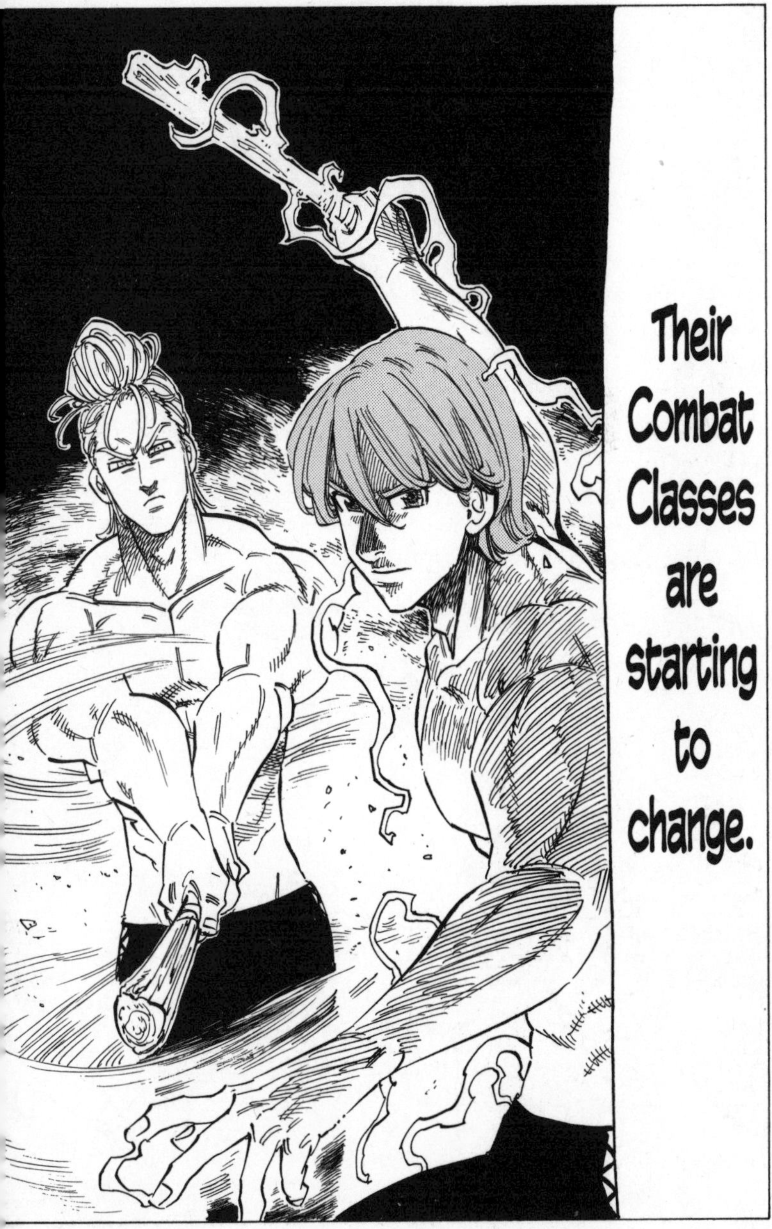
Their Combat Classes are starting to change.

Chapter 133 - Impatience & Anxiety

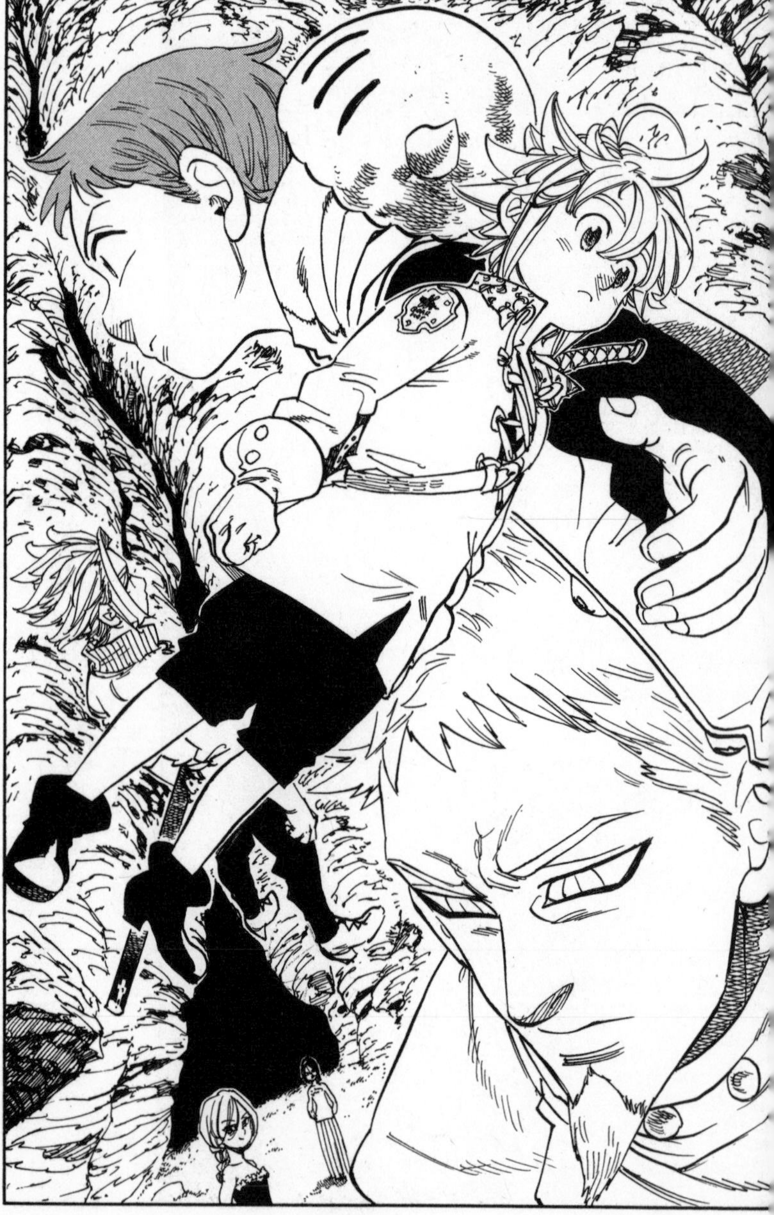

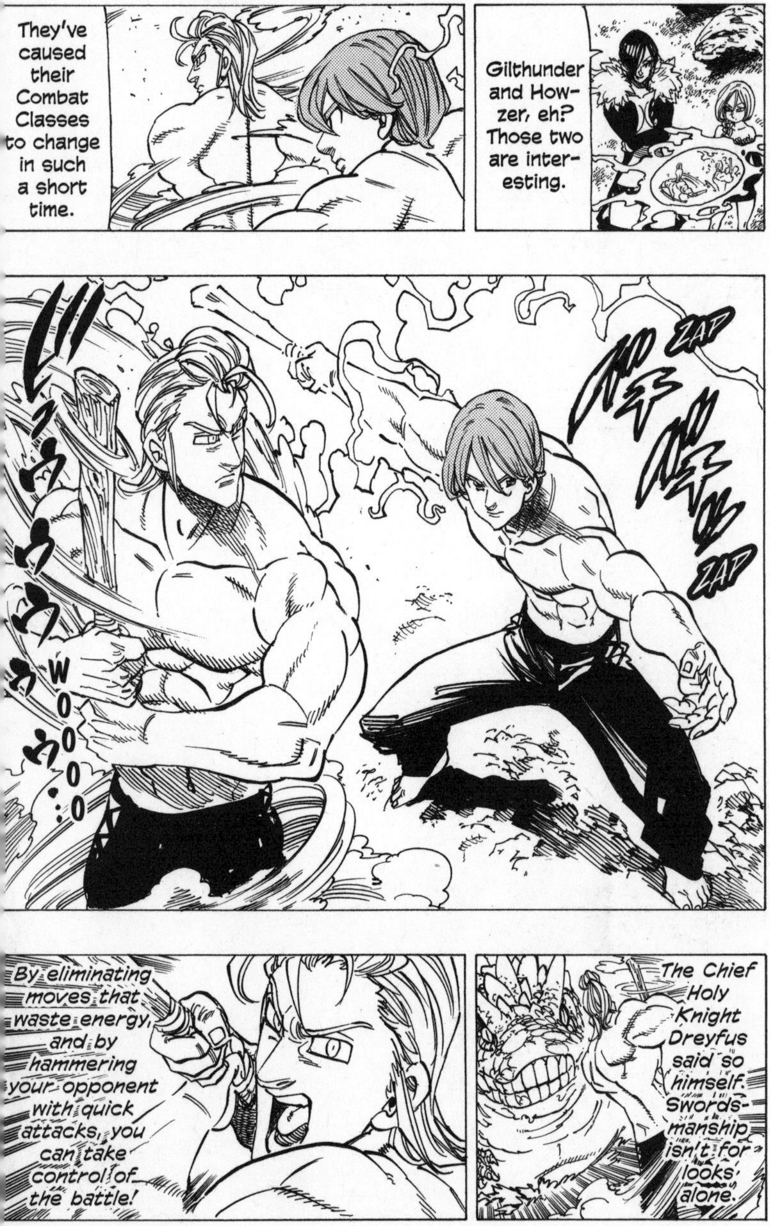
Gilthunder and Howzer, eh? Those two are interesting.
They've caused their Combat Classes to change in such a short time.
ZAP
ZAP
WOOOO...
The Chief Holy Knight Dreyfus said so himself. Swordsmanship isn't for looks alone.
By eliminating moves that waste energy, and by hammering your opponent with quick attacks, you can take control of the battle!

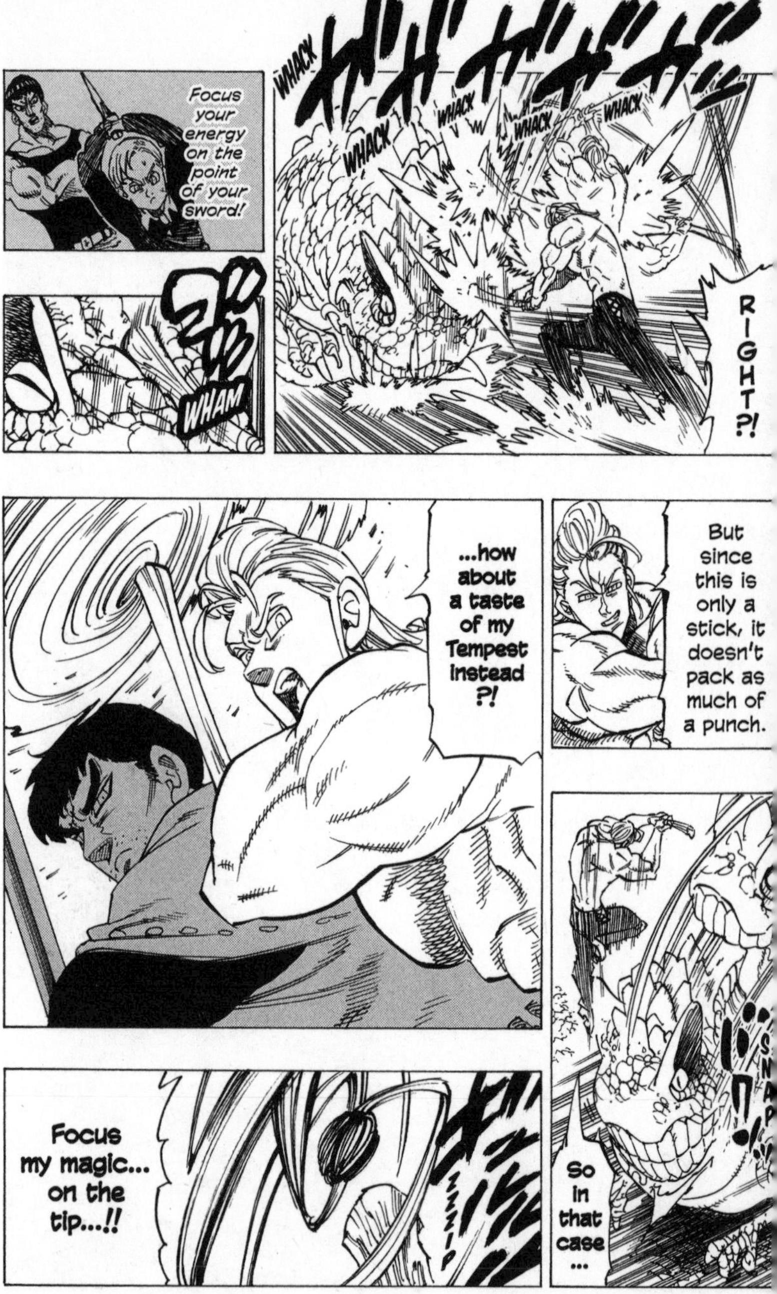
WHACK
WHACK
WHACK
WHACK
WHACK
RIGHT?!
Focus your energy on the point of your sword!
WHAM
But since this is only a stick, it doesn't pack as much of a punch.
SNAP
So in that case...
...how about a taste of my Tempest instead?!
Focus my magic... on the tip...!!
ZZZIP

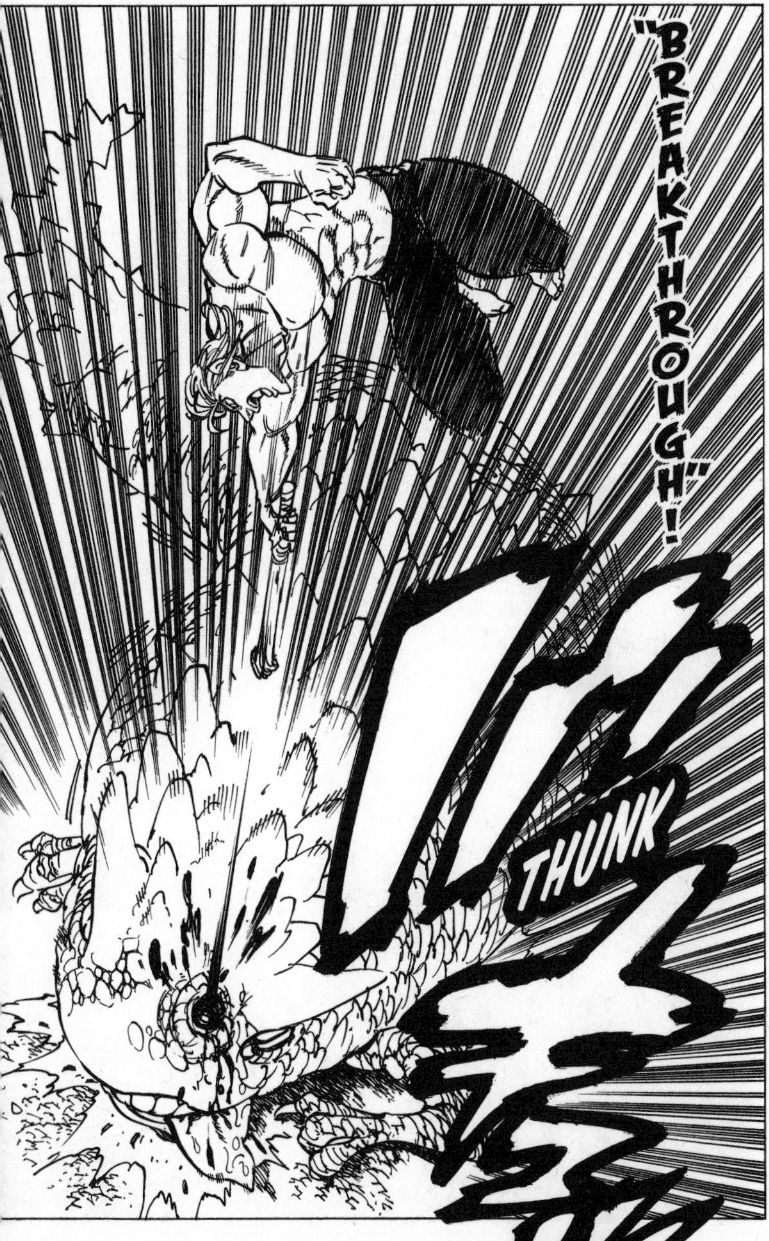
"BREAKTHROUGH!"
THUNK

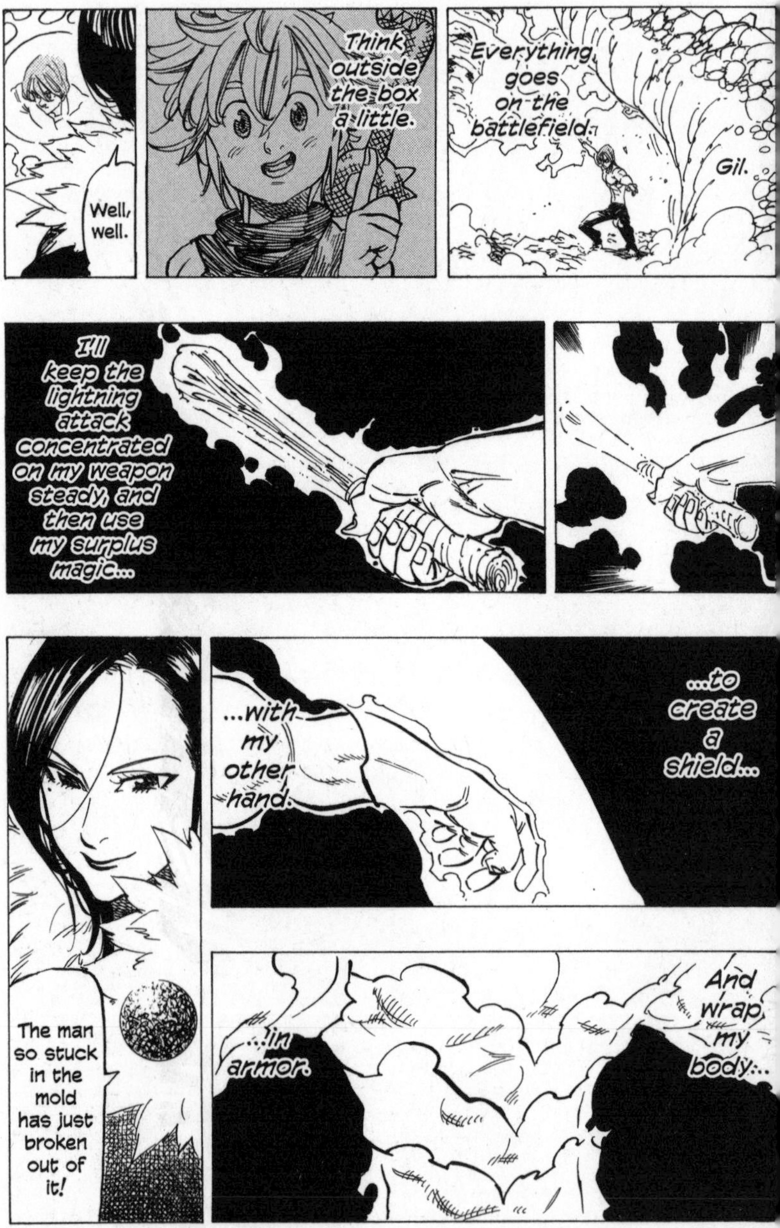
Everything goes on the battlefield.
Gil.
Think outside the box a little.
Well, well.
I'll keep the lightning attack concentrated on my weapon steady, and then use my surplus magic...
...to create a shield...
...with my other hand.
And wrap my body...
...in armor.
The man so stuck in the mold has just broken out of it!

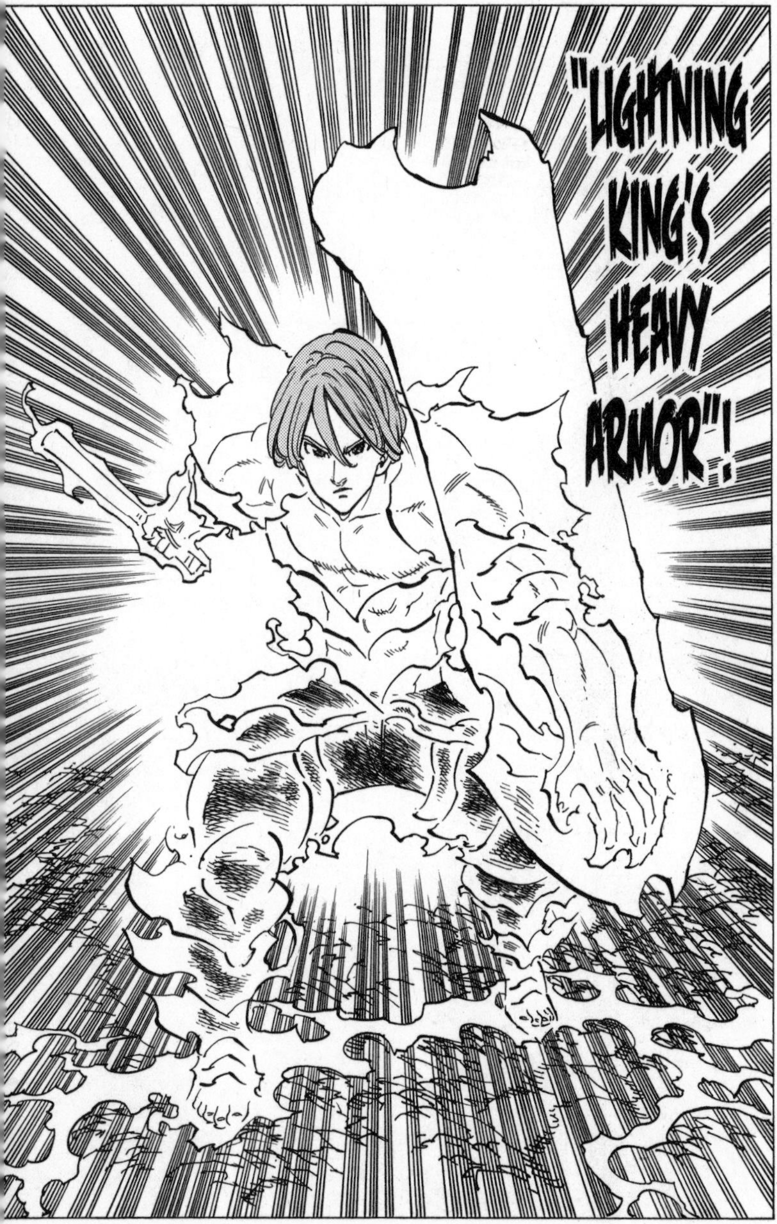
"LIGHTNING KING'S HEAVY ARMOR"!

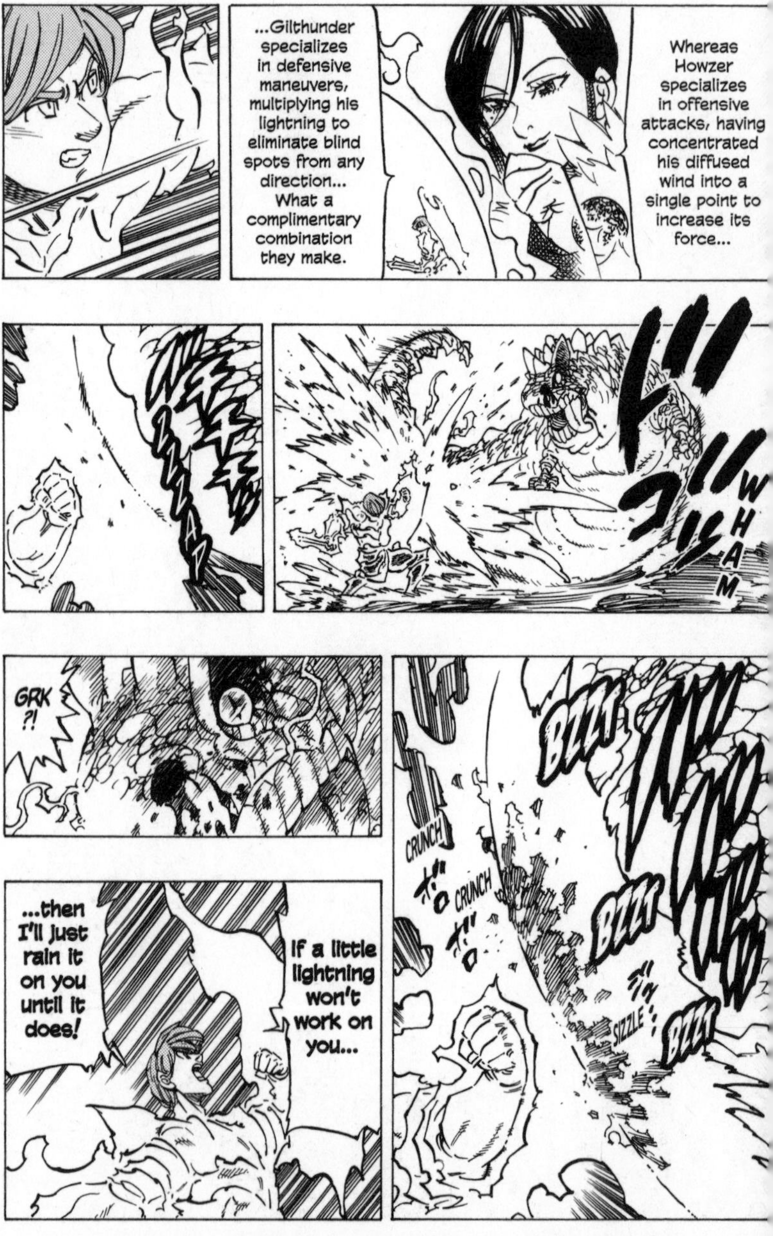
Whereas Howzer specializes in offensive attacks, having concentrated his diffused wind into a single point to increase its force...
...Gilthunder specializes in defensive maneuvers, multiplying his lightning to eliminate blind spots from any direction... What a complimentary combination they make.
WHAM
ZZZZAP
BZZT
CRUNCH
CRUNCH
BZZT
SIZZLE
BZZT
GRK ?!
If a little lightning won't work on you...
...then I'll just rain it on you until it does!

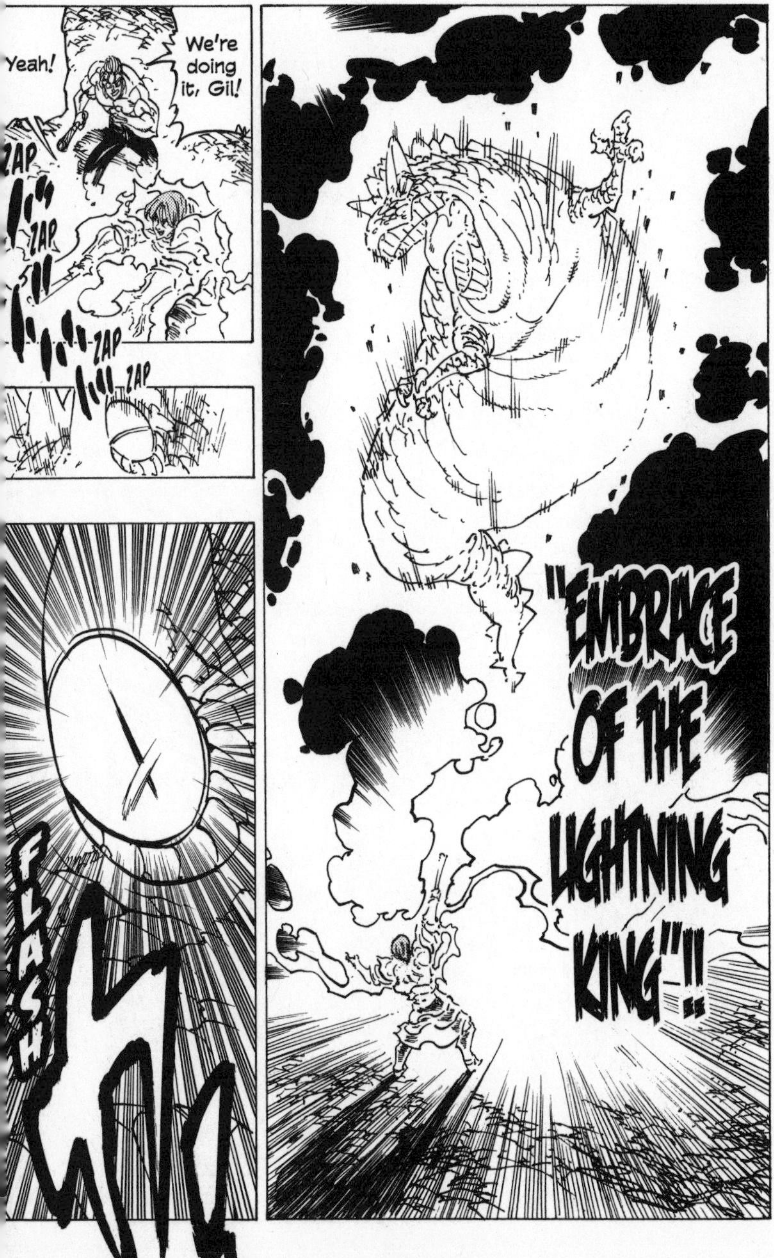
"EMBRACE OF THE LIGHTNING KING"!!
We're doing it, Gil!
Yeah!
ZAP
ZAP
ZAP
ZAP
FLASH

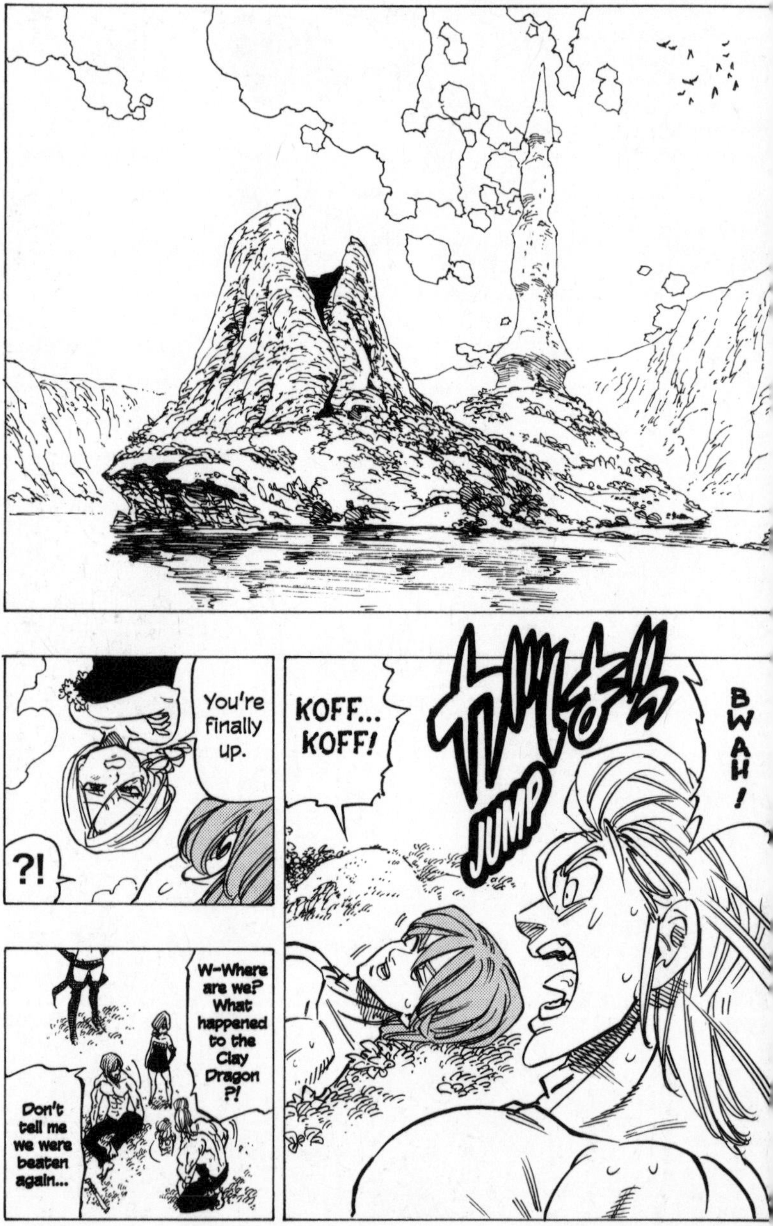
BWAH!
JUMP
KOFF... KOFF!
You're finally up.
?!
W-Where are we? What happened to the Clay Dragon?!
Don't tell me we were beaten again...

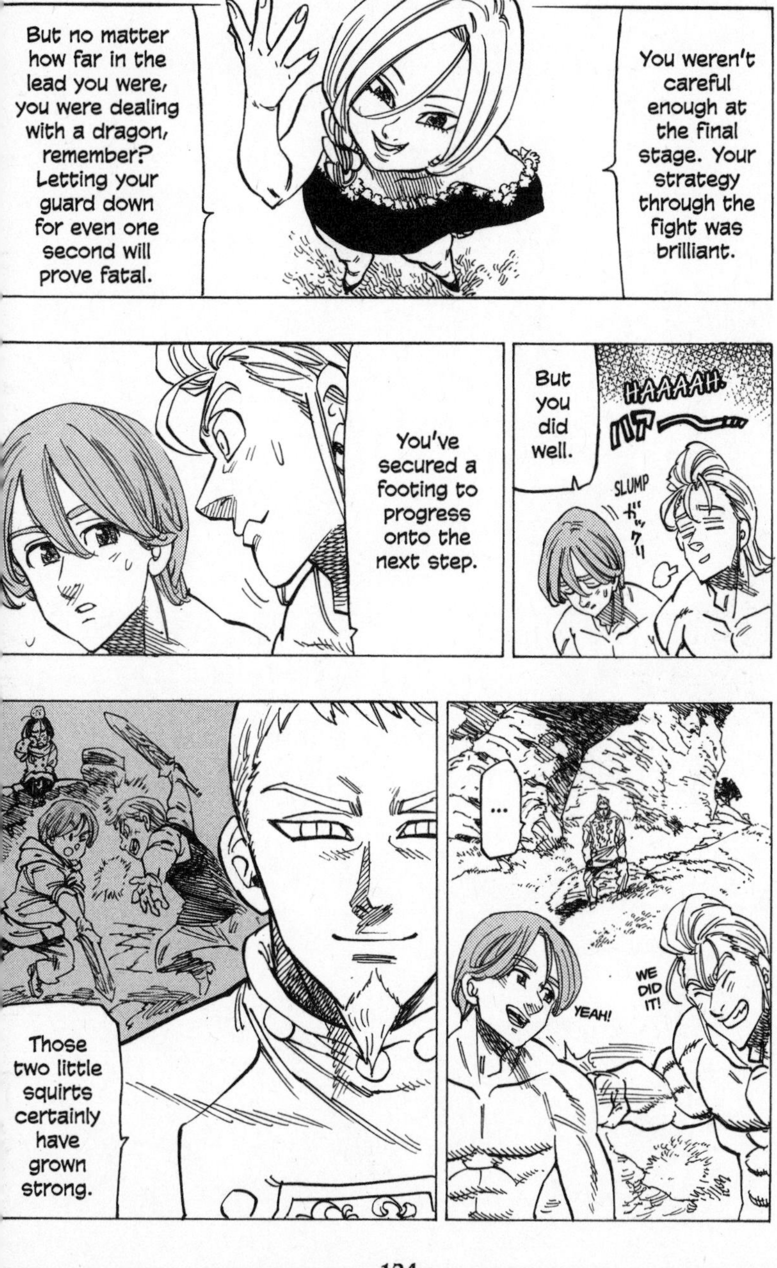
You weren't careful enough at the final stage. Your strategy through the fight was brilliant.
But no matter how far in the lead you were, you were dealing with a dragon, remember? Letting your guard down for even one second will prove fatal.
HAAAAH
But you did well.
SLUMP
You've secured a footing to progress onto the next step.
...
WE DID IT!
YEAH!
Those two little squirts certainly have grown strong.

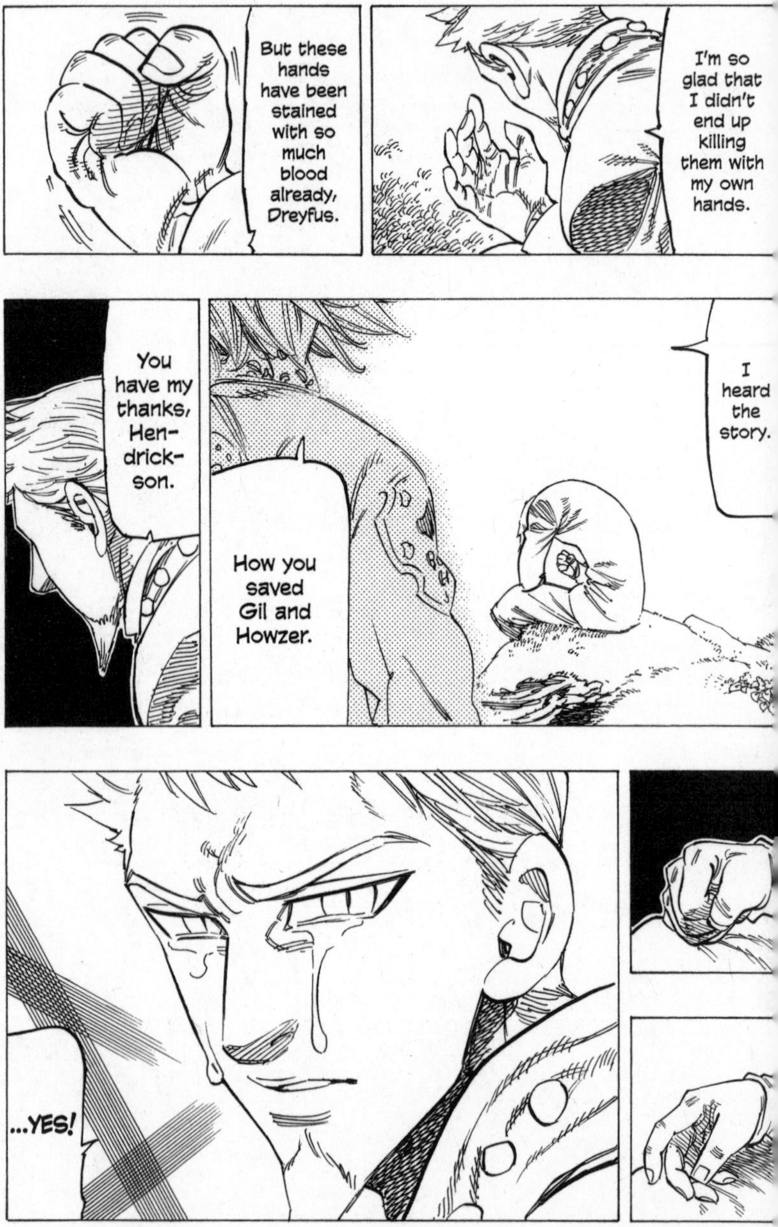
I'm so glad that I didn't end up killing them with my own hands.
But these hands have been stained with so much blood already, Dreyfus.
I heard the story.
How you saved Gil and Howzer.
You have my thanks, Hen-drick-son.
...YES!

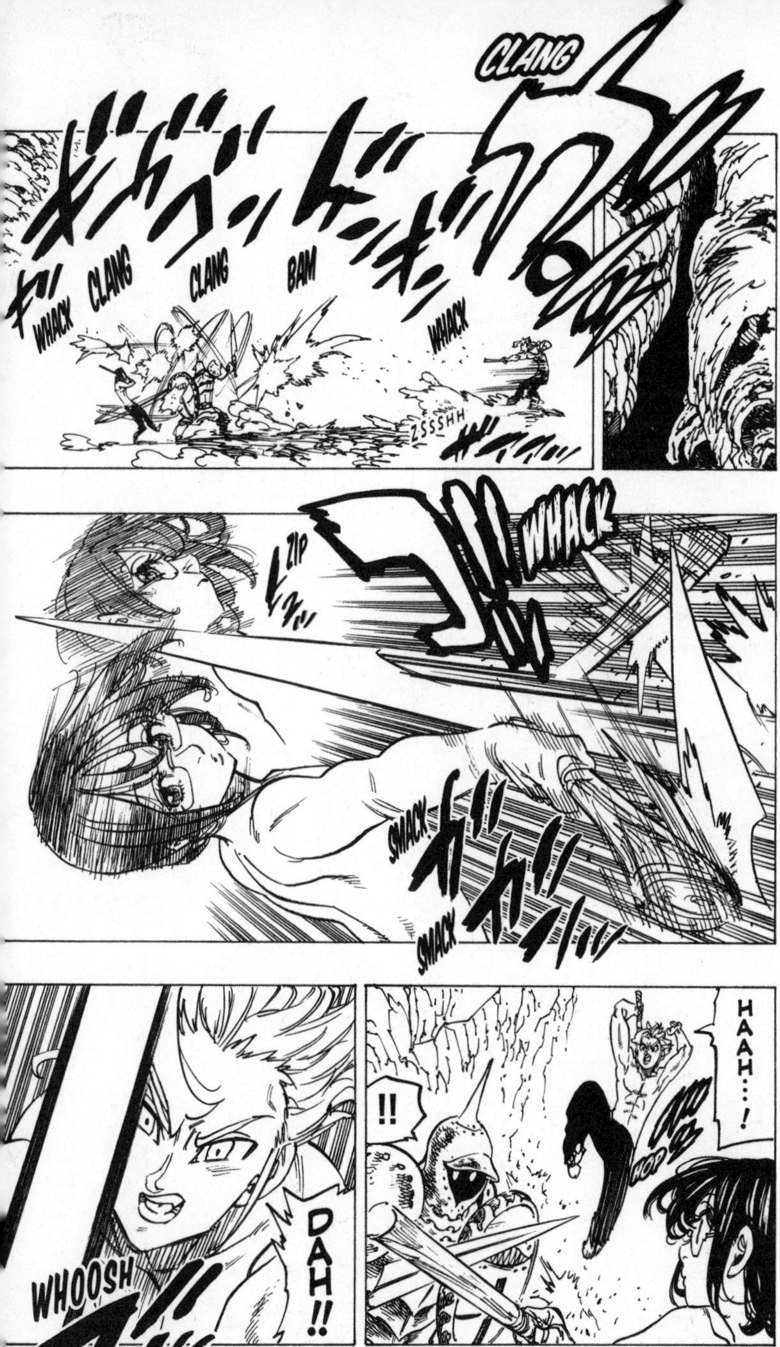
CLANG
WHACK
ZSSSHH
BAM
CLANG
CLANG
WHACK
WHACK
ZIP
SMACK
SMACK
HAAAH...!
HOP
!!
DAH!!
WHOOSH

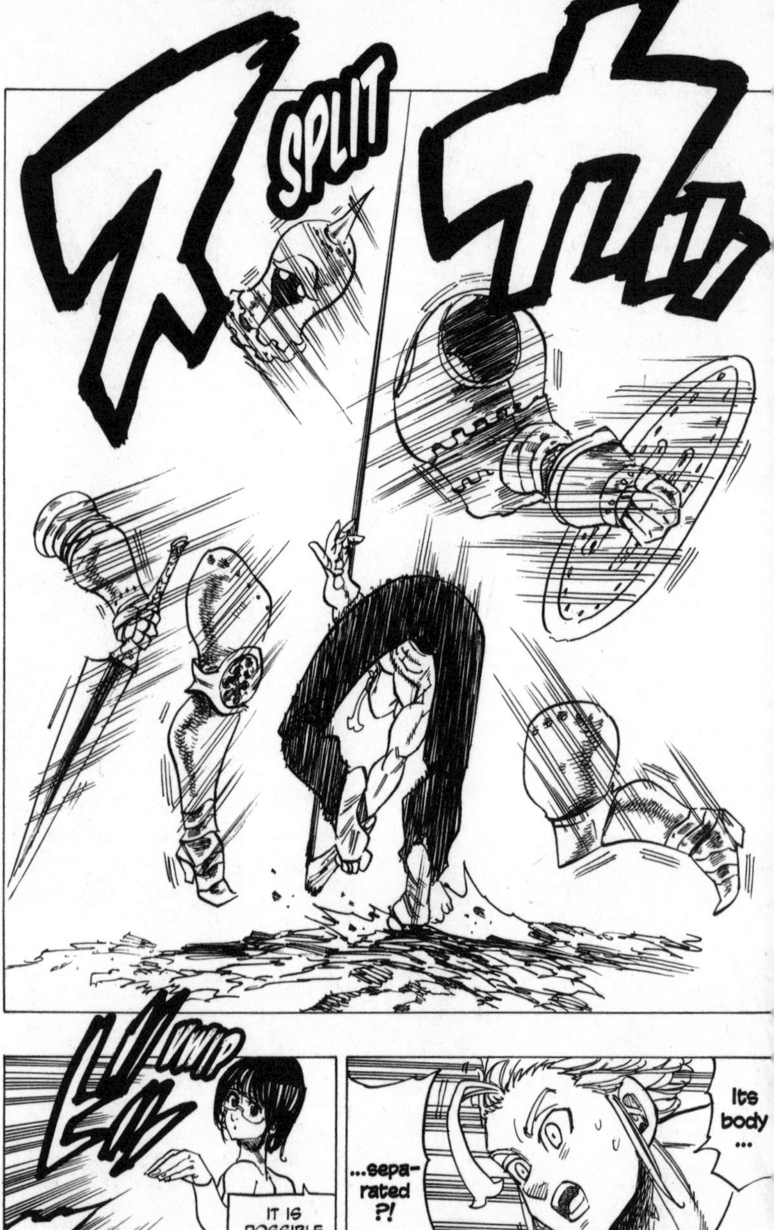
SPLIT
Its body ...
...separated ?!
VWIP
IT IS POSSIBLE IT IS A VARIETY OF GOLEM.

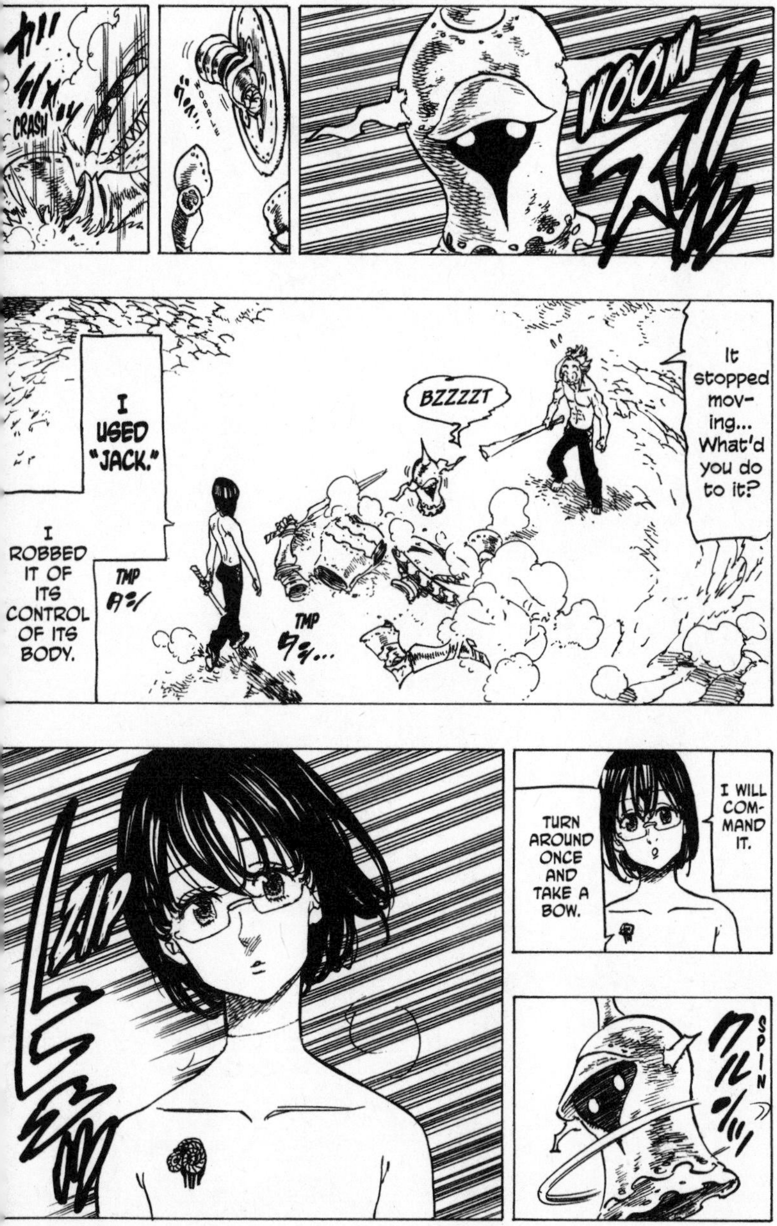
VOOM
WOBBLE
CRASH
It stopped moving... What'd you do to it?
BZZZZT
I USED "JACK."
TMP
I ROBBED IT OF ITS CONTROL OF ITS BODY.
TMP
I WILL COMMAND IT.
TURN AROUND ONCE AND TAKE A BOW.
SPIN
ZIP

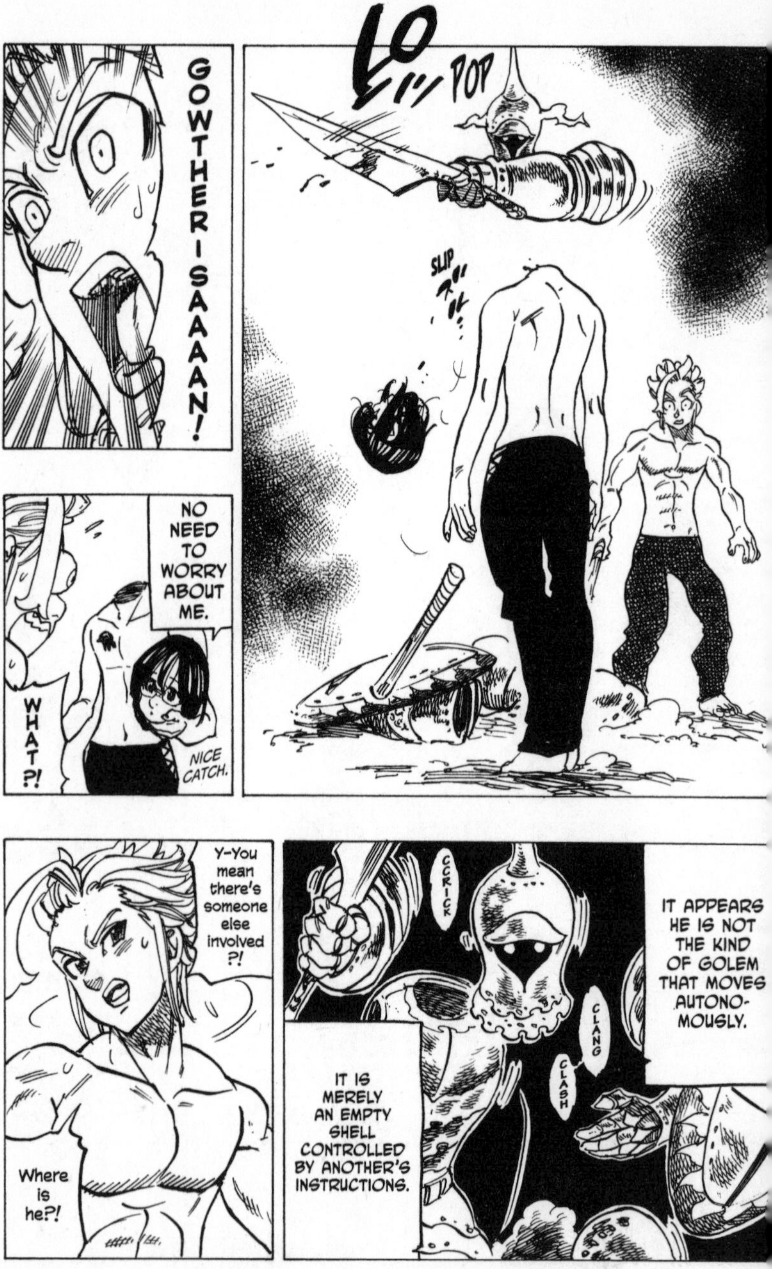
LO
POP
SLIP
GOWTHER-ISAAAAAN!
NO NEED TO WORRY ABOUT ME.
WHAT?!
NICE CATCH.
IT APPEARS HE IS NOT THE KIND OF GOLEM THAT MOVES AUTONOMOUSLY.
CCRICK
CLANG
CLASH
IT IS MERELY AN EMPTY SHELL CONTROLLED BY ANOTHER'S INSTRUCTIONS.
Y-You mean there's someone else involved?!
Where is he?!

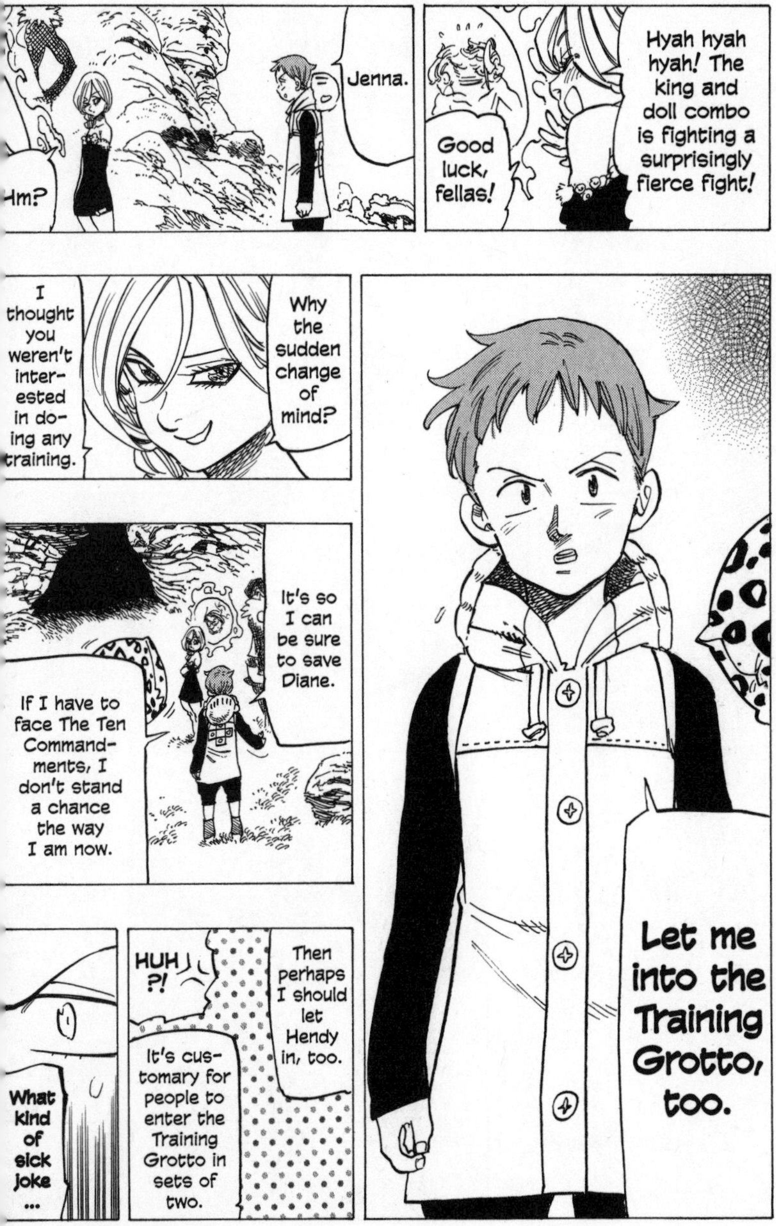
Hyah hyah hyah! The king and doll combo is fighting a surprisingly fierce fight!
Good luck, fellas!
Jenna.
Hm?
Let me into the Training Grotto, too.
Why the sudden change of mind?
I thought you weren't interested in doing any training.
It's so I can be sure to save Diane.
If I have to face The Ten Commandments, I don't stand a chance the way I am now.
Then perhaps I should let Hendy in, too.
HUH?!
It's customary for people to enter the Training Grotto in sets of two.
What kind of sick joke ...

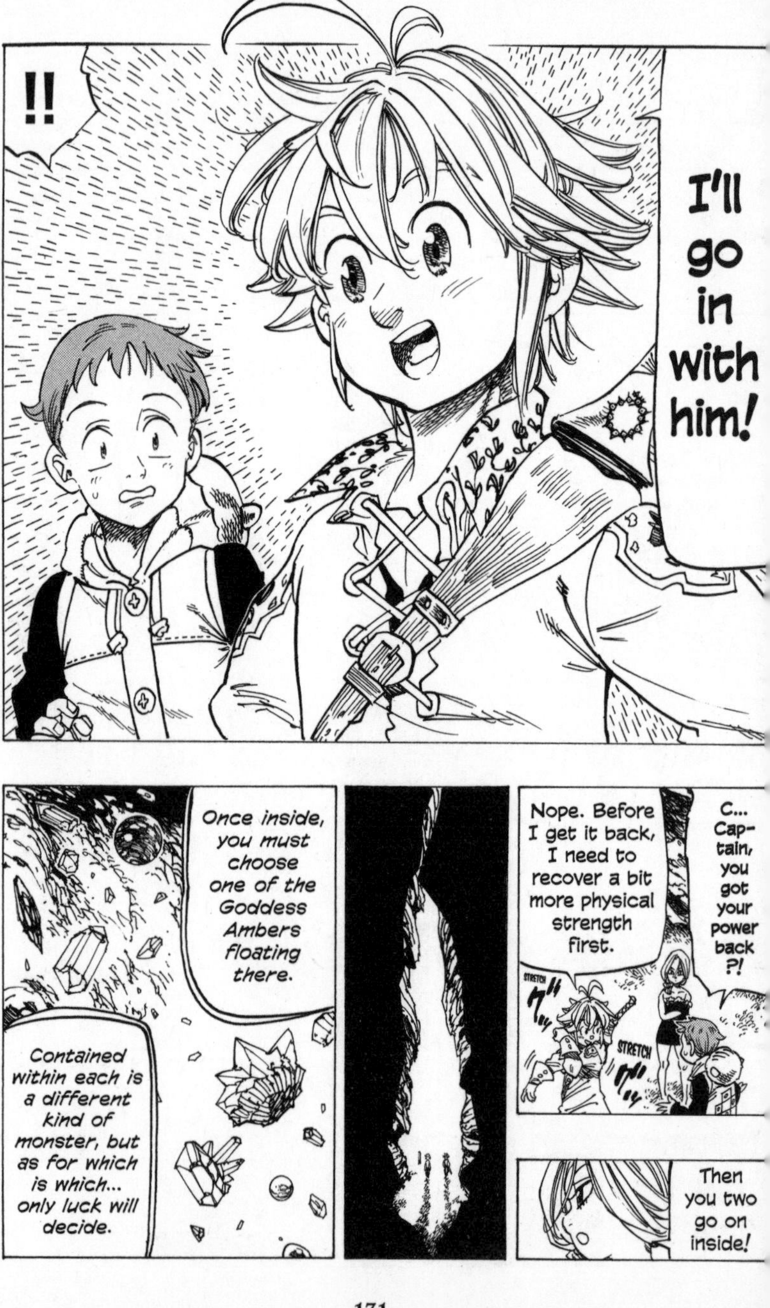

I'll go in with him!
!!
C... Captain, you got your power back?!
Nope. Before I get it back, I need to recover a bit more physical strength first.
STRETCH
STRETCH
Then you two go on inside!
Once inside, you must choose one of the Goddess Ambers floating there.
Contained within each is a different kind of monster, but as for which is which... only luck will decide.

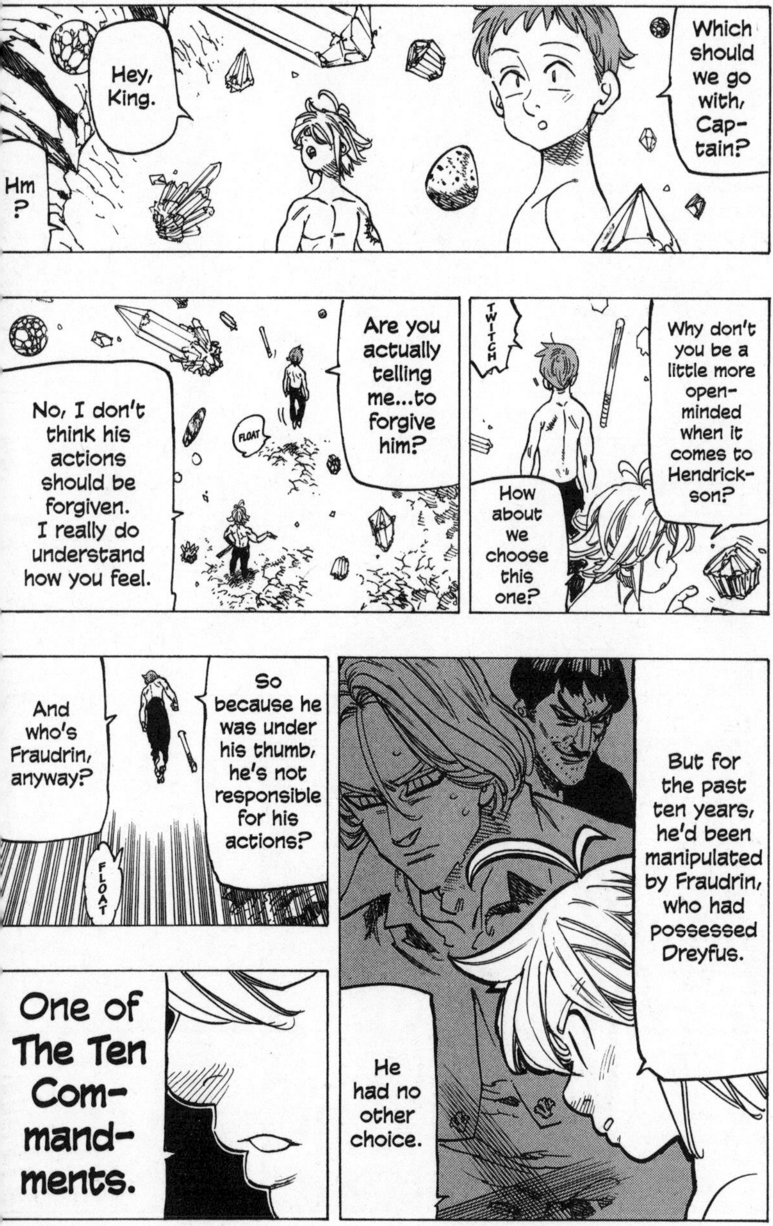
Which should we go with, Captain?
Hey, King.
Hm?
Why don't you be a little more open-minded when it comes to Hendrickson?
TWITCH
How about we choose this one?
Are you actually telling me...to forgive him?
FLOAT
No, I don't think his actions should be forgiven. I really do understand how you feel.
But for the past ten years, he'd been manipulated by Fraudrin, who had possessed Dreyfus.
He had no other choice.
So because he was under his thumb, he's not responsible for his actions?
And who's Fraudrin, anyway?
FLOAT
One of The Ten Commandments.

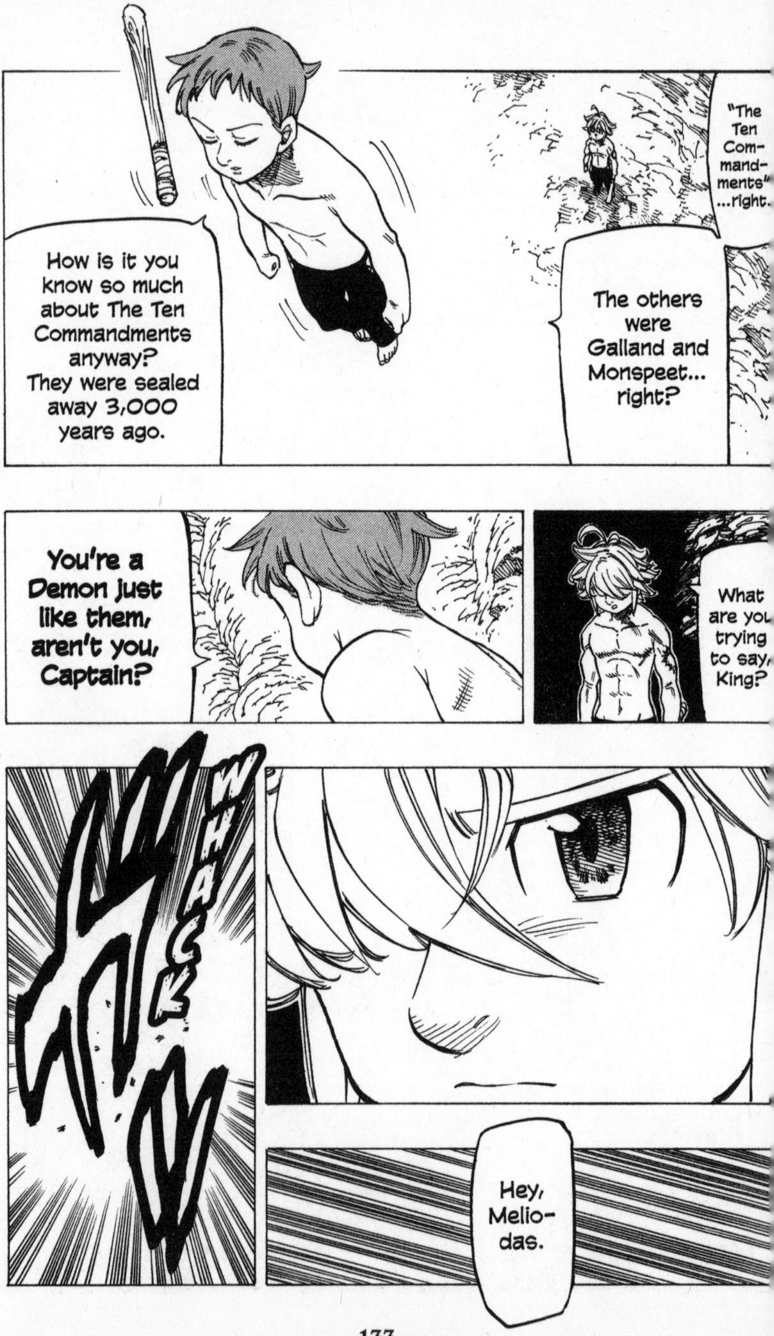
"The Ten Commandments" ...right.
The others were Galland and Monspeet... right?
How is it you know so much about The Ten Commandments anyway? They were sealed away 3,000 years ago.
What are you trying to say, King?
You're a Demon just like them, aren't you, Captain?
Hey, Melio-das.
WHACK

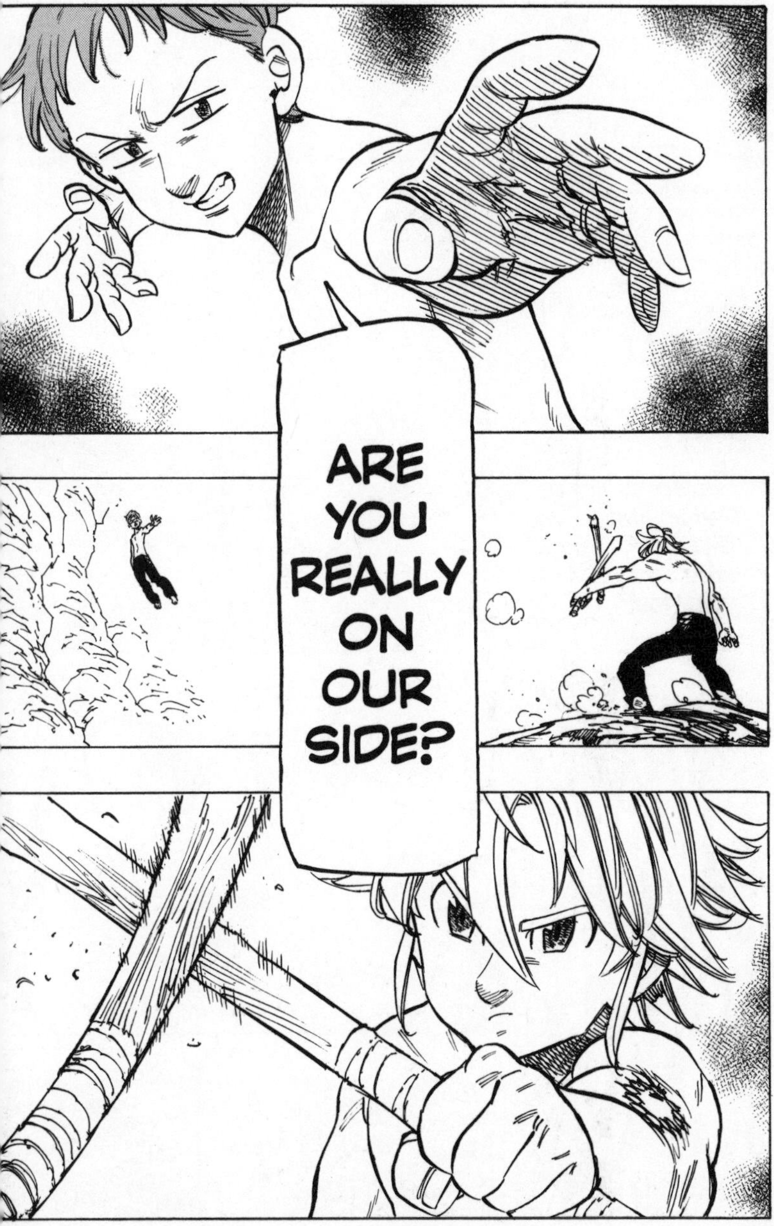
ARE YOU REALLY ON OUR SIDE?

Chapter 134 - To You, Who is No Longer Captain

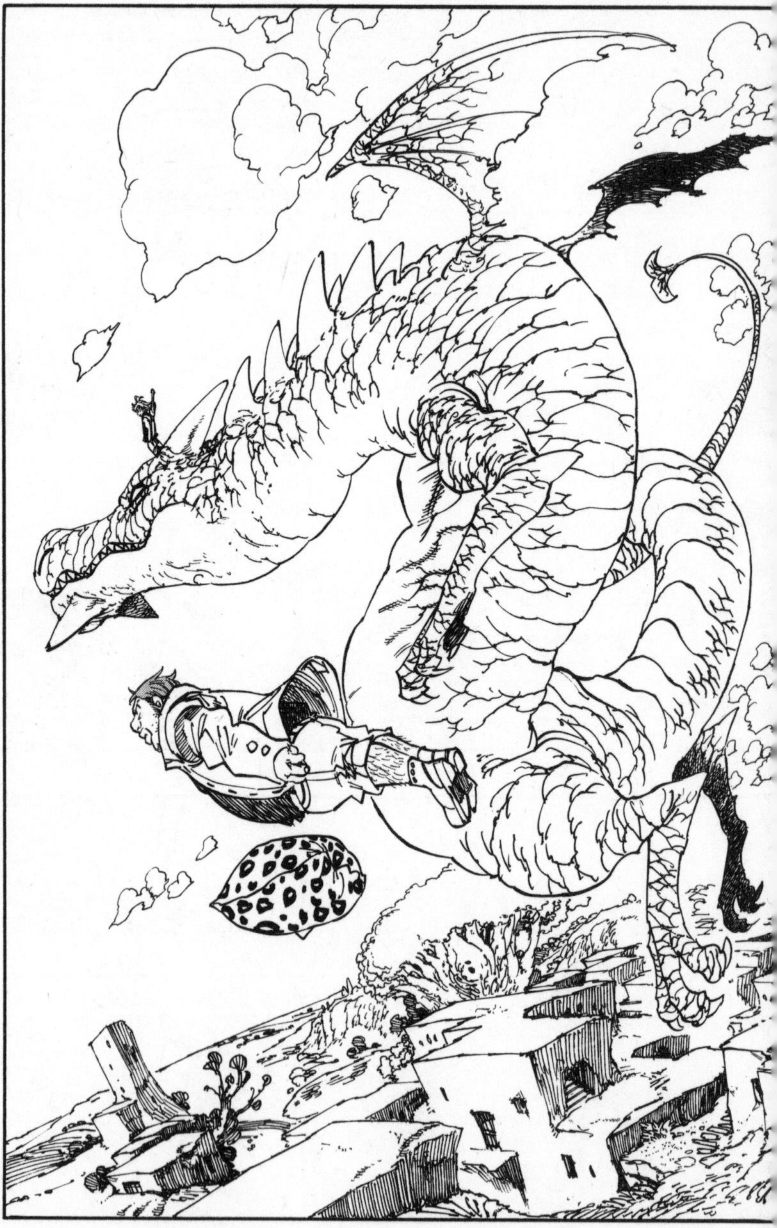

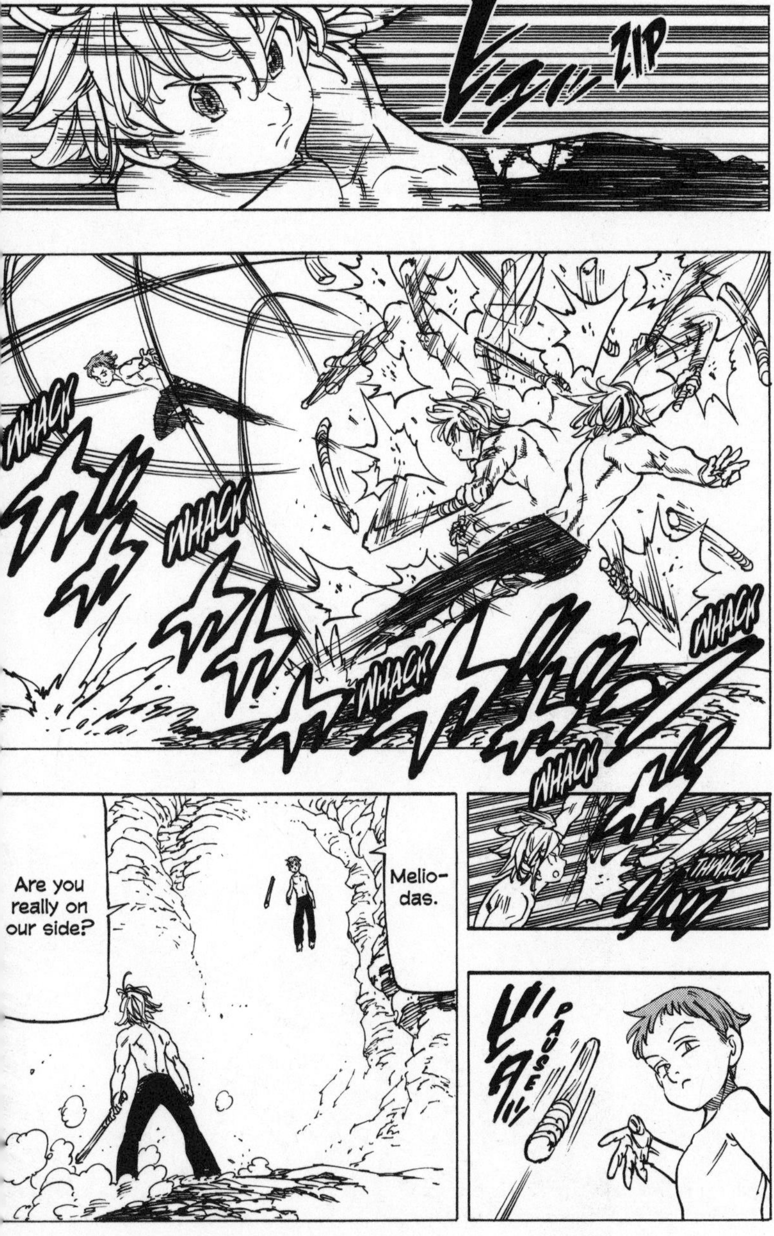
ZIP
WHACK
WHACK
WHACK
WHACK
WHACK
THWACK
PAUSE
Melio-das.
Are you really on our side?

W...What the?! They're suddenly fighting!
What does it mean, Jenna-sama?! Why would they turn on each other?
How should I know?!
...!!
Depends on what constitutes being on your side.
If you mean to turn on Elizabeth and The Seven Deadly Sins, then I'm your enemy.
Don't change the subject!
WHIP
Tell me what it is you're after!

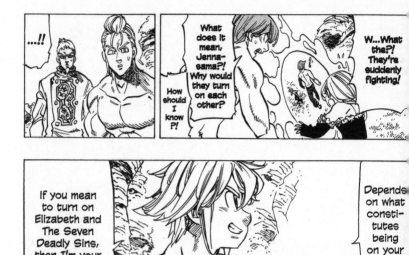

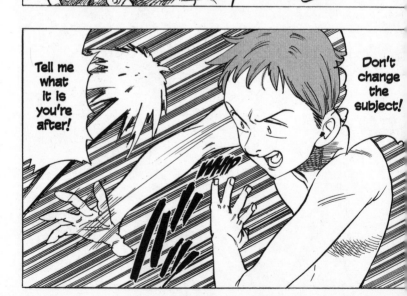

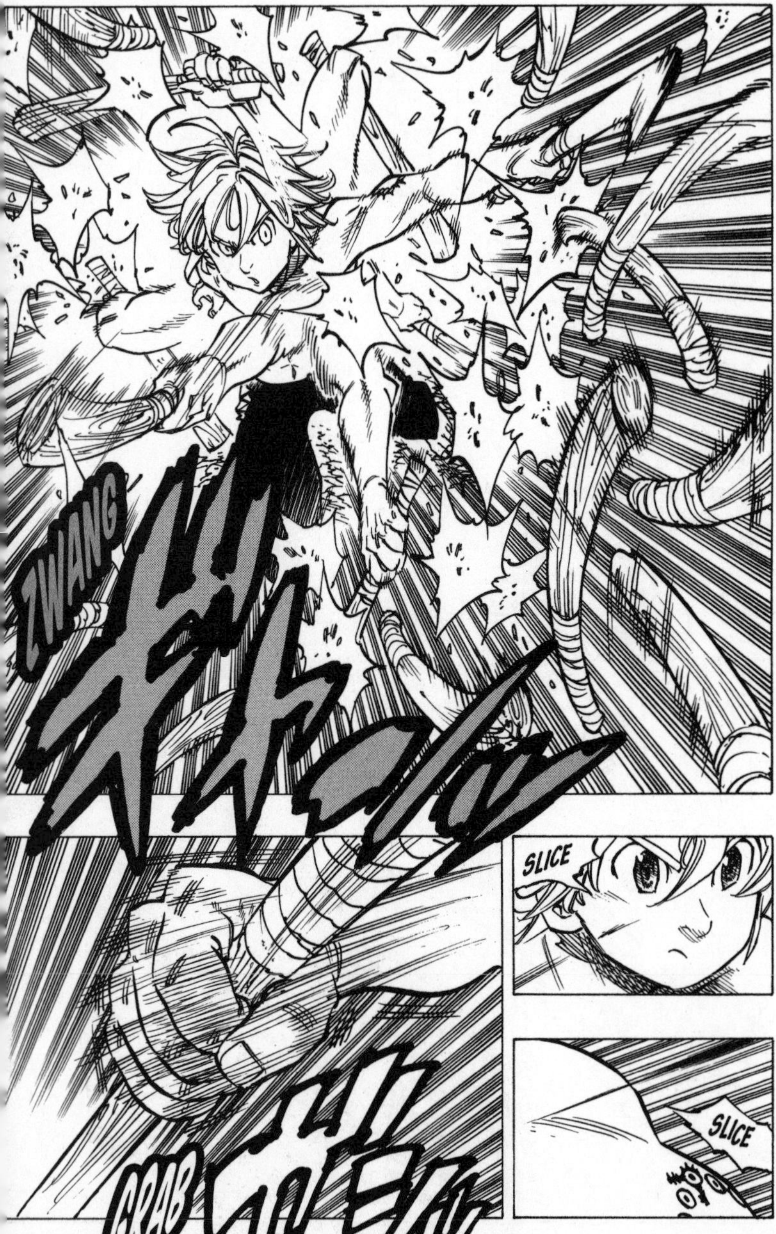
ZWANG
SLICE
GRAB
SLICE

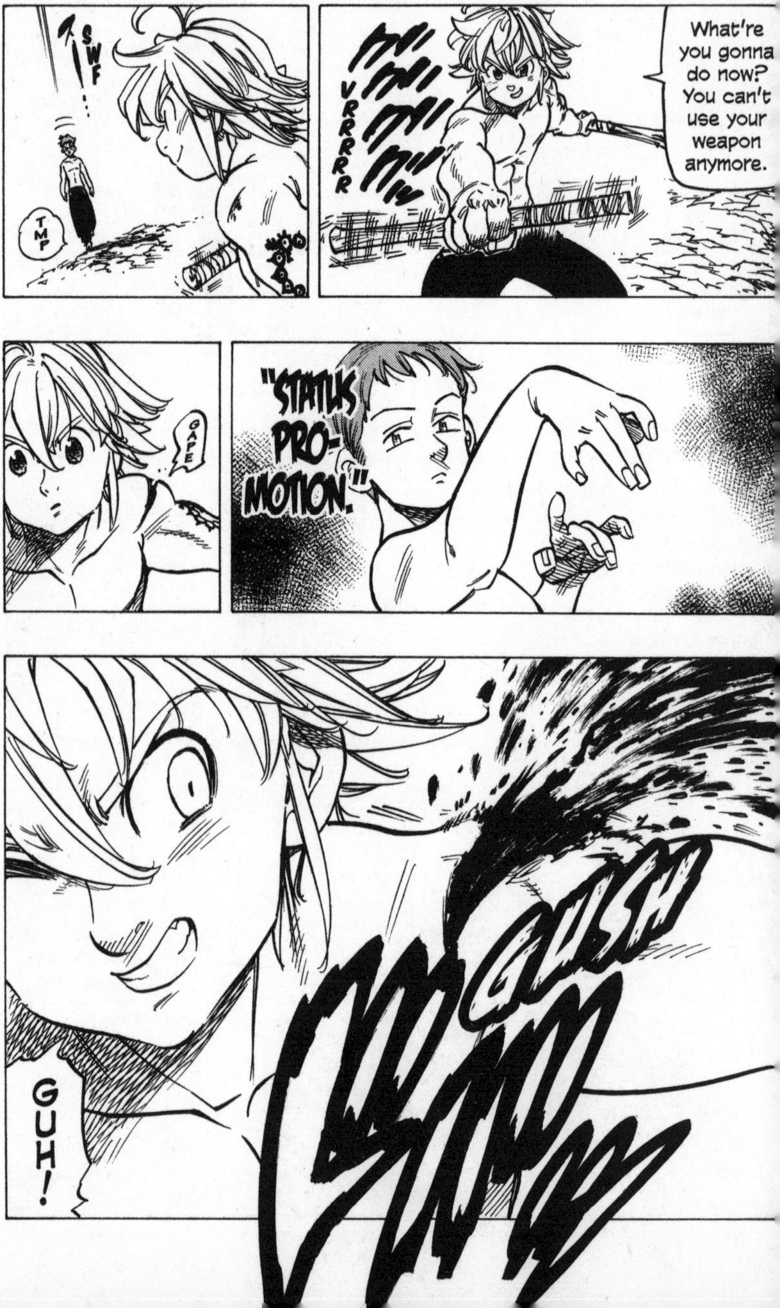
What're you gonna do now? You can't use your weapon anymore.
VRRRRR
SWF
TMP
"STATUS PRO-MOTION."
GAPE
GUSH
GUH!

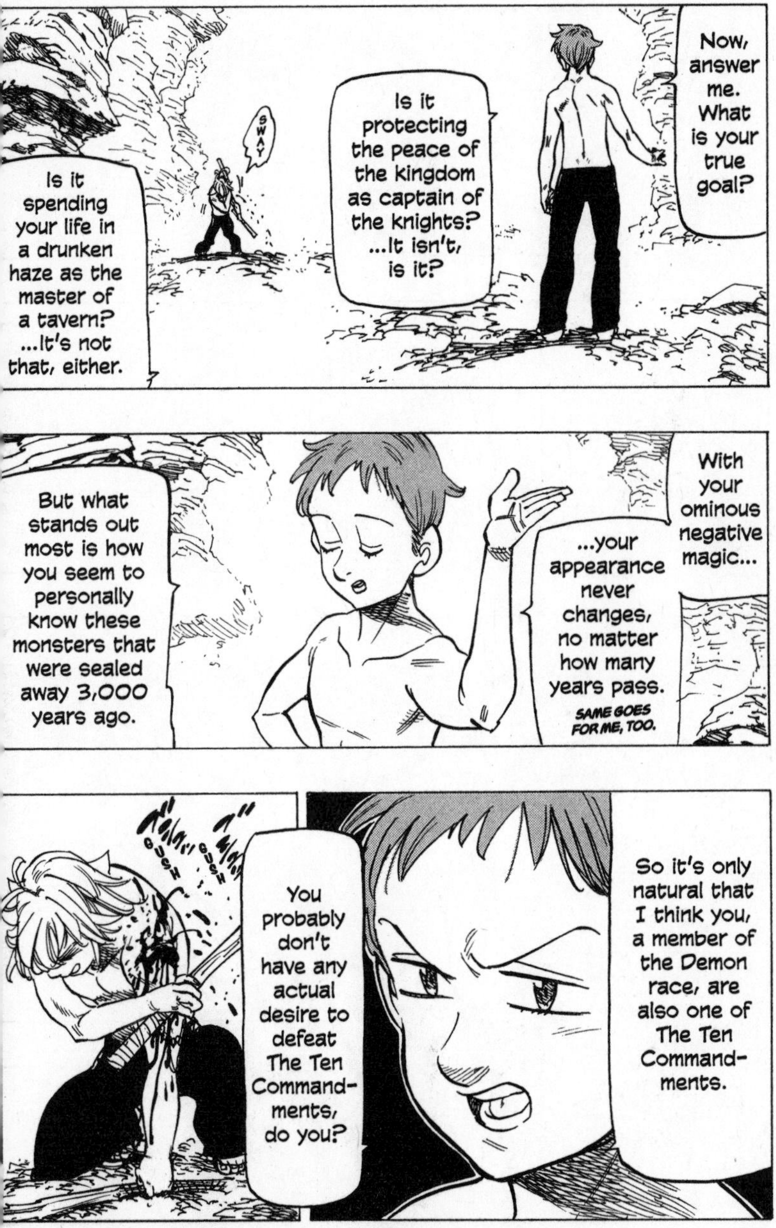
Now, answer me. What is your true goal?
Is it protecting the peace of the kingdom as captain of the knights? ...It isn't, is it?
SWAY
Is it spending your life in a drunken haze as the master of a tavern? ...It's not that, either.
With your ominous negative magic...
...your appearance never changes, no matter how many years pass.
SAME GOES FOR ME, TOO.
But what stands out most is how you seem to personally know these monsters that were sealed away 3,000 years ago.
So it's only natural that I think you, a member of the Demon race, are also one of The Ten Commandments.
You probably don't have any actual desire to defeat The Ten Commandments, do you?
GUSH
GUSH

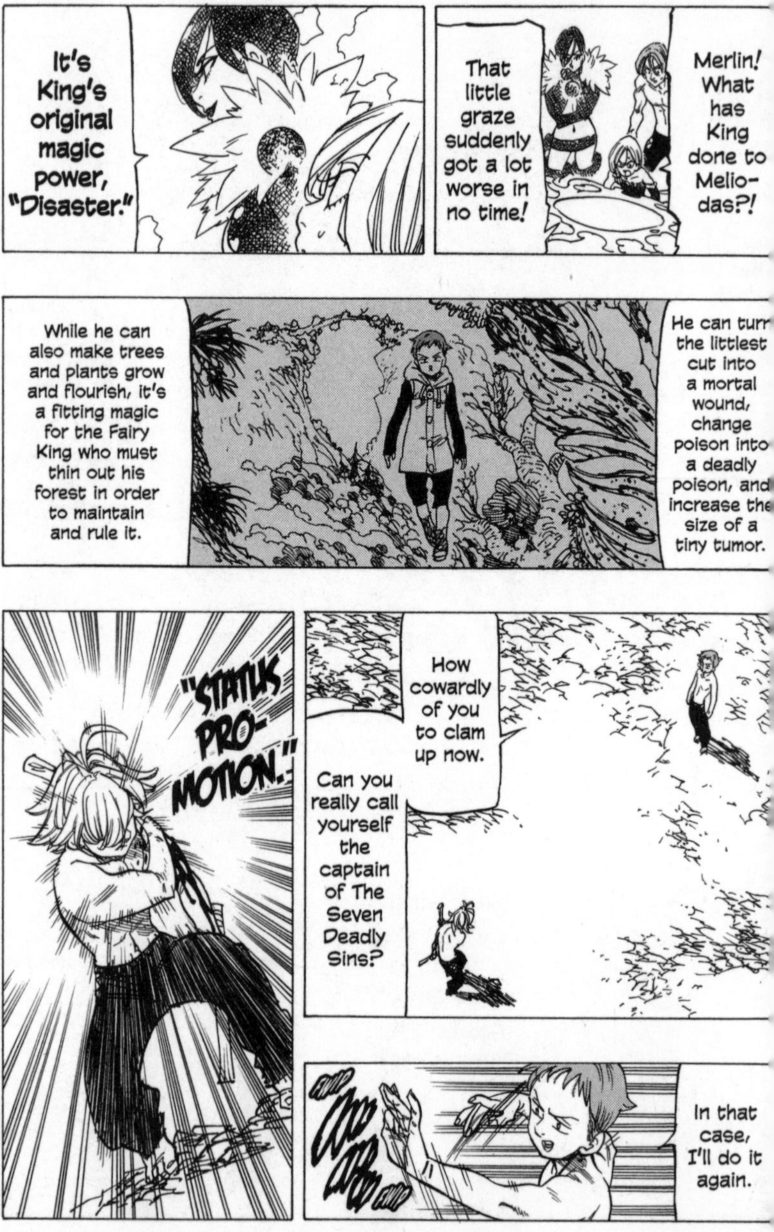
Merlin! What has King done to Melio-das?!
That little graze suddenly got a lot worse in no time!
It's King's original magic power, "Disaster."
He can turn the littlest cut into a mortal wound, change poison into a deadly poison, and increase the size of a tiny tumor.
While he can also make trees and plants grow and flourish, it's a fitting magic for the Fairy King who must thin out his forest in order to maintain and rule it.
How cowardly of you to clam up now.
Can you really call yourself the captain of The Seven Deadly Sins?
In that case, I'll do it again.
"STATUS PRO-MOTION."

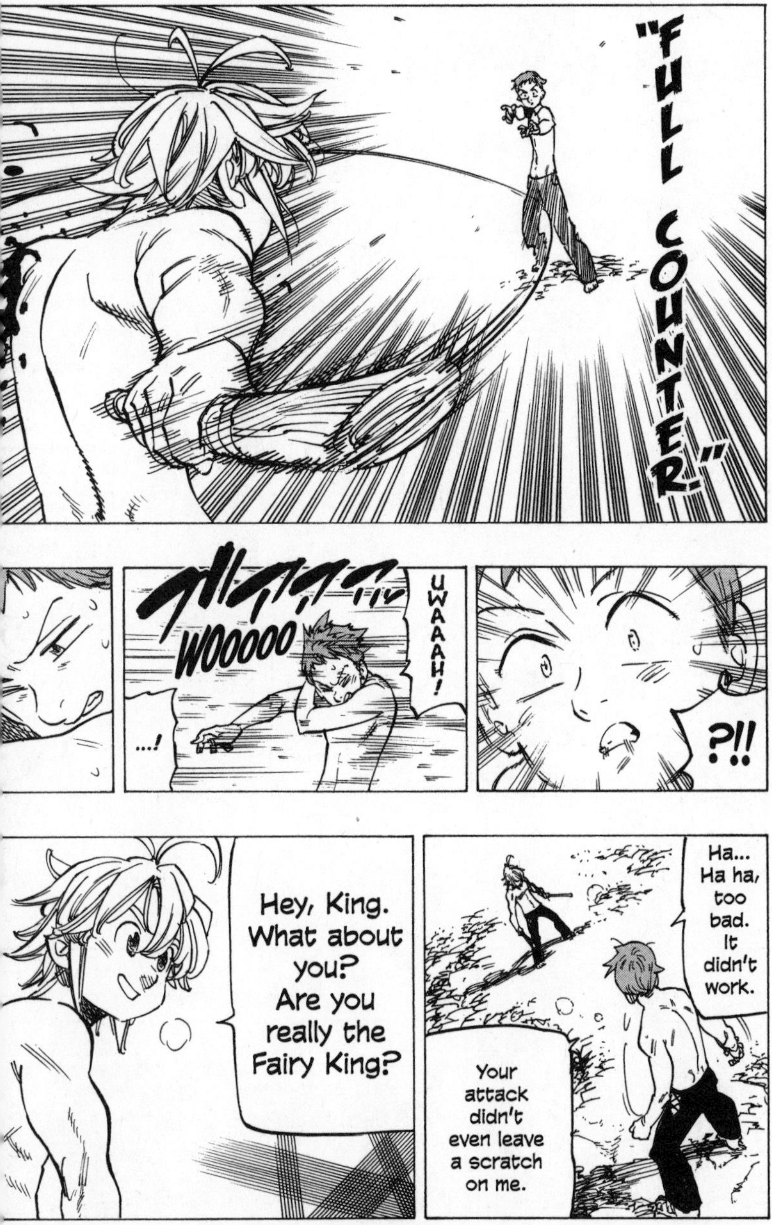
"FULL COUNTER."
?!!
UWAAAAH!
WOOOOO
...!
Ha... Ha ha, too bad. It didn't work.
Your attack didn't even leave a scratch on me.
Hey, King. What about you? Are you really the Fairy King?

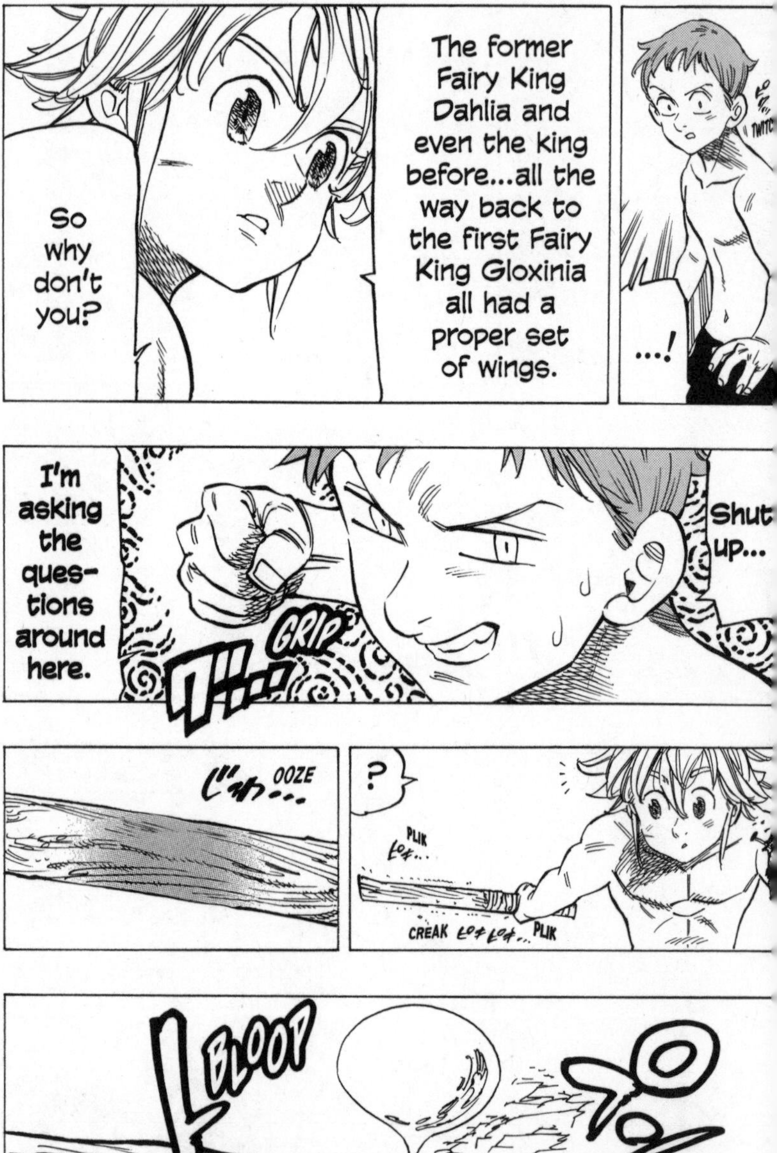
TWITC
...!
The former Fairy King Dahlia and even the king before...all the way back to the first Fairy King Gloxinia all had a proper set of wings.
So why don't you?
Shut up...
I'm asking the ques-tions around here.
GRIP
?
PLIK
CREAK
PLIK
OOZE
BLOOP

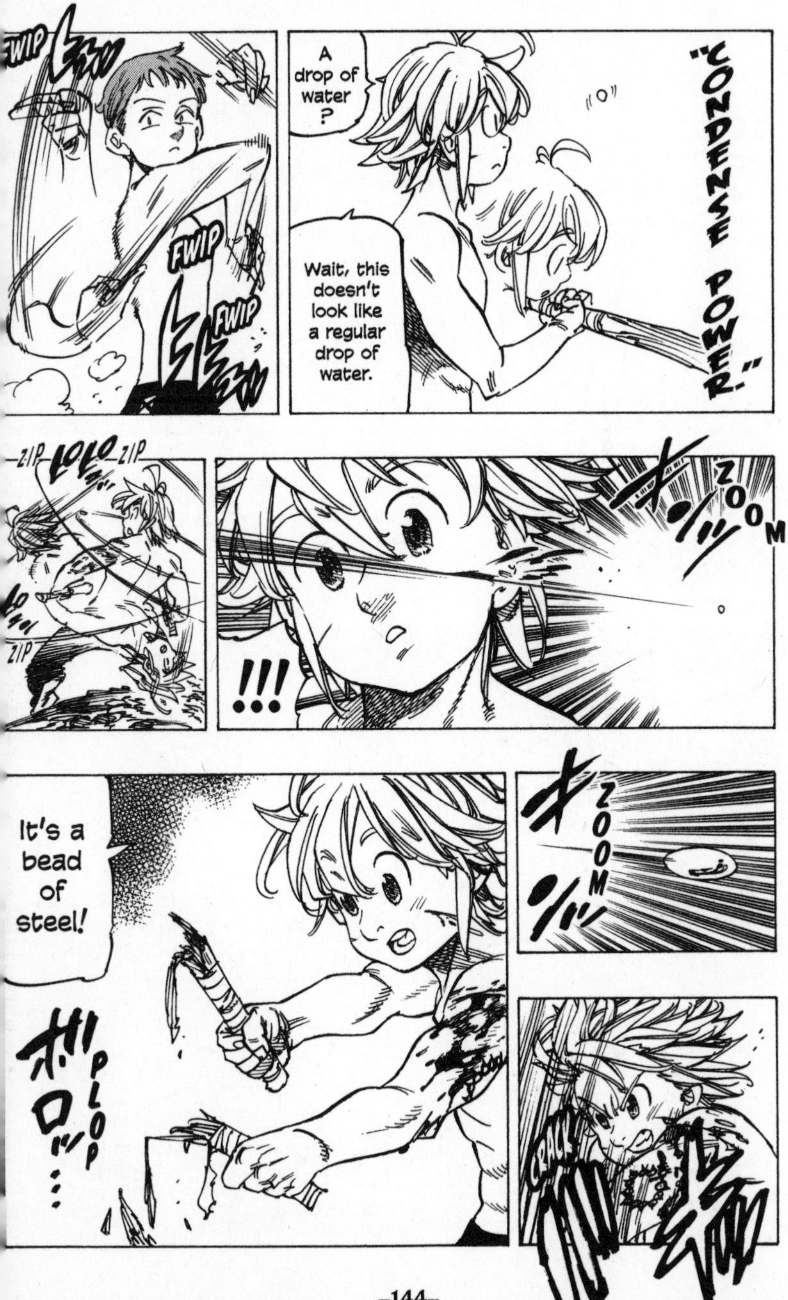
"CONDENSE POWER."
A drop of water?
Wait, this doesn't look like a regular drop of water.
FWIP
FWIP
FWIP
ZOOM
!!!
ZIP
ZIP
ZIP
ZOOM
CRACK
It's a bead of steel!
PLOP...

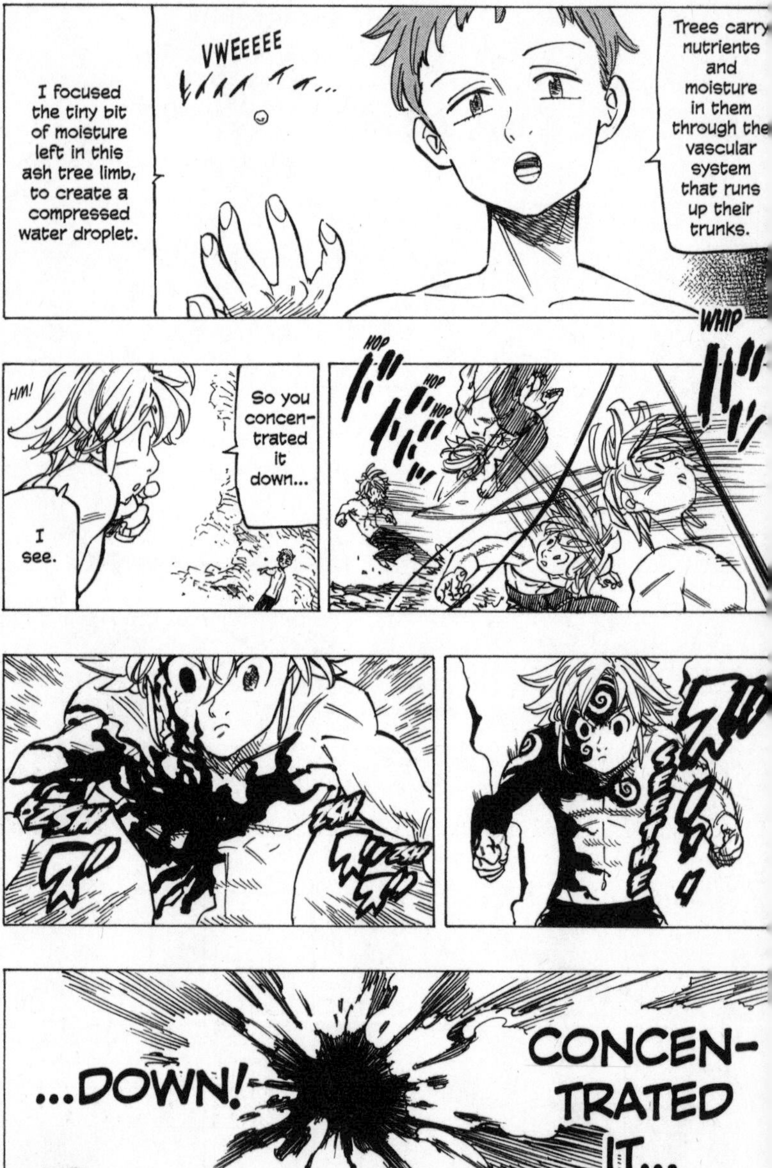
Trees carry nutrients and moisture in them through the vascular system that runs up their trunks.
VWEEEEE
I focused the tiny bit of moisture left in this ash tree limb, to create a compressed water droplet.
WHIP
HOP
HOP
HOP
So you concen-trated it down...
HM!
I see.
SEETHE
ZSH
ZSH
ZSH
CONCEN-TRATED IT...
...DOWN!

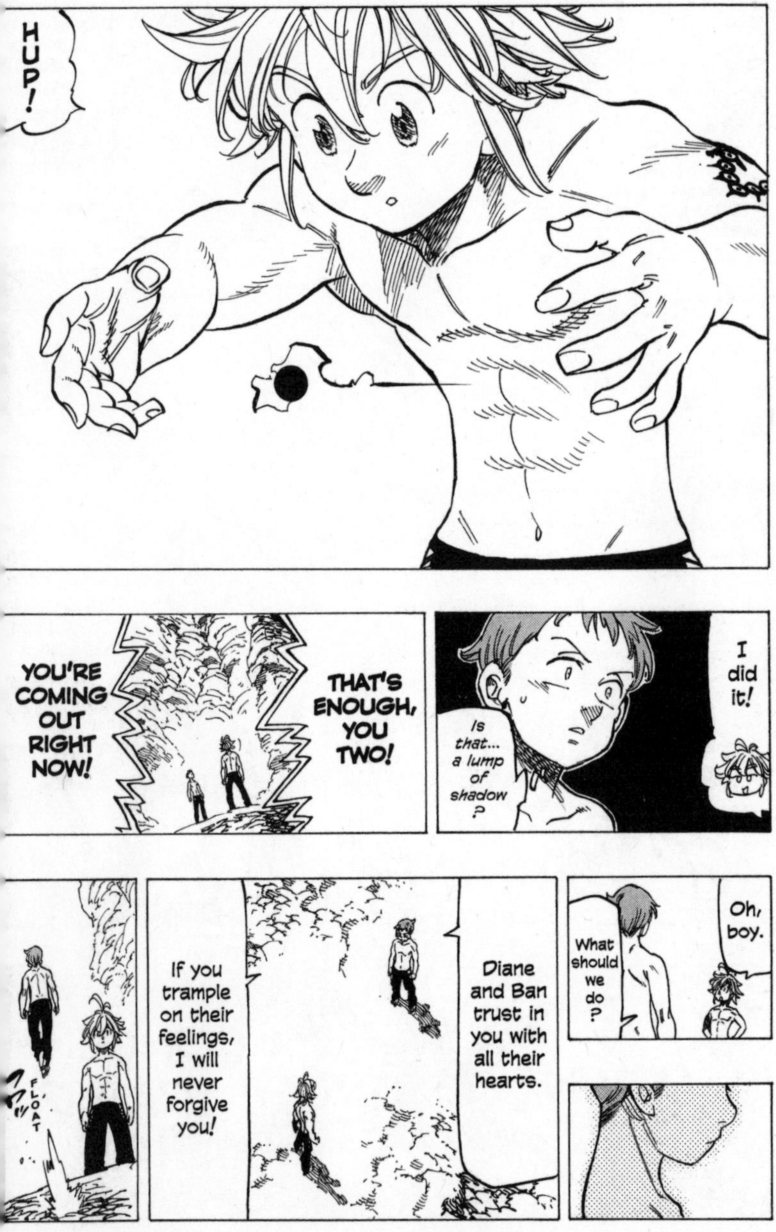
HUP!
I did it!
Is that... a lump of shadow?
THAT'S ENOUGH, YOU TWO!
YOU'RE COMING OUT RIGHT NOW!
Oh, boy.
What should we do?
Diane and Ban trust in you with all their hearts.
If you trample on their feelings, I will never forgive you!
FLOAT

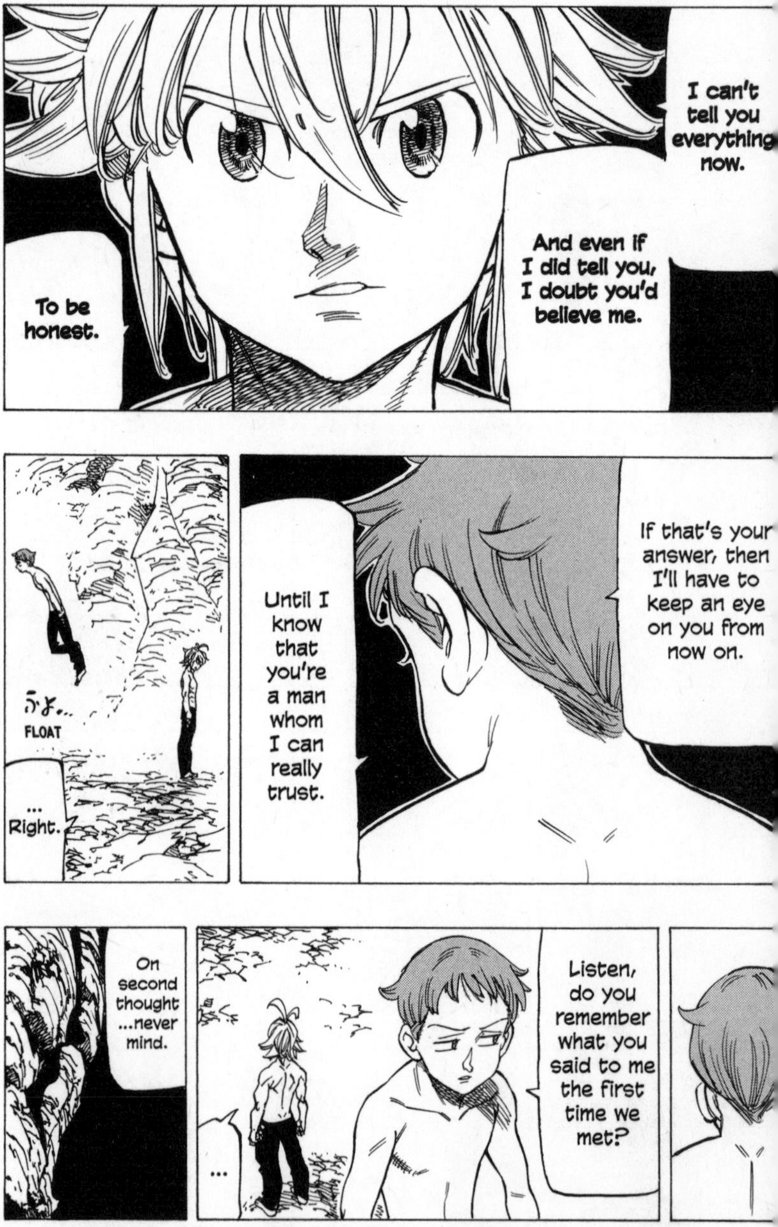
I can't tell you everything now.
And even if I did tell you, I doubt you'd believe me.
To be honest.
If that's your answer, then I'll have to keep an eye on you from now on.
Until I know that you're a man whom I can really trust.
ふよ…
FLOAT
... Right.
Listen, do you remember what you said to me the first time we met?
...
On second thought ...never mind.

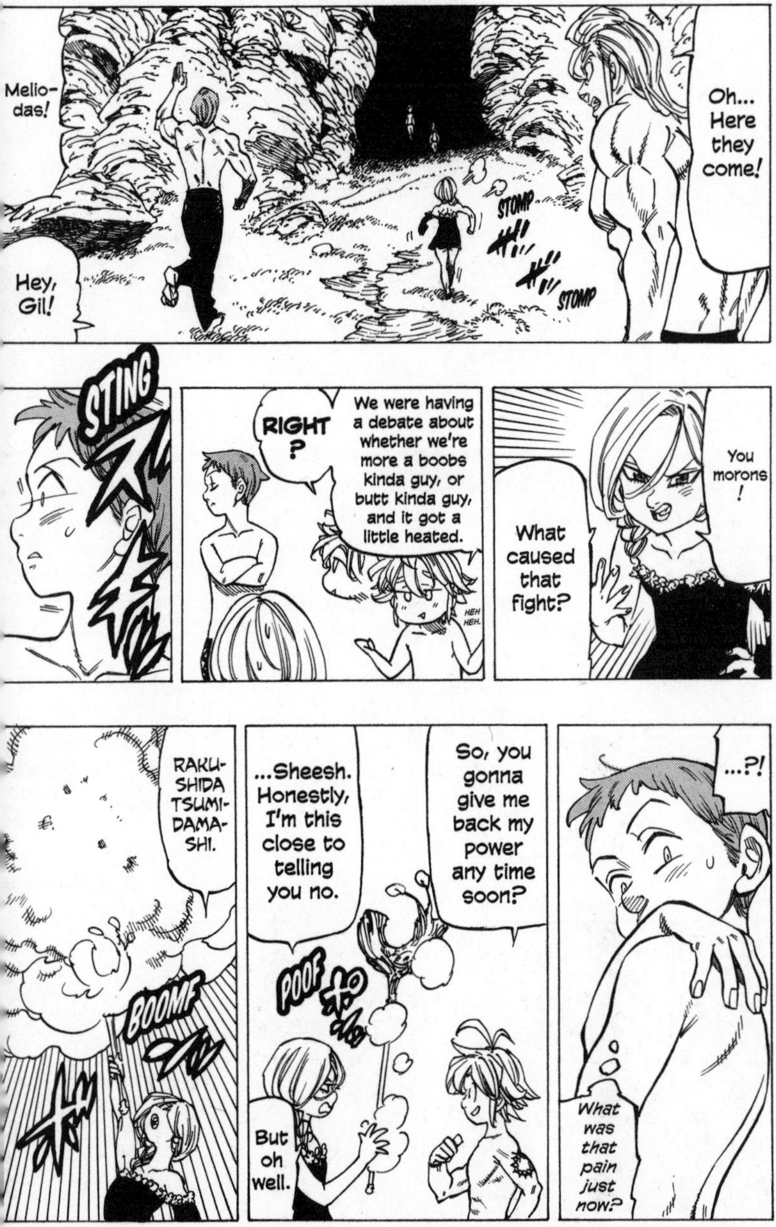
Oh... Here they come!
STOMP
STOMP
Melio-das!
Hey, Gil!
You morons!
What caused that fight?
We were having a debate about whether we're more a boobs kinda guy, or butt kinda guy, and it got a little heated.
RIGHT?
HEH HEH.
STING
...?!
What was that pain just now?
So, you gonna give me back my power any time soon?
...Sheesh. Honestly, I'm this close to telling you no.
POOF
But oh well.
RAKU-SHIDA TSUMI-DAMA-SHI.
BOOMF

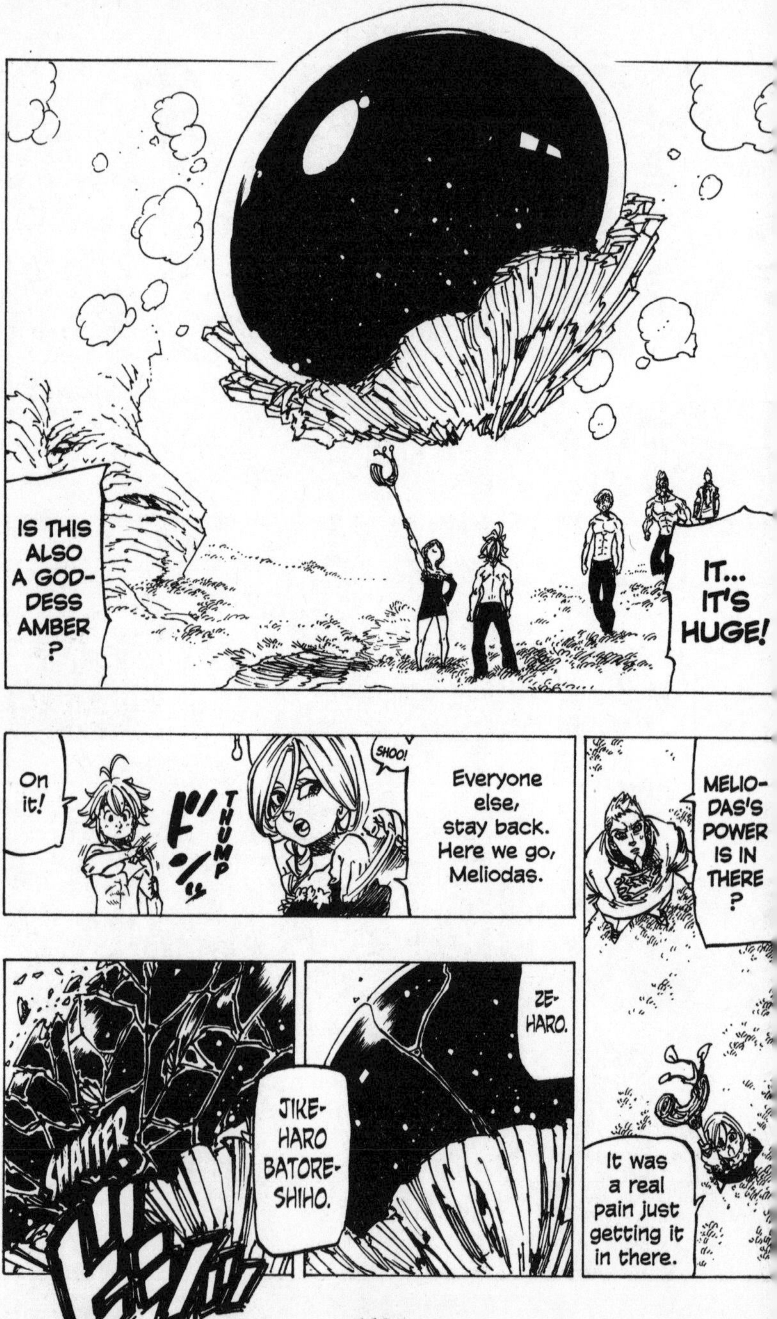
IT... IT'S HUGE!
IS THIS ALSO A GODDESS AMBER?
MELIODAS'S POWER IS IN THERE?
It was a real pain just getting it in there.
Everyone else, stay back. Here we go, Meliodas.
SHOO!
THUMP
On it!
ZEHARO.
JIKEHARO BATORESHIHO.
SHATTER

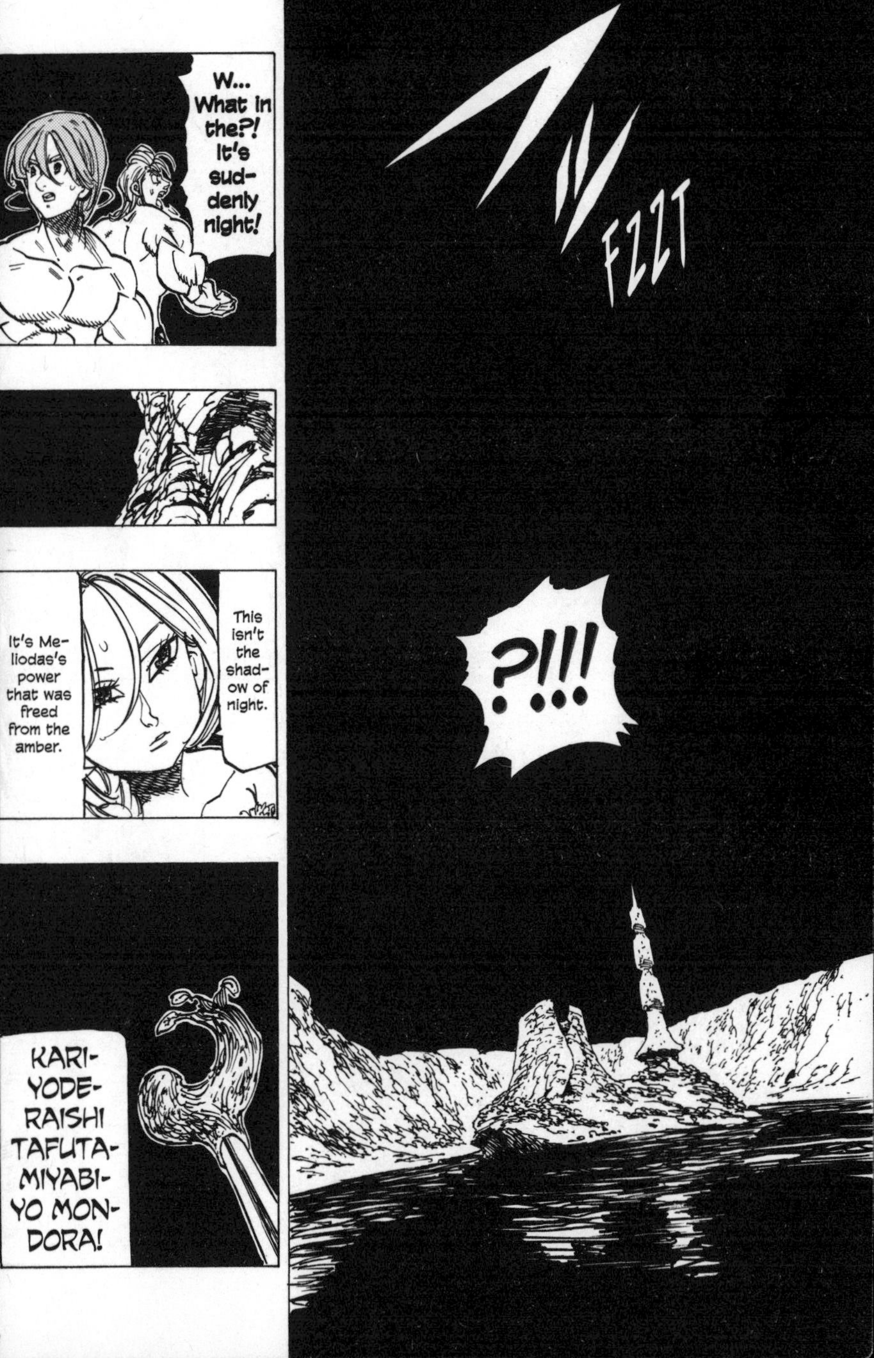
FZZT
?!!!
W... What in the?! It's sud-denly night!
This isn't the shad-ow of night.
It's Me-liodas's power that was freed from the amber.
KARI-YODE-RAISHI TAFUTA-MIYABI-YO MON-DORA!

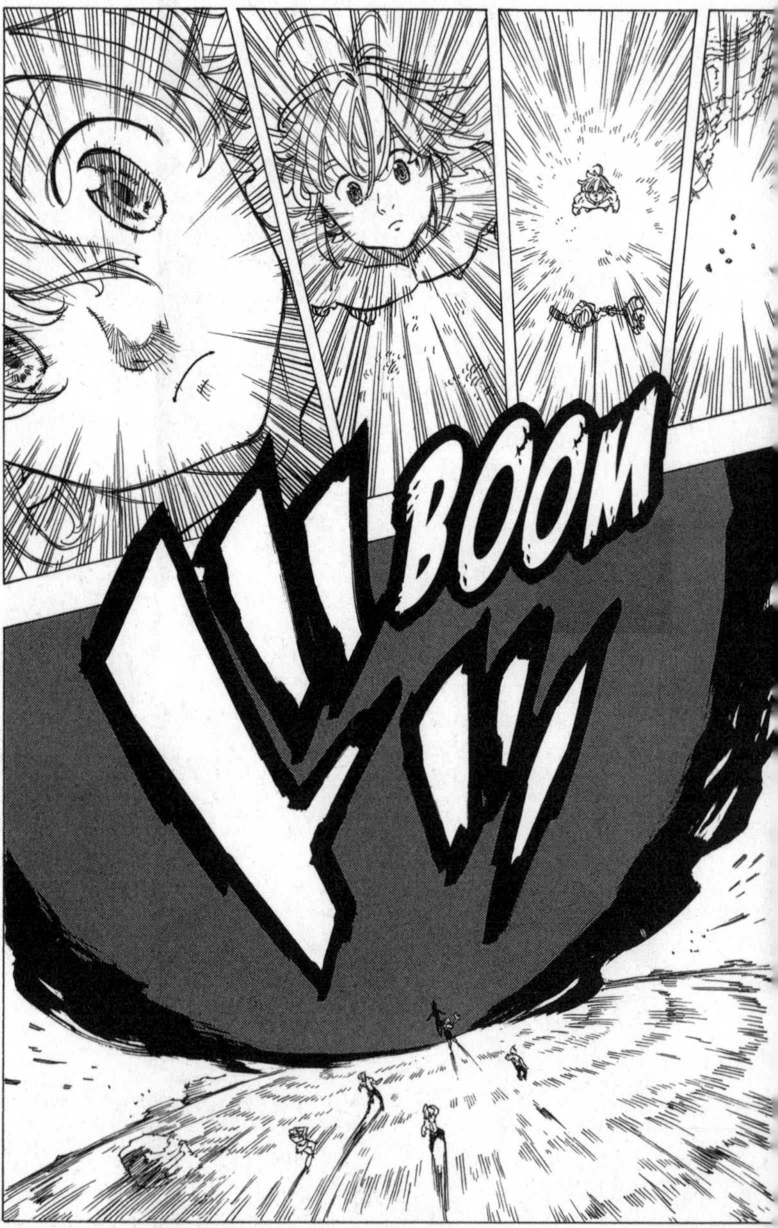
BOOM

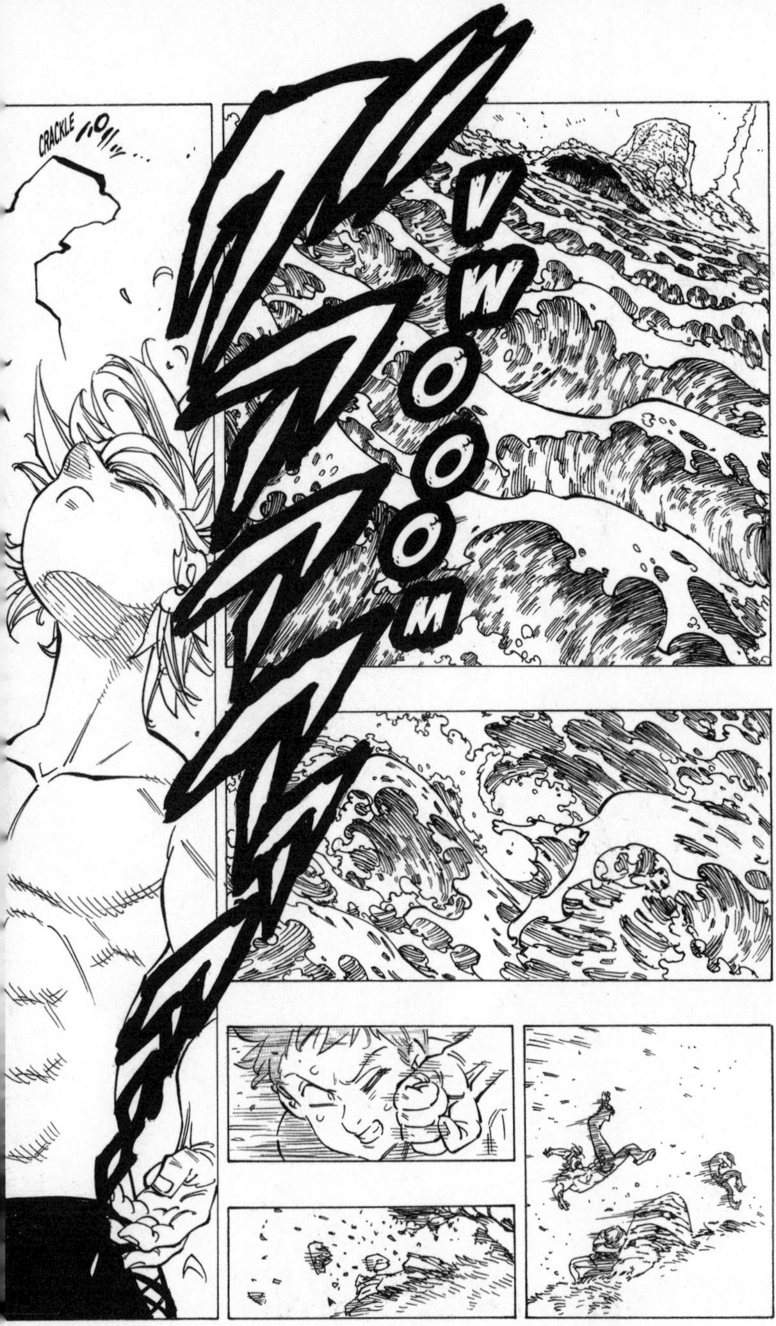
CRACKLE
VWOOOOM

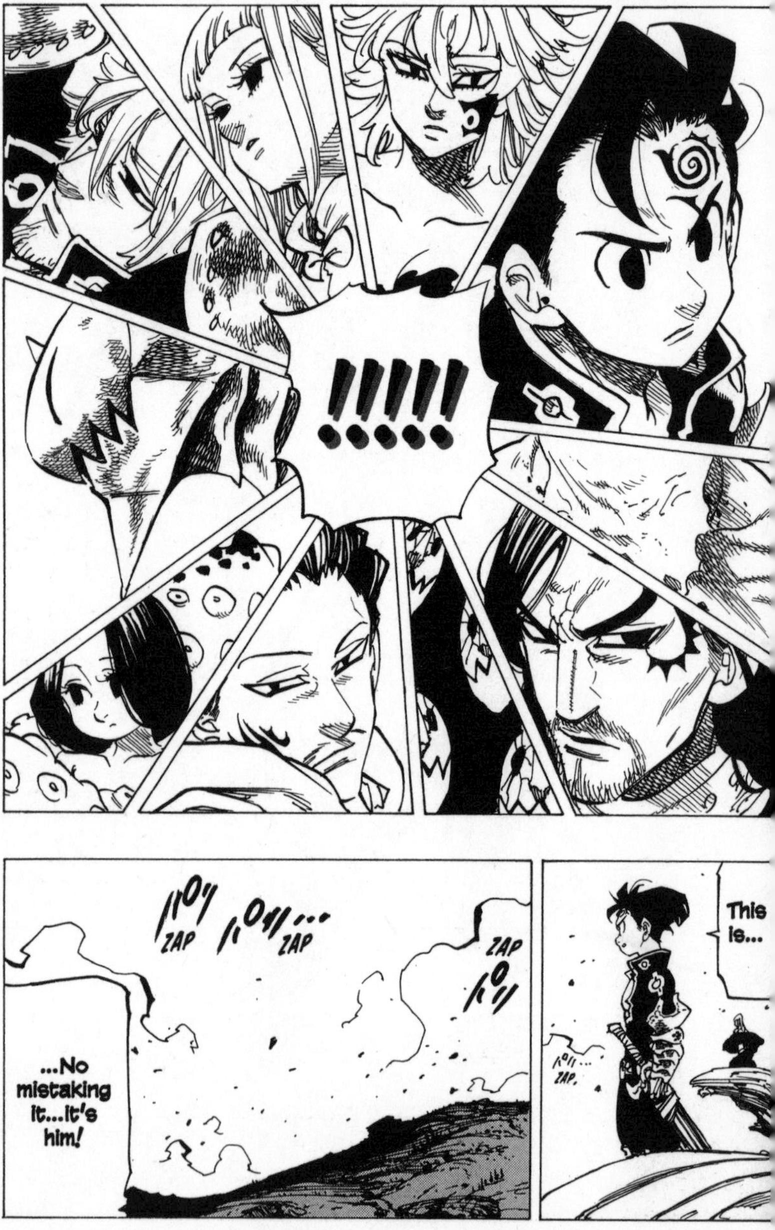
!!!!!
This is...
ZAP.
ZAP
ZAP
ZAP
...No mistaking it...it's him!

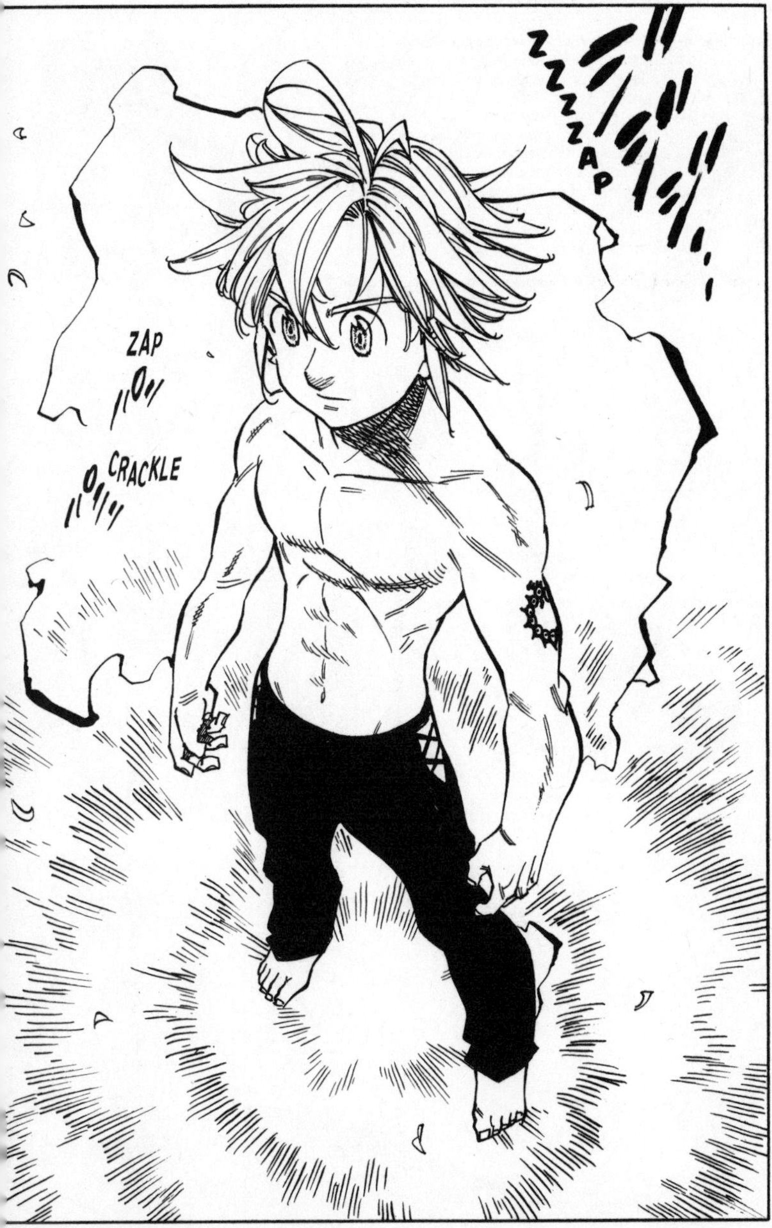
ZZZZZAP
ZAP
CRACKLE

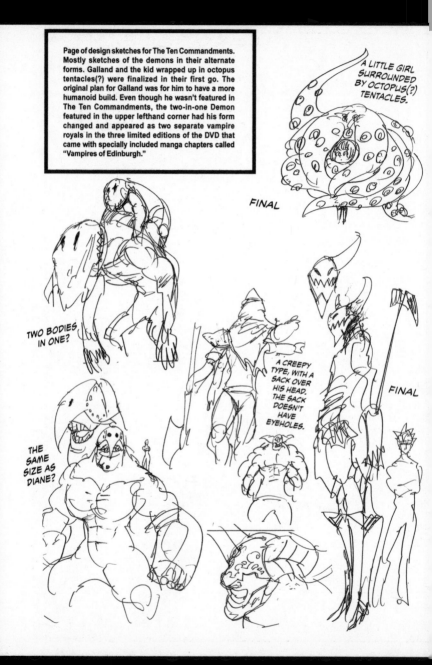

Page of design sketches for The Ten Commandments. Mostly sketches of the demons in their alternate forms. Galland and the kid wrapped up in octopus tentacles(?) were finalized in their first go. The original plan for Galland was for him to have a more humanoid build. Even though he wasn't featured in The Ten Commandments, the two-in-one Demon featured in the upper lefthand corner had his form changed and appeared as two separate vampire royals in the three limited editions of the DVD that came with specially included manga chapters called "Vampires of Edinburgh."

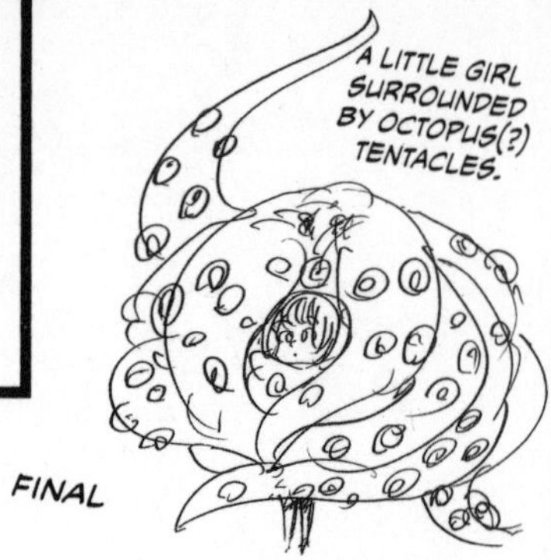
A LITTLE GIRL SURROUNDED BY OCTOPUS(?) TENTACLES.
FINAL

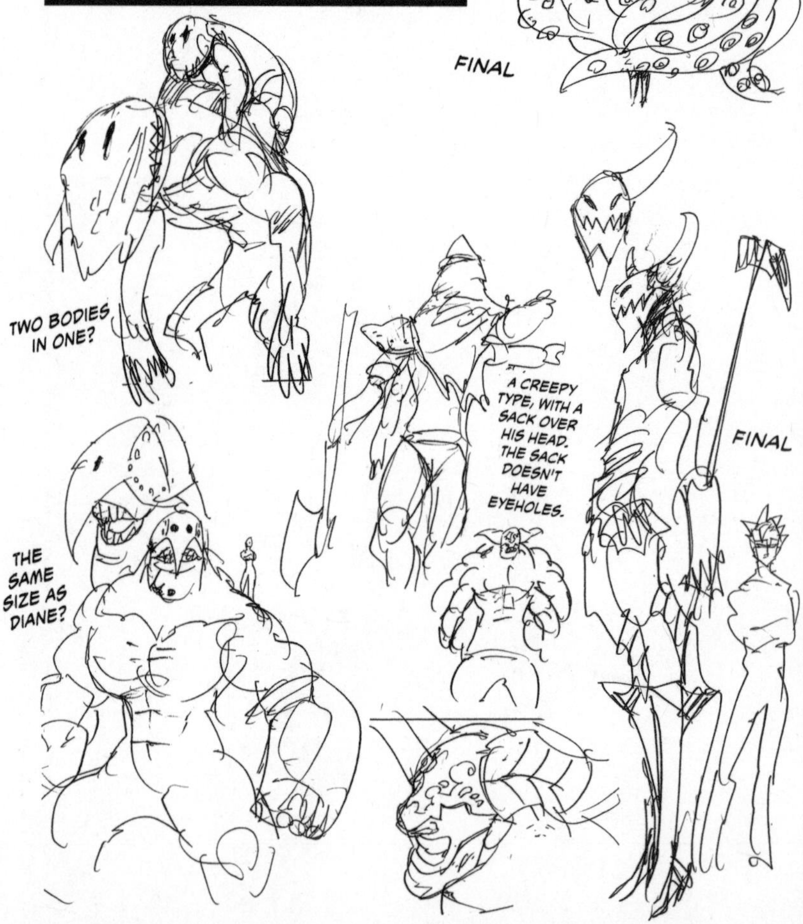
TWO BODIES IN ONE?
A CREEPY TYPE, WITH A SACK OVER HIS HEAD. THE SACK DOESN'T HAVE EYEHOLES.
FINAL
THE SAME SIZE AS DIANE?

Chapter 135 - A Little Greeting

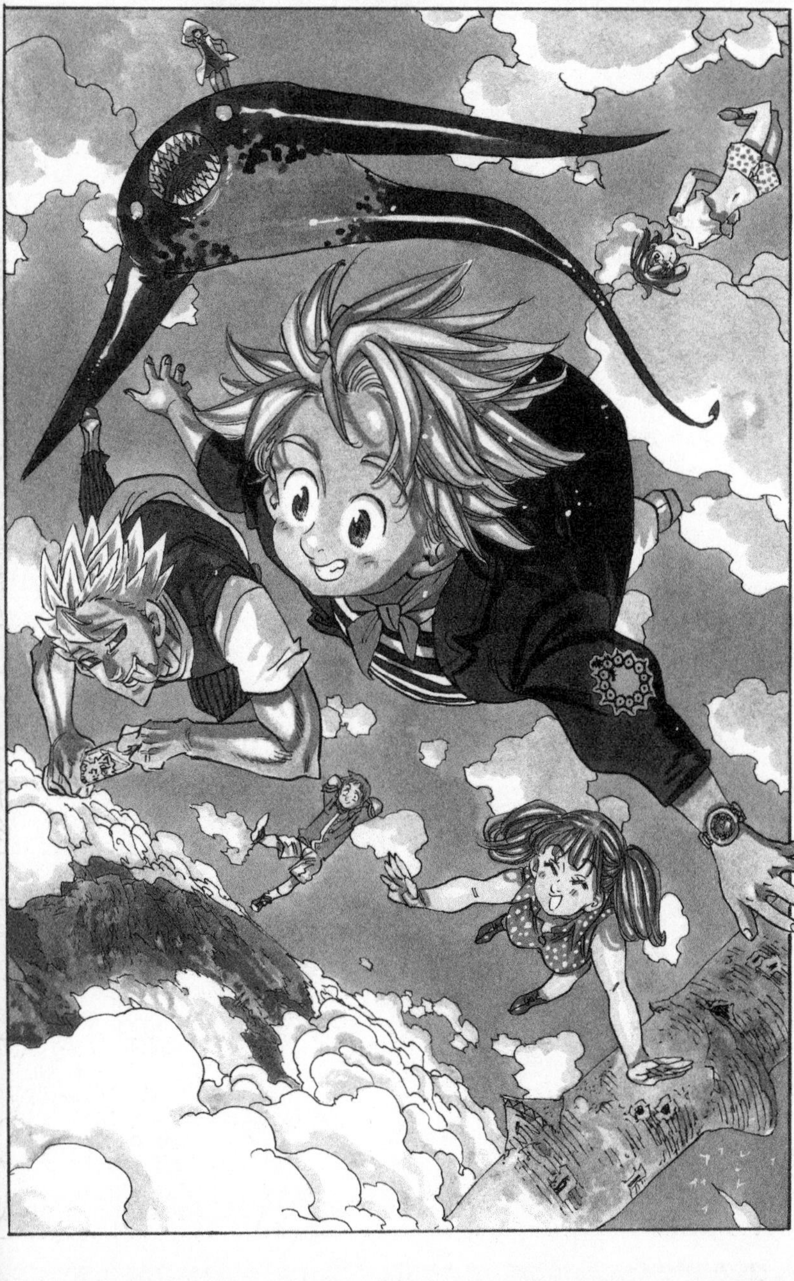

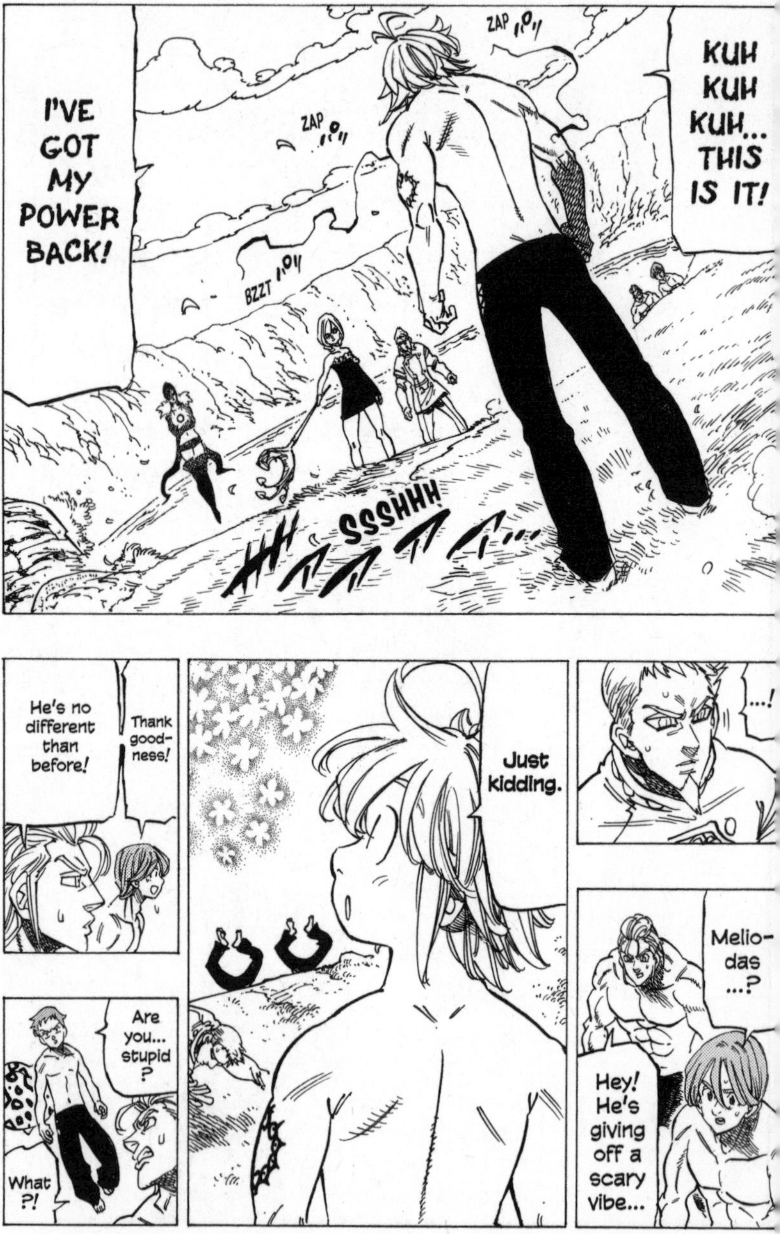
ZAP
KUH KUH KUH... THIS IS IT!
ZAP
I'VE GOT MY POWER BACK!
BZZT
SSSHHH
...!
Melio-das ...?
Hey! He's giving off a scary vibe...
Just kidding.
Thank good-ness!
He's no different than before!
Are you... stupid ?
What ?!

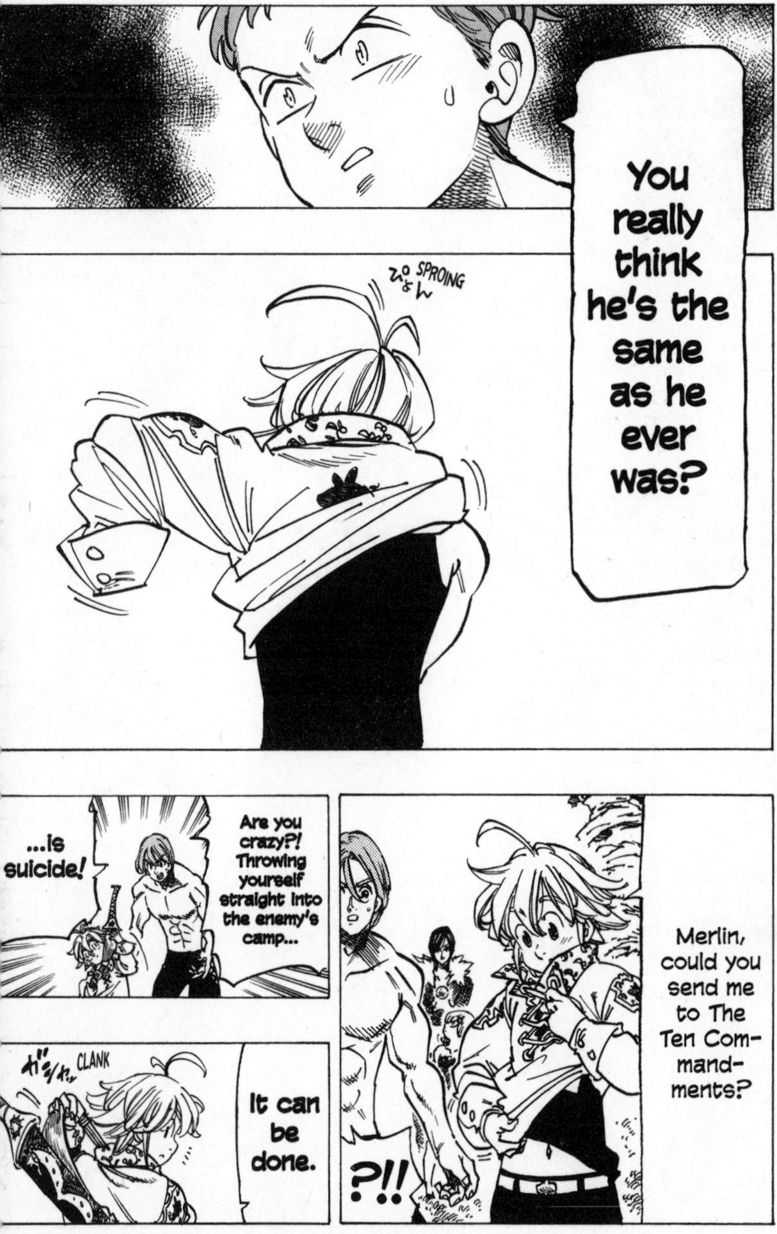
You really think he's the same as he ever was?
SPROING
ぴょん
Merlin, could you send me to The Ten Commandments?
?!!
Are you crazy?! Throwing yourself straight into the enemy's camp...
...is suicide!
CLANK
It can be done.

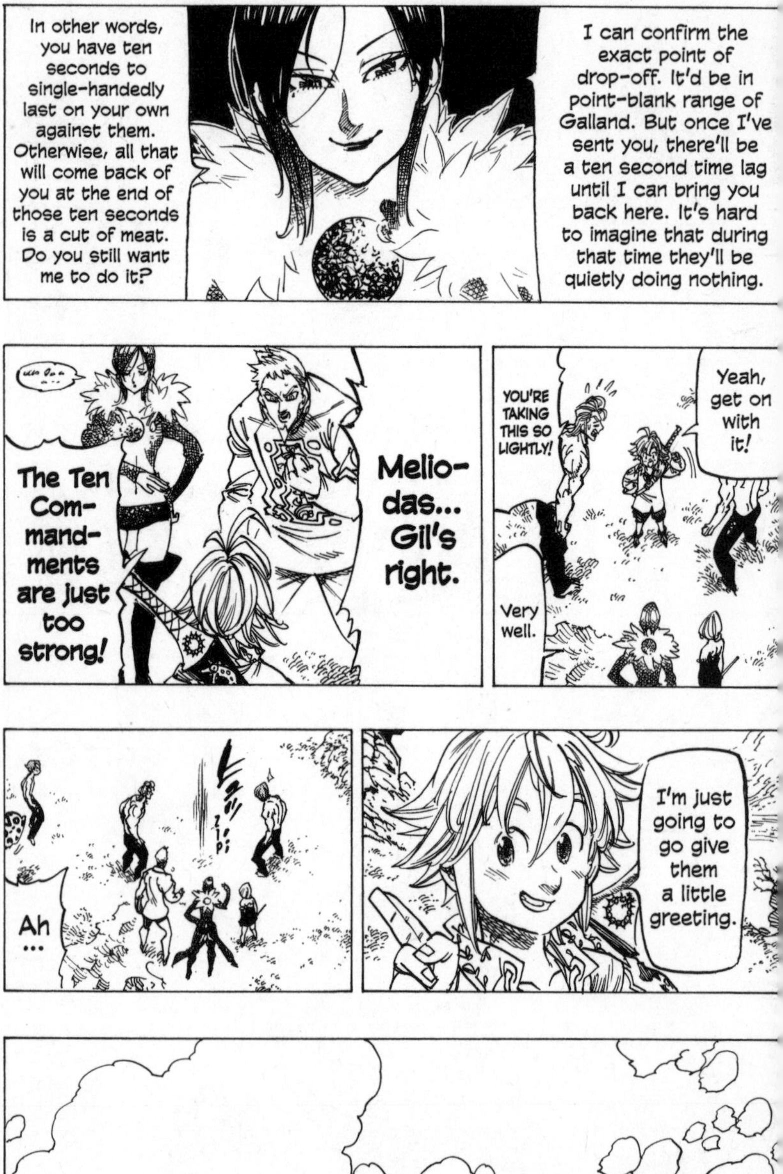

I can confirm the exact point of drop-off. It'd be in point-blank range of Galland. But once I've sent you, there'll be a ten second time lag until I can bring you back here. It's hard to imagine that during that time they'll be quietly doing nothing.
In other words, you have ten seconds to single-handedly last on your own against them. Otherwise, all that will come back of you at the end of those ten seconds is a cut of meat. Do you still want me to do it?
Yeah, get on with it!
YOU'RE TAKING THIS SO LIGHTLY!
Very well.
Meliodas... Gil's right.
The Ten Commandments are just too strong!
I'm just going to go give them a little greeting.
ZIP
Ah...

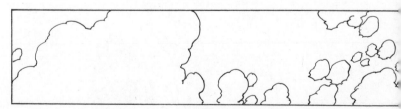

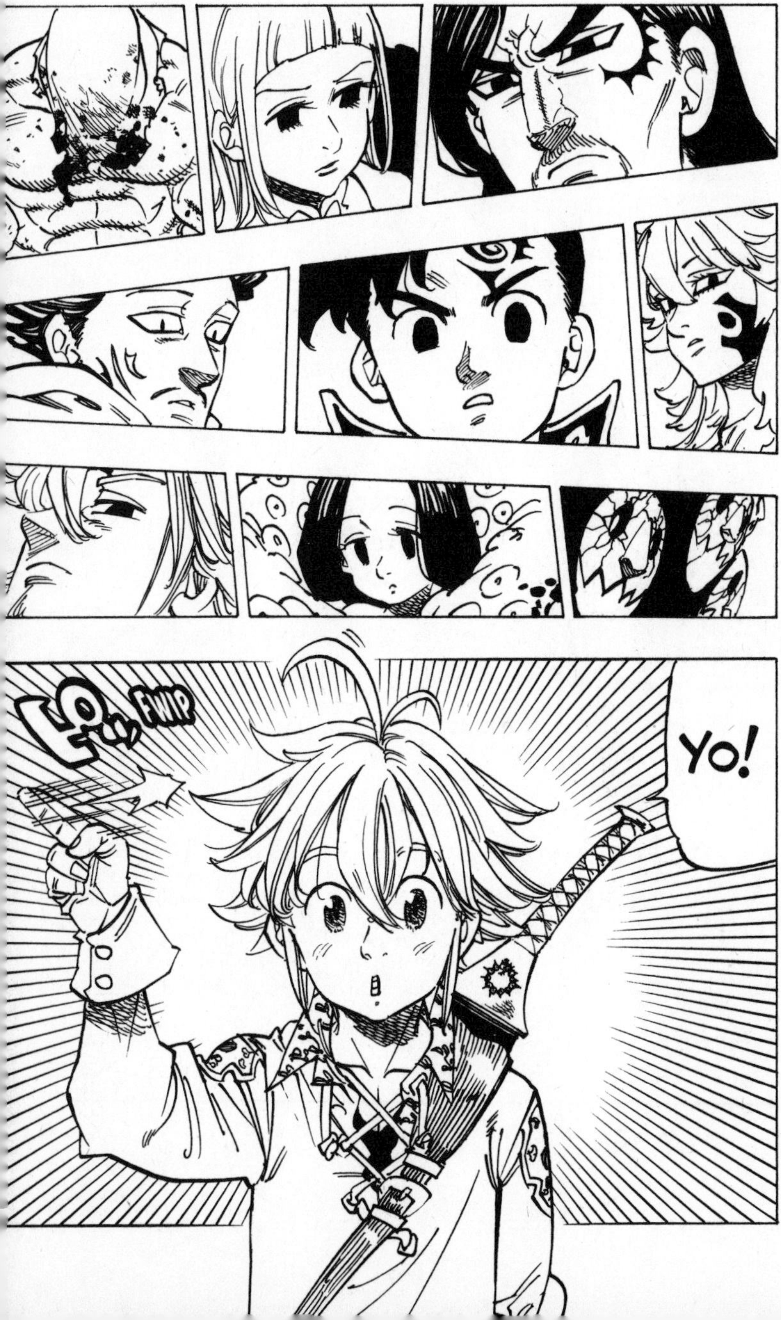
YO!
FWIP

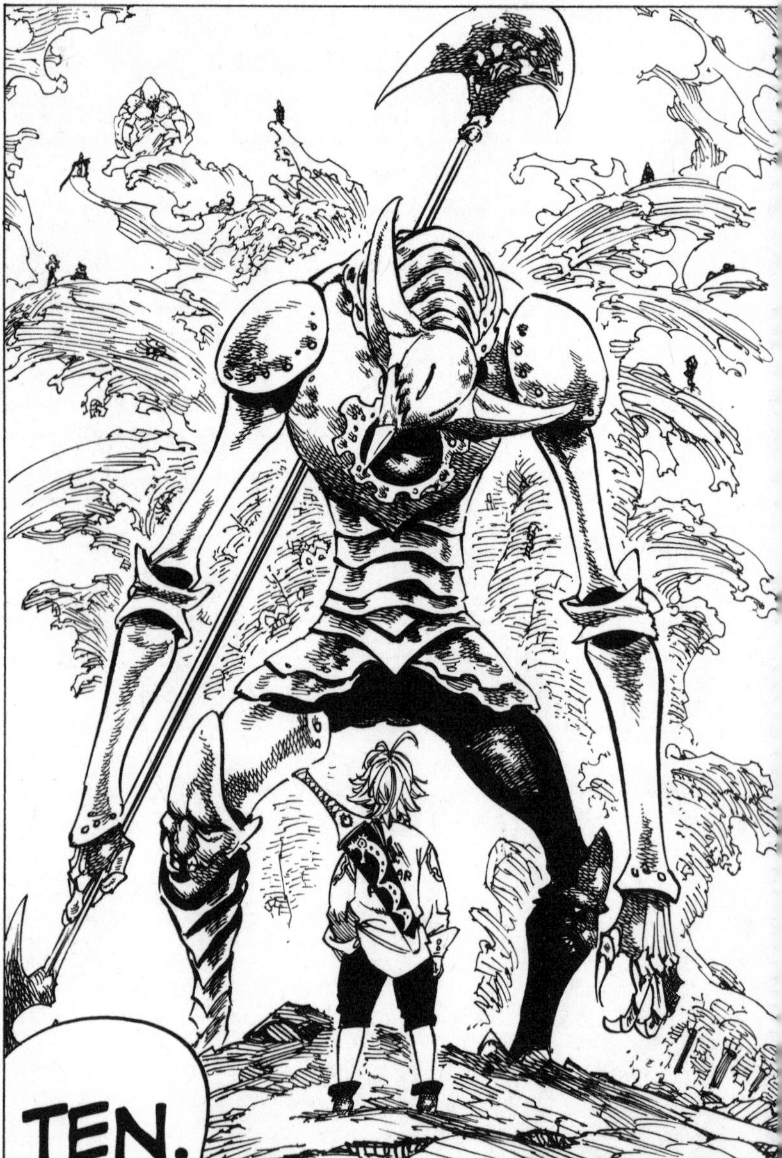
TEN.

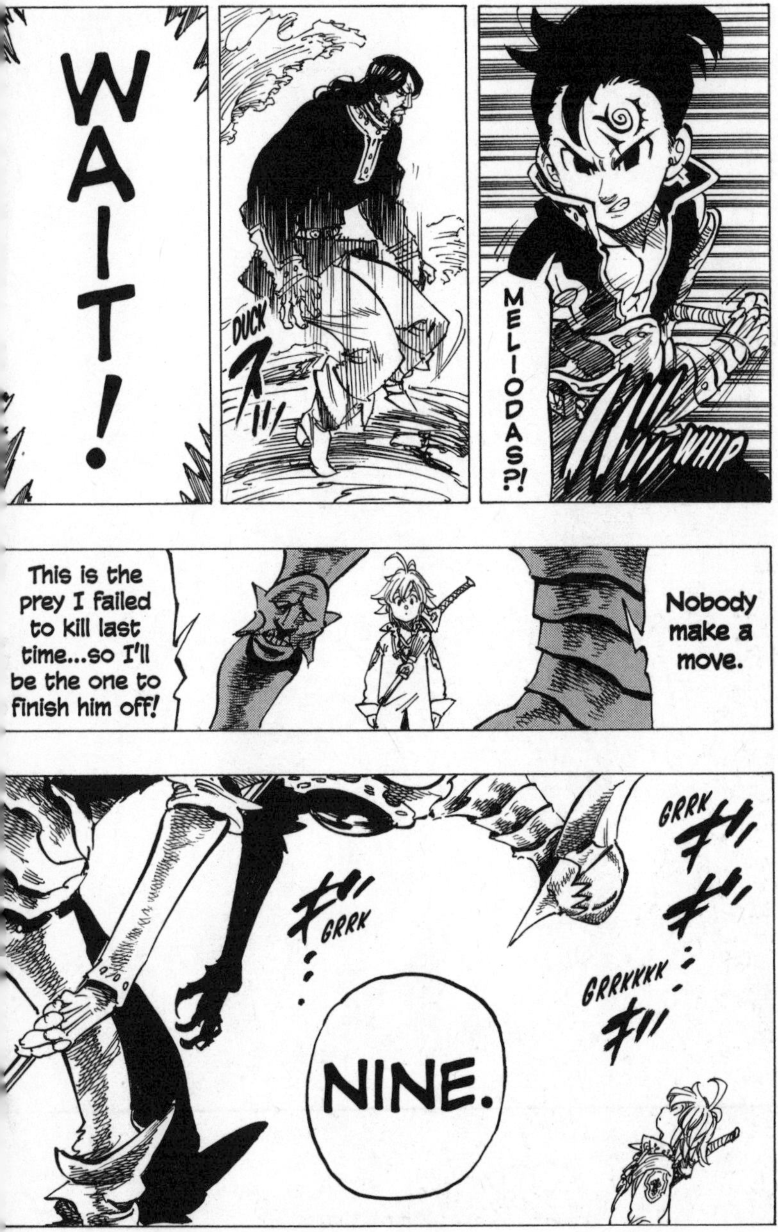
MELIODAS?!
WHIP
DUCK
WAIT!
Nobody make a move.
This is the prey I failed to kill last time...so I'll be the one to finish him off!
GRRK
GRRKKKK
GRRK
NINE.

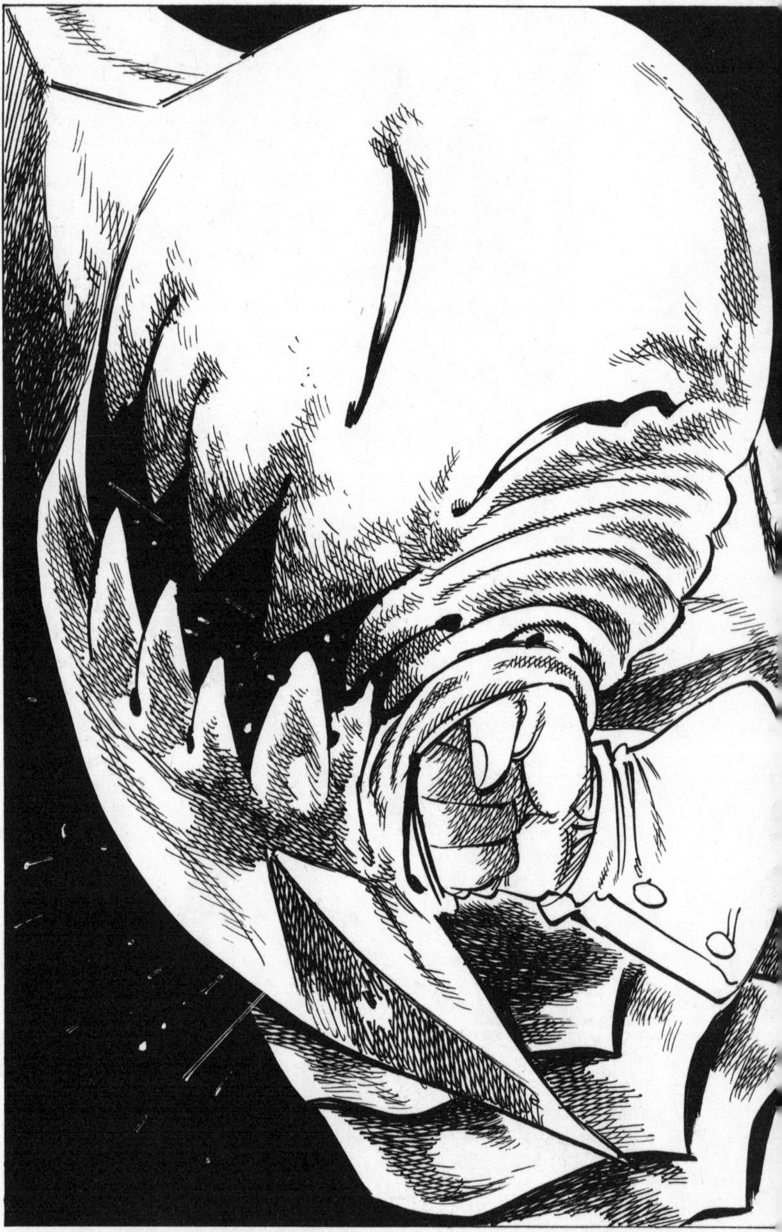

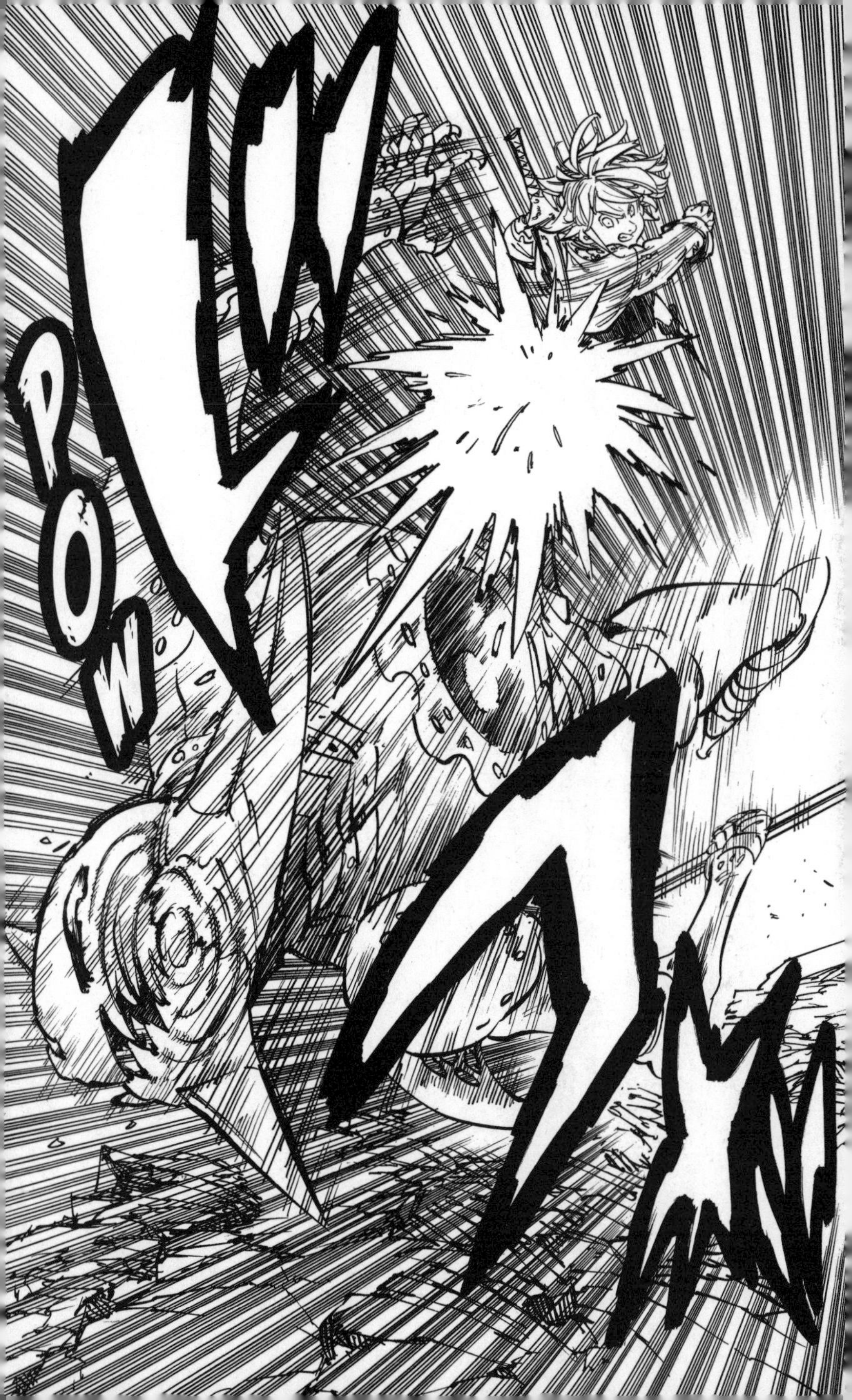
POW

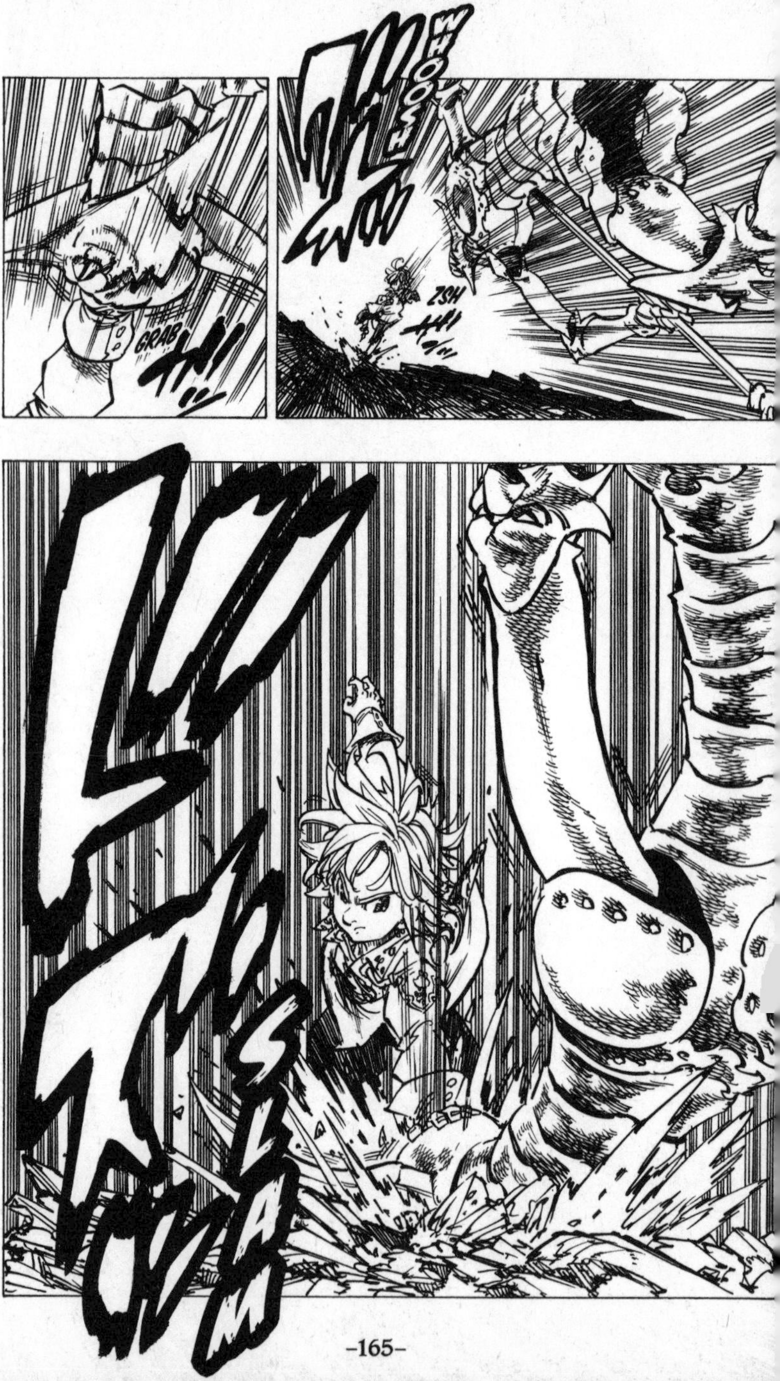
WHOOSH
ZSH
GRAB
SLAM

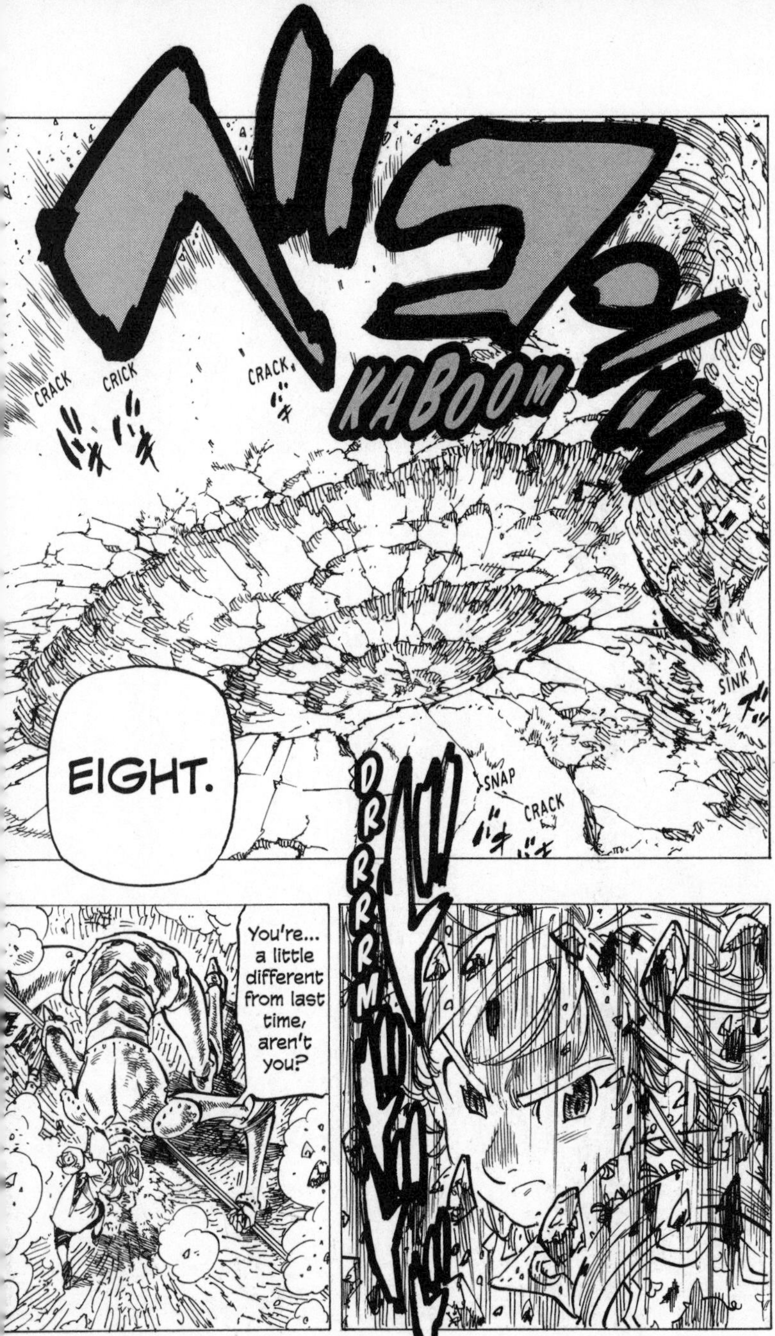
KABOOM
CRACK
CRICK
CRACK
SINK
SNAP
CRACK
EIGHT.
DRRRRM
You're... a little different from last time, aren't you?

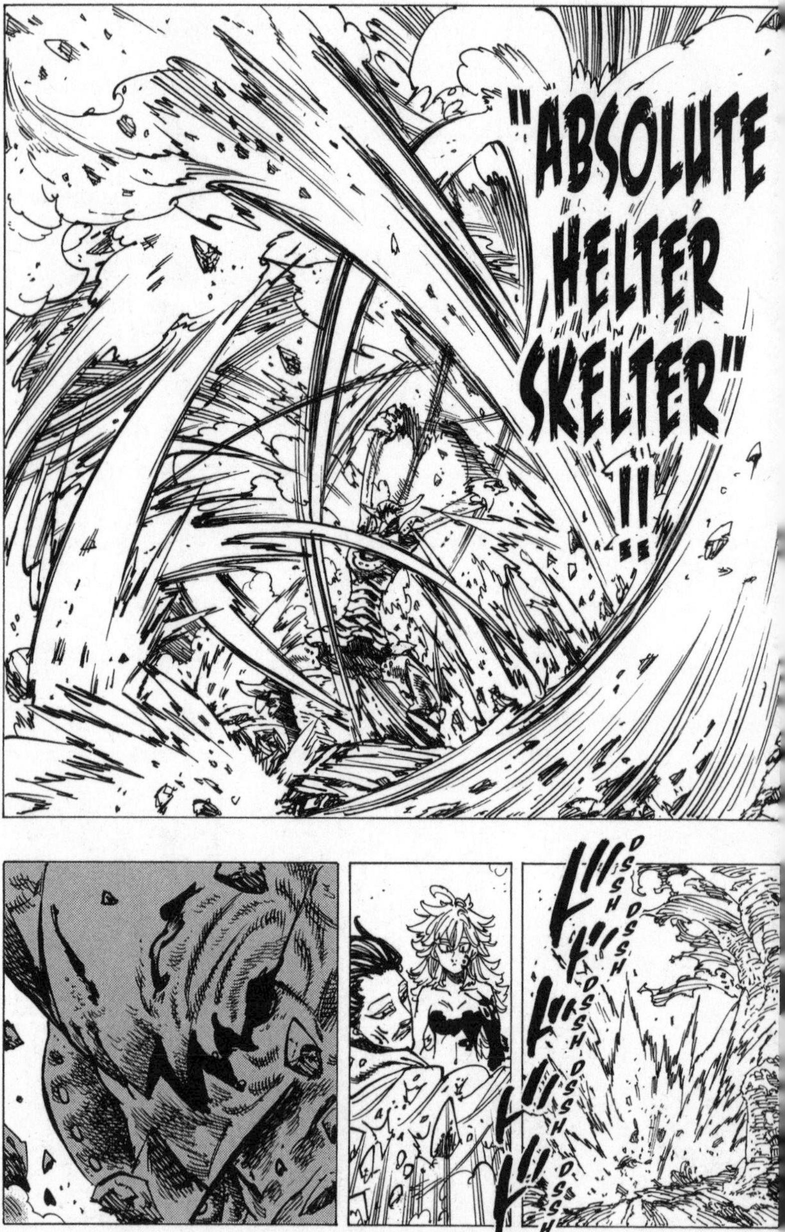
"ABSOLUTE HELTER SKELTER"!!
DOSSH
DOSSH
DOSSH
DOSSH
DOSSH

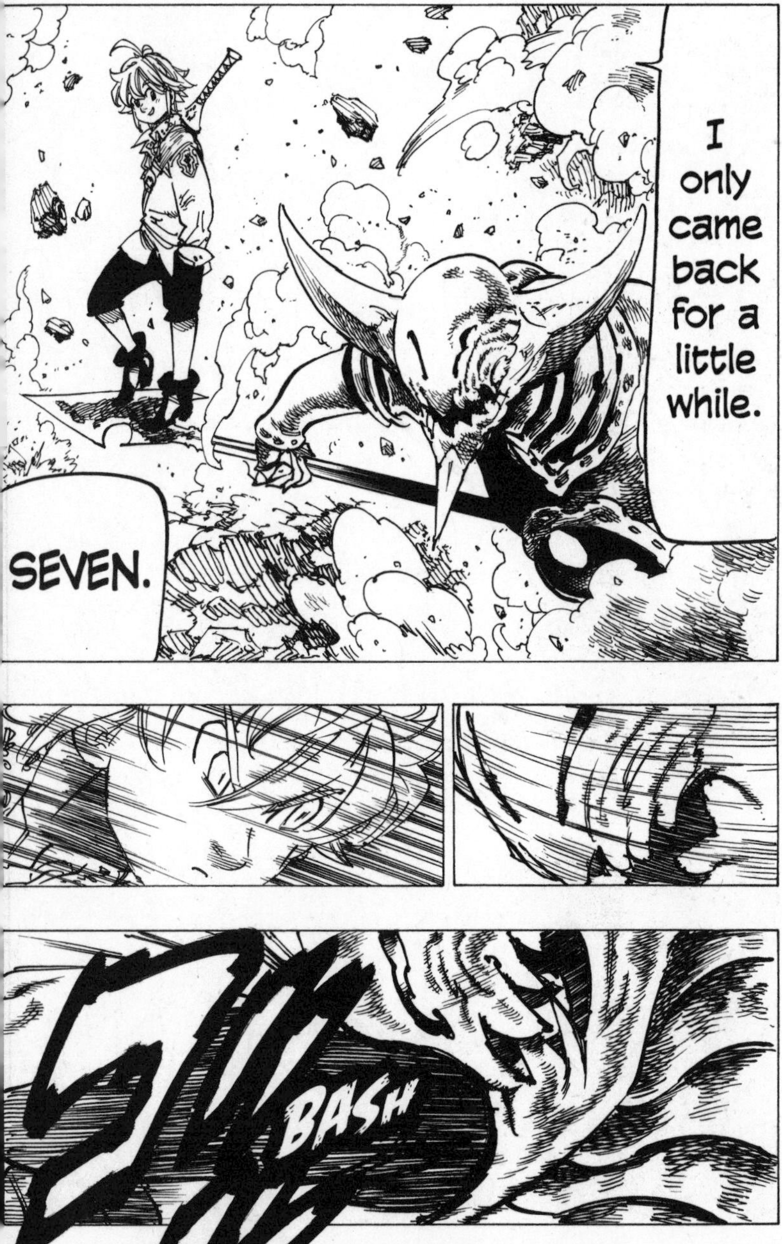
I only came back for a little while.
SEVEN.
BASH

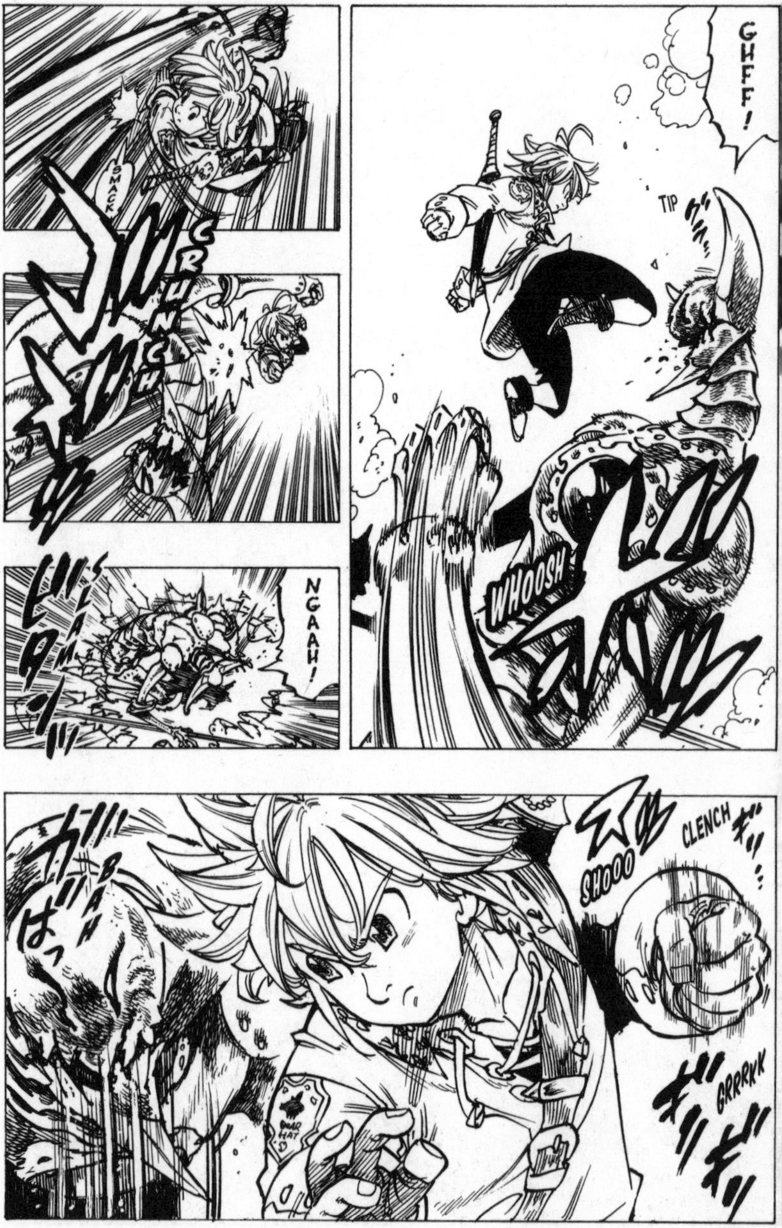
GHFF!
TIP
WHOOSH
SMACK
CRUNCH
SLAM
NGAAH!
CLENCH
SHOOO
GRRRKK
BAH

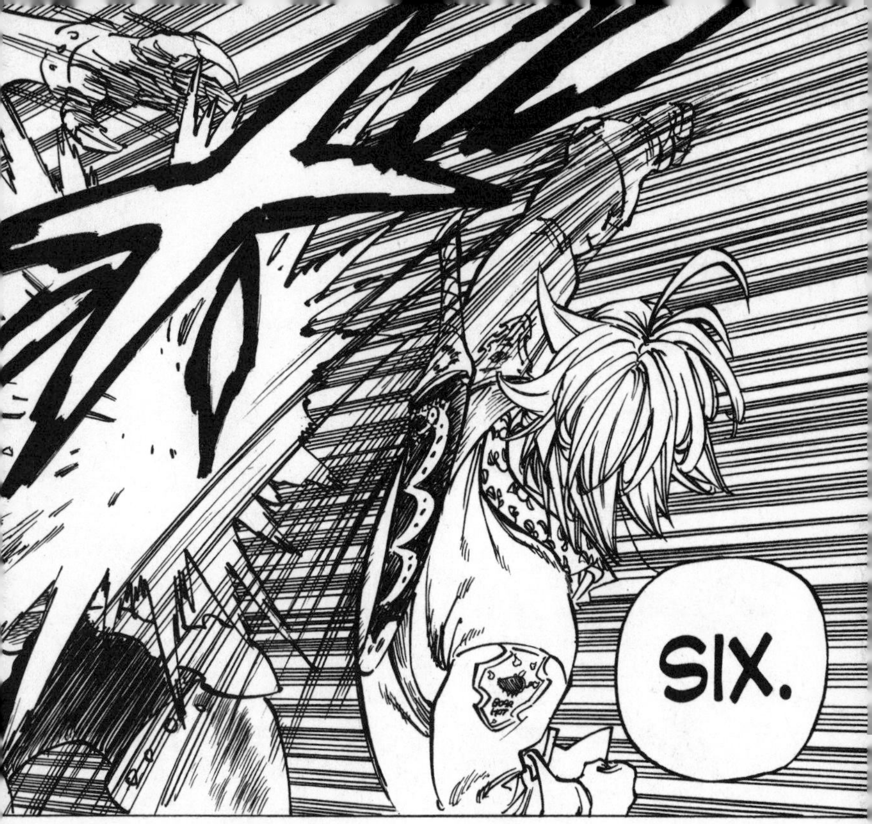
SIX.

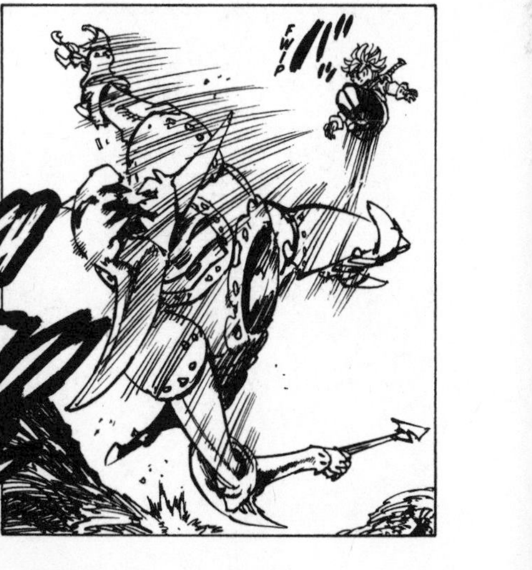
FWIP

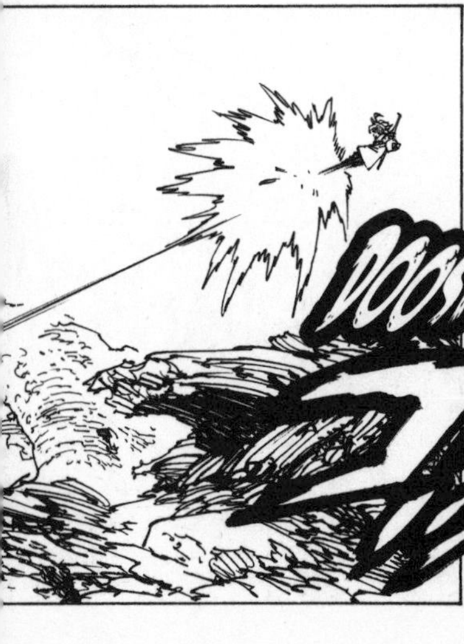
DOOSH

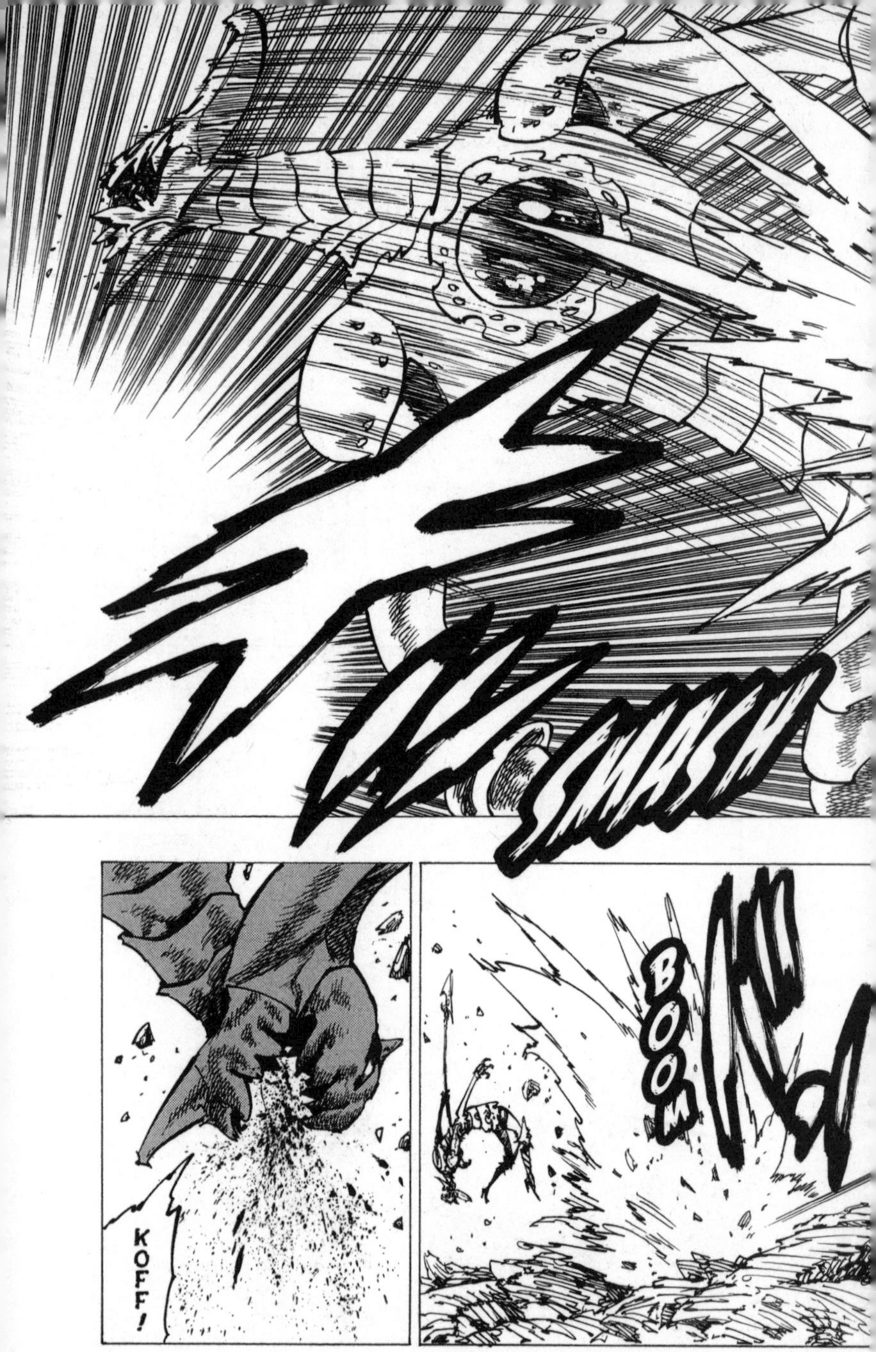
SMASH
BOOM
KOFF!

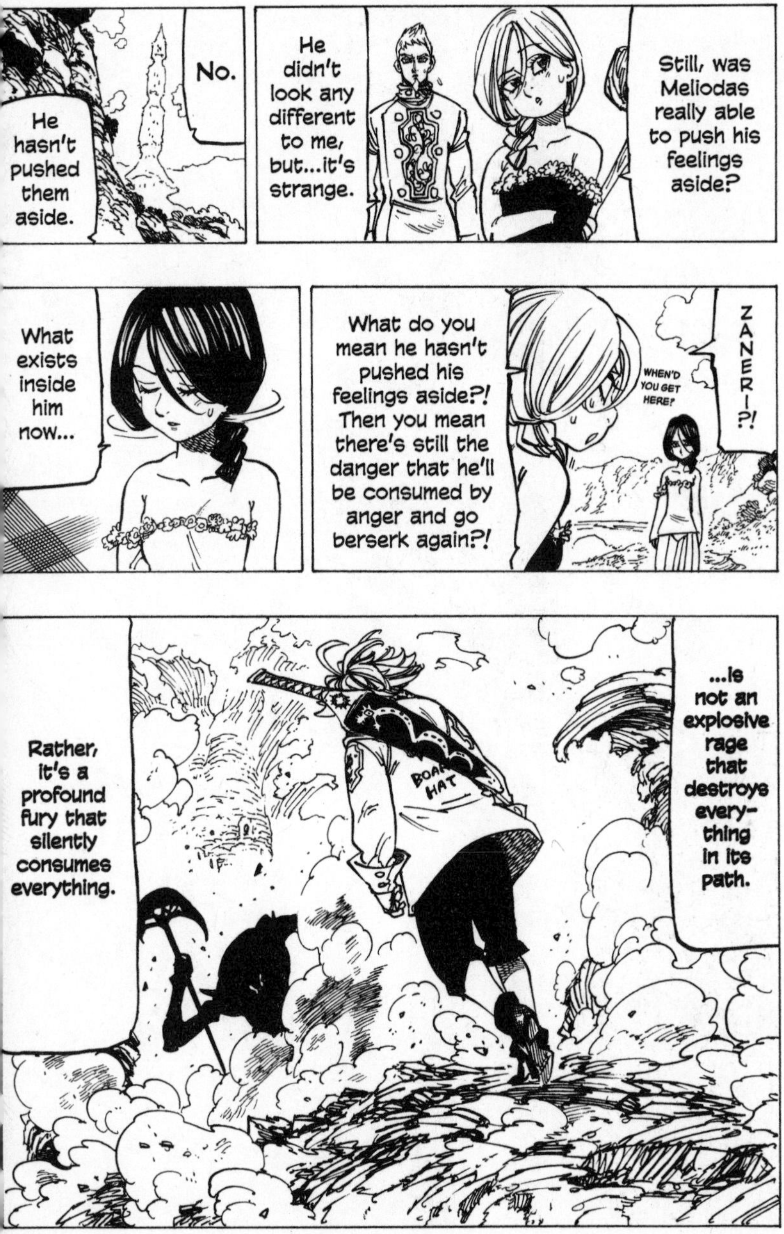
Still, was Meliodas really able to push his feelings aside?
He didn't look any different to me, but...it's strange.
No.
He hasn't pushed them aside.
ZANERI-?!
WHEN'D YOU GET HERE?
What do you mean he hasn't pushed his feelings aside?! Then you mean there's still the danger that he'll be consumed by anger and go berserk again?!
What exists inside him now...
...is not an explosive rage that destroys everything in its path.
Rather, it's a profound fury that silently consumes everything.

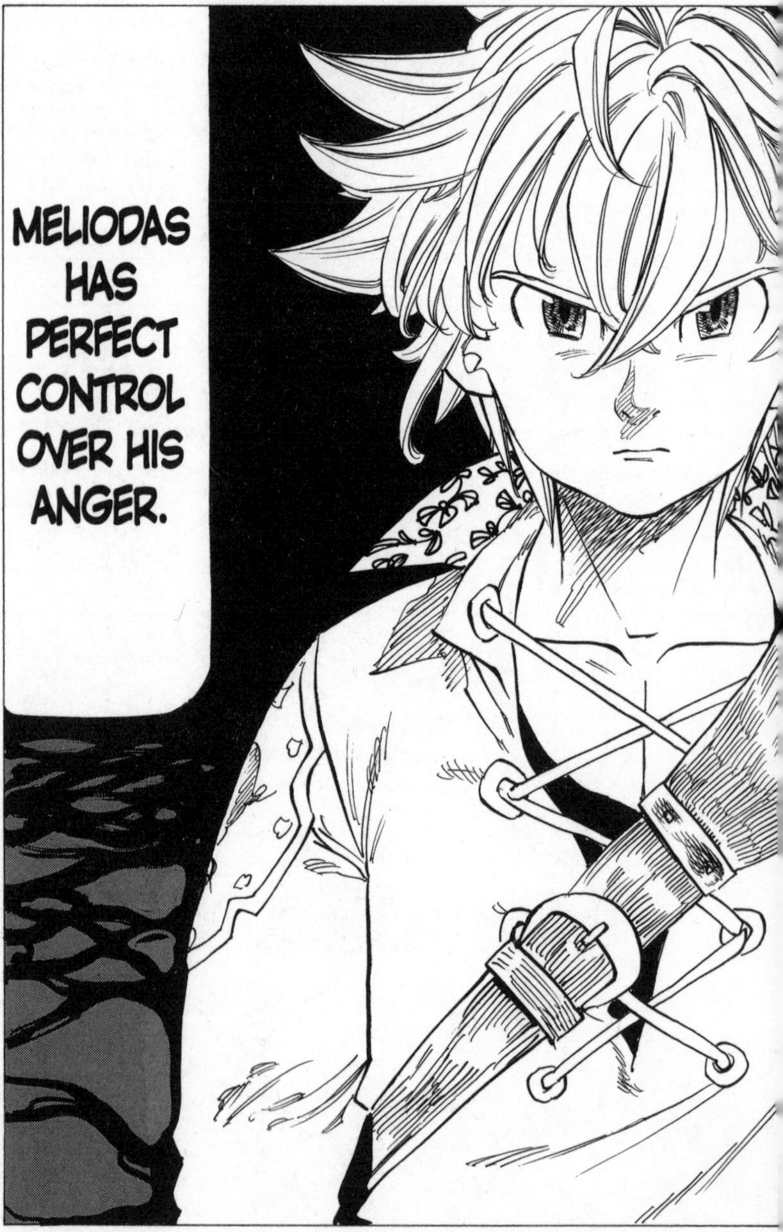
MELIODAS HAS PERFECT CONTROL OVER HIS ANGER.

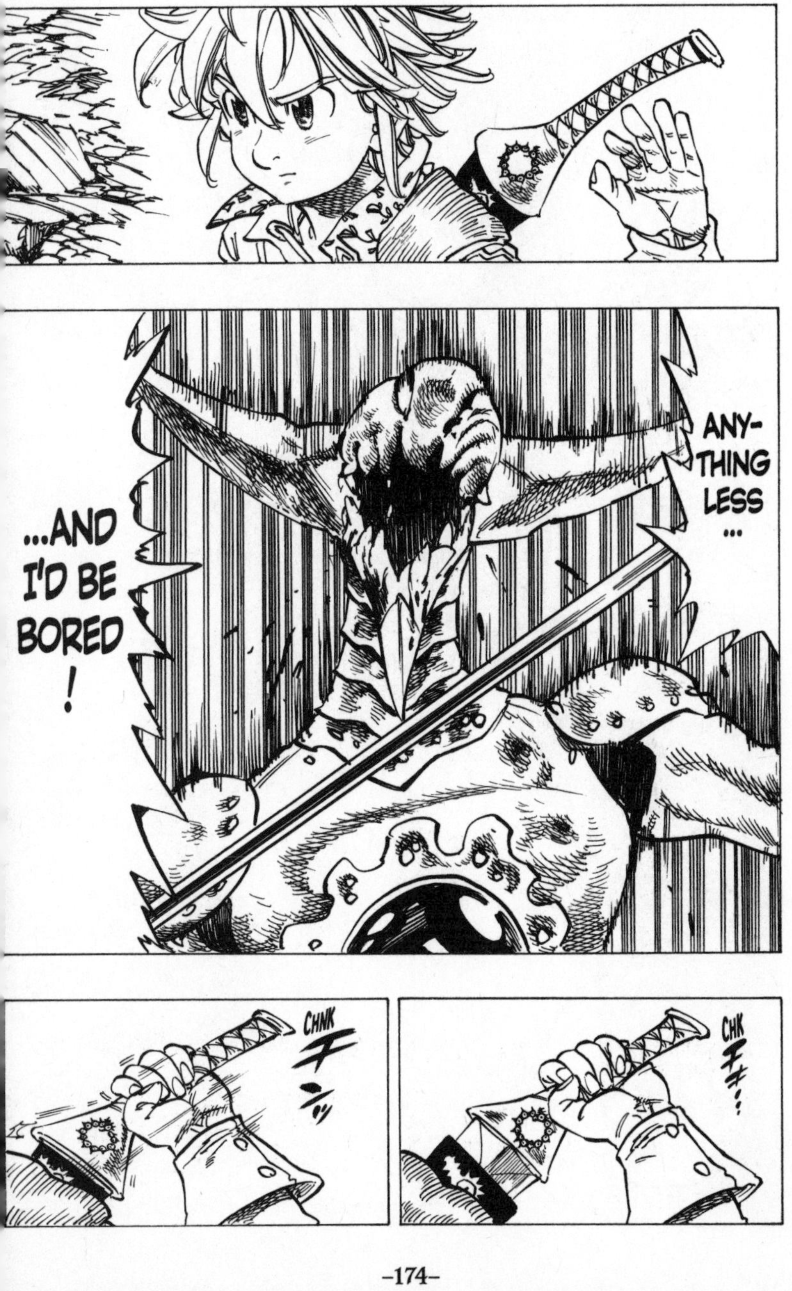
ANY-THING LESS ...
...AND I'D BE BORED!
CHK
CHNK

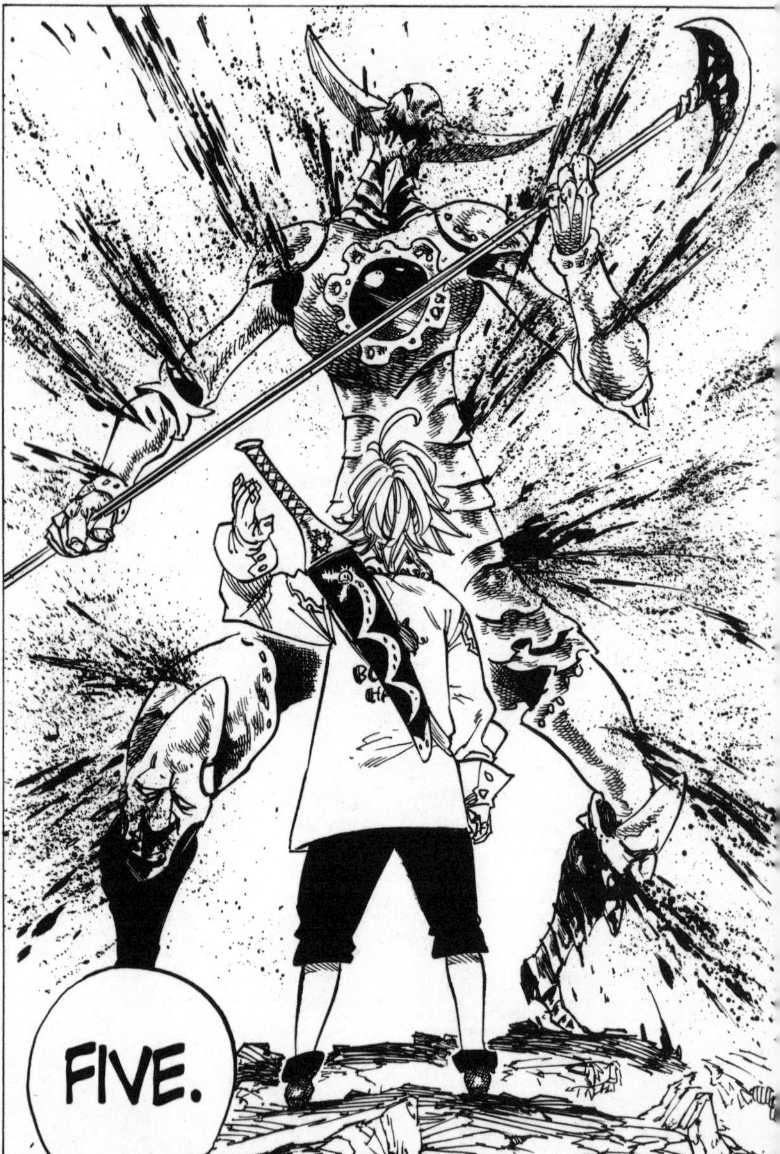
FIVE.

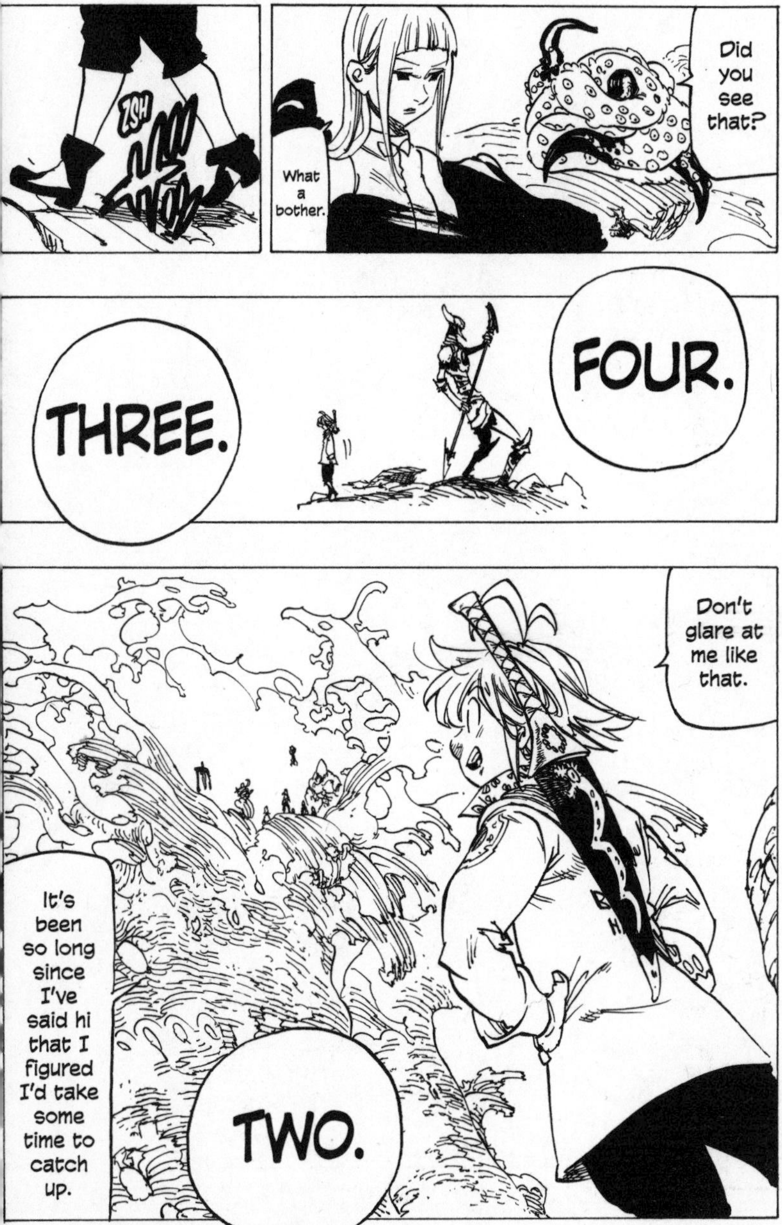
Did you see that?
What a bother.
ZSH
FOUR.
THREE.
Don't glare at me like that.
It's been so long since I've said hi that I figured I'd take some time to catch up.
TWO.

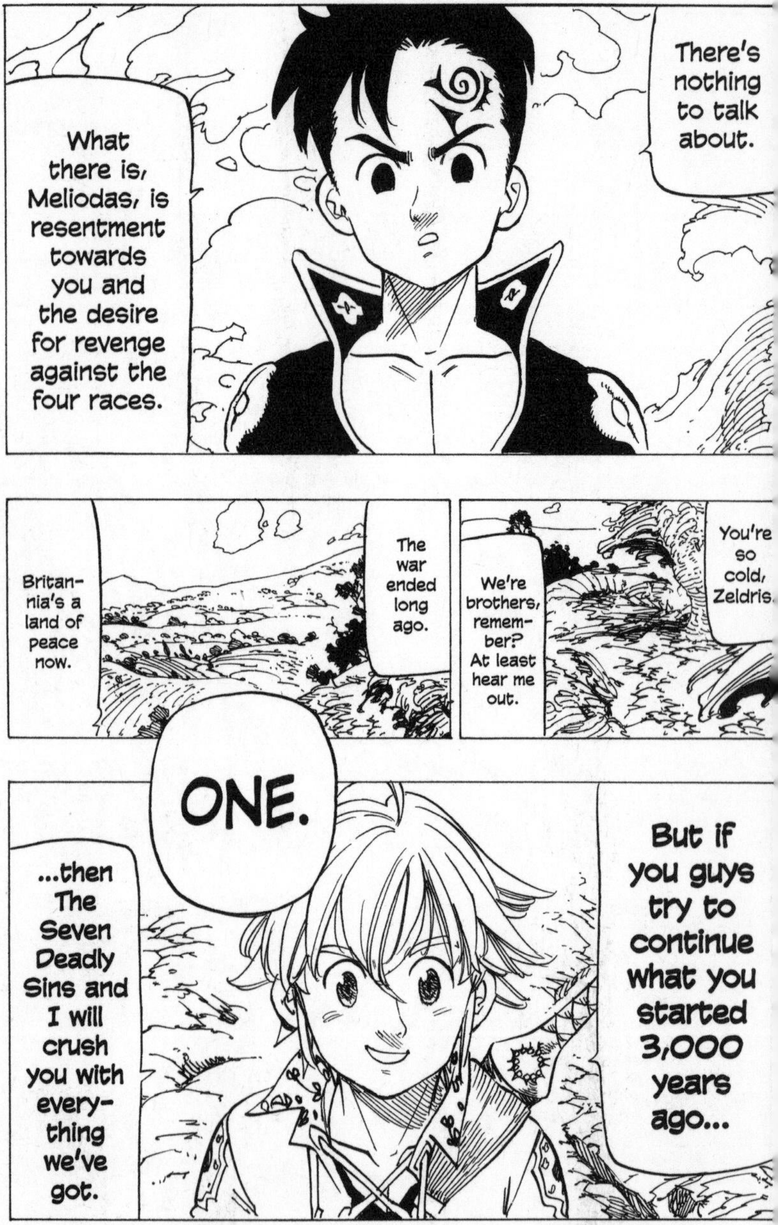
There's nothing to talk about.
What there is, Meliodas, is resentment towards you and the desire for revenge against the four races.
You're so cold, Zeldris.
We're brothers, remember? At least hear me out.
The war ended long ago.
Britan-nia's a land of peace now.
ONE.
But if you guys try to continue what you started 3,000 years ago...
...then The Seven Deadly Sins and I will crush you with every-thing we've got.

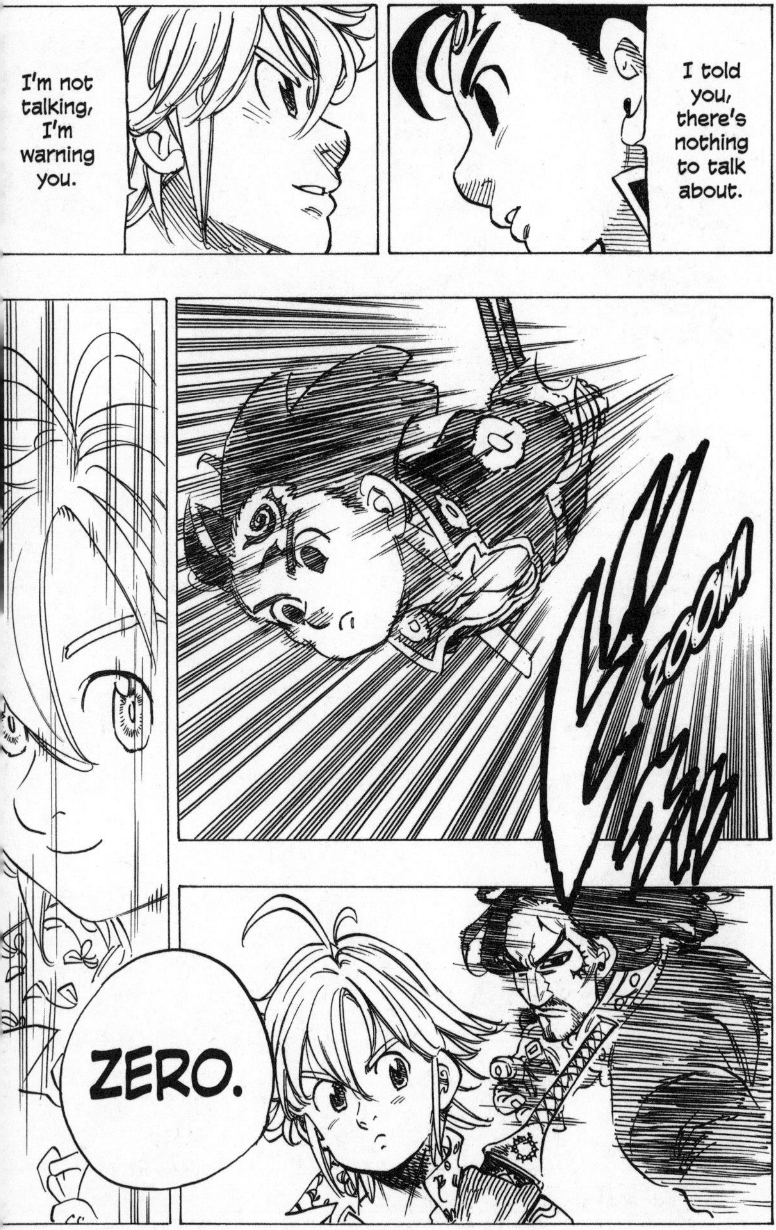
I told you, there's nothing to talk about.
I'm not talking, I'm warning you.
ZOOM
ZERO.

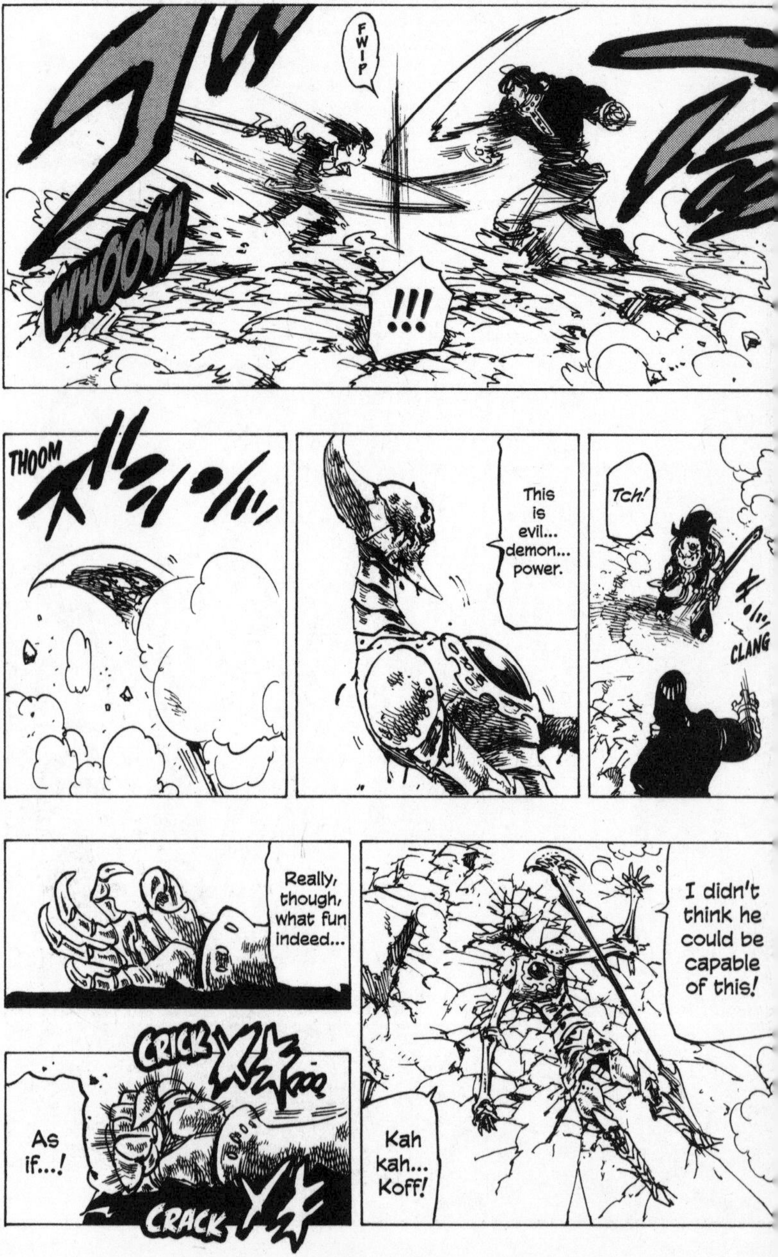
FWIP
WHOOSH
!!!
Tch!
CLANG
This is evil... demon... power.
THOOM
I didn't think he could be capable of this!
Kah kah... Koff!
Really, though, what fun indeed...
CRICK
As if...!
CRACK

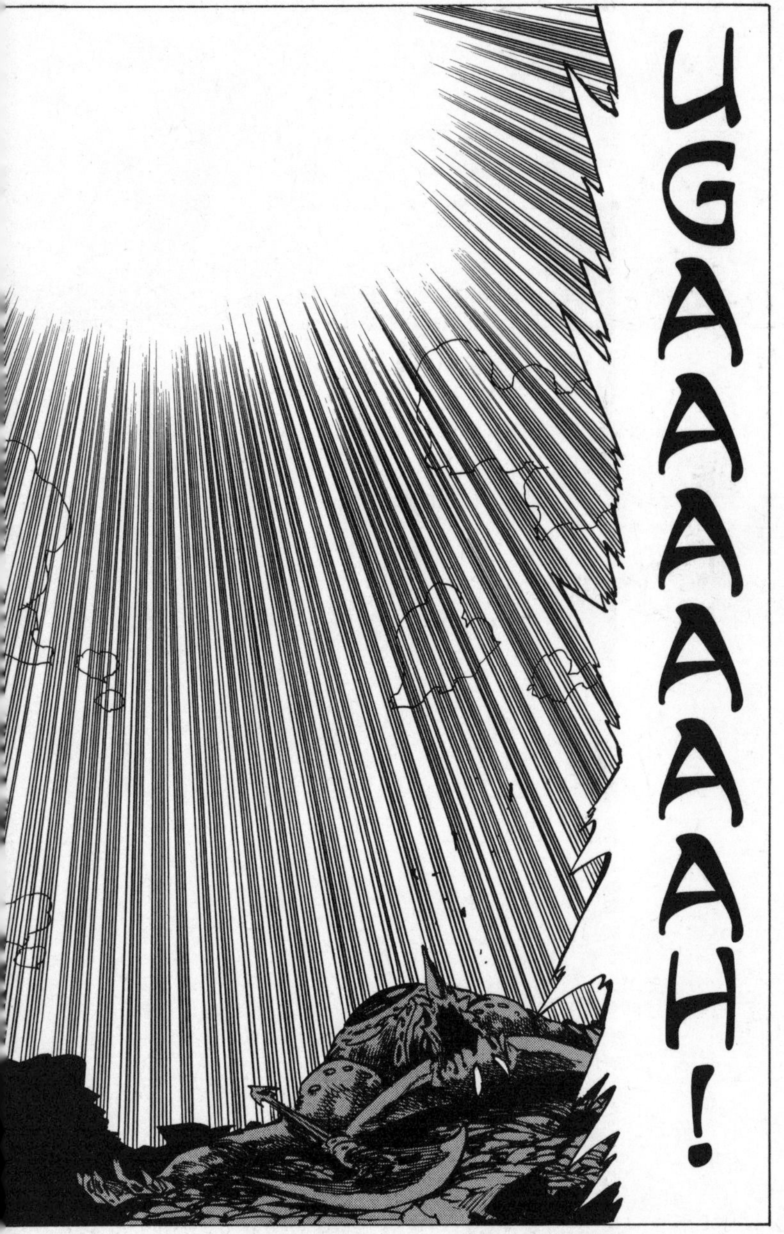
UGAAAAAAH!

To Be Continued in Volume 18...

"THE SEVEN DEADLY SINS" Q&A CORNER

"CHATTING KNIGHTHOOD"

Be sure to include your name and location with your submission!!

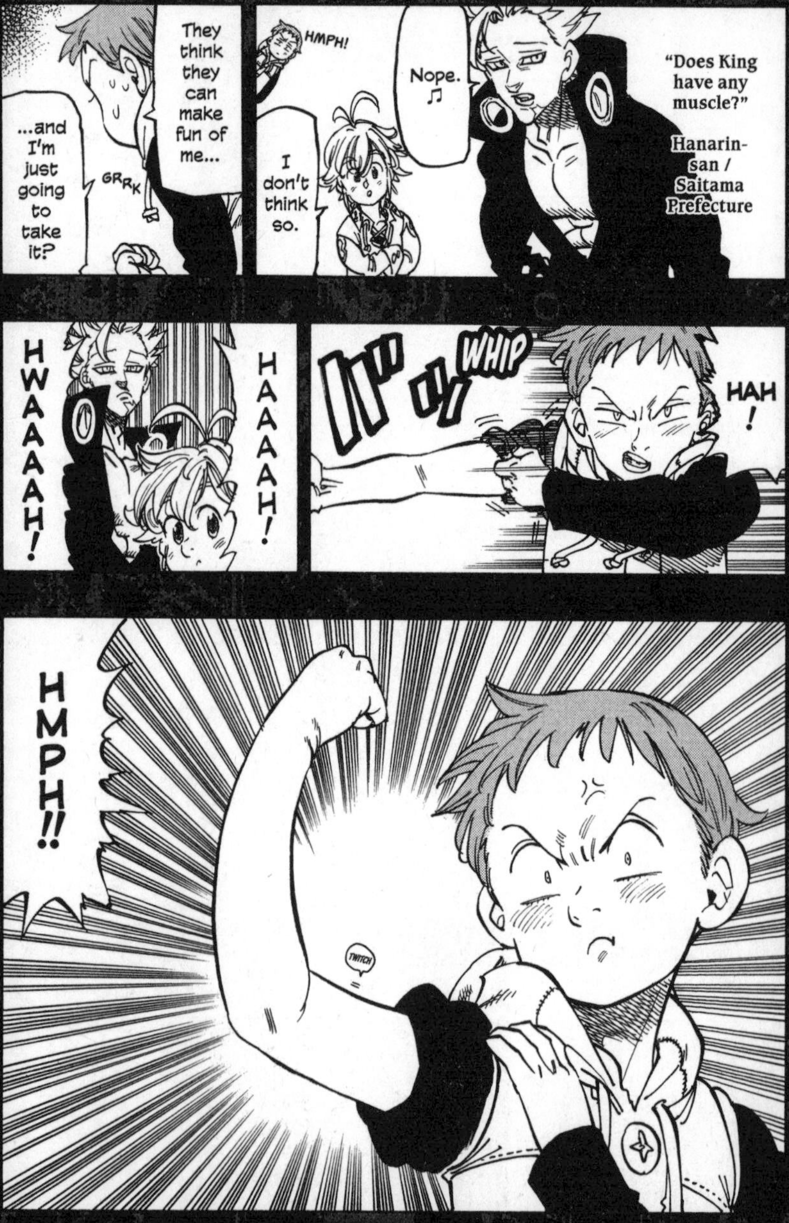

"Does King have any muscle?"
Hanarin-san / Saitama Prefecture
Nope. ♫
HMPH!
I don't think so.
They think they can make fun of me...
...and I'm just going to take it?
GRRK
WHIP
HAH!
HAAAAAH!
HWAAAAAH!
HMPH!!
TWITCH

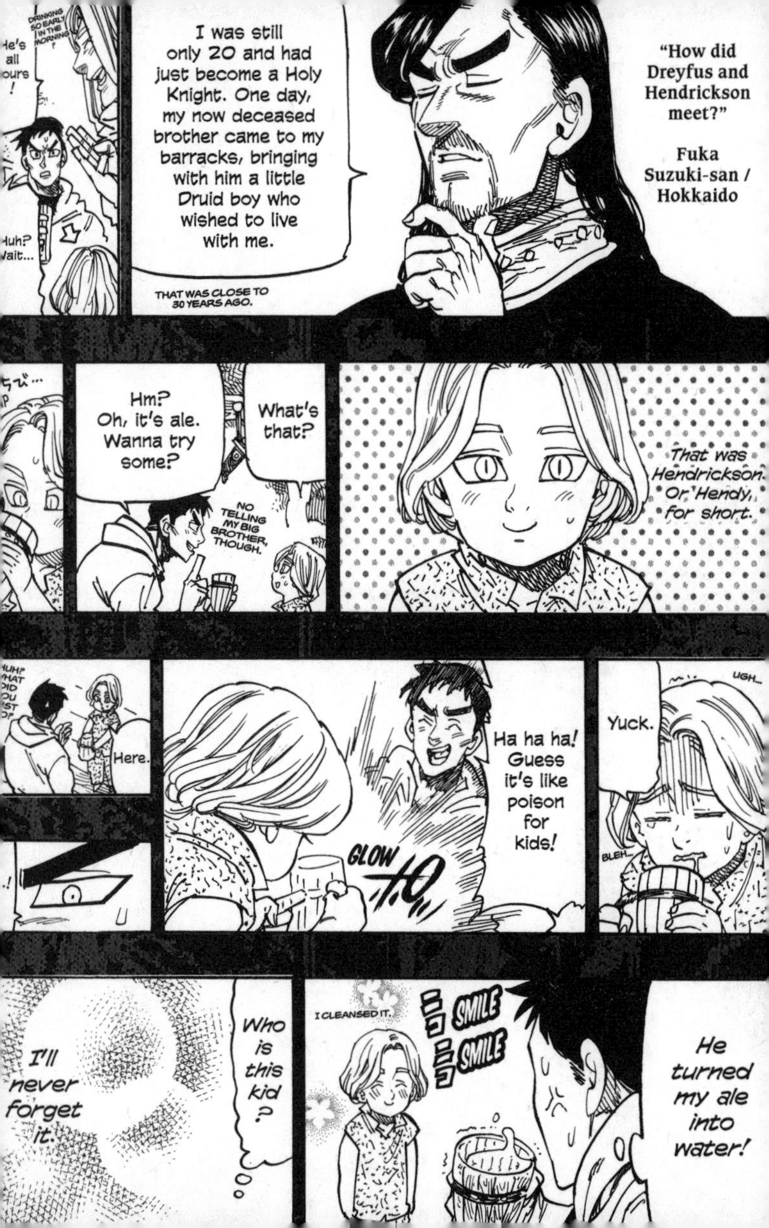
"How did Dreyfus and Hendrickson meet?"
Fuka Suzuki-san / Hokkaido
I was still only 20 and had just become a Holy Knight. One day, my now deceased brother came to my barracks, bringing with him a little Druid boy who wished to live with me.
THAT WAS CLOSE TO 30 YEARS AGO.
DRINKING SO EARLY IN THE MORNING?
That was Hendrickson. Or Hendy, for short.
What's that?
Hm? Oh, it's ale. Wanna try some?
NO TELLING MY BIG BROTHER, THOUGH.
UGH...
Yuck.
BLEH...
Ha ha ha! Guess it's like poison for kids!
GLOW
Here.
He turned my ale into water!
SMILE SMILE
I CLEANSED IT.
Who is this kid?
I'll never forget it.

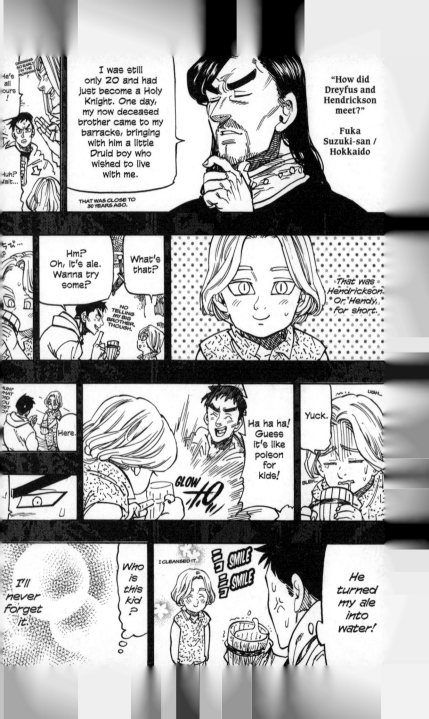

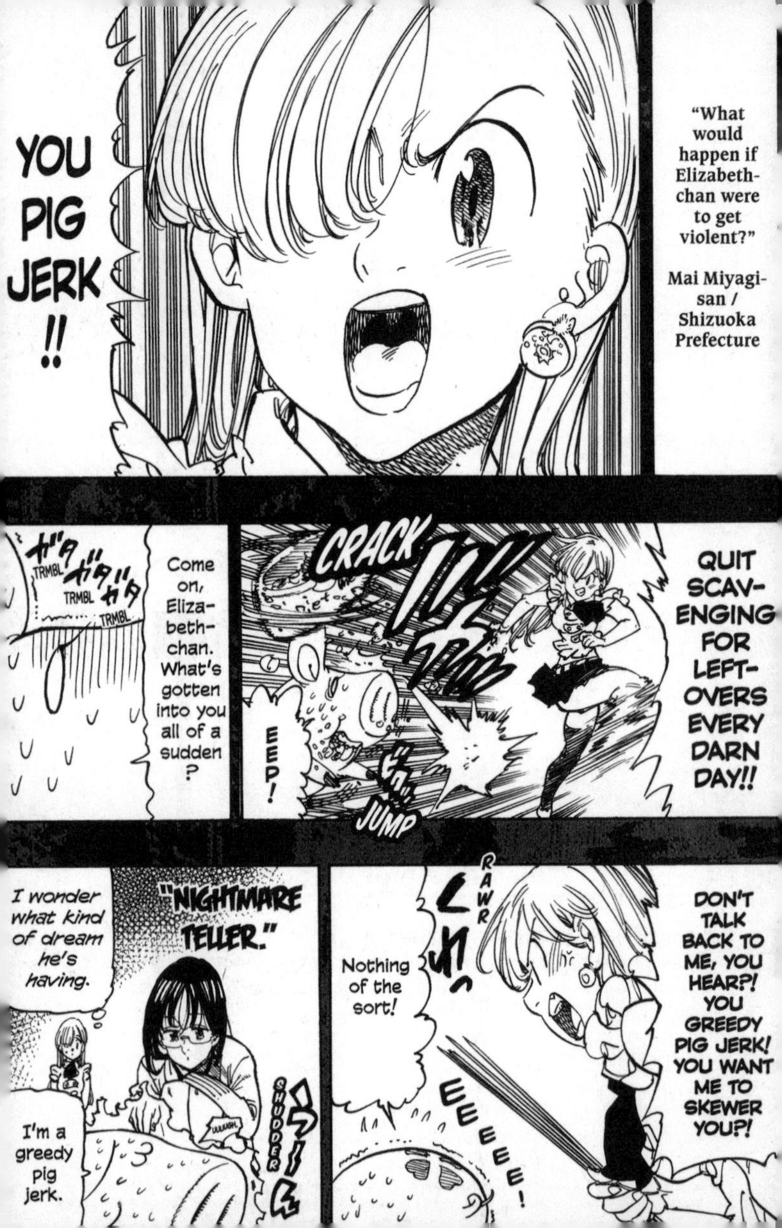
"What would happen if Elizabeth-chan were to get violent?"
Mai Miyagi-san / Shizuoka Prefecture
YOU PIG JERK!!
QUIT SCAVENGING FOR LEFTOVERS EVERY DARN DAY!!
CRACK
EEP!
JUMP
TRMBL
TRMBL
TRMBL
Come on, Elizabeth-chan. What's gotten into you all of a sudden?
DON'T TALK BACK TO ME, YOU HEAR?! YOU GREEDY PIG JERK! YOU WANT ME TO SKEWER YOU?!
RAWR
Nothing of the sort!
EEEEEE!
"NIGHTMARE TELLER."
I wonder what kind of dream he's having.
SHUDDER
I'm a greedy pig jerk.

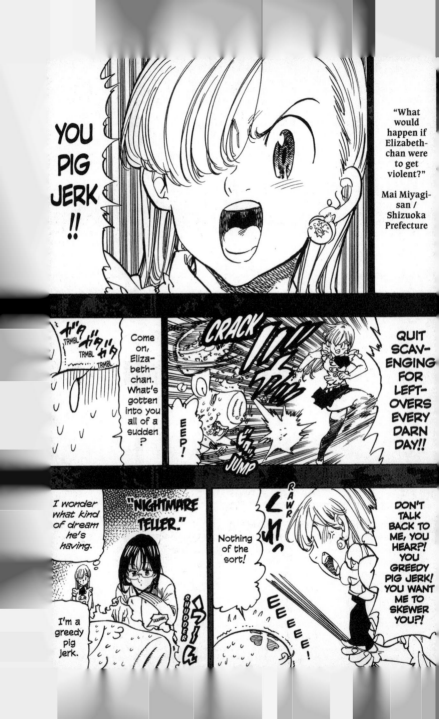

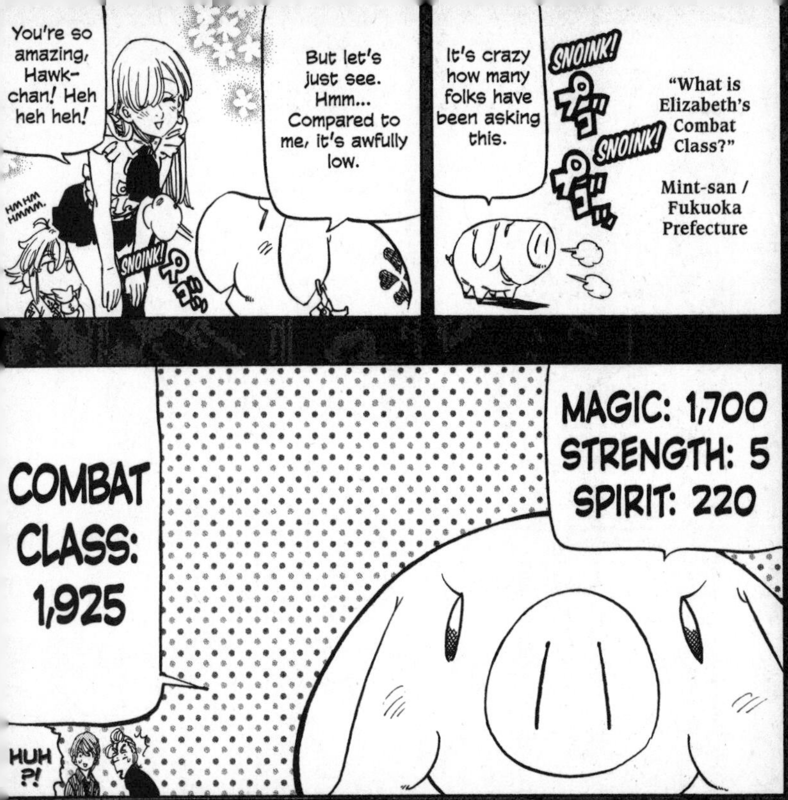

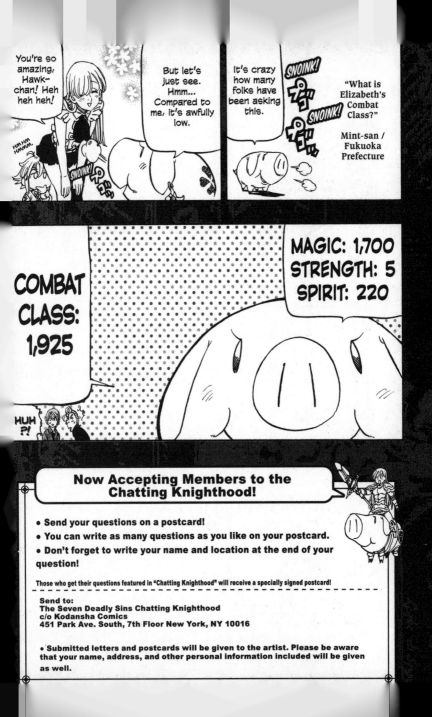

"What is Elizabeth's Combat Class?"
Mint-san / Fukuoka Prefecture
SNOINK!
SNOINK!
It's crazy how many folks have been asking this.
But let's just see. Hmm... Compared to me, it's awfully low.
You're so amazing, Hawk-chan! Heh heh heh!
HM HM HMMM.
SNOINK!
MAGIC: 1,700
STRENGTH: 5
SPIRIT: 220
COMBAT CLASS: 1,925
HUH?!

Now Accepting Members to the Chatting Knighthood!

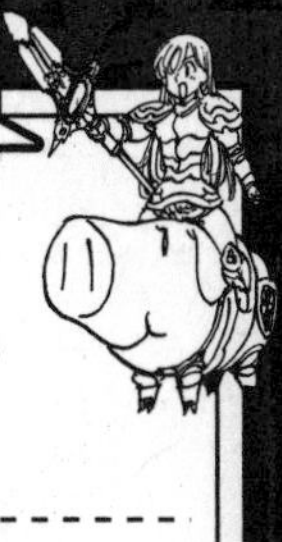

- Send your questions on a postcard!
- You can write as many questions as you like on your postcard.
- Don't forget to write your name and location at the end of your question!

Those who get their questions featured in "Chatting Knighthood" will receive a specially signed postcard!

Send to:
The Seven Deadly Sins Chatting Knighthood
c/o Kodansha Comics
451 Park Ave. South, 7th Floor New York, NY 10016

- Submitted letters and postcards will be given to the artist. Please be aware that your name, address, and other personal information included will be given as well.

"THE SEVEN DEADLY SINS" ILLUSTRATION CORNER

"THE DRAWING KNIGHTHOOD" SPACE

Be sure to include your name and address on your postcard!

SPECIAL PRIZE

"Whoa... What the heck is this?!"

"Now, now. Don't get mad."

"I'm not mad. I just want to know who these handsome gents are!"

"That's what you have to say?! You've got to be kidding, right?!"

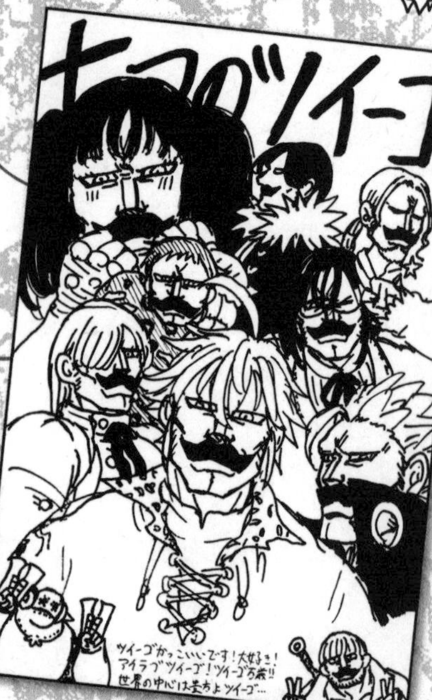

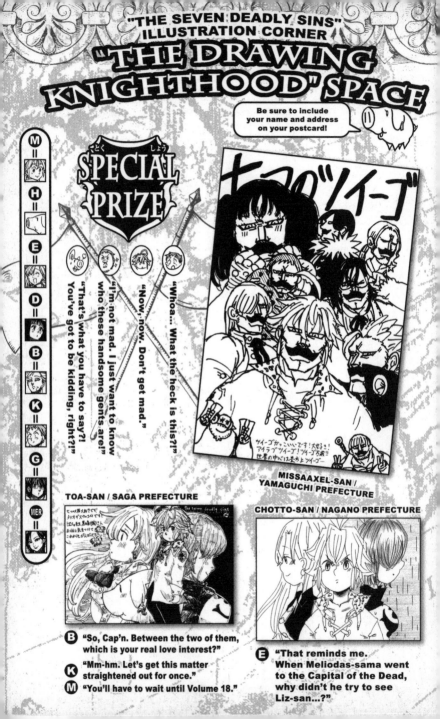

MISSAAXEL-SAN / YAMAGUCHI PREFECTURE

TOA-SAN / SAGA PREFECTURE

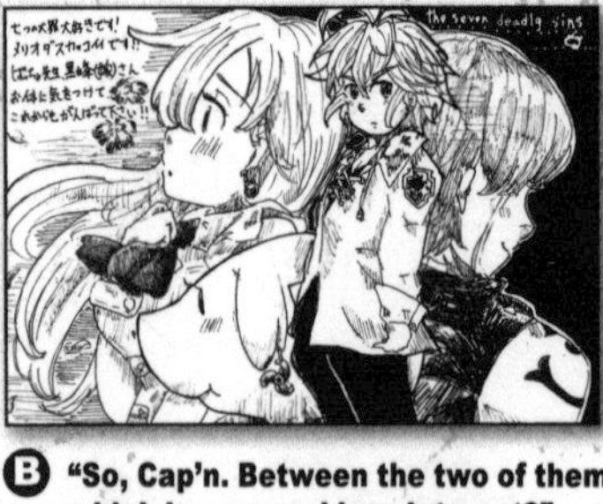
the seven deadly sins

B "So, Cap'n. Between the two of them, which is your real love interest?"

K "Mm-hm. Let's get this matter straightened out for once."

M "You'll have to wait until Volume 18."

CHOTTO-SAN / NAGANO PREFECTURE

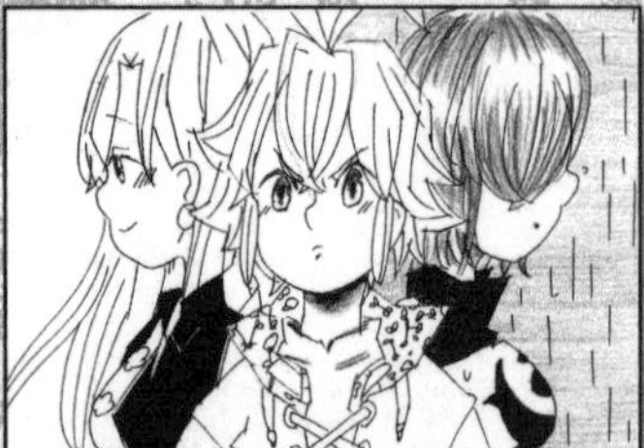

E "That reminds me. When Meliodas-sama went to the Capital of the Dead, why didn't he try to see Liz-san...?"

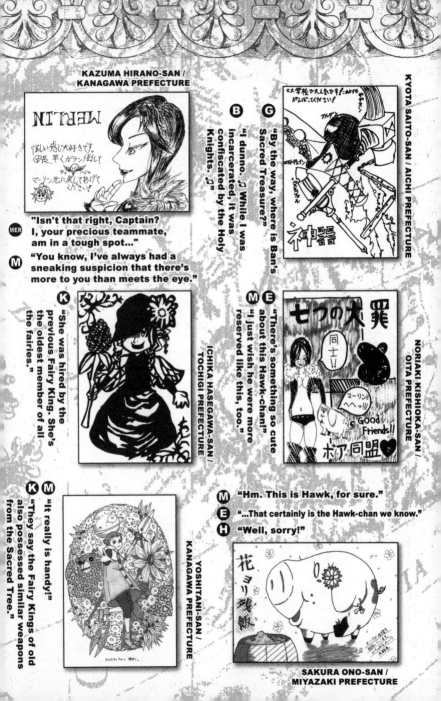

KYOTA SAITO-SAN / AICHI PREFECTURE

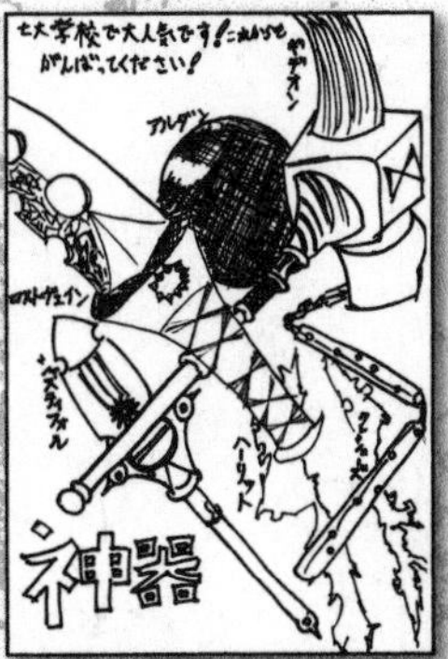
神器

G "By the way, where is Ban's Sacred Treasure?"

B "I dunno. ♫ While I was incarcerated, it was confiscated by the Holy Knights. ♫"

KAZUMA HIRANO-SAN / KANAGAWA PREFECTURE

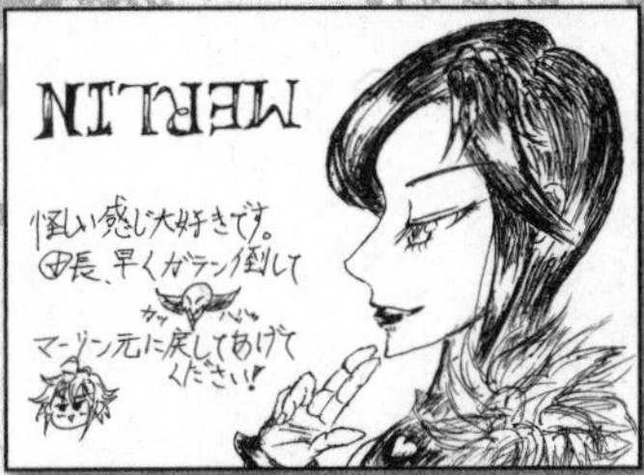
MERLIN
怪しい感じ大好きです。
団長、早くガラン倒して
マーリン元に戻してあげてください!

MER "Isn't that right, Captain? I, your precious teammate, am in a tough spot..."

M "You know, I've always had a sneaking suspicion that there's more to you than meets the eye."

NORIAKI KISHIOKA-SAN / OITA PREFECTURE

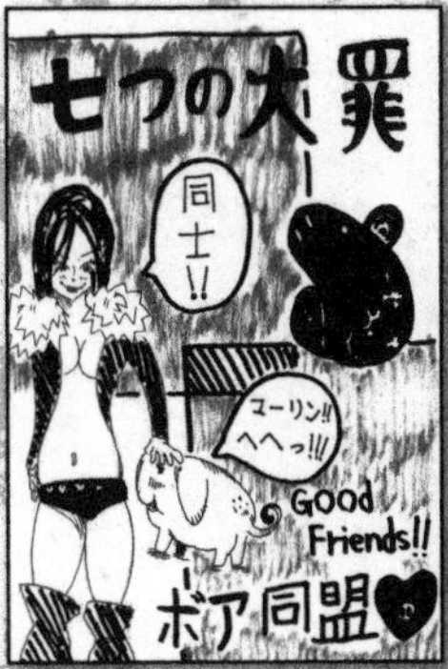
七つの大罪
同士!!
マーリン!! へへっ!!!
GOOD Friends!!
ボア同盟

E "There's something so cute about this Hawk-chan!"

M "I just wish he were more reserved like this, too."

ICHIKA HASEGAWA-SAN / TOCHIGI PREFECTURE

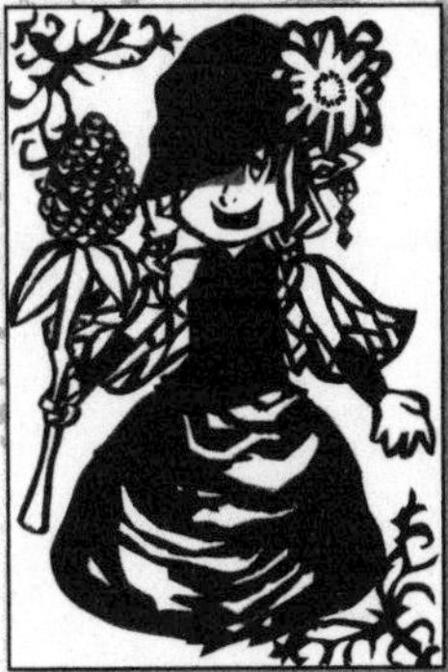

K "She was hired by the previous Fairy King. She's the oldest member of all the fairies."

M "Hm. This is Hawk, for sure."

E "...That certainly is the Hawk-chan we know."

H "Well, sorry!"

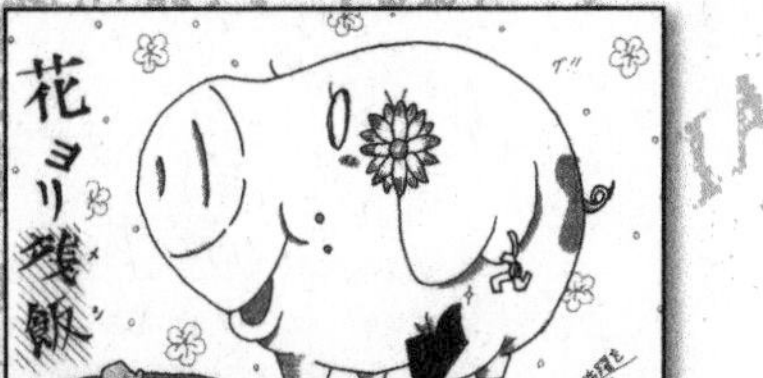
花ヨリ残飯

SAKURA ONO-SAN / MIYAZAKI PREFECTURE

YOSHITANI-SAN / KANAGAWA PREFECTURE

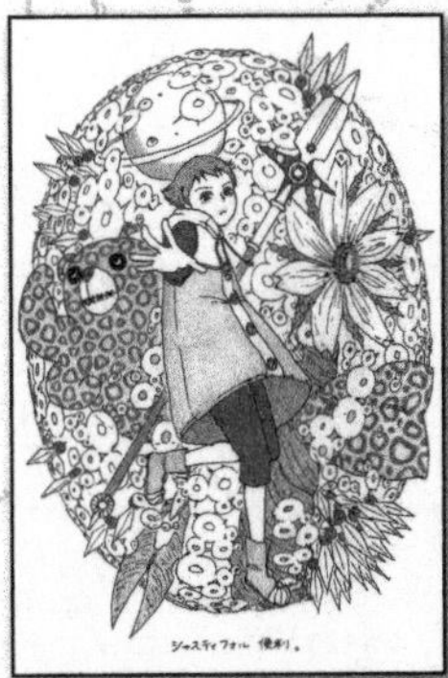

M "It really is handy!"

K "They say the Fairy Kings of old also possessed similar weapons from the Sacred Tree."

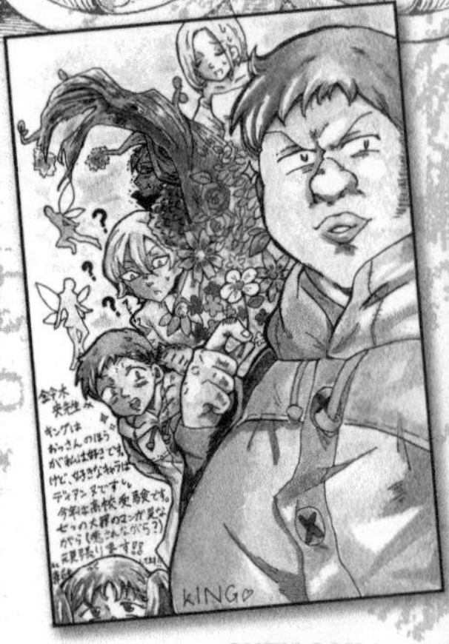
KING♡

SUZU-SAN / NAGASAKI PREFECTURE

"How come when I take this form, everyone keeps their distance? Is it too much for them to take?"

"Just die already."

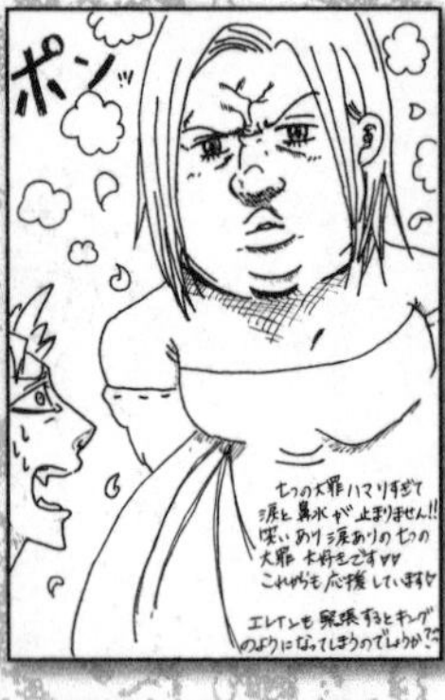
ポン

LITTLE NIGHT KID-SAN / NAGANO PREFECTURE

B "Hey, King! Don't mix up that failure of a big brother with Elaine!"

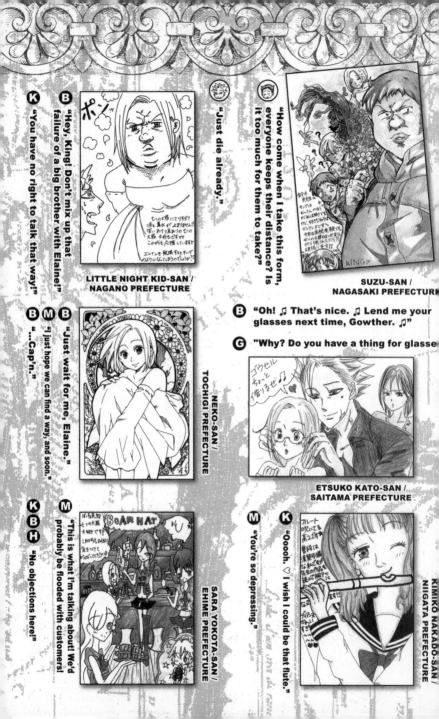

K "You have no right to talk that way!"

B "Oh! ♫ That's nice. ♫ Lend me your glasses next time, Gowther. ♫"

G "Why? Do you have a thing for glasse

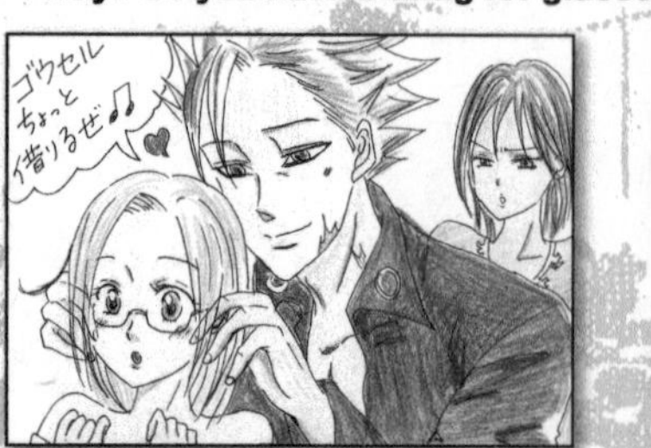
ゴウセル
ちょっと
借りるぜ♫

ETSUKO KATO-SAN / SAITAMA PREFECTURE

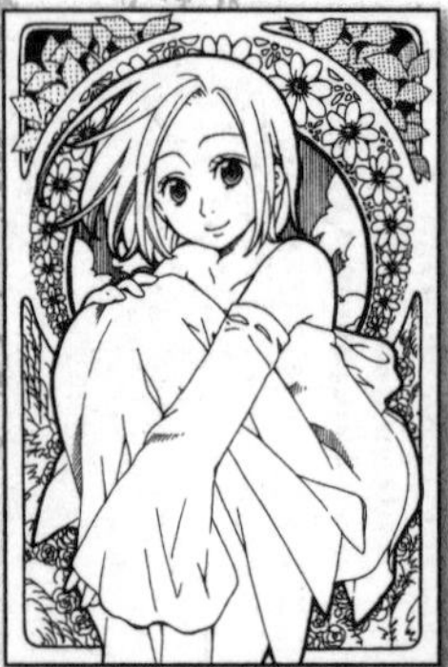

NEKO-SAN / TOCHIGI PREFECTURE

B "Just wait for me, Elaine."

M "I just hope we can find a way, and soon."

B "...Cap'n."

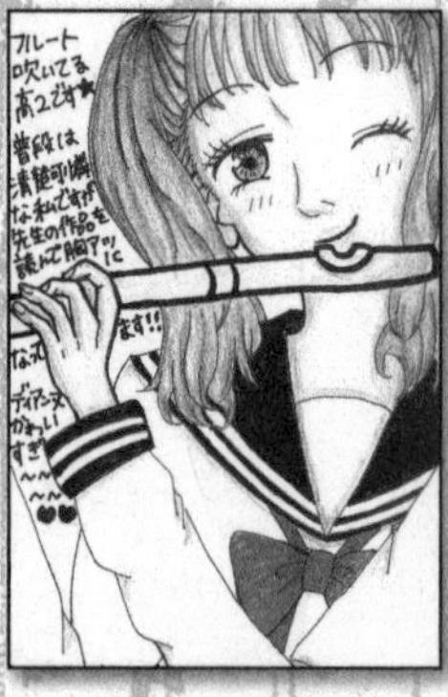

KIMIKO NAKADO-SAN / NIIGATA PREFECTURE

K "Ooooh. ♡ I wish I could be that flute."

M "You're so depressing."

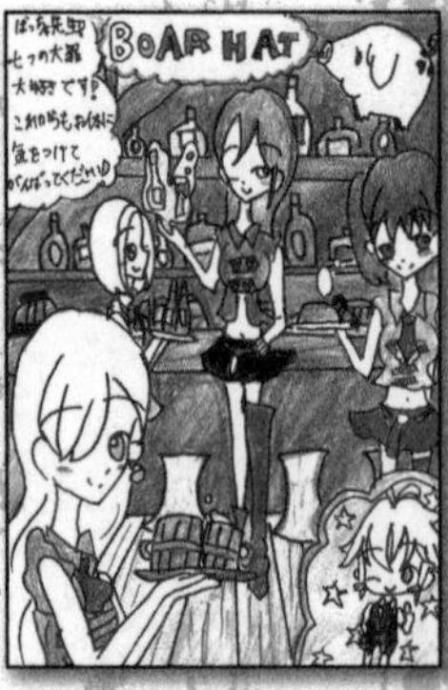
BOAR HAT

SARA YOKOTA-SAN / EHIME PREFECTURE

M "This is what I'm talking about! We'd probably be flooded with customers!"

K B H "No objections here!"

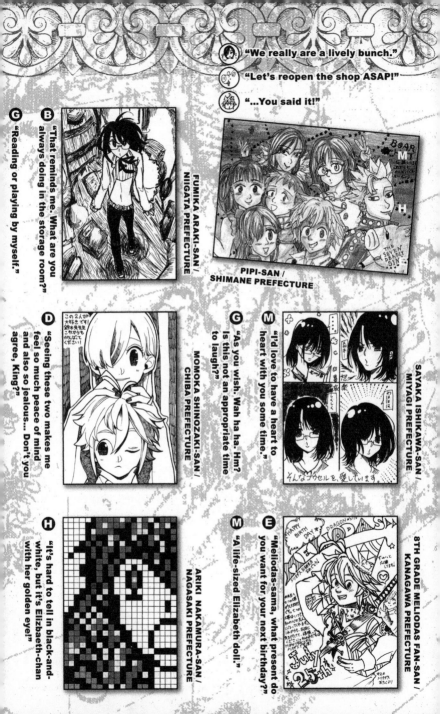

"We really are a lively bunch."

"Let's reopen the shop ASAP!"

"...You said it!"

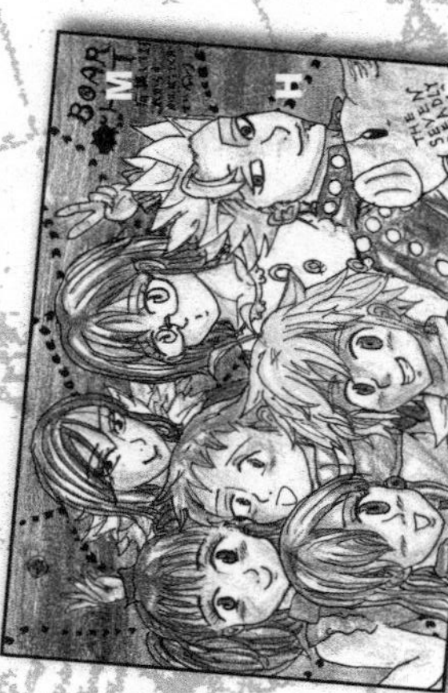

BOAR HAT
M
H
THE SEVEN DEADLY SIN

PIPI-SAN / SHIMANE PREFECTURE

SAYAKA ISHIKAWA-SAN / MIYAGI PREFECTURE

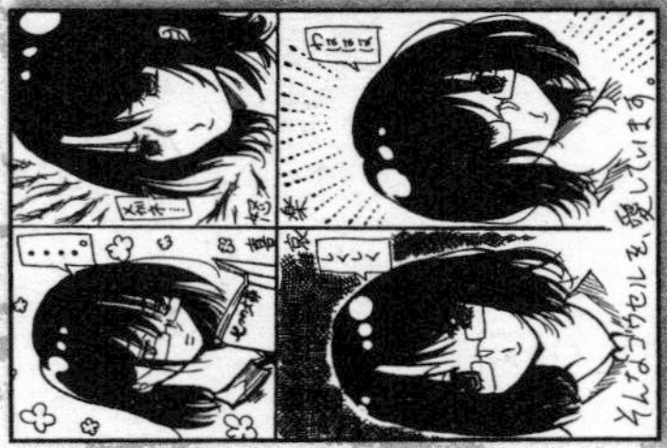

喜
怒
哀
楽
そんなゴウセルを、愛しています。

M "I'd love to have a heart to heart with you some time."

G "As you wish. Wah ha ha. Hm? Is this not an appropriate time to laugh?"

8TH GRADE MELIODAS FAN-SAN / KANAGAWA PREFECTURE

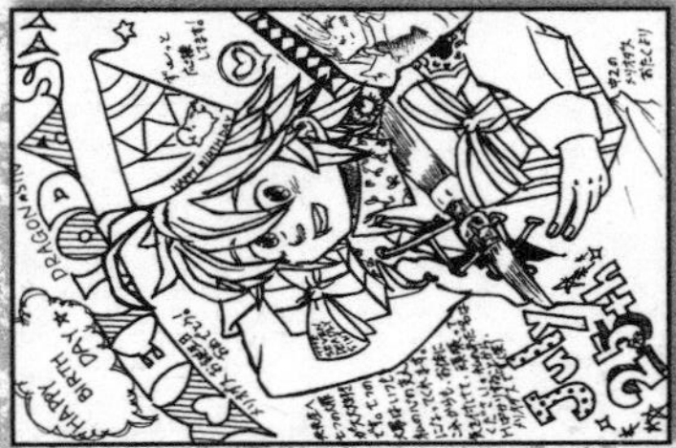

HAPPY BIRTHDAY☆
DRAGON SIN
July 25th

E "Meliodas-sama, what present do you want for your next birthday?"

M "A life-sized Elizabeth doll."

FUMIKA ARAKI-SAN / NIIGATA PREFECTURE

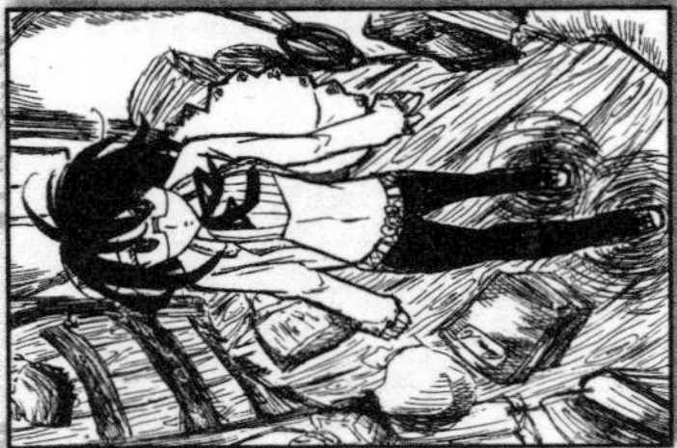

B "That reminds me. What are you always doing in the storage room?"

G "Reading or playing by myself."

MOMOKA SHINOZAKI-SAN / CHIBA PREFECTURE

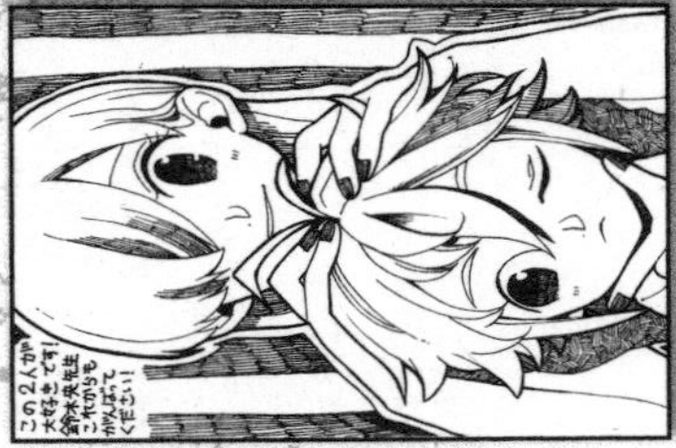

この2人が大好きです! 鈴木央先生これからもがんばってください!

D "Seeing these two makes me feel so much peace of mind and also so jealous... Don't you agree, King?"

ARIKI NAKAMURA-SAN / NAGASAKI PREFECTURE

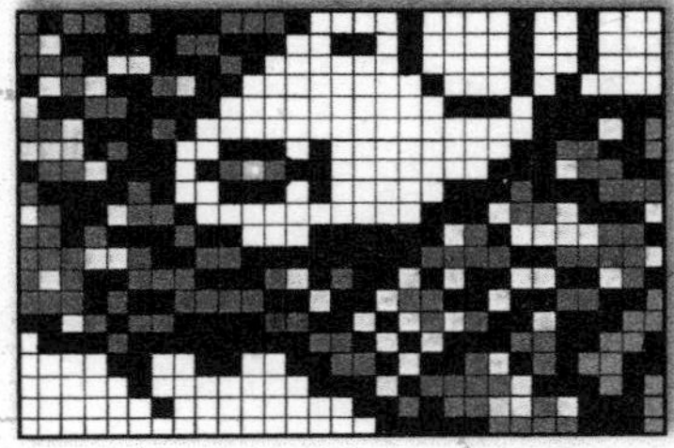

H "It's hard to tell in black-and-white, but it's Elizbaeth-chan with her golden eye!"

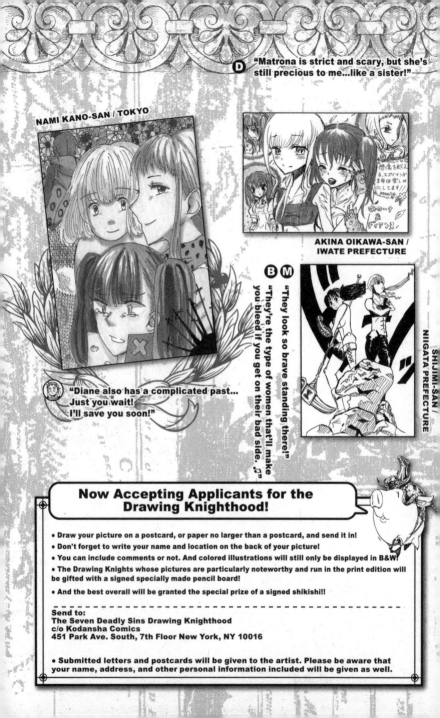

D "Matrona is strict and scary, but she's still precious to me...like a sister!"

NAMI KANO-SAN / TOKYO

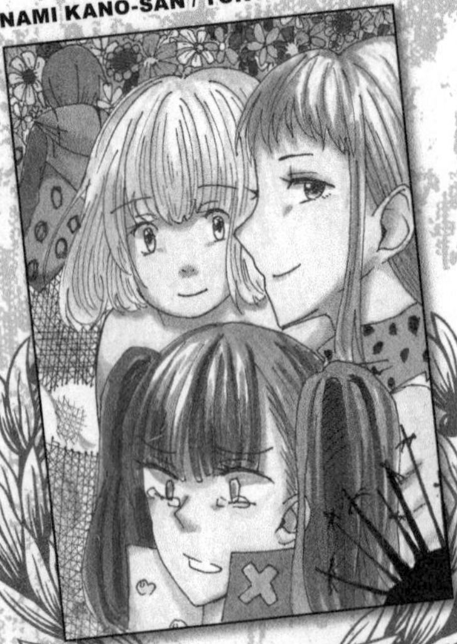

"Diane also has a complicated past... Just you wait! I'll save you soon!"

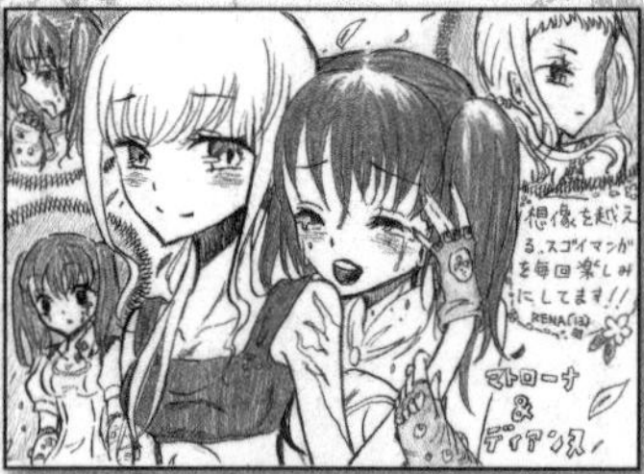

想像を越える、スゴイマンガを毎回楽しみにしてます!!
RENA(13)
マトローナ & ディアンヌ

AKINA OIKAWA-SAN / IWATE PREFECTURE

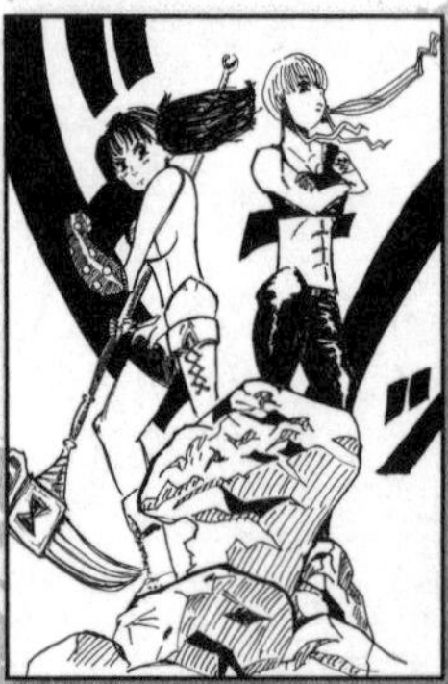

SHIJIMI-SAN / NIIGATA PREFECTURE

B "They look so brave standing there!"

M "They're the type of women that'll make you bleed if you get on their bad side. ♫"

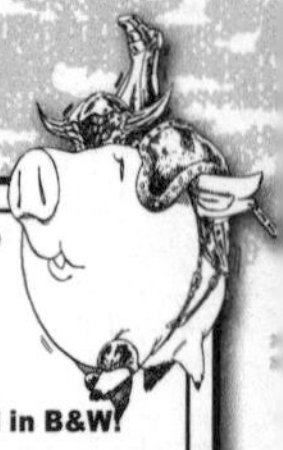

Now Accepting Applicants for the Drawing Knighthood!

- Draw your picture on a postcard, or paper no larger than a postcard, and send it in!
- Don't forget to write your name and location on the back of your picture!
- You can include comments or not. And colored illustrations will still only be displayed in B&W!
- The Drawing Knights whose pictures are particularly noteworthy and run in the print edition will be gifted with a signed specially made pencil board!
- And the best overall will be granted the special prize of a signed shikishi!!

Send to:
The Seven Deadly Sins Drawing Knighthood
c/o Kodansha Comics
451 Park Ave. South, 7th Floor New York, NY 10016

- Submitted letters and postcards will be given to the artist. Please be aware that your name, address, and other personal information included will be given as well.

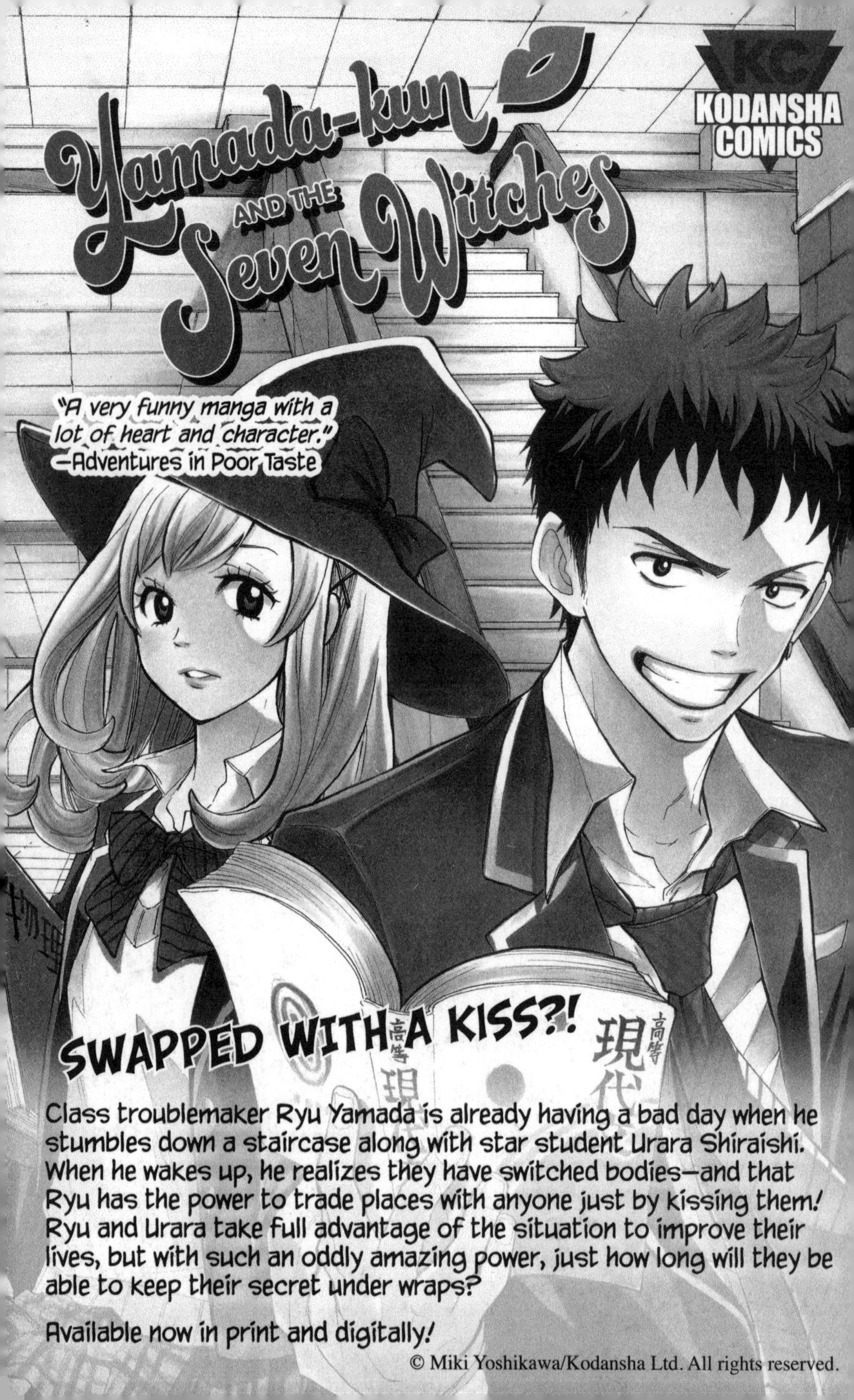
Yamada-kun AND THE Seven Witches
KC KODANSHA COMICS
"A very funny manga with a lot of heart and character."
—Adventures in Poor Taste
SWAPPED WITH A KISS?!
Class troublemaker Ryu Yamada is already having a bad day when he stumbles down a staircase along with star student Urara Shiraishi. When he wakes up, he realizes they have switched bodies—and that Ryu has the power to trade places with anyone just by kissing them! Ryu and Urara take full advantage of the situation to improve their lives, but with such an oddly amazing power, just how long will they be able to keep their secret under wraps?
Available now in print and digitally!
© Miki Yoshikawa/Kodansha Ltd. All rights reserved.

The Seven Deadly Sins volume 17 is a work of fiction. Names, characters, places, and incidents are the products of the author's imagination or are used fictitiously. Any resemblance to actual events, locales, or persons, living or dead, is entirely coincidental.

A Kodansha Comics Trade Paperback Original.

Published in the United States by Kodansha Comics, an imprint of Kodansha USA Publishing, LLC, New York.

Publication rights for this English edition arranged through Kodansha Ltd., Tokyo.

First published in Japan in 2015 by Kodansha Ltd., Tokyo.

ISBN 978-1-63236-293-3

Printed in the United States of America.

www.kodanshacomics.com

9 8 7 6 5 4 3 2 1

Translation: Christine Dashiell
Lettering: James Dashiell
Editing: Lauren Scanlan
Kodansha Comics edition cover design: Phil Balsman